The Trans-Appalachian Frontier in 1850

The Trans-Appalachian Frontier

The Trans-Appalachian Frontier

Frontier

People, Societies, and Institutions
1775–1850

MALCOLM J. ROHRBOUGH

New York
OXFORD UNIVERSITY PRESS
1978

Copyright © 1978 by Oxford University Press, Inc.

Library of Congress Cataloging in Publication Data
Rohrbough, Malcolm J
The trans-Appalachian frontier.
Bibliography: p.
Includes index.
1. Northwest, Old—History—1775–1865.
2. Frontier and pioneer life—Northwest, Old.
3. Southwest, Old—History. 4. Frontier and
pioneer life—Southwest, Old. 5. Appalachian
region—History. 6. Frontier and pioneer life—
Appalachian region. I. Title.
F484.3.R64   977'.02   77-28492
ISBN 0-19-502209-2

Printed in the United States of America

Dedicated to
VERNON CARSTENSEN
with
deep appreciation
and highest esteem

Acknowledgments

Many people and several institutions have contributed to this project over eight years. I should like to acknowledge these debts here.

To begin with, I should like to express my appreciation to the directors and librarians of the following institutions for their assistance: Alabama Department of Archives and History, Montgomery, and especially to Milo B. Howard, Jr. for his kind hospitality; University of Alabama Library, University; American Antiquarian Society, Worcester, Massachusetts; Arkansas History Commission, Little Rock; Division of Manuscripts and Division of Maps, Library of Congress, Washington, D.C.; P. K. Yonge Library of Florida History, University of Florida, Gainesville; Widener Library, Harvard University, Cambridge, Massachusetts; Chicago Historical Society, Chicago; Illinois Historical Survey, University of Illinois Library, Urbana, with appreciation to Robert M. Sutton for his many kindnesses; Illinois State Historical Library, Springfield; University of Chicago Library, Chicago; Indiana Historical Society, Indianapolis; Indiana State Library, Indianapolis; Indiana University Library, Bloomington; Iowa State Department of History and Archives, Des Moines; State Historical Society of Iowa, Iowa City; University of Iowa Library, Iowa City; Filson Club, Louisville; Margaret I. King Library, University of Kentucky, Lexington; Department of Archives, Louisiana State University Library, Baton Rouge, and especially to John Milton Price (now editor of *Southern Studies*) and Margaret Anne Fisher; Louisiana Division, New Orleans Public Library; Michigan Historical Collections, Bentley Historical Library, University of Michigan, Ann Arbor, with special thanks to my old friend and colleague, Kenneth P. Scheffel; William L. Clements Library, University of Michigan, Ann Arbor; Mississippi Department of Archives and History, Jackson, and especially to Laura D. S. Sturdivant; University of Mississippi Library, University; State Historical Society of Missouri, Columbia, with appreciation to Jo Lankford; Case–Western Reserve University Library, Cleveland; Ohio Historical Society, Columbus; Ohio State University Library, Columbus; Western Reserve Historical Society, Cleveland; Public Library of Knoxville and Knox County, Knoxville; McClung Historical Collection, Lawson-McGhee Library, Knoxville; Tennessee Historical Society, Nashville; Tennessee State Library and Archives, Nashville; University of Tennessee Library, Knoxville; State Historical Society of Wisconsin, Madison; University of Wisconsin Library, Madison.

I am also grateful to these students of the Department of History, University of Iowa, for their research assistance: Robert Burchfield, David DeLeon, William Douglas, Timothy N. Hyde, Alan F. January, Walter Kopsa, Gerald Patton, Jane Reister, and William Silag.

Several scholars took of their time to read part or all of this manuscript and to make valuable suggestions. I should like to express my deep appreciation to Paul F. Bourke, Flinders University of South Australia; Vernon Carstensen, University of Washington; Robert R. Dykstra, University of Iowa; Dorsey D. Ellis, University of Iowa; Peter T. Harstad, State Historical Society of Iowa; John Lankford, University of Missouri-Columbia; and Michael L. Olsen, New Mexico Highlands University.

G. I. Rohrbough and A. N. Gustine provided financial assistance for this project. I am grateful to both. The Graduate College of the University of Iowa helped to defray the cost of typing part of the final draft of the manuscript.

Eunice M. Prosser cheerfully typed the manuscript—several times.

Special thanks are due Barbara, Beth, Justin, and Peter, who helped in many ways.

I assume sole responsibility for errors.

"Rockholme"   M.J.R.
Gloucester, Massachusetts
July 1977

Contents

Maps

Tables

Abbreviations

Books and Periodicals

AHQ	*Alabama Historical Quarterly*
AI	*Annals of Iowa*
AJLH	*American Journal of Legal History*
AR	*Alabama Review*
ArHQ	*Arkansas Historical Quarterly*
FCHQ	*Filson Club Historical Quarterly*
FHQ	*Florida Historical Quarterly*
IJH	*Iowa Journal of History*
IJHP	*Iowa Journal of History and Politics*
IMH	*Indiana Magazine of History*
JAH	*Journal of American History*
JISHS	*Journal of the Illinois State Historical Society*
JMH	*Journal of Mississippi History*
JSH	*Journal of Southern History*
LH	*Louisiana History*
LHQ	*Louisiana Historical Quarterly*
M-A	*Mid-America*
MH	*Michigan History*
MHM	*Michigan History Magazine*
MHR	*Missouri Historical Review*
MPHC	*Michigan Pioneer and Historical Collections*

MVHR   *Mississippi Valley Historical Review*
OAHQ   *Ohio Archaeological and Historical Quarterly*
OHQ   *Ohio Historical Quarterly*
RKSHS   *Register of the Kentucky State Historical Society*
SAQ   *South Atlantic Quarterly*
THM   *Tennessee Historical Magazine*
THQ   *Tennessee Historical Quarterly*
TP   *Territorial Papers of the United States*, ed. Clarence E. Carter and
        John Porter Bloom (27 vols. to date, Washington, D.C., 1934–)
WMH   *Wisconsin Magazine of History*

Manuscript Depositories and Microfilm Collections

ADAH   *Alabama Department of Archives and History, Montgomery*
AHC   *Arkansas History Commission, Little Rock*
CHS   *Chicago Historical Society, Chicago*
ESR   *Early State Records on Microfilm, Library of Congress*
HRS   *Historical Records Survey, a division of the Works Progress Adminis-
        tration*
IHS   *Indiana Historical Society, Indianapolis*
IHS-U   *Illinois Historical Survey, University of Illinois Library, Urbana*
ISHL   *Illinois State Historical Library, Springfield*
ISL   *Indiana State Library, Indianapolis*
LSU   *Department of Archives, Louisiana State University Library, Baton
        Rouge*
McHC   *McClung Historical Collection, Lawson-McGhee Library, Knoxville*
MHC   *Michigan Historical Collections, Bentley Historical Library, Univer-
        sity of Michigan, Ann Arbor*
MIK   *Margaret I. King Library, University of Kentucky, Lexington*
OHS   *Ohio Historical Society, Columbus*
PKY   *P. K. Yonge Library of Florida History, University of Florida, Gaines-
        ville*
SHSI   *State Historical Society of Iowa, Iowa City*
SHSW   *State Historical Society of Wisconsin, Madison*
TSLA   *Tennessee State Library and Archives, Nashville*
UT   *University of Tennessee Library, Knoxville*

A Note on Citations, Quotations, Maps, and Place-Names

Throughout this volume I have not cited secondary literature except where it bears directly on a specific point under discussion. The size of the bibliography of literature on the trans-Appalachian frontier makes complete citations impossible. Unpublished theses and dissertations are cited by degree, institution, and date. All quotations are reproduced in the original form, except where taken from edited editions, in which case I have included the editor's corrections and emendations in brackets.

The preparation of the necessary maps revealed a number of problems. Counties are important for this study, but county boundaries changed frequently, and I found it especially difficult to locate them in three or four states for the same year. The passage of time and settlement patterns have left their changes elsewhere. Some early towns have disappeared, even from maps. In meeting the challenge of changes in names, and, within names, of variations in spellings, I have opted for the modern usage wherever possible. Three sources of maps deserve special mention here: the many maps in the Map Division of the Library of Congress; a set of maps for Mississippi reprinted by the Mississippi Historical Society in 1969; and Herman R. Friis, "A Series of Population Maps of the Colonies and the United States, 1625–1790," *Geographical Review*, 30 (1940): 463–79.

The Trans-Appalachian Frontier

Introduction

This is a book about the first American frontier. Specifically, it is about the experiences of people, the rise of societies, and the development of institutions on the trans-Appalachian frontier from 1775 to 1850.

The people came first. From the middle of the eighteenth century, ambitious and adventurous men and women in growing numbers penetrated into the region west of the Appalachian mountains. It was a fertile land, well watered and a storehouse of game; above all, it was remote. The obstacles to settlement were distance, physical barriers in the form of mountains, forests, and rivers, and especially the Indians of the Ohio Valley. International rivalries also affected settlement of people in the trans-Appalachian region. For almost a century, the English and French had fought for control of the interior of the continent. In 1756 a new war broke out—a fourth and, as it turned out, decisive conflict. At the Treaty of Paris in 1763 the French ceded their continental empire to the English. The English thus enormously enlarged the physical dimensions of their empire in the New World, but in attempting to govern, they became aware of the changed nature of their subjects. Seventeenth-century Englishmen and Englishwomen had turned, over the course of five generations in the New World, into Anglo-Americans. They were English in allegiance (thus far) and institutional heritage, but they were also something more. They were on the way to becoming Americans. The term "Anglo-American," as used hereafter, identifies both the institutional roots of the past and the impending changes of the future, and

3

implies the growing differences between the two cultures and the political independence that would become a reality in 1783.

These ultimate changes seemed unlikely in 1763. Yet, even as they celebrated their victory, the English began to confront imperial problems, principally in defense, finances, and Indian relations. The solution was a proclamation forbidding settlement in the West, but an imaginary line drawn along the crest of the mountains did not prevent hunters, trappers, explorers, and land viewers from advancing into the interior of the continent. For the next decade, Anglo-Americans crossed the mountains regularly, and, as early as 1773, some staked out claims in the broad expanse known as Kentucky.

This impulse to go west stretched back more than one hundred and sixty-five years—five generations—to the flats of the James River. Here, in the spring of 1607, the first English settlers had raised a palisade. Among the bench marks of the expansion inland were the occupation of the Connecticut Valley in the 1630's, the movement of population into the Shenandoah Valley of Virginia, the extension down the Great Valley of the Appalachians in the decade of the 1730's, and the spread of settlement across the northern Appalachians into western Pennsylvania after 1763. Not since the first permanent English colonies at Jamestown and Plymouth, however, had the Anglo-American people colonized in such hostile country and at such distance from established institutions of government and law as they did in the trans-Appalachian West. Just as the first settlers at Jamestown, Plymouth, and other plantations scattered along the East Coast had been separated from their homeland by the broad and often stormy Atlantic Ocean, those who crossed into the Appalachians and beyond were separated from their "homeland" by a land ocean of trees, mountains, and swift-flowing streams. They went to the West richer in experience, however, than the first English people who had come to the continent. They had one hundred and sixty-five years of colonizing behind them, with all that meant in terms of learning to live on the land and in terms of developing institutions to serve their needs (or adapting them from English models). But they, like the Virginians and Plymouthians, would have to accommodate, adjust, and make do. The men and women who crossed the mountains to the "western waters," for so the land was called, probably gave little thought to such matters. They sought good lands, and to this end they would manage their own affairs. In a fertile country, surrounded by danger and hardship, they first sought physical security from hostile forces; once physical security was assured, they sought a stable world. From 1775 to 1850 three generations of people repeated the experience of immigrating to the frontier. They were an infinitely varied people, from many places in America and from across the ocean. Some were literate and fair-spoken, others spoke in the vernacular of the day, and still others spoke no English at all. Their economic circumstances covered an equally broad range. They would come to spread over a vast area, for the trans-Appalachian frontier stretched from the Holston to the Arkansas, from Detroit and Des Moines to New Orleans and Mobile. In seventy-five years, barely exceeding the Biblical lifespan for a single individual, a rush of settlers occupied the middle third of the continent.

This work is also a description, analysis, and comparison of the several societies that developed on the trans-Appalachian frontier. The movement of people across the mountains—or through the mountains, since many of them already lived in mountain valleys—was more than simply the migration of individuals from one place to another. It involved partly the transference of an old society, partly the creation of a new one. The word "society" is here used in its broadest sense, to identify the ways in which people related to one another, to suggest common experiences, present circumstances, future hopes, and, throughout, a sense of shared values and priorities. The frontier provided fertile soil for the growth of societies. In the dark mold of the rich lands relations between and among people grew apace with corn and cotton. The different requirements of new land settlement imposed new demands on the societies in process of taking shape. Just as the multiplication of undifferentiated cells that appear at first so much alike in time produces organs with different functions, so new settlements, at first much like each other, and like those on the East Coast a century or more earlier, in time developed into different societies in response to different social, political, and economic opportunities and imperatives.

Even on the distant frontiers men and women remained social people. At first they joined together for protection from a lonely and hostile wilderness, travelling in companies for the sake of mutual help and security. Once arrived, they located near to one another insofar as their interests in landholding would allow. The basic unit of land settlement in early Kentucky was the "station," where people came together for safety from the Indians. North of the Ohio River the compact settlements of the

Ohio Company stressed the communal values of New England and the responsibilities of the settlers for one another. In the first years of the trans-Appalachian frontier, the world of the wilderness was simply too vast for any one person, the labors too numerous, and the dangers too great. A few people had sought the solitude of the woods, and the first generation of settlers valued their talents, for woodsmen such as Daniel Boone spied out the lands and led the fight against the Indians. The bulk of the immigrants, however, sought a more stable world. Later, with the larger numbers of people and the fading Indian threat, people no longer needed to live in stations, but their associations continued. Whether the pioneer to the western country came from the neat villages of New England, the more random countryside of Virginia and the Carolinas, or the closed societies of Europe—and all these homelands were represented in the western country—he was accustomed to some degree of order, law, precedent, and tradition. If some of these societies were narrow and confining (especially in an economic and social sense), they were also secure, ordered, and rational. Frontier societies, on the other hand, conveyed a sense of chaos, confusion, and disorder. In the beginning observers loosely defined frontier society as those who lived west of the Appalachians. Later, others commented on the different societies north and south of the Ohio River. Slavery was the distinguishing feature of this difference, with its implication of staple crop agriculture and a plantation economy. Elsewhere, deep-seated cultural differences were a salient feature. The Louisiana Purchase contained societies of Spanish and French heritage separate and different from the Anglo-American. Beyond these large-scale distinctions, various smaller societies appeared on the frontiers as the cells further differentiated themselves.[1]

This book is also a study of the creation and re-creation of institutions. The story of the trans-Appalachian frontier from 1775 to 1850 comprises, in large part, the experiences of people in an agricultural society moving west into a promised land, of their taking up the land and placing it under cultivation. Simultaneously, the immigrants established economic, social, and political institutions to protect these gains and preserve their values. Institutions provided a framework of social

1. Carl Bridenbaugh, *Myths & Realities: Societies of the Colonial South* (Baton Rouge, 1952), ch. 3, discusses the large-scale distinctions between societies. Bridenbaugh does not deal with the smaller societies into which the "Back Settlements" (as he calls them) were subdivided.

organization, defining the way in which people arranged themselves in relationship to one another. Institutions fixed the outer limits of human activity. They imposed form and structure on the lives of the frontier people; they established standards of human conduct. Institutions might be formally imposed from above, as in the case of government, courts, and law; or they might evolve with the consensus of the community, in a form suited to the frontier environment and circumstances, as in the case of lay preachers, circuit riders, and itinerant teachers. The first settlers in Kentucky, Tennessee, and, to a lesser extent, the Ohio Valley, had to improvise. As they did so, they repeated a process that had begun with the Mayflower Compact and extended in varying degrees across the breadth of the American frontier to the opening of the Cherokee Strip.

American colonial society eventually became a structured society. People on the frontier could not escape—and most did not want to escape—this condition. Even people in the remote reaches of the Carolina back-country sought the rudimentary order characterized by a sheriff, justice of the peace, and court of law. If the tax collector was close behind, then he would be served or evaded in various ways. The need remained. The church, the county, and deference to one or all of several leading public figures formed the foundation of order in the colonial world. In the same fashion, leaders in political and economic life emerged on the frontier of Anglo-American settlement. They were neither the town fathers of New England nor the county lieutenants of Virginia and the Carolinas, but they gave frontier society leaders who could be called upon when needed. The first pioneers across the Appalachians carried this tradition into Kentucky and Tennessee. The county, the militia, and the leading military and economic figures of the area provided a focus of authority on the distant frontiers.[2]

This story opens in 1775 and continues until 1850. Thus, it is an account of the first frontier of the new American nation. Continuity with the past remained important, however, for what happened drew on English ori-

---

2. Note the picture of life and politics in Virginia in Charles S. Sydnor, *Gentlemen Freeholders: Political Practices in Washington's Virginia* (Chapel Hill, 1952); and of economic and political power in an early New England town in Sumner Chilton Powell, *Puritan Village: The Formation of a New England Town* (Middletown, 1963). On life in the Carolina backcountry, see Bridenbaugh, *Myths & Realities*, ch. 3.

gins. The new Americans knew a lot about Sir William Blackstone and his doctrines of property and its conveyance; they were familiar with traditional ways of joining for redress of grievances by memorial and petition; they knew the outlines of the court system and trial by jury; they recognized the influence and administrative authority of the county court. In this sense, they were like the American Revolutionaries who threw off the yoke of English oppression in 1775 (or said they did), but who bore the imprint of generations of English influence to a greater degree and in more ways than some would have liked to admit.

But what happened drew on American experience as well, stretching back over one hundred and sixty-five years to the first settlements at Jamestown. By 1775 five generations of frontier peoples had created an Anglo-American tradition (call it a frontier tradition, if you like). And with political independence, a broad strain that was strictly American influenced frontier development. Among the most important results were the ordinances of 1785 and 1787. These ordinances were the codification of experience since 1607, adopted to the values and needs of a new and independent American nation. Recognizing the influence of the past, this study looks to and describes the future—that is to say, the three generations after 1775—and so a description of the trans-Appalachian West as the first American frontier seems appropriate.

All this is not to say that there were not other significant frontier traditions in the settlement of the New World. There were at least three. The French had established in North America a vast empire that stretched in a crescent from the St. Lawrence by way of the Great Lakes down the Mississippi to the Gulf of Mexico. French influence is still dominant today in parts of Canada and remains significant in portions of the old Louisiana Purchase. The Spanish also left their imprint on a large section of the continent. Their heritage is a dominant feature of the American Southwest and survives in several forms in Florida. Finally, of course, there remains the frontier experience of the Native American. In a sense, the American Indian witnessed the advance of the frontier from the wrong end of a loaded gun. It was a unique vantage point. All of these traditions are worthy of careful study and consideration; each should receive its own analysis. Such study is not undertaken here, however, where the emphasis is on the Anglo-American and American frontier people, societies, and institutions. Only to the extent that the others—French, Spanish, and Native American—affected the American experience are they considered.

One other point needs to be made. With few exceptions, this is a book about an agricultural world. If, as is suggested here, the frontier west of the Appalachians gave rise to many societies, a universal interest in the soil joined almost all of them. The acquisition, cultivation, exploitation, and eternal search for more fertile and cheaper lands provide a common theme from the Appalachians west to the line of semiaridity (and even beyond), from the Great Lakes to the Gulf of Mexico. So this study does not deal with explorers, significant as their contributions may have been. Nor are we concerned here with the fur trade, a basic economic enterprise in the eighteenth century. Interest in the fur trade dictated the relationship of the Europeans (including the Anglo-Americans) to the Indians in the eighteenth century. In the nineteenth century it was the land. The fur trade allowed the Indians to remain on the land, but the transition to an abiding interest in landownership doomed them to removal. One other point needs to be made by way of introduction: agriculture was not the only kind of economic enterprise that men and women pursued on the trans-Appalachian frontier. People mined early and energetically for lead and later for copper; they also engaged in large-scale lumbering and established small industries as opportunities presented themselves. Urban development gradually appeared across the breadth of the frontier, but urban areas reflected interest in and dependence upon their agricultural hinterlands. Agriculture, the land, and the agrarian values remained basic and continuing themes.

Between 1775 and 1850 pioneer peoples physically occupied the trans-Appalachian West. In about the same length of time—that is to say in three generations since Frederick Jackson Turner's address in 1893—historians have labored with the concept of the American frontier. The results have been mixed. The ascendancy of Turner and his students and disciples marked the first generation. The second was a reaction against the first and was dominated by the critics of Turner's ideas. A third generation has worked to find new paths and to cast off the continuing influence of Turner, without marked success. Central themes throughout are the uniqueness of the frontier experience and a description and analysis of an emerging frontier society, which is generally treated as monolithic for purposes of contrast with more settled areas. Both concepts are grounded in Turner's essay.[3]

A next step was the study of the frontier in national and international affairs. Here emphasis fell on the frontier in nineteenth-century politics as exemplified in figures like William Henry Harrison and Andrew Jackson and issues like land legislation, transportation, and, by the middle of the century, slavery. Along with the rise of the West as a separate "section"—a Turnerian word—and its influence in national affairs was the central place of the frontier in war, diplomacy, and international affairs. This theme focused on expansion as a basic force in American life from the opening of the seventeenth century to the close of the nineteenth. Beginning in 1775 war and independence led to extended diplomatic negotiations with England, France, and Spain, and several Indian tribes in the 1780's and 1790's, culminating in diplomatic and military successes. For the next decade and a half, the new American nation pursued its economic and physical expansion in the context of a general European war. Among the diplomatic triumphs of this period was the purchase of Louisiana Territory in 1803; its failures included the onset of a war with England for which the nation was unprepared. After 1815 the dominant theme was expansion and acquisition by war and diplomacy. Within little more than a generation, settlers filled in the major part of the continential nation, to the Great Bend of the Missouri River. War and diplomacy added Texas, California, the Far Southwest, and the Oregon country. By the opening of the Civil War, the continental nation had taken final shape.[4]

3. A basic volume in this tradition is Ray Allen Billington, *America's Frontier Heritage* (New York, 1966). A conventional study of the rise of the West remarkable for its detail is R. Carlyle Buley, *The Old Northwest: Pioneer Period, 1815–1840* (2 vols., Indianapolis, 1950). A series of variations on this model are three studies by Thomas P. Abernethy: *The Formative Period in Alabama, 1815–1828* (Montgomery, 1922), which emphasizes geography and political sectionalism; *From Frontier to Plantation in Tennessee: A Study in Frontier Democracy* (Chapel Hill, 1932), a fuller study that carries through the frontier period; and *Three Virginia Frontiers* (Baton Rouge, 1940), three essays on different frontier periods that take issue with Turner but stay within the Turner model.

4. Two standard works on the West in the affairs of the nation are Frederick Jackson Turner, *The Rise of the New West, 1819–1829* (New York, 1906); and Turner, *The United States, 1830–1850* (New York, 1935). A recent study that emphasizes national and international affairs is Francis S. Philbrick, *The Rise of the West, 1754–1830* (New York, 1965).

Within the last generation, a few historians have moved to a more systematic study of the frontier. Their work has focused on analysis, model building, and hypothesis rather than on description. Some of these studies have examined the evolution of institutions on the frontier. The emphasis has been on political institutions, albeit political institutions defined broadly enough to include economic development. Although these accounts have covered a wide range in time and space—from New England in the seventeenth century to the Pacific Coast in the nineteenth century—some of the most important studies have dealt with the trans-Appalachian frontier.[5] Other writers have broken away from the Turner model in different ways. One group has produced a series of studies on the contributions of the frontier experience to the American character and cultural traits as revealed in myth and symbol. In their search for large-scale values, some of these studies have a remote and ghostly quality about them. A problem that generally plagues them—and the work of more traditional historians, too—is the confusion between the terms "frontier" and "West." The two words have blended to the point where the distinction between them is lost, a circumstance that does nothing to clarify the concept of the frontier. This problem has been intensified in recent years as the study of the frontier has shifted to the study of the trans-Mississippi region and so more specifically the "West" in a geographic sense.[6] Yet the turn to new directions in recent years has produced a few historical studies of noteworthy insight. Among the most important is a consideration of the role of urbanization on the frontier, a

5. The most influential and widely read of the recent studies is Stanley Elkins and Eric McKitrick, "A Meaning for Turner's Frontier," *Political Science Quarterly*, 69 (1954): 321–53, 565–602. Their articles should be read in connection with a study of model building in Robert R. Dykstra, "Stratification and Community Political Systems," *American Behavioral Scientist*, 16 (1973): 698–707. An early statistical study directed to questions of democracy in politics and economics is Merle Curti, *The Making of an American Community: A Case Study of Democracy in a Frontier County* (Stanford, 1959), which analyzes Trempealeau County (Wisconsin) for the period from 1854 to 1880.
6. The most important of the works on the American West as symbol is Henry Nash Smith, *Virgin Land: The American West as Symbol and Myth* (Cambridge, 1950). Smith's book is not really concerned with the frontier. Other volumes in the same tradition are Arthur K. Moore, *The Frontier Mind: A Cultural Analysis of the Kentucky Frontiersman* (Lexington, 1957); and Richard Slotkin, *Regeneration through Violence: The Mythology of the American Frontier, 1600–1860* (Middletown, 1973). Among the historians whose works suffer from confusion between the terms "West" and "frontier" are Louis B. Wright, *Culture on the Moving Frontier* (Bloomington 1955), chs. 2 and 3; and Daniel J. Boorstin, *The Americans: The National Experience* (New York, 1965), pt. 2.

condition in which almost all frontiers shared sooner or later. Another fruitful avenue of inquiry is the place of abundance in American life, and specifically the part of the frontier in producing this abundance and in consuming it. The study of individual communities or societies also offers promise for the future, in assessing the way in which the early frontier experience produced both cooperation and conflict.[7]

This book focuses on societies and institutions in order to identify the differences between and among those areas that we generally call frontiers. Although it makes distinctions between and among different frontiers, this story generally uses the word "frontier" in the singular when it describes new land settlements. The frontier experience was shaped by many forces, among them changes in technology and the expanding values and influences of the longer-settled sections. As these changed, so did the frontier. At the same time, this account tries to preserve some sense of the impact of these institutional forces and the land itself on the individual pioneer. The migration to the West was undertaken by a vast cross-section of humanity that included male and female, young and old, black and white, affluent and poor, native-born and immigrant, and over three generations. The people formed themselves into the frontier societies. They shaped institutions and were, in turn, shaped by them.[8]

The words "frontier" and "West" have different meanings here. The "frontier" is the new land settlements, often with primitive economic, political, and social development. It is also the outer limits of American population settlement. The frontier is almost always a temporary circumstance—sometimes very brief—followed, in turn, by the rural world of nineteenth-century America, with its own kinds of hardships and frustrations. The "West" is a geographic designation. In this study, it

7. Among the most important studies in these areas are Richard C. Wade, The Urban Frontier: The Rise of Western Cities, 1790–1830 (Cambridge, 1959), whose value is limited by the select sampling of cities in both time and place and the failure to clarify the difference between "frontier" and "West"; David Potter's essay, "The Frontier of Abundance," in The People of Plenty: Economic Abundance and the American Character (Chicago, 1954), ch. 7; and Robert R. Dykstra, The Cattle Towns (New York, 1968).
8. Articles useful for the study of institutions are Earl Pomeroy, "Toward a Reorientation of Western History: Continuity and Environment," MVHR, 41 (1954–55): 579–600, which stresses continuity of institutions and values; Rowland Berthoff, "The American Social Order: A Conservative Hypothesis," American Historical Review, 65 (1960): 495–514, which argues that mobility in American society after 1815 helped to shape the nation in the nineteenth century; and Allan G. Bogue, "Social Theory and the Pioneer," Agricultural History, 34 (1960): esp. 30–34.

refers to the lands west of the Appalachian mountains, beginning with the new land settlements in Kentucky. This study of the trans-Appalachian frontier also includes Florida, Spanish in heritage, but American in its frontier experience after 1819. In the beginning, that is to say 1775, all those areas west of the Appalachians were frontiers; by 1815 this was no longer true. And by 1850 only parts of the trans-Appalachian West were still frontiers.

Professor James C. Malin, a remarkable man whose work is too little known and not enough remembered, once commented that all history is a progress report.[9] History is constantly written, and what appears at any one time represents at best only the most recent updating of information with interpretations. Such a comment is applicable to this book. It generalizes about a vast geographic area—larger than many European nations—and millions of pe ple. Such is the scope and power of the advance of population, the distances involved, and the long time period that much has been described in brief, other aspects not at all. Many of the topics identified herein invite full-scale investigations in their own right. This work should be thought of as a progress report, outlining some of the conceptual problems and suggesting solutions relative to this seventy-five years of the American frontier experience.

9. James C. Malin, *The Grassland of North America: Prolegomena to Its History* (Lawrence, Kan., 1947), vi.

I

Across the Mountains

The year 1775 opened on a motionless America. For one hundred and sixty-five years of permanent Anglo-American settlement, occupation of the continent had proceeded inland, but never rapidly. Indians, political intrigue, imperial considerations, vast distances, and physical obstacles had all slowed the advance. After five generations, settlements had reached the mountain ranges that barred the way to the interior. Along the seaboard a heavy commerce with European nations and a high quality of life achieved by several wealthy, leisured, and cultured societies (with great differences among them) testified to the maturity of the colonies. A class of educated men had developed politics and economics to a fine art. In that fateful year the cities along the eastern seaboard—and there were important urban centers—were in a ferment over the continuing quarrel with Great Britain. What had begun as a dispute about taxation and the payment of war debts had grown into a conflict over principle, calling into question the basic relationship between Great Britain and her colonies three thousand miles to the west. Inland from the great seaports, however (and not so far inland), life went on as it had for generations. The business at hand was scratching a living out of the soil, the acquisition of land, growing a few surplus crops or some livestock for market, always with a watchful eye on the forests for marauding Indians. Here life had changed little from that experienced by the first English settlers in the New World. Technological innovations—principally in firearms—provided a degree of security, but all around these people swelled the great forest, much as it had encompassed their fathers and grandfathers. The immensity of the wilderness that remained everywhere dwarfed cabins and clearings, and the more so as one moved west to the great Appalachian range.

The year 1775 was also a time of monentous events. In the East armed conflict broke out against King George III. This clash directed the colonies upon a course that would lead to a great struggle for independence. At the same time that gunfire sounded across the Lexington Green, in the remote wilderness west of the mountains a group of promoters, speculators, fur traders, land-hungry settlers, and free spirits were beginning the settlement of the trans-Appalachian region. In a short time they would establish another Lexington. Their proposal was no less dramatic, their dangers no less real, and their responsibilities for the future no less awesome for themselves and for the life of the new nation. Despite Indian hostility, official disapproval, isolation, and economic hardship, men and women embarked upon a venture in the interior of the continent so remote from the settled and secure portions of the colonies as to represent a new kind of frontier experience.

That this new departure in expansion to the West coincided with the outbreak of the American Revolution and a new departure in government raises the question of whether there was a connection between the two. In fact there was not. The first pioneers west of the mountains did think of themselves as engaged in a struggle for political and economic independence from proprietors and other colonial officials, but their interests were eminently practical. They were concerned with protection from the Indians, clear land titles, and good markets for their surplus crops. Whoever could provide these conditions—within reason—met their views of a good government, whether it be George III or George Washington. In truth, they did not long remain aloof, for the War for Independence came to the West as an Indian war. If there was one thing that the early pioneers agreed upon, it was the threat from the Indians, and the often-voiced sentiment that the Indians represented the British was enough to ally many frontier people with the independence movement in the East. Even so, it was a long time before the men and women of the western waters thought in terms of national allegiance. Immediately ahead lay a series of confrontations with Indians, with states, and eventually with a new national government.

The establishment in 1775 of permanent settlements in that area known as Kentucky marked a dividing line in this long expansion to the West. Although it was carried out by men and women less interested in their contributions to the welfare of the evolving nation than in their own prosperity and physical safety, nonetheless their actions opened the way to the interior of the continent. Even before the end of the Revolutionary War, boats began to drift down the Ohio. Singly and at first few in number, they only contrasted with the great river and the silent deserted shores. They were the harbingers of a powerful force, however, that in the years ahead would settle the interior of the continent for the new nation, force the Indians to move from their hunting grounds, push the Spanish into opening the Mississippi River, pressure the English into a reluctant evacuation of the Northwest posts, and, in short, lay the basis of the occupation of the continent to the Mississippi River and even beyond. So rapid and persistent was this movement during the years of the war itself that, by the coming of peace, it was no longer possible to confine the settlements to the east of the mountains. To make good her claim, the American nation embarked on a military struggle against the Indians and their British allies. For several years it was an equal contest. The inability of the Indians to unite in the face of the American advance balanced the inability of the weak, newly independent nation, suffering from severe financial burdens and internal discord, to carry on a military campaign at a distance of several hundred miles from its sources of strength on the East Coast.

The pioneer people who crossed the mountains into Kentucky and Tennessee and their children and grandchildren who acted out the next stages knew a great deal about occupying new land, learned from their parents and through years of experience in the woods and on the land. They knew how to fell a tree in a certain direction, how to build a log cabin, how to handle livestock, how to clear, plant, cultivate, and harvest. They also knew how to supplement their diet in the woods by hunting and fishing and how to trap fur-bearing animals whose skins would be useful in clothing the family. The women knew how to churn, bake, spin, weave, and sew. Above all, they knew how to raise their children to assist on the farm and to give them the skills they would need for a similar life ahead. These might include the ability to read and write, or it might not. The pioneers also knew how to accept the demands of the land and the physical hardships that it imposed. Gradually, advances in technology came to the frontier people, and, if the requirements were the same, the tasks became somewhat easier. Better axes and a steel plow, stronger wagons for hauling families and produce, and improved materials for constructing roads slowly made their influences felt. After 1815 came the steam engine, and with it an economic revolution for nation and frontier alike. Steam moved people across the water and, more important, upstream. It could run saws and millstones that in an earlier but still recent age had depended upon waterpower. These changes would affect the life of the frontier, but only gradually.

It was well for the frontier people that they had skills and experience in dealing with the wilderness, for even the mitigating circumstances of technological innovation could not relieve the physical presence of the new country. Around them lay a world as new and unformed as Eden. Natural forces of enormous power—great storms, fires, and floods—mixed with the promise of the land. The deep forests produced a pall of gloom that hung over travellers for days, and settlers for much longer periods. People saw sunlight occasionally filter through the canopy of trees, but they rarely travelled or lived in it. Balanced against this melancholy, however, were beautiful clear streams of running water and a variety and abundance of bird and animal life. Added to the force of nature was the sense of distance and loneliness. The earlier settlers went in small groups, but few could escape the feeling of having cast off from land and left a harbor to put to sea, without the prospect of a safe anchorage ahead. Behind lay family, friends, society—those forces that seemed to protect people from the danger; ahead lay the unknown.

In a manner strongly reminiscent of Marc Bloch's description of the age of feudalism, the early settlers across the mountains were surrounded by powerful forces—human and natural—that they could not control. Babies died at birth, and pioneer peoples of all ages and stations succumbed to diseases that few understood and no one could cure. Men ventured into the woods and never returned. The constant presence of injury and death, the sense of man as frail and vulnerable, gave rise to both a fatalistic view of life and a strong religious fervor as men and women vented their frustrations at the presence of such impersonal and seemingly uncontrollable forces. They also gave rise to superstition and folk remedies in medicine and religion, for where fate seemed to play such a significant role in the lives of people, fate must be analyzed, appeased, evaded. These people lived close to the earth. The rhythm of the seasons conditioned their lives, with an agricultural cycle, hunting interludes, and natural catastrophes. At the same time, hostile Indians who had mastered so much of the forbidding wilderness plagued them. As the tillers of land in the Middle Ages stayed near the castle, the pioneers of the trans-Appalachian frontier huddled close to their forted stations, casting an anxious eye on the sky, and then on the great forest, even as they rejoiced in the promise of the land.[1]

1. Marc Bloch, *Feudal Society* (Chicago, 1961), 72–75.

I

The Struggle for Security

In June of 1774 a group of adventurers led by James Harrod laid out a settlement near the headwaters of the Salt River in that broad expanse of land south of the Ohio River known as Kentucky. This act was the climax of the new, intense interest in the fertile region west of the mountains that made settlers disregard the official restriction of colony and crown and the dangers posed by powerful Indian tribes. Like other parties wandering through Kentucky, Harrod's group spent much time spying out the land and plotting future settlements. On an especially attractive site near a salt lick, Harrod and his men laid out a town, built cabins, staked out lots, cleared land, planted a crop of corn, and departed, leaving their pre-emptive marks on the surrounding countryside.[1]

James Harrod was not the first white man to visit the wilderness west of the mountains; he was not even the first Anglo-American. Many others, including the celebrated Daniel Boone, had been in and out of the region, especially since 1763. But Harrod's expedition and improvements of 1774 signified the beginning of permanent occupation. Some time during the following autumn or winter, a party of Indians came upon the deserted settlement and destroyed it. In doing so, the Native Americans acted out another scene in the drama between the retreating Indian civilization and the advancing Anglo-Americans. For more than a

1. Neal O. Hammon, "The Fincastle Surveyors in the Bluegrass, 1774," *RKSHS*, 70 (1972): 287–88.

century and a half the white settlers had tried to change the wilderness
and the Indian resisted. The persistence and numbers of the Anglo-
Americans gradually gained them the upper hand in this struggle. However often the Indian destroyed the isolated cabins, killed the livestock,
laid waste the cultivated fields, and even killed the settlers, the Anglo-
Americans continued to come. When members of Harrod's party returned in March of 1775, they found others already at the ruins of their
site. The two groups began at once to rebuild. The result was a crude
palisaded fort that endured. This structure may be considered the first
permanent Anglo-American settlement in that broad reach of territory
stretching from the Tennessee River to the Ohio, variously known as
Kentucky, the western country, or the land of the western waters.

At almost the same time that the palisades of Harrodstown (later Harrodsburg) provided settlers with a degree of physical protection in Kentucky, an entrepreneur named Richard Henderson, Virginian by birth
but North Carolinian by choice, dreamed of a speculative scheme that
would make him the head of a large proprietary colony in the trans-
Appalachian West. He represented the attraction of the lands west of the
mountains to investors and speculators and created an organization, the
Transylvania Company, that proposed to control large tracts of Kentucky by Indian leases and to sell these lands to immigrants. He intended to retain his rights to the lands in a manner characteristic of
proprietary colonies in the seventeenth century. This proprietorship
would be the foundation of a new colony—the fourteenth—and the first
west of the mountains. Henderson had a measure of grudging acquies-
cence from the Indians, achieved by long bargaining and plentiful distribution of trade goods to several chiefs at the Treaty of Sycamore
Shoals in March 1775. Buoyed with self-confidence and entranced by the
beauty of his Eden, he journeyed to Kentucky in April 1775. There, at a
site selected by his employee, Daniel Boone, he laid out Boonesboro, the
economic and political center of his proposed empire. The new settlement's first planned structure was a fort, symbolic of the immediate
needs for security that pressed from all sides.[2]

2. James M. Gaver, "The Boonesborough Experience: Revolution in the 'Dark and Bloody
Ground' " (B.A., Princeton, 1964), esp. ch. 4, analyzes Henderson's planning, prepara-
tions, execution, and the reasons for the proprietor's failure, especially the determination of the prospective settlers not to accept the old relationship between landlord and
tenant.

The establishment of the proposed Transylvania Colony and its promise of land attracted a number of immigrant land seekers. Henderson employed Daniel Boone and a company of axemen to cut a track to the settlement. The Wilderness Road, as it came to be called, ran from Long Island on the Holston River through the Cumberland Gap to the center of the new colony at Boonesboro. Even with a trail marked and cut, the journey was hard. William Calk, who went west with the Transylvanians in the spring of 1775, left a short but descriptive account. Here is a part of it:

> April satd first [1775] this morning there is ice at our camp half inch thick we Start Early & travel this Day along a verey Bad hilley way cross one creek whear the horses almost got Mired Some fell in & all wet their loads we cross Clinch River & travell till late in the Night & camp on cove creek. . . .

> tuesday 11th this is a very loury morning & like for Rain But we all agree to Start Early we Cross Cumberland River & travel Down it about 10 miles through Some turrabel Cainbrakes as we went down abrams mair Ran into the River with Her load & Swam over he followd her & got on her & made her Swim Back agin it is a very Raney Eavening we take up camp near Richland Creek they Kill a Beef Mr Drake Bakes Bread with out Washing his hands we Keep Sentry this Night for fear of the indians— [3]

Calk met some families returning to Virginia, but many of those who went to the western country stayed. The lure was the land. On the eastern side of the mountains were worn-out fields, high prices, and quitrents; ahead, at the end of the long immigrant road, the pioneer "began to discover the pleasing and rapturous appearance of the plains of Kentucky." So wrote Felix Walker, another 1775 immigrant. The experience was euphoric to an agriculturist. Walker wrote of "a sight so delightful to our view and grateful to our feelings, almost inclined us, in imitation of Columbus, in transport to kiss the soil of Kentucky, as he hailed and saluted the sand on his first setting his foot on the shores of America." [4] This second discovery of America drew families forth to the wilderness. Forted stations at Logan's and Boiling Springs appeared near the settlements at Harrodsburg and Boonesboro in the area later known as the

3. William Calk, "The Journal of William Calk, Kentucky Pioneer," *MVHR*, 7 (1920–21): 367–68.
4. Felix Walker, "The First Settlement of Kentucky," *De Bow's Review*, 16 (1854): 152.

Bluegrass. By the summer of 1775, as the new Continental Army gathered to lay siege to Boston, one hundred and fifty men were in Kentucky and two hundred acres planted in Indian corn. In the autumn of 1776 Virginia organized the new trans-Appalachian settlements into Kentucky County, an official recognition of their permanent nature.

The occupation of western North Carolina took place in two stages, one antedating the first permanent settlements in Kentucky. As early as the summer of 1771, pioneer families appeared west of the mountains along the Watauga and Holston rivers. Refugees from the Regulator defeat at Alamance swelled the numbers. Unlike the dramatic movement of people through the Cumberland Gap and into the Kentucky Bluegrass, expansion into the Watauga-Holston area was an extension of the North Carolina settlements. Here, in the mountain valleys of the Appalachians, pioneers struggled to cultivate the soil, to organize their settlements, and to make peace with the strong Indian tribes that surrounded them. In sharp contrast to this gradual growth was the founding of a permanent settlement along the Cumberland River in 1779. Inspired by the entrepreneurial genius of Richard Henderson, a group of pioneers (including John Donelson, whose daughter later became the wife of Andrew Jackson) chose to locate his new land grant on the distant Cumberland. In winter a large immigrant party moved by water down the Kentucky to the Ohio and thence up the Tennessee. Surviving both Indian hostility and a smallpox epidemic, the settlers established the village of Nashborough (later Nashville), built shelters, and, with the coming of spring, planted a corn crop. This second Tennessee settlement—some two hundred miles west of the Watauga-Holston frontier—lasted and grew. North Carolina eventually recognized its western settlements with the formation of Washington County in 1777 to serve the settlements just beyond the mountains and, in 1783, Davidson County, to accommodate the pioneers in the valley of the Cumberland River.

The ratification of a formal peace treaty recognizing American Independence in 1783 coincided with a period of increased immigration and intensified Indian warfare west of the mountains. People moved in great numbers from the Piedmont regions along the Wilderness Road and through the Cumberland Gap, then down the Ohio River by way of Pittsburgh. Richard Henry Lee wrote to James Madison of the "powerful emigration" from the interior parts of Virginia to Kentucky. He found two specific causes: "the desire of removing from heavy taxes and the search after land." For a variety of reasons, life in the New Country west of the mountains seemed more attractive than life in the Old. New immigrants went especially to Kentucky. The settlements there were already established and institutions of government, economy, and society more developed than elsewhere in the western country. The richness and fertility of Kentucky and other western lands were widely advertised. Virginia land warrants, redeemable in Kentucky lands, and the activities of land speculators helped to speed the movement of population.[5] (See table 1.)

Table 1. Growth of Kentucky and Tennessee, 1775–90

	Kentucky	Tennessee
1775	150	. . . . .
1776	. . . . .	7,700
1777	5,000 in the region south of the Ohio	. . . . .
1780	3,000 men able to bear arms	. . . . .
1782	8,000 inhabitants	. . . . .
1783	12,000	. . . . .
1784	30,000	. . . . .
1787	50,000	. . . . .
1788	. . . . .	25,000
1790	73,677	35,691

Source: These figures are from a more complete listing in Evarts B. Greene and Virginia D. Harrington, *American Population before the Federal Census of 1790* (New York, 1932), 192–94. The figures for 1790 come from the first federal census. Herman R. Friis, "A Series of Population Maps of the Colonies and the United States, 1625–1790," *Geographical Review*, 30 (1940): map for 1790, facing p. 464, gives a sense of the distribution of population in Kentucky and Tennessee.

To the south, settlements in the Tennessee Valley and the Watauga-Holston region grew slowly after 1783. A dispute with North Carolina over sovereignty added to the problems of warfare with the Indians and the great distances between the settlements. The year after North Carolina established Davidson County (the Nashville settlements), the Watauga-Holston settlements—North Carolina's county of Washington—declared their independence and formed the state of Franklin. The struggle between Franklin and North Carolina, which lasted for four years, disrupted orderly government, confused economic development

5. Richard Henry Lee to James Madison, Nov. 20, 1784, in Lee, *The Letters of Richard Henry Lee*, ed. James C. Ballagh (2 vols., New York, 1911), 2: 300. On immigration to Kentucky and the activities of speculators, see Patricia Watlington, *The Partisan Spirit: Kentucky Politics, 1779–1792* (New York, 1972), 17–23.

by calling land titles into question, and led to violence. Despite mani-
festos and courthouse raids, a number of people continued to arrive, and
settlement expanded along the French Broad, Powell, and Clinch (all
tributaries of the Tennessee), and, farther to the west, along the Cumberland. In 1788 the Franklinites capitulated, but they gained a measure
of independence from North Carolina two years later when Congress
created the Territory South of the River Ohio. The territorial governor
was a leading land speculator, William Blount. Whether the former
Franklinites thought Blount an improvement over the nabobs of Raleigh
is not clear, but he was more accessible and he did try to provide settlers
with protection from the Indians. Blount located the territorial capital at
Knoxville, a small village deep in the hills of the eastern Tennessee country. The trans-Appalachian settlements experienced a decade of steady
growth after the close of the Revolution.

The pioneers who moved to the trans-Appalachian frontier between
1775 and 1795 shared certain basic needs, principally food, shelter, and
physical security from the dangers of the wilderness. A distinguishing
feature of this first trans-Appalachian frontier was its anxiety over the
Indian. In later years the Native American would be relegated to the role
of a nuisance, an unpleasant obstacle in the movement of the American
peoples westward, and, finally, an improvident ward thrown on the
charity of the nation. The first generation of trans-Appalachian pioneers
knew a far different Indian: a brave and skilled adversary in warfare, a
cunning negotiator of equal stature around the council fire, a people
whose brilliant wilderness lore had been borrowed wholesale by the
Spanish, the French, the English, and eventually the Americans. In
time, security would come to mean an orderly society guaranteeing protection of private property; for the first pioneers of the trans-Appalachian
West, security meant simply protection from the Indian. The Indian
threat was especially severe in 1777 and 1781. Within a few years after
1775, men had come to the western country in such numbers as to make
it impossible for the Indians to drive them out, yet the nature of Indian
warfare, with its surprise attack and rapid withdrawal, disrupted the
agrarian society of the early pioneers. Frontier society, with its small,
scattered agricultural settlements and lack of a centralized military force,
had always been vulnerable to such attacks. For the years of the Ameri-

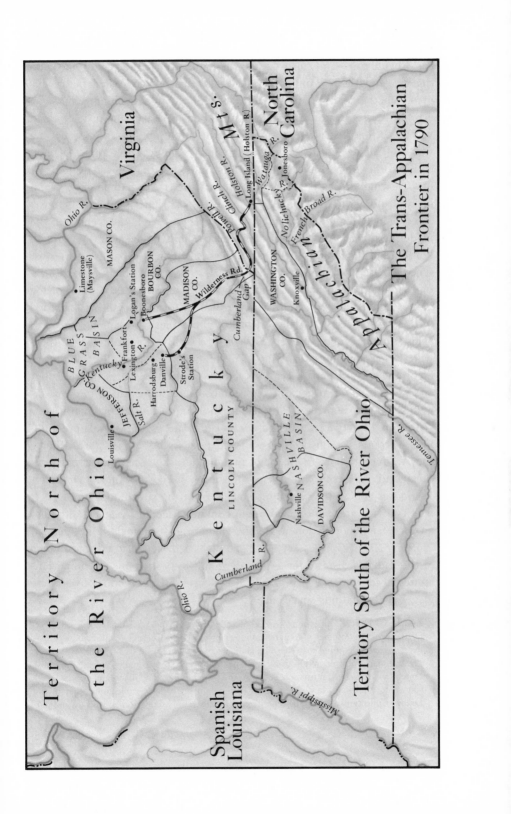

The Trans-Appalachian Frontier in 1790

can Revolution—and for a decade thereafter—no settler could look into
the forest without wondering whether death lay concealed before his
eyes, whether it was safe to fetch the family cow at evening, whether a
cry for assistance was a neighbor in need or an Indian ambush. No man
ventured from his cabin unarmed. A generation of children grew up in a
world of silence and hasty midnight trips to the nearest station. Women
endured the long absences of their husbands, but they never waited easily. Clearing and cultivating the land that the settler had come so far to
possess and endured so much to hold was hard, lonely, and dangerous.

To achieve conditions under which the pioneer could penetrate the
wilderness, clear the land, plant his crops, and at the same time protect
himself and his family, the early settlers relied on two basic institutions.
One of these, the frontier station, was new; a second, the organized militia, had roots deep in the colonial past. The station was a group of log
houses connected by a high wooden wall to form a primitive palisaded
fort. The pioneer Benjamin Allen described Biles's Station as "20 or 30
steps square, a house at every corner, & a family in each house." Others
were larger and more elaborate. The houses were generally two stories
high, the second floor serving as a firing station. Settlers cleared trees
and underbrush in order to secure unobstructed observation in every direction and to deprive the attacking Indians of cover. Men with early
claims on attractive sites or those who came later with Virginia pre-emption warrants established most of the first stations; like Harrodsburg,
they frequently bore the name of the founder. The early settlers of Kentucky and Tennessee found that the station suited their needs perfectly.
Its houses and walls were built of logs from the surrounding forests. It
had its own water supply and might contain space for livestock, although
an increasing population made the sheltering of animals less practical.
Nothing else was necessary. The station was designed to take advantage
of the Indian's distaste for a long siege and to destroy his one important
strategic advantage—surprise. It was successful. Individual lives were
lost, but the stations survived.[6]

6. Lyman C. Draper Collections, 11 CC 68, SHSW. Lyman Copeland Draper (1815–91)
filled a series of volumes with personal interviews of early Kentucky and Tennessee pioneers. He also acquired materials of a similar nature from the estate of John D. Shane, a
Presbyterian minister. While these volumes represent an invaluable source, one must
remember that the information is transcribed by Draper and Shane and comes in response to questions they posed. Like material in many large collections, that in the
Draper Collections tends to be repetitive, generally emphasizing Indian warfare and pio-

The settlers first lived within the walls of a station, but slowly the pressure of population and the gradual ebb of Indian warfare made it not only possible but also necessary for families to move outside the palisade. Once released from the stations by the lifting of a siege, settlers simply camped near the gates. Sometimes they constructed the first homes in an ever-widening arc around the station, to which people might return to fort up in time of emergency. Sarah Graham noted that her father built his first cabin in a clearing about seventy yards from Fisher's Station, in the Kentucky Bluegrass. As late as 1793, a threatened uprising of tribes in the southwestern Tennessee country led Governor William Blount to comment: "The families in general on the frontiers are collected at stations. at one which I lately visited (John Craig's) there are 280 people, men women and children, living in a miserable manner in small huts." Blount's diplomacy and liberal distribution of whiskey ("of which I considered it the interest of the United States to be as liberal as [Chief] Watts and his party were thirsty") finally quieted the Tennessee frontier, and the pioneer families dispersed to their homes.[7]

A more traditional instrument of defense was the militia. The role of the civilian-soldier had its roots in colonial America and, before that, in the English countryside. It reflected the traditional Anglo-American distrust of standing armies, and it was also inexpensive. The first militia units south of the Ohio were unofficial and simply included all men associated with a station or settlement. Each of the several rudimentary governments on the trans-Appalachian frontier provided for a militia, beginning with Richard Henderson's Transylvania Colony proprietorship and the Watauga Association—an unofficial government of the first settlers in eastern Tennessee—and extending through the state of Franklin and county governments under Virginia and North Carolina, to the territories northwest and south of the Ohio River. The requirements were almost always the same. The law or custom required that all men of arms-bearing age (generally eighteen to forty-five) enroll and muster on a regular basis. On the earliest and most exposed frontiers of Kentucky and Tennessee, serviceable equipment and skill in the field counted for more than the fine points of military organization and fancy

neer hardships. Several of the accounts collected by Draper and Shane have been published in the *FCHQ*.

7. Draper Collections, 12 CC 46; William Blount to Henry Knox, April 11, 9, 1793, in *TP*, 4: 251, 250.

uniforms. Sarah Graham, who had come to Kentucky in 1780, commented that the early militia units "had no other shirts than buckskin hunting shirts; and wore moccasins and bear-skin hats." Regulations gradually became detailed. A *Kentucky Gazette* notice specified the Kentucky requirements in 1787.

> Every non commission officer and private is by law directed to furnish himself with a good clean musket, containing an ounce ball, three feet eight inches long in the barrel, with a good Bayonet and iron ramrod, well fitted thereto, a cartridge box, properly made, to contain and secure twenty cartridges fitted to his musket; a good musket, and canteen; and to have at every muster one pound of good powder, and four pounds of lead, including twenty blind cartridges; and every serjeant to have a pair of moulds fit to cast balls, in their respective companies.[8]

The militia served needs of the frontier in addition to military defense. Regimental musters twice yearly and company musters quarterly were a center of political activity. Each militia company, for example, elected one delegate to the Danville Convention of 1784. The law specified that militiamen should elect their own officers, and many who had failed to meet the property qualifications for suffrage in one of the older states were thus given their first opportunity to cast a ballot or run for office. Militia activities also had a social side, for musters were the largest gathering of people on the trans-Appalachian frontiers until the great religious revivals at the turn of the century. They often coincided with court day, and after drills men would gather in small groups to play at politics, swap horses, engage in rough and tumble, debate the leading questions of the day (the price of land and crops), or simply exchange news.[9]

Private military organizations in the form of local volunteer units played a shadowy role in the first survival years. Their establishment resulted from the apparent inability of the militia to cope with the nature of Indian warfare. In the face of sudden raids, the militia seemed cum-

---

8. Draper Collections, 12 CC 45; Lexington *Kentucky Gazette*, Aug. 18, 1787. Under Kentucky law, militiamen might substitute a rifle for musket. The governor's declaration that all shirkers would be prosecuted (Lexington *Kentucky Gazette*, Aug. 25, 1787) suggests that not all those eligible served willingly.
9. George F. Taylor, "Suffrage in Early Kentucky," *RKSHS*, 61 (1963): 23; Margaret Kinard, "Frontier Development of Williamson County," *THQ*, 8 (1949): 25, 32; Margaret Burr DesChamps, "Early Days in the Cumberland Country," *THQ*, 6 (1947): 223–24.

bersome and inefficient. Private military groups, however, operated spontaneously and without the restraints of the militia. In their independence from higher authority and their single-minded determination for revenge, these groups may be considered antecedents of American vigilante movements. With a strongly vested personal interest, they were highly motivated and fought well on the distant reaches of the frontier. These groups focused on the threat at hand and were less inclined to drill and muster in approved fashion or on a regular basis. The political and social functions of the militia were probably less significant for private military organizations, although a few successful leaders, such as John Sevier of Tennessee, laid the basis of future political careers in such groups. These unofficial military units disappeared with the decline of the threat from the Indians.[10]

The need for physical security remained paramount on the early trans-Appalachian frontier, and it affected every aspect of life, especially patterns of settlement and travel. Most of the early immigrants to the trans-Appalachian regions north and south of the Ohio travelled in groups. The local newspapers carried notices of departure, stressing that those intent on joining should come armed. Prospective travellers assembled the night before to organize themselves; the expedition began promptly at daylight the following morning. Sometimes those returning to the east along the Wilderness Road joined together in a pledge of mutual support reminiscent of the Mayflower Compact. The itinerant Methodist circuit rider, Francis Asbury, has left an account of his participation in one such trip undertaken in 1790.

> We set out on our return through the wilderness with a large and helpless company; we had about fifty people, twenty of whom were armed, and five of whom might have stood fire. To preserve order and harmony, we had articles drawn up for, and signed by, our company, and I arranged for people for travelling according to the regulations agreed upon. Some disaffected gentlemen, who would neither sign nor come under discipline, had yet the impudence to murmer when left behind.[11]

10. Mariella Davidson Waite, "Political Institutions in the Trans-Appalachian West, 1770–1800" (Ph.D., Florida, 1961), 48, discusses Sevier. Simon Kenton's organization of the Mason County Minute Men is described in G. Glenn Clift, *History of Maysville and Mason County* (2 vols., Lexington, 1936), 1: 54.

11. Francis Asbury, *The Journals and Letters of Francis Asbury*, ed. Elmer T. Clark et al. (3 vols., Nashville, 1958), 1: 640; see also Lexington *Kentucky Gazette*, Jan. 15, May 7, 1791; April 27, 1793.

As late as the 1790's, men going up and down the Ohio to Limestone and Pittsburgh continued to advertise in the newspapers for well-armed companions.

That the station, the militia, and other institutions of frontier life emphasized self-assistance was just as well. Lack of federal military protection against the Indians was a continuing grievance of the frontier areas. In the period from 1775 to 1795 the national government made only sporadic efforts to protect the pioneers of the trans-Appalachian region. During the first decade, the new government fought a war for its independence against the strongest military power in the western world; in the second, the uncertain financial condition of the new independent nation worked against vigorous military action. Officials in the East often stressed that defense must be cheap, whatever its effectiveness.[12] When help was forthcoming, the force was undermanned, poorly provisioned, and badly led. Not until the twin military disasters of Josiah Harmar and Arthur St. Clair in the Northwest did the national government mount a vigorous campaign against the Indians.[13]

As basic as the need for physical security was the need for daily subsistence. The America of 1775 was a land of small farmers. The first pioneers of the trans-Appalachian frontiers were also farmers, and they reacted to the frontier experience of the trans-Appalachian West accordingly. The Anglo-American struggle for land in the New World had already been under way for a century and a half by the time the pioneers penetrated to the interior of the continent. It had been a long conflict in which the land seekers had fought against the Indians, colonial proprietorships, landlords, and quitrents. This quest for land drove men and women into the backcountry of the Carolinas, across the mountains in Pennsylvania, and into northern New England. The vision of rich, fertile, cheap lands now sent pioneers across the Appalachians, and with them, sometimes ahead of them, came the land speculators. By the decade of the 1790's, people had settled the central region known as the Kentucky Bluegrass, land had become expensive, and social and economic distinctions were already evident. Francis Asbury, who saw much

12. Note, for example, Henry Knox to Winthrop Sargent, Nov. 9, 1789, in *TP*, 2: 220–21.
13. Watlington, *The Partisan Spirit*, 29–30, discusses frontier resentment over the lack of military support from absentee Virginia landowners and from the state of Virginia.

of the western country, detected the conflict between the glorious lands of this western world and the spiritual glory of the next. "Good religion and such good land are not so easily matched together," he wrote.[14]

The pioneering experience began with the departure to the new land, and what the pioneer chose to carry with him was vital. Primitive transportation facilities placed a premium on weight. Tools and seed were the most commonly carried items. Although the settler was an agriculturist whose ultimate destiny was linked to the soil, his immediate survival depended on his skill with a variety of tools—the axe, knife, hoe, and rifle—and his ability to keep them in good working order. Joseph Doddridge remembered the several talents that his father brought to the frontier. The elder Doddridge could make shoes, cooper ware, and "farming utensils," which his son described as the best around. He could also spin thread, repair rifles, and build a cabin, hewed log house, or shingled house with equal facility. Furthermore, as the most literate man in the neighborhood, he served as a kind of public secretary for the community, writing "letters, bonds, deeds of conveyance, etc." These were all talents not only useful but even necessary to the frontiersman, although Doddridge perhaps possessed them to an unusual degree.[15]

Agricultural development ran from a small clearing in the forest or near a station with the first critical crop of corn, to a sufficiency, and ultimately to a surplus for sale. On arriving at his destination, the immigrant unloaded his horses and built a shelter for his family and supplies. Later he built a log cabin. Both the lean-to and cabin could be built from materials at hand, and often simultaneously with clearing the land. In the course of the next several years—if the settler remained in one spot—this first shelter might be supplemented or changed. If he moved again, the lean-to and log cabin cycle probably recurred. But, in every case, construction of buildings was a continuous process. The pioneer was always engaged in building or repairing barns, shelters, outbuildings, and additions to the house.

Coincident with the construction of shelter came cultivation of the soil. This invariably meant planting the first crop of corn. "They Begin laying off lots in the town and prearing for peopel to go to worek to

14. Asbury, *Journals and Letters*, 2: 83. Watlington, *The Partisan Spirit*, 38–44, lists some of the largest landowners, many of whom had come to Kentucky as surveyors.
15. Joseph Doddridge, *Notes on the Settlement and Indian Wars of the Western Parts of Virginia and Pennsylvania, from 1763 to 1783, Inclusive* (2d ed., Albany, 1876), 166–67.

make corn," wrote William Calk of the first arrivals in Boonesboro in the spring of 1775.[16] If the pioneer lived in or near a station, he would plant in one of the quarter-acre garden plots that surrounded the walls, or perhaps in a common field without fencing. In the woods, a suitable site would have to be cleared. Whatever the location and circumstances, corn was the universal crop on the trans-Appalachian frontier. It needed little cultivation. It grew rapidly in the fertile, black soil of the Bluegrass and the Nashville basins. Without this gift of the Indian, so easy to plant and so adaptable to frontier conditions, so nourishing and with so many uses, the cycle of life and labor on the early frontier would have been different. From the time of his arrival, the main effort of the early settler was directed to the cultivation of his corn crop. Seed was often scarce, family supplies limited, and the pioneer completely dependent upon the land for food through the next winter. At no other time was the pioneer so vulnerable as he was on the first harvest.[17]

Accounts of station life and early economic enterprise emphasize again and again that the family was an institution of central importance. The pioneers moved in family groups, both for physical protection and for mutual assistance in economic enterprise. The accounts collected by Draper, Shane, and others make constant reference to the family unit. Everyone worked on the first trans-Appalachian frontier—men, women, children, and older people—and they worked harder in the first years, when the farm was barely self-sufficient. The task of opening up the new land was all consuming. The routine chores were endless, with clothes and soap to make, cotton to pick and spin, corn to grind, and all the daily tasks that had to be done again and again. The family also lent an air of stability and purpose to the frontier scene. The Legislative Council of the Northwest Territory commented that "the foundation of public prosperity and happiness must be laid in private families;—every well ordered family is a little amiable community." [18]

The western country was a land of great promise, but plenty and prosperity lay in the future. Many of the early settlers came with little. A decade of war intensified their poverty. Recalling these early years for Draper or Shane, several pioneers noted how little the first generation of settlers had in the way of material goods. William Clinkenbeard im-

16. Calk, "Journal," 369.
17. Harriette Simpson Arnow, "The Pioneer Farmer and His Crops in the Cumberland Region," *THQ*, 19 (1960): 291–327.
18. Journal of the Legislative Council, 1800–01, ESR, Ohio, p. 90.

migrated to Kentucky with his father in 1780. It was a ragged procession, he explained, "Pressly Anderson was barefooted and bare legged (rolled up his pantaloons); his W.[ife] was walking and carrying her child." The Clinkenbeards settled at Strode's Station, north of Boonesboro, where they sought both safety and land. Strode let Clinkenbeard and others use land rent free until the close of the war. It was a good way to attract enough able-bodied men around the station to defend it in case of Indian attack. Each family had a garden just outside the palisade, a communal unfenced field, laid off into quarter-acre plots. There the Clinkenbeards and others cultivated their first Kentucky soil. Clinkenbeard remembered the early days in these terms: "The women the first spring we came out, wo'd follow their cows to see what they ate, that they might know what greens to get. My Wife and I had neither spoon, dish, knife, or any thing to do with when we began life. Only I had a butcher knife." While Clinkenbeard tilled the land, he also tried to assemble a herd of livestock. Domestic animals—whether cattle, sheep, or horses—were a promise of future income, for they were a prospective surplus crop and one that could walk to market in a world where land transportation was virtually nonexistent.[19]

Like other early farmers in Kentucky, Clinkenbeard also hunted and trapped, selling the meat and skins. He bought a set of trenchers from Enos Terry of Strode's Station, of whom he commented, "He turned dishes & bowls—& being no hunter exchanged them for meat & tallow to us hunters." Deer and buffalo were among the favorite early targets of the Kentucky hunters, especially the buffalo, which was often shot simply for sport. If we are to believe the accounts that have come down to us, every pioneer remembered shooting his first buffalo. Buffalo meat was also widely consumed. "Buffalo was mighty coarse meat; good deal like corn bread. Had it for bread," noted Benjamin Allen. "Then bear was fat, and we had it for meat." Pioneers also hunted turkey. John Hedge recalled of the early years in Kentucky: "We had turkey-pot-pie till I got so tired I never wanted to eat any more as long as I lived." Gradually the market hunter emerged, who sold his kill to later arrivals. "I supported the family, mostly with my gun," remembered John Graves.[20]

After clothes brought on the journey wore out, people made their

19. Draper Collections, 11 CC 54–66. Another account of livestock in the first years of settlement is Benjamin Allen's in *ibid.*, 11 CC 68.
20. Draper Collections, 11 CC 55, 122, 69, 22.

own, as they had earlier, east of the mountains. Jeptha Kemper commented that "every family had to wear their own make. They had no stores, and if they had, they had no money to take to them." Sometimes home-woven cloth supplemented the skins of the forest. Sarah Graham remembered that her mother brought four pounds of cotton seed and planted it. From this "she raised 14 lbs: of picked cotton the 1st year, besides letting Aunt Sooky Holtzclaw and Mrs. Copeland also have of some of the seed, from which they also raised cotton. Mother gave 7 yds: of cotton for one sow shoat. With 9 yds: she got some salt on Beargrass and a little money besides."[21]

Clinkenbeard, Allen, Hedge, and others came out in search of land. They found people there before them already in control of large tracts. These were entrepreneurs of means and luck—early on the scene in strategic locations subject to pre-emption rights under a Virginia law of 1779—who intended to make fortunes and build great landed estates. John Floyd of Virginia was one of these. Floyd came to Louisville at the falls of the Ohio in the winter of 1779. He immediately established a station on his land. He hoped to find pioneers to settle and make improvements. "I have no fear of not getting Settlers at my station in abundance, as they are *very sickly at the falls*," he wrote. While his family lived in a tent for ten weeks, Floyd built five cabins for his prospective tenants. Although a family of means, the Floyds endured the hardships shared by all pioneer families. The winter of 1779–80 was an exceptionally severe one. A freeze in mid-December closed the Ohio to traffic. Floyd's outlook on life changed from the confidence of an entrepreneur to the anxiety of a man struggling for survival. He asked relatives or friends making the trip west that winter please to bring "a little Flour," an item that he called "as dear as gold dust." Corn rose to $165 a bushel at Louisville, "and people seem desirous to have every other article in proportion to that. Money is of no account here." Floyd also appealed to his friends in Virginia to send clothes for his wife and son. But throughout the winter he continued to make reference to "all the advantages we expect in the future" and to "my Land where I shall soon have a fine plantation and Fort." With the coming of spring, Floyd's prospects rose with the swollen Ohio. He wrote of his changed fortunes:

> I am sorry I made such complains to you in the winter about Bread as we now have plenty. I think near *three hundred large Boats have arrived at the Falls this spring* with families, & *corn* can be bought now for thirty

21. Draper Collections, 12 CC 130, 46.

Dollars — We have *six stations* on B. Grass with not less *than 600 men.*
You would be surprised to see 10 or 15 Waggons at a time going to &
from *the falls* every day with Families & corn.[22]

The simplest kinds of economic transactions characterized the
economy of the early trans-Appalachian frontiers. People concentrated
on the immediate needs of life, which they found in the soil and the
woods. To the extent that they made economic contact with the outside
world, it was through the fur trade. On all the frontiers from western
Pennsylvania to Georgia, the earliest trade with the East was in peltry.
The relatively high value of furs justified their transportation for long
distances over poor roads. Doddridge commented of early western Pennsylvania, "Fur and peltry were the people's money. They had nothing
else to give in exchange for rifles, salt, and iron, on the other side of the
mountains." The first Kentucky and Tennessee pioneers also traded in
furs and ginseng. The numbers of fur-bearing animals gradually diminished, as the large numbers of immigrants (especially after 1783) cut
down the forests. Trapping continued, however, and Kentucky newspapers in the Bluegrass country advertised for furs as late as 1795, suggesting a continued supply and a commodity of consistent value.[23]

Such accounts suggest, too, the barter economy that accompanied agricultural self-sufficiency. Hard currency was scarce on the early trans-
Appalachian frontier. Immigrants carried a small supply of cash with
them for corn, seed, meat, and other necessities such as nails, tools, or
salt, but few of the new settlers had much money. Merchants in urban
Lexington, the commercial center of the Bluegrass, permitted the pioneer to pay for goods in the products of the farm and the forest. If the
merchant wished to do business, he had no choice. Early Kentucky surveying fees were paid in tobacco, dressed deerskins, and second-rate
cows and calves. John Hedge remembered that "the currency of the
country then was cows and calves, and horses. More current than our
bank notes now. Have heard a horse cried off in Paris at so many cows
and calves."[24]

22. John Floyd to Col. William Preston, Montgomery County, Virginia, Oct. 30, Nov.
26, Dec. 19, 1779; Jan. 19, May 5, 1780, Draper Collections, 17 CC 120–25, 185–87.
Indians killed Floyd in 1783. On his life and career, see Watlington, *The Partisan Spirit,*
35–37.
23. Doddridge, *Notes on the Settlement,* 148; Lexington *Kentucky Gazette,* Jan. 3, 1795.
24. Charles Richard Staples, *History of Pioneer Lexington, 1779–1806* (Lexington, 1939),
31–33, 37; William Chenault, "The Early History of Madison County," *RKSHS,* 30
(1932): 142; Draper Collections, 11 CC 19.

The immigrants developed a number of frontier industries and utilized a variety of mechanical skills to meet their basic needs. Production of salt and iron usually received attention first. Saltworks early appeared in Kentucky, capitalizing on the many salt licks and the importance of meat in the frontier diet. Salt was one of the few items that the frontiersman purchased at a store. Another was iron. Blacksmiths established furnaces, and such facilities were almost invariably profitable. With the universal dependence on firearms and livestock, the blacksmith was one of the most valued of frontier tradesmen. A Cincinnati doctor, Daniel Drake, who grew up on the Kentucky frontier, later wrote, "The mechanic acts practiced at that time were only those which are inseparable from civilization. The blacksmith, house carpenter, turner, tanner, shoemaker, tailor, weaver, and such like, made the whole, and all were very commonplace in skill." Drake concluded, "The great occupation was clearing off the forest and cultivating the rich and fresh new soil."[25]

The gristmill was the most widespread of the early industries; it processed corn, the basic frontier crop. The mills of the trans-Appalachian frontier depended for power on the many swift streams that fed the large river system of the Ohio Valley. Perhaps two hundred tributaries of the Tennessee and Cumberland rivers alone had sufficient power for mills. The reliance on waterpower made milling a seasonal operation, for mills could not operate during periods of low water. At floodtime, they might be washed away. Even with all the inconveniences and expenses of heavy stones and dam construction, mills early appeared almost everywhere, and pioneers flocked to the mills with their corn.[26] Robert McAfee remembered a mill built in the vicinity of Harrodsburg as early as 1778, widely used although the "large hand mill stones . . . ground but slowly, and after filling the hopper it was often left to itself for half a day at a time. The wild turkies often resorted to it to get their breakfast." In 1783 the McAfees moved away from the station and immediately felt the need of a mill. McAfee's father, "with the assistance of his brothers . . . and one or two hired hands built a log dam across Salt River and put up a small Tub mill which afterwards done a good business for many years, and settlers from Benson near Frankfort often came to his mill with

25. Harriette Simpson Arnow, *Seedtime on the Cumberland* (New York, 1960), 249–50, 252–54; Daniel Drake, *Pioneer Life in Kentucky, 1785–1800* (Cincinnati, 1870), 179.
26. Kenneth McDonald, "Milling in Middle Tennessee, 1780–1860" (M.A., Vanderbilt, 1938), 239–44.

packhorses loaded with grain." Mills in Tennessee, western Virginia, and Pennsylvania followed the same pattern. Such was the demand for their services that laws and local custom controlled their use. The law usually provided that each take his turn at the mill. A wait was almost always involved, perhaps even a stay overnight. For this reason, a young boy often carried the corn or grain to the mill and returned with the flour. It was a fine opportunity for social contact, and the wait with contemporaries offered a chance to skylark, visit, play games, and exchange news. For his services, the miller collected a portion of the flour, generally one-eighth. As an enterprise that provided a most necessary economic service, the mill achieved the status of a public utility.[27]

The struggle against the Indians, the Revolution under way in the East, and the physical conditions of the new land all affected the quality of life on the first trans-Appalachian frontier. Immigrants crowded into stations, diet was limited, and sanitary conditions grew worse with the passage of time. John Floyd noted the aggravations of confined quarters and restricted diet. "People this year seem generally to have lost their health: but perhaps it is owing to the disagreeable way in which we are obliged to live," he wrote, "crowded in forts where the air seems to have lost all its purity and sweetness." Floyd's son was ill, and he was "much afraid we shall lose the child, and if we do I shall impute it to nothing but living in dirt and filth."[28]

Despite all the hardships, dangers, and lack of material things, immigrants came across the mountains in increasing numbers. People came during the Indian warfare of 1777; they came before, during, and after the severe winter of 1779–80; they came throughout a decade of Indian hostility that began after the Treaty of 1783. These numbers ensured the survival of the first American frontier. A sea of farms and land seekers submerged the early stations. And if the frontier experience had a certain physical hardness about it, the seemingly infinite fertility of the soil repaid the effort. The economic returns of these first years were limited, but most settlers had sufficient food and fiber to support life. Robert

---

27. Robert B. McAfee, "Sketches of the First Settlements in Kentucky," Draper Collections, 4 CC 98; McAfee, "The Life and Times of Rbt. B. McAfee and His Family Connections; Written by Himself, Commenced April 23, 1845," *RKSHS*, 25 (1927): 113; Arnow, *Seedtime on the Cumberland*, 278, 394; Mary A. Stephenson, "Some Early Industries of Mercer County," *RKSHS*, 13 (1915): 47.
28. Floyd to Preston, June 1780, Draper Collections, 17 CC 182–83.

McAfee commented that the people had enough to live on, "and their stock of Hogs & cattle as well as horses increased rapidly."[29] This rapid growth of the settlements moved the pioneers into a new stage of development.

29. McAfee, "The Life and Times," 113.

2

The Search for Stability

At some point in the frontier experience, the pioneer turned his attention from security to stability. When the immediate demands of physical safety, shelter, and subsistence were satisfied, or nearly so, the question was then how best to safeguard the economic advantages of land and to realize the high expectations that had sent most families to the western country. The distinction between desire for security and desire for stability was not always a clear one. The two conditions were not mutually exclusive but often overlapped, or the second followed so closely on the first as to be indistinguishable from it. Yet to achieve stability, a more complicated economic life was necessary, and the organization of government, law, and social institutions. Economic prosperity assured the survival of new settlements, their growth, and the eventual appearance of a more complex society. In such a world people had the leisure to ponder their condition and to work effectively for its improvement. Government established a framework within which men pursued their interests in an orderly fashion, following generally accepted rules of behavior. Those who deviated could be confined and punished. A legal code regulated personal conduct and encouraged people to risk their capital. The amorphous, random, chaotic world of the early frontier had to be formed into some sort of viable society. The West had to become, sooner or later, a place where people wanted to live permanently, not simply where they endured.

At the root of the transition was a growing economic prosperity. By the end of the first year, the frontier family generally had sufficient harvest to meet its immediate needs; by the end of the second, there was enough to feed livestock as well. The third year, a surplus sometimes remained. When the harvests of the field and the forest exceeded the needs of the family, the pioneer began to think of a way to turn this surplus into needed goods and services. Sometimes he found a market near at hand in new immigrants, with whom he exchanged corn and meat for cloth, iron, tools, and perhaps even hard money. Robert McAfee remembered that in 1786 his father "raised an abundant crop which he sold to new settlers which poured into Kentucky every year." Eventually the new settlements produced agricultural surpluses so large that they could no longer be absorbed locally. At this point an accessible and reliable market had to be found in the outside world. The Ohio and Mississippi rivers (fed by the Cumberland and Kentucky, among others) were among the great river systems of the world, and the logical market was the port of New Orleans. But in the 1780's trade downriver developed slowly, impeded by distance, the uncertain nature of the market, and the bureaucratic confusion and diplomatic intrigue with Spanish officials over American rights of navigation on the Mississippi.[1]

From the beginning of its growth at the end of the Revolution, the settlers of the trans-Appalachian frontier searched for a commercial crop with an intensity reminiscent of their Virginia ancestors. The answer was the same: tobacco. Until 1783 hemp was the more significant crop, and tobacco raised only in small quantities. Therefore, tobacco cultivation spread over much of the Bluegrass and Nashville basins. In the manner of the early Virginia experience, tobacco became the circulating medium of the day. Taxes, fines, fees, debts, and so forth could all be paid in tobacco. As early as 1783, an inspection system certified the quality of the exportable product. Three warehouses—two on the Kentucky River, the third at the falls of the Ohio—became the centers of the

1. William Flinn Rogers, "Life in East Tennessee near the End of the Eighteenth Century," East Tennessee Historical Society, *Publications*, 1 (1929): 32–35; Robert McAfee, "The Life and Times of Rbt. B. McAfee and His Family Connections; Written by Himself, Commenced April 23, 1845," *RKSHS*, 25 (1927): 116. On the difficulties of trade with Spanish New Orleans in the 1780's, see Arthur P. Whitaker, *The Spanish American Frontier, 1783–1795: The Westward Movement and the Spanish Retreat in the Mississippi Valley* (Boston, 1927), 94–96. Several theses discuss transportation and trade the best is Henry Hendricks Gauding, "Water Transportation in East Tennessee prior to the Civil War" (M.A., Tennessee, 1933), ch. 2.

inspection system. The farmers took tobacco to the warehouse, where inspectors graded it and issued a receipt. This receipt circulated as currency. Until 1795 counterfeiting a tobacco warehouse receipt was a crime punishable by death. The rise in tobacco as an export commodity necessitated a more complex economic system, and the scale of the trade created enlarged opportunities for the specialization of economic function.[2]

Merchants became an integral part of this world. They were already important economic figures on the early trans-Appalachian frontiers, arriving just behind the first settlers. The business of the merchant was to supply the pioneers with needed items. He was the first contact of the subsistence frontier with the commercial East, and he served as an intermediary figure in bringing commerce to the western country. The career of Lardner Clark of Nashville is one example. As early as 1783, Clark sold goods to the new citizens of Nashville and Davidson County. It was an uncertain and risky undertaking. He offered credit and accepted payment in whatever products the frontiersman might bring forward. As a result, he found himself constantly involved in litigation to recover claims. At the other end of the scale from his impoverished western clientele were the creditors of the East, with their large offices, safe homes, and dunning form letters. Clark exemplified the burdens and the risks. In spite of his handsome house (one of the finest in early Nashville) and his many public offices, he was constantly in debt and had to sell off portions of his landholdings. He died in 1801 virtually bankrupt.[3]

As the size and scope of trade expanded on the trans-Appalachian frontier, so did the functions of the merchant. He gradually became a middleman in the export of western products. In order to trade, merchants had to take agricultural produce; of necessity, they became shippers. Flatboats carrying large quantities of bulk produce received in payment for store goods were among the first to venture down the Mississippi. Merchants began to assume banking functions—offering credit,

2. Leland Smith, "A History of the Tobacco Industry in Kentucky from 1783 to 1860" (M.A., Kentucky, 1950), ch. 1. The expansion of tobacco culture may be traced on a map of the inspection stations and the dates of their founding (p. 30).

3. W. A. Provine, "Lardner Clark, Nashville's First Merchant and Foremost Citizen," *THM*, 3 (1917): 28–50, 115–33; the inventory of Clark's estate is on pp. 126–27. Margaret Burr DesChamps suggests that the average annual family expenditure at the local store, "a center of the community," did not exceed twenty dollars. "Early Days in the Cumberland Country," *THQ*, 6 (1947): 211.

making loans, discounting notes, serving as brokers in financial transactions. John Sanders, for example, established a bank in Louisville, issuing bills of credit based on goods received. The commodities bound downriver were still frontier staples and tobacco, but the quantities increased, and to save transportation costs merchants gradually took on processing functions, turning hogs into pork, cattle into beef, and wheat into flour. Processing represented a new stage in development. Elisha Winters of Lexington advertised his business in 1794 as a mixture of trade, shipping, and processing. He and his partners had a large assortment of goods to sell for

> Tobacco, Hemp, Wheat, beef, Pork, Hempseed, Flax, Hog's Lard, Peltry, Bees wax, Hog's Bristles, or Cash—They will contract (on generous terms) for the ensuing crop of Hemp. They want immediately to employ a number of men that understands Boat building. Also two good Coopers that understands either right work or flour barrels, and great wages will be given to a Miller who can come well recommended.[4]

The trans-Appalachian frontier experienced dramatic changes in the 1780's—physical expansion, increased population, and rising trade. Stations became towns; farms grew into plantations. The pioneers and adventurers of the early years found themselves supplanted by new arrivals. Virginians and Carolinians of substance came across the mountains, carrying land warrants or acquiring them on their arrival. Joining them were former Revolutionary War officers and professional men, especially lawyers. In a sense, all these people were the harbingers of a more stable society. The 1780's also witnessed the rise of the tobacco culture. Lands in the Bluegrass region became valuable, and this broad belt of limestone soil became more and more the economic, social, and political center of a growing population.[5]

In this decade government became a powerful influence. Government was one of the first institutions on the trans-Appalachian frontier. It appeared in some form with the construction of the first station, with agreements for travelling together, or in making arrangements to cultivate a field of corn communally. Early government was often closely

4. Lexington *Kentucky Gazette*, Feb. 15, 1794. Cf. the career of Andrew Jackson as a merchant near Nashville in 1795 in Thomas P. Abernethy, "The Early Development of Commerce and Banking in Tennessee," *MVHR*, 14 (1927–28): 311–12.
5. Delbert P. Eagle, "Aspects of the Kentucky Frontier" (M.A., Kentucky, 1938), ch. 1.

related to questions of security and hence to the militia, and the creation of one often led to another. Where the military organization appeared first, the command structure might gradually assume civil functions. As the needs of the frontier became more complex, people gave government powers to direct the orderly distribution of land, to keep necessary records, and to afford merchants a degree of protection. Whether it was security or stability they sought, frontier people turned to frontier government to serve where state government did not function or functioned inadequately (in the case of Virginia and North Carolina) or to supply services that individuals by themselves could not provide—protection from the Indians, construction of roads and bridges, delivery of the mail, and, eventually, custody of the poor and orphaned.[6]

Early frontier governments were much alike in objectives and structure. In a petition to North Carolina, dated 1775, the upper Watauga River settlers stated their reasons for coming together.

> Finding ourselves on the Frontiers, and being apprehensive that, for the want of a proper legislature, we might become a shelter for such as endeavoured to defraud their creditors; considering also the necessity of recording Deeds, Wills, and doing other public business; we, by consent of the people, formed a court for the purposes above mentioned . . . [this] was done by the consent of every individual.[7]

The members of the Watauga Association chose five commissioners to serve as "a court" that would decide contested issues. The settlers, through the association, also negotiated with the surrounding Indian tribes for a lease to their lands. Pioneers on the Nolichucky and in Carter's Valley eventually joined the Watauga settlement. Growth in numbers led to a gradual expansion of the role of government, and the "court" eventually employed a clerk and sheriff. Commissioners began to hold sessions at regular intervals. As a basis for judgment, the settlers used the laws of Virginia, the legal code familiar to the largest number.[8]

6. Two general accounts of government in the trans-Appalachian West are George Henry Alden, *New Governments West of the Alleghenies before* 1780 (Madison, 1897); and Mariella Davidson Waite, "Political Institutions in the Trans-Appalachian West, 1770–1800" (Ph.D., Florida, 1961).

7. Quoted in J. G. M. Ramsey, *The Annals of Tennessee to the End of the Eighteenth Century* . . . (Philadelphia, 1853), 134–38.

8. John Haywood, *The Civil and Political History of the State of Tennessee from Its Earliest Settlement up to the Year* 1796 (Nashville, 1891), 50–61; Waite, "Political Institutions in the Trans-Appalachian West," ch. 1.

Other rudimentary governments on the trans-Appalachian frontier followed the lines of the Watauga model. Judge Richard Henderson was a dominant figure in the formation of two governments: the Transylvania Company (1775) and the Cumberland Association (1780). In May 1775, as proprietor of the Transylvania Company, he called for representatives of the Kentucky settlements to meet at Boonesboro for purposes of making "such Laws" as necessary for the safety and good order of the new settlements. Seventeen representatives responded and debated for five days in this first legislative activity on the new trans-Appalachian frontier. The emphasis fell on the needs for protection of the people in the new settlements and of the property that they had and hoped to acquire. The bills passed convey the range of concerns shared by frontier people.

1. An Act for establishing Courts of Jurisdiction, and regulating the practice therein.
2. An Act for regulating a Militia.
3. An Act for the Punishment of Criminals.
4. An Act to Prevent Profane Swearing and Sabbath Breaking.
5. An Act for Writs of Attachment.
6. An Act for ascertaining Clerks' and Sheriff's Fees.
7. An Act to Preserve the Range.
8. An Act for Improving the breed of Horses.
9. An Act for Preserving Game.[9]

The Cumberland Association, Henderson's government for the new Nashville settlements, emphasized military organization and judicial machinery for the adjustment of disputes, especially those surrounding land title. A preamble to the articles of organization listed the many duties of the association and the reasons for its establishment. It specifically mentioned "the manifold suffering and distresses" endured by the settlers, the desertion of many who became discouraged, and the subsequent condition under which "all administration of justice seemed to cease from amongst us." The authors applauded the return of settlers with the conclusion of the war and thought the time appropriate to move to a more organized society. They wrote:

9. Quoted in James M. Gaver, "The Boonesborough Experience: Revolution in the 'Dark and Bloody Ground' " (B.A., Princeton, 1964), 83. It should be borne in mind that the proprieters, especially Henderson, exercised much authority at this time, and they probably also influenced legislation, especially the attention to legal forms and the courts.

It appears highly necessary that for the common weal of the whole, the securing of the peace, the performance of contract between man and man, together with the suppression of vice, again to revive our former manner of proceedings, pursuant to the plan agreed upon at our first settling here, and to proceed accordingly, until such times as it shall please the Legislature to grant us the salutary benefit of the law duly administered amongst by their authority.

The "several Stations" chose twelve men to meet at Nashville on January 7, 1783. The Committee, for so it was called, gave much attention to the problem of defense. Security was clearly still a paramount concern.[10]

None of these rudimentary governments survived; nor did they develop striking new forms or foster the emergence of a new group of leaders. Instead, the forms of government on the trans-Appalachian frontier were much like those found east of the mountains, and the leaders generally came from the first rank of property holders. What these first experiences at government did suggest was a common core of needs, chiefly over matters of security, external and internal. External security meant protection from outside threats such as Indians, by negotiations and, if necessary, by military organization. Internal security meant the peaceful resolution of disputes between and among members of the settlement, with legal machinery for the arrest, trial, and punishment of those who flouted or disobeyed established rules of conduct. Conflicts often concerned land, and a committee (or court) was often set up to arbitrate them. Most of the pioneers had settled on land that they held solely by right of occupation and without vestige of legal title, and they sought guarantees to their land. They also wanted stability in their relations with one another and with people and institutions in the outside world. Stability meant record keeping, and early frontier governments gave much attention to writing, recording, and validating land claims. This same emphasis on bookkeeping is found in the mining camps of the trans-Mississippi West a century later. As the pioneer acquired

10. "Records of the Cumberland Association," *American Historical Magazine*, 7 (1902): 115–16, 123. In addition to the usual emphasis on the militia, the Committee "agreed that six spies be kept out to discover the motions of the enemy, so long as we shall be able to pay them. Each to receive 75 bushels of Indian corn per month." Unlike Watauga, Westsylvania, and Transylvania, the state of Franklin had full executive, legislative, and judicial branches. Note Waite, "Political Institutions in the Trans-Appalachian West," 10.

property and as property became a compelling force, record keeping expanded to include stock marks, surveys, probate, and marriage records.[11]

When Virginia extended county governments to Kentucky in 1776, the trans-Appalachian frontier had its first official government. The concept of the country as a basic unit of local government had its roots in England. It was a form familiar to most frontier peoples. In an era of primitive transportation, long distances, and deferential societies, county government was a powerful element in individual lives. Its leaders were the most important men in the county, and often the largest landowners. They had much in common with their colleagues at the seat of colonial and later state government and were unlikely to do anything to upset the existing political or economic framework. The machinery of government established in Kentucky County was unexceptional. Virginia authorities named five judges, chose Harrodsburg as the county seat, and in September 1777 the judges convened the first county court of quarter sessions, where they set in motion the military and civil provisions of the act creating Kentucky County. The militia, already organized, became a part of the Virginia militia system. The court also named a number of auxiliary officers, including a clerk of the court, sheriff, surveyor, and ten justices of the peace, one for each of the stations scattered across the Kentucky frontier.[12]

County government gradually expanded its authority to include jurisdiction over the construction and maintenance of roads, support for the poor, the licensing of public facilities from taverns to gristmills, and the admission of lawyers to the bar. The number of offices and the machinery of government increased with the added duties. Plural officeholding was common, and most of the important local figures held several positions of public trust. Sitting in separate judgment or together as a court, the justices had enormous power to define the limits of their authority and to inflict summary punishment. They also levied taxes and allocated tax monies. The county court was self-perpetuating, for its

11. John D. Barnhart, *Valley of Democracy: The Frontier versus the Plantation in the Ohio Valley, 1775–1818* (Bloomington, 1953), 46–50; Jack M. Sosin, *The Revolutionary Frontier, 1763–1783* (New York, 1967), ch. 11, esp. pp. 166–71. The importance of organization against both internal and external dangers in one county is discussed in Raymond Clifford Seeber, "A History of Anderson County, Tennessee" (M.A., Tennessee, 1928), 25–26.

12. Robert S. Cotterill, *History of Pioneer Kentucky* (Cincinnati, 1917), 118–20.

members filled vacancies as they occurred. When the numbers of people grew too large or when people settled at too great a distance from the county seat, new counties were laid off, and the process repeated itself.[13]

Hand in hand with government came law and the court system. The pioneers of the western country looked forward to the material rewards of their efforts, but they could not help feeling apprehensive over the disorganized state of frontier society. Men and women had dispersed over vast areas without any force to make them respect one another's rights. Early law came in many forms. For the rudimentary governments of the Watauga, Boonesboro, and Cumberland settlements, it was largely informal. The early court provided machinery to resolve disagreements within the settlement and prevent violence in a society already uneasy over the unsettled nature of wilderness life. Law, if such existed, was local custom. Men presented their grievances against one another to neighbors sitting as elected commissioners; these considered the case in the context of local custom and rendered a verdict. With the arrival of county government from Virginia and North Carolina, the law and court system became both more formal and wide ranging. There were soon several courts dispensing Virginia or North Carolina law. At the bottom were the justice of the peace courts, single judge tribunals of great power and authority delivering summary justice at the local level, with jurisdiction over cases involving small sums and minor infractions of civil law. At the next level were the county courts, a basic judicial unit on the frontier. In a large cabin or even a private home at the county seat, justices of the peace (generally three to five) sat in judgment. The convening of the county court (it generally met four times a year) was a social as well as judicial occasion. County courts spread over the trans-Appalachian region with settlement, and, by 1790, frequently in advance of population. Above the county court was the circuit court, and, at the top, the supreme or superior court for the territory or state. Both of

---

13. Harriette Simpson Arnow, *Seedtime on the Cumberland* (New York, 1960), 315–16. Compare the structure and operation of the Kentucky county court system with that of Virginia a generation earlier in Charles S. Sydnor, *Gentlemen Freeholders: Political Practices in Washington's Virginia* (Chapel Hill, 1952). A discussion of the enormous continuing influence of the Kentucky county court is Robert M. Ireland, *The County Courts in Ante-bellum Kentucky* (Lexington, 1972).

these higher courts met at set intervals. Along with the county court appeared the general court of quarter sessions, which dealt with a variety of frontier administrative problems like roads, taxes, the poor, and public improvements; it also appointed constables and assumed a quasi-legislative function for the citizens of the country. In counties of the South, the general court also established patrols to control the local slave population. The orphans court and the probate court were offshoots of the general court and handled specialized business.

A few case studies will help to show how several frontier courts of the trans-Appalachian region functioned. The first court in the "upper East Tennessee" met at the cabin of Charles Robertson, near Jonesboro, on February 23, 1778. The court opened by choosing a full slate of subordinate officers. Then, exercising judicial, administrative, and legislative powers, it proceeded to the problems of the district. Within its judicial authority were matters of crime, principally theft, violence, and disruption. The court was especially sensitive to what it viewed as insults to its authority. Fines for contempt were common. The first one was levied against John Sevier, Jr., a son of John Sevier, the clerk of the court. Administrative duties included registering brand marks for livestock, collecting taxes, and recording land titles. The court exercised great authority over the economy of this developing region, for it examined money in circulation, set prices, approved mill construction, established ferries, and built roads (forty-two roads by 1792). The court also provided for orphans and for the probate of wills. The early deliberations of the Washington County Court took place at a moment of national crisis, deep in the wilderness, and surrounded by foes. The court reflected the tensions of war and spent little time on the protection of individual rights. It administered a loyalty oath to the citizens of the county. It also ordered that transients be interviewed to determine their character, means of support, and reasons for being abroad. In short, the court appeared on the scene to administer the law, found the region in a period of crisis and moved aggressively to meet it. Those who violated the law as interpreted by the Washington County Court suffered harsh and sometimes violent punishment. Branding and whipping were common sentences, fines universal, and sentences of death imposed (in at least one case after a jury had recommended mercy). For vague actions against the good of the community and a conviction for horse stealing, the court sentenced Elias Pybourn to be confined to the public Pillory one Hour. That he have both his ears nailed to the Pillory and severed from his Head; That he receive at the Publick Whipping post thirty-nine lashes well laid On; and be branded on the Right cheek with the letter H, and on his left cheek with the letter T. and that the Sheriff of Washington County put this sentence in execution between the hours of Twelve and Two this day.[14]

The proceedings of the first court of Davidson County provide another glimpse into the frontier court system. The act of the North Carolina legislature that created "a District County westward of Cumberland Mountain To be known by the name of Davidson County and to include the Settlement on Cumberland River &c" also provided for a court of pleas and quarter sessions to convene four times yearly. At its first meeting, in October 1783, the gentlemen of the court elected a clerk, sheriff, entry taker, surveyor of county, and a constable for each station. The court then made plans for the construction of a courthouse (eighteen feet square) at Nashville. It should be "Built at the expense of the Publick" to be furnished with the necessary benches Barr Table &c fit for the reception of the Court," and a prison (fourteen feet square) "of Hewed Logs of a foot square both Walls Loft & floor, Except the same shall be Built on a Rock." Plans to receive bids for the buildings, the swearing in of a grand jury, and the organization of the militia followed in short order. The initial grand jury case, in the January 1784 term, charged John Chism "for cohabiting w^t a woman not his wife." It was the first of a series of cases involving bastardy, adultery, and fornication. The standard punishment for parties duly convicted of adultery, fornication, or giving birth to an illegitimate child was a fine of twenty-five shillings. Routine administrative duties pertaining to the concerns of a frontier community occupied the bulk of the court's time: probating estates, stock markings, strays, licensing lawyers, approving gristmill sites, licensing taverns (called "ordinaries"), establishing a ferry on the Cumberland River (especially important at Nashville), and setting rates for liquors and places of public entertainment.[15]

14. Quoted in John Allison, *Dropped Stitches in Tennessee History* (Nashville, 1897), 44; see also Howard M. Browning, "The Washington County Court, 1779–1789: A Study in Frontier Administration," *THQ*, 1 (1942): 328–43; and Miriam L. Fink, "Judicial Activities in Early East Tennessee," East Tennessee Historical Society, *Publications*, 7 (1935): 38–49. A case study of a frontier court after the Revolution is Lucien Beckner, "History of the County Court of Lincoln County, Va.," *RKSHS*, 20 (1922): 170–90.
15. Davidson County, Minute Book A, 1783–91, pp. 1–25, UT.

A final example shows the variety of the court experience. In Virginia's trans-mountain counties, the Jefferson County Court convened in 1780. Throughout the next decade it transacted routine and continuing business, including wills, warrants of survey, inventories of estates, stock marks, and polls taken and recorded (such as the election for the Virginia Assembly in the spring of 1782). After 1784 it gave much attention to laying out roads. The pages of its minutes recorded the financial transactions of the county, for the court was the universal source of record for its citizens. The record of the county court was the public information journal of the day, the dispenser of charges and apologies alike. Mylassah Mayfield denied before a magistrate of the Jefferson County Court, for example, that he had said Robert Floyd and his family had "Mulatoo blood." The number of the court's various transactions and the amount of its business grew over time, especially with the heavy immigration after 1781. The financial transactions display the economy of the day: land, slaves, and crops. Currency was varied. One man sold a tract of land for £300 "Current money of Virginia in hand"; James Patton and Benjamin Pope exchanged 660 acres of second-rate land for 165 gallons "of good merchantable whiskey." There were several indentures. James Steward apprenticed his son, John, to Michael Humble, who

> will use his utmost endeavors, to learn, & interest the above named John Steward in the aforementioned art, & mystery[s] of blacksmith & Gun Smith, & every other mechanical art, . . . & that he will, at no time, expose him the said John to the dangers of the Enemy, more than the Common custom, or usage of one of his Circumstances, and that he will find him sufficient meat, drink & clothing.

The court tried several suits between parties. It also charged some citizens with breach of the laws. George Pomeroy was convicted for breaking a law with respect to "Divulgers of false news," fined two thousand pounds of tobacco, and ordered to post bond for his good behavior. The court fined John Nelson five shillings "for profane swearing in open Court." One entry read simply, "Ordered that Squire Boone be fined agreeable to Law for not attending as a witness in the Suit . . . when he was duly sum[d]." A dominant theme running through all the testimonials, transactions, and recordings associated with the civil, criminal, and administrative duties was a sense of the dignity of the court. Isaac Cox, George May, Richard Chinewith, and William Oldham were "Gentlemen Justices." They were so described in the records; they clearly expected to be treated as such.[16]

Despite the economic opportunity associated with the frontier period, the county court exercised much direct control over economic affairs. It licensed gristmills and sawmills, fixed the price of whiskey, laid out and maintained roads, and protected property. The Bourbon County Court also set the prices for taverns: warm dinner, 1/6; cold dinner, 1/; breakfast with tea, coffee, or chocolate, 1/3; breakfast without, 1/1; "lodging in Clean Sheats," 6d. The court admonished that "Ordinary keepers in this County take pay according to the above rates and no more." The power of the court extended to the right to tax. Land, polls, slaves (where applicable), and luxuries were the most common targets for levies. Taxes were often reckoned in tobacco and collected in kind. The county court heard suits brought for the collection of debts. The sums involved were often quite small. Matthew Anderson sued Nicholas Moyers for an unpaid note in the sum of "One Pound Seven Shillings and four pence." William Alexander brought suit to recover from James McCulloch a debt of fifty bushels of Indian corn.[17]

As the needs of the frontier became more complex and litigation expanded in like proportion, the legal system grew. The settlers on the frontiers west of the Appalachians were a litigious group in the 1780's. The expansion of the courts and the growing number and complexity of cases coming before them enhanced the status and professional opportunities of a corps of professionals. Lawyers appeared early on the frontier of the trans-Appalachian West, and their numbers increased with conflicts over land claims and the expansion of commercial activity. They came to exercise enormous influence. The lawyer was the first professional man on the frontier, and his work carried him to the heart of the frontier's interest in economic advantage. In the struggle for acquisition of property, amidst the fluid economic condition and numerous opportu-

16. Jefferson County, Court Orders, Minute Book A, 1780–83; Minute Book #1, 1784–85, MIK. The indenture is dated May 7, 1782; Boone's fine, May 6, 1784.

17. Bourbon County, Order Book, 1786–93, entry for June Court, 1786; Mercer County, Circuit Court, Judgements (Suits), 1780–1801, suits dated 1789 and 1790, MIK. Margaret Kinard comments that the counties built on the frontier experience of contiguous areas, specifically that Williamson County benefited from the earlier settlement of the Nashville region. She observes that the militia and county court were "the stabilizing influences on development." "Frontier Development of Williamson County," *THQ*, 8 (1949): 12–13, 153.

nities for advancement of the western country, lawyers almost everywhere prospered. Men whose talents would not carry them into the first
rank in the East came to the frontier; men of greater talents whose family
connections did not give them easy access to high places joined them.
Early legal activity focused on land and land titles. One observer commented of Kentucky in 1786, "There is scarce a tenth man in Kentucky
who has land with certain title." The confused land titles in Kentucky
and, to a lesser extent, in Tennessee laid the basis of several legal fortunes. Henry Clay's was the best example, but far from the only one. Financial reward and influence went hand in hand. Success in law became
the basis for investment in lands or a career in politics or both.[18]

As the size and duties of the court system expanded, so did the rewards of officeholding. The early county governments of Kentucky and
Tennessee functioned under the eighteenth-century doctrine that the
best men in a community had an obligation and right to participate in its
governance. Officeholding also meant profits for a select few. The sheriff
and various land officers, such as surveyors and the recorder of land
titles, collected fees for their work. Surveying also offered opportunities
for extralegal gain. The profits of the county clerk were especially attractive. The enumeration of the fees to the clerk and sheriff in the minutes
of the Committee of the Cumberland Association for 1783 suggests the
complexity of business in an early court and consequent opportunities
for income. The clerk and sheriff charged a fee for every separate trans-
action—issuing a summons, administering an oath, writing a warrant, or
recording a stock mark and brand—and the whole added up to a sizable
return.[19]

Whatever its form and the court system, law was not easy to enforce
in the wilderness. Some frontiersmen found the restraints of law incon-
venient or even repugnant. To an indeterminate number of those who
deliberately flouted the law must be added large numbers who obeyed

---

18. "Journal of General Butler," Jan. 2, 1786, *Olden Time*, 2 (1847): 507. Harriette Simpson
    Arnow calls lawyers "the closest thing to a professional the pioneers knew." She clas-
    sifies medicine as a business rather than a profession. "Education and the Professions in
    the Cumberland Region," *THQ*, 20 (1962): 140, 146. Patricia Watlington, *The Partisan
    Spirit; Kentucky Politics, 1779–1792* (New York, 1972), ch. 1, discusses the confusion of
    land claims.
19. "Records of the Cumberland Association," 116–17. The same fee schedules are also
    found in the proceedings of the Hamilton Court District of East Tennessee. See
    Hamilton District Court Papers, McHC.

the law selectively. Many pioneers felt no inclination to refrain from settling on lands guaranteed to Indian tribes by solemn treaty. Territorial
officers found it almost impossible to remove such trespassers, and most
of them did not try to do so. Settlers also committed random acts of violence against Indians with confidence that a jury of their peers would
never convict them. "If the mode of bringing to trial, those who have in-
jured Indians, rests with the people at large, the consequence will be that
the aggressors will go unpunished," Judge David Campbell of the Territory South of the River Ohio advised President George Washington in
1791, adding, "It will be well if the present form of Government continues for some years, in the Territory, at least until the people are
taught to obey the Law and pay due Respect to Treaties."[20]

Selective enforcement of the law carried over into other areas as well:
the public domain (state or federal) was considered the property of all;
the debts owed merchants were evaded or ignored without guilt. In
small settlements united by common hardship and similar interests, the
pioneers banded against an outside threat, whether it be Indians, the
government, or strangers, and did so whatever the law might say. Even
where the machinery of law functioned, a basic instinct took hold: protecting one's own, suspicion of the outsider, the strength of local power
and influence. On the frontier, law and justice were personal things, as a
letter concerning a recently lost court case, tried at a distance from
home, points out. "James believes that *complete* Justice has not been
done," wrote Charles McClung to his brothers, "I believe, nor can you
expect to have complete Justice done, there, or at any place, where your
connections and friends are absent, and at a distance." He went on,
"Human nature is such now, and as I believe always has, and always
will be, those in power, and who are in such circumstances, and situated
as to act, can get more than Justice, those otherwise situated will get
less."[21]

The appearance of higher courts west of the Appalachians was very
significant, and the introduction of the federal court system under the
Judiciary Act of 1789 had a force approaching a revolution. In the case of
Kentucky, for example, the presence of higher courts dramatically asserted the authority of English law in all its forms and traditions. Due

20. David Campbell to George Washington, Nov. 9, 1791, in *TP*, 4: 101.
21. Charles McClung to James W. McClung, Feb. 6, 1815, Charles McClung Papers,
McHC.

process, dependence on English precedence, and the force of tradition gave the high courts of the western country a legal structure much like that of the East. Such was the authority of the higher courts that lower courts had to conform, at least to a substantial degree. These developments provided great stability and promoted a high regard for tradition in societies both newly created and already well advanced.

The men who served on the bench exemplified the impact and direction of the federal courts. Harry Innes is a case in point. He came to Kentucky from Virginia in 1783, and two years later was made Kentucky's second attorney general. In 1789 he became judge of the United States Court for the District of Kentucky. He did not so much grow up with the country as he shaped the country to his judicial standards. In his capacity as a leading public figure, he worked for the better defense against the Indians, promoted manufacturing, and improved agriculture and education. Innes's most significant contribution, however, was in the courts. He steadfastly conformed to the English practices and the respect for precedent. His views were shaped by a profound regard for the law and precedent and a rather low opinion of human nature. Throughout a long career on the bench, Innes did everything within his considerable power to give stability to a society rapidly moving beyond the frontier stage.[22]

The Kentucky Constitutional Convention of 1792 represents one of the few decisive struggles over institutional direction on the trans-Appalachian frontier. At stake were the traditional institutions gradually carried into and adopted in the western country in the twenty years since the first permanent Anglo-American settlement at Harrodsburg. These dealt specifically with the protection of property and the adoption of the English common law, with its large body of precedent and widespread use of lawyers. Before the opening of the convention, a group of reformers called for a new institutional departure, including the abolition of slavery and taxation of uncultivated lands—both of which threatened an emerging planter class; a unicameral legislature, free suffrage by ballot including the vote for women; and the exclusion of "immoral men"

22. Mary K. Bonsteel Tachau, "The Federal Courts in Kentucky, 1789–1816" (Ph.D., Kentucky, 1972), chs. 1 and 2; Watlington, *The Partisan Spirit*, 57–59, 137–38. The influence of the national government also made itself felt in the absorption of the Kentucky militia at the time of statehood. See "Act Establishing a Uniform Militia throughout the United States." 1 Stat. 271–74 (May 8, 1792).

from office. The reformers also asked for adoption of a simplified system
of law and courts. What they sought, in short, was a law that could be
understood and used by everyone. It was a proposal that struck directly
at the already powerful lawyer class.

In this confrontation, the forces supporting traditional institutions and
the common law emerged victorious. The constitution that passed provided for separate branches of government at the executive, legislative,
and judicial levels. With a bicameral legislature—the lower house elected
by free manhood suffrage and the upper hedged by property qualifications—and a governor chosen by electors, the sources of power in the
proposed commonwealth of Kentucky were removed from the direct influence of the individual ballot. The resolution to provide for the gradual
emancipation of slaves without compensation failed, and, instead, the
delegates approved the principle of emancipation only with the full con-
sent of slave owners and only with full compensation. The doctrine of
the common law was fully accepted and, indeed, never seriously debated. The end result was a document much like articles of government
in the eastern states. In the scarcely one generation since James Harrod
and his party slashed a few trees and planted some Indian corn, Kentucky had undergone a full-scale transformation into a political unit with
institutional values reflecting the new gentry class that had emerged to
prominence and power.[23]

Important to the settlement of the trans-Appalachian frontier was the
creation of institutions concerned with the quality of life. The western
country was a good place to acquire property, but was it a good place to
live? Jane Stevenson commented of early Lexington, "We had no notion
of raising our children among that sort of people."[24] Of the institutions
that gradually softened this harsh existence and diluted the materialism
of the frontier, the two most important were the school and the church.
Education on the trans-Appalachian frontier between 1775 and 1795 was

23. Watlington, *The Partisan Spirit*, 209–22; Barnhart, *Valley of Democracy*, chs. 5 and 6,
argues that the "radicals"—as he calls them—won "a substantial victory" (p. 105). An
excellent article on the adaptation of English law throughout the trans-Appalachian
frontier is William B. Hamilton, "The Transmission of English Law to the Frontier of
America," *SAQ*, 67 (1968): 243–64.
24. Lyman C. Draper Collections, 13 CC 138, SHSW. This letter probably dates from
1779.

largely haphazard and unstructured. The primary focus of the early settlers was security: their concerns were conflict with the Indians, the search for land, the struggle to clear, plant, and market. All left their mark. Schoolbook learning was lower on the scale of priorities. But in some form, it was present from the beginning. The early Kentucky stations had informal schools. With the dispersal of settlers into the wilderness, instruction took place in the home, if it took place at all. The role of the family was central. Much depended on the parents. Who were they? What was their station in life? What sort of place in life did they seek for their children? Those who saw themselves as "gentlemen"—and there were such on the trans-Appalachian frontier from almost the very beginning—placed schooling high in their priorities. Theirs was a tradition of classicial education stemming from the landed aristocracy of early Virginia, who first sent their sons to English universities and later, after suitable institutions had been set up in the colonies, to colleges here. The question of school was largely one of class distinction and served as an early indicator of the appearance of a landed aristocracy on the trans-Appalachian frontier.

For these established and ambitious landed gentry, the basic educational institution that emerged was the academy, a private subscription school, taught by an itinerant master, who signed articles of agreement for the season with the parents of the pupils whom he taught. To this center of learning went the young scholars whose parents could afford the tuition, who were interested in their children's education, and who lived close enough that their sons and daughters could walk to school. A few pupils might board with friends. In 1788 Messrs. Jones and Worley opened a school with a classical curriculum in Lebanon (Kentucky). Their advertisement requested: "For diet, washing and house room, each scholar pay three pounds in cash or five hundred weight of pork on entrance, and three pounds cash on the beginning of the third quarter. It is desired that as many as can would furnish themselves with beds." Pupils paid one half of their fees in cash and the other half in produce at the cash price.[25] Yet the proportion of school-age children on the trans-Appalachian frontier in this twenty-year period who saw the inside of a schoolhouse or experienced any kind of formal instruction was probably not large. The accounts that have survived suggest it was small, and that

25. Lexington *Kentucky Gazette*, Jan. 5, 1788.

those children who did attend school went for brief periods only. The early schools were centered in towns, giving urban dwellers an advantage over those who lived in the woods. The latter received their real education on the land.[26]

In the rural schools the educational experience varied widely. Itinerant masters, of varied origins and competences, taught pupils on an individual basis without regard to formal grades or textbooks. The subject matter was elementary. Boys learned to read in order that they might understand newspapers and business transactions, to write in order to draw up contracts and agreements, and to do basic sums for balancing accounts on the farm or in the mercantile house. Formal education for girls was almost nonexistent; instead girls helped around the house, making a contribution to the family and serving the proper apprenticeship to an early marriage. Cooking, weaving, sewing, working with skins, milking and churning, maintaining the vegetable garden near the home, these were appropriate and sufficient skills for a young woman on the frontier. Considering the overwhelming emphasis on practicality in frontier life and the frequent interruptions necessitated by work on the farm, Indian alarms, and changes of teachers, it is surprising that children even had the opportunity to acquire the rudiments of a formal education. For those who were uninterested, or whose parents were indifferent, schooling was brief.

For a few, however, school brought inspiration. Reading opened the horizons of a small number of frontier youths to the world of literature, ideas, and abstractions. From the perspective of forty years, Daniel Drake wrote, "Now, comparing myself with other boys of my age, I think I had a taste for study rather greater than the bulk of them, and if books had been within my reach, it is probable that I should have made some proficiency by solitary study at night and on rainy days." Drake was an exception. He founded the first medical school in the Ohio Valley and became the cultural leader of early Cincinnati. His comments for the Kentucky frontier of the 1790's convey the experience of the majority

26. Eagle, "Aspects of the Kentucky Frontier," ch. 6; Arnow, "Education and the Professions in the Cumberland Region," 120–38; Rogers, "Life in East Tennessee near the End of the Eighteenth Century," 41–42. Almost every local history has a chapter on early education. Two of the best are Frank Merritt, "Selected Aspects of Early Carter County History, 1760–1861" (M.A., Tennessee, 1950), ch. 4; and Paul Atkins Counce, "Social and Economic History of Kingsport before 1908" (M.A., Tennessee, 1939), ch. 3.

of people: "Our preachers and teachers were, in general, almost as destitute as the people at large, many of whom could neither read nor write,
did not send their children to school, and of course, kept no books in the
house."[27]

In most frontier communities the church was a more important and
wide-spread institution than the school. The enlightened skepticism of
the late eighteenth century, widespread in Europe and in certain social
and intellectual circles on the eastern seaboard, scarcely penetrated to the
wilderness in the interior of the continent. The appeal of religion to a
frontier people was emotional rather than intellectual. In the frontier
climate formal theological training counted for little and the power of the
spirit for much. Religion embraced all members of the family, and
religious gatherings, which brought together adults and children of varying ages, were social occasions in a society where opportunities for getting together were all too limited.[28]

Baptist laymen moved right along with the frontier, farming during
the week and preaching in fervent but untrained fashion on Sunday.
These Baptist lay preachers soon had help (or competition) in ministering to the needs of the frontier. Francis Asbury brought the Methodist
gospel to the Kentucky-Tennessee area about 1786, and he provided the
leadership for a growing number of Methodist circuit riders. The itinerant Methodist circuit riders serving several congregations were different
from the part-time resident ministers of other denominations, especially
the Baptists. Asbury himself travelled to the most remote parts of the
trans-Appalachian frontier between 1786 and 1815. His routine was typical of the circuit riders of the period. He arrived late in the afternoon at
the home of one of the faithful supporters, preached to the families that
gathered to hear him, slept for a few hours, and left at daybreak the next
morning to head for the next house and gathering. Sometimes he
lingered to baptize, marry, receive members into the church, conduct a
prayer meeting, or simply rest for a day. His journal recorded the primi-

---

27. Daniel Drake, *Pioneer Life in Kentucky, 1785–1800* (Cincinnati, 1870), 161–62.
28. A good general study for Kentucky is Eagle, "Aspects of the Kentucky Frontier," ch.
   5. Almost every local and county history also has a chapter on early religious development. Note especially the unpublished theses of Counce, Merritt, and Seeber. A
   useful specialized study is Allen James Ledford, "Methodism in Tennessee,
   1783–1866" (M.A., Tennessee, 1941), esp. chs. 1–3.

tive condition of the land and its people. Of his work and the people whom he served, he wrote:

> I am of opinion it is as hard, or harder, for the people of the west to gain religion as any other. When I consider where they came from, where they are, and how they are called to go further, their being unsettled, with so many objects to take their attention, with good health and good air to enjoy, and when I reflect that not one in a hundred came here to get religion, but rather to get plenty of good land, I think it will be well if some or many do not eventually lose their souls.[29]

Churches tended to be a calming influence on the frontier. Where other institutional direction was still weak, the church became a direct arbiter and enforcer of social order. Sermons emphasized moral behavior as taught in the Bible and prophesied a sad end for those who strayed from the path as indicated therein. With churches established on a permanent basis, though without full-time resident ministers, authority was vested in the elders, who ran the church and the lives of its members. The elders served as arbiters in disputes to prevent resort to the courts and perhaps even violence. With the sanction of the church behind it, the board of elders made its decisions hold up. The Methodist *Discipline* recited a solemn code under which sinners might be tried, and the circuit riders preached that this law should be carried out to the letter. In matters of personal conduct, church members might be brought to trial for a variety of sins, temporal as well as spiritual. Offenses varied from drunkenness, adultery, fighting, disorderly conduct and habits, and delinquency in attendance to communing with another sect, criticizing the church, celebrating the Fourth of July, and taking part in Indian (heathen) festivities. Those convicted might be dismissed or placed on probation, depending on the seriousness of the crime. The records of the Great Crossings Church in Scott County (Kentucky) reveal how the deacons worked to get people out to church and keep them on the straight and narrow path to salvation. Those who did not were brought up short. The Sheltons "are Excluded fellowship with this Church for Disorderly Conduct" and "Benjamin Appelgate is Excluded from this Church for Fighting & Drinking to Excess," read the minutes. Members took their dismissal seriously. Severance from the church denied families

29. Quoted in Samuel C. Williams, *Early Travels in the Tennessee Country, 1540–1800* (Johnson City, 1928), 305.

one of the centers of frontier social life. Churches could be generous with those who confessed their sins, but the fallen had best confess hard and keep at it.[30]

Life for most of the settlers on the first frontier west of the Appalachians was basic and close to nature; its unifying characteristic was physical labor. The occasional struggles of the pioneers against the Indians have obscured the fact that frontiersmen spent most of their time in the fields, clearing, planting, harvesting, but always at work. With the added duties of home construction and repair, hunting, and livestock manage-ment, little time remained for other activities. Men filled their lives with work and outdoor activities of the most arduous kind. Women lived lonely and isolated lives, their monotonous routines broken only by childbirth, which came with painful regularity. It was a rare frontier family that did not welcome visitors; the settlement of another family nearby was cause for rejoicing. Little wonder, then, that frontier families embraced religion as an emotional outlet and derived great pleasure from such gatherings as the husking bee or a barn raising. Any enterprise that brought people together was welcome. Against this background, social activities among men often ran to excesses of drinking and fighting. It was a physical world and prowess with arm and rifle was the standard by which early frontiersmen judged one another. Daniel Drake wrote of gatherings "composed of men and boys only, for raising houses, stables, and barns, for rolling logs, for husking corn, for opening new roads, and other purposes; all of which I have repeatedly attended, and well recol-lect that profanity, vulgarity, and drinking were their most eminent characteristics."[31]

The drudgery of frontier life, with its emphasis on subsistence and

30. Leland Winfield Mayer, ed., "The Great Crossings Church Records, 1795–1801," *RKSHS*, 34 (1936): 10–11. On the struggle of the Presbyterians to keep doctrine untar-nished west of the mountains and to discourage "disorderly and unsound Ministers," see Robert B. McAfee, "The History of the Rise and Progress of the First Settlement on Salt River and the Establishment of the New Providence Church," *RKSHS*, 29 (1931): 5–10.

31. Drake, *Pioneer Life in Kentucky*, 181–82. It should be remembered that by the time Drake wrote this account he was a leading citizen of Cincinnati, head of a medical school, and influential in the cultural life of the rising city. These circumstances may have influenced his recollections of earlier days.

fear of Indian alarms, did not wholly retard the appearance of culture and economic and social distinctions. In Lexington, or other parts of the Kentucky Bluegrass by 1795, the wealthy could purchase an "elegant PHAETON," take lessons in ballroom dancing or French, attend any one of several private schools, be tutored in needlework, and choose from a large stock of books in two bookstores. The leisured gentleman might also avail himself of the opportunity to join any one of several social and cultural institutions, including a subscription library, Masonic Lodge No. 25, the Mercer Society for the Encouragement of Agriculture, or the Society of the Cincinnatus. The breeding of horses was already a strong interest, and horse racing well organized. Those who saw the value of higher education, probably its social as well as intellectual aspects, had established a college, Transylvania Seminary.[32] At the same time, scarcely sixty miles distant from the cultural-economic-political center of the Bluegrass, a frontier population lived in conditions of cultural deprivation and economic subsistence. Over the twenty years from 1775 to 1795, a New World emerged with an institutional framework much like the Old. The institutional structure that evolved assisted materially in the preservation of property rights. The new trans-Appalachian settlements had conferred benefits on thousands of families in the form of land. Not surprisingly, some had benefited more than others.

32. Lexington *Kentucky Gazette*, Dec. 22, 1792; Sept. 28, 1793; May 3, June 28, July 5, Oct. 11, 1794; July 11, 1795.

3

Security and Stability
in the Territory
Northwest of the Ohio

To the north of the expanding frontiers of Kentucky and Tennessee lay a fertile and dangerous land. The early French fur traders had discovered and advertised its beauty. It lay next to one of the great water transportation arteries of the continent, the broad, placid Ohio. But it was the land of the powerful Indian tribes of the valley, the Shawnee and the Delaware. Even as the Ohio River became a route for immigrants to Kentucky after 1783, the forbidding forests north of the river and the reputation of the Indian tribes deterred most settlers. The first American occupants were probably anonymous trappers who established temporary camps on the Ohio and its tributaries. Some may have attempted a crop of corn, although it seems unlikely that they stayed in one place for so long, for those in Indian country were always on the move. With the close of the American Revolution, a growing tide of immigration swept from Pittsburgh down the Ohio and, not surprisingly, deposited a few hardy, adventurous, and less affluent souls on the north side of the river. Some of these stayed.

The new American government viewed these squatters with hostility, for it hoped to demonstrate its strength in the West and also to restore amiable relations with the Indian tribes so recently allied with the British. Trespassers might provoke the Indians north of the Ohio into a war that the United States was ill equipped to fight and one that its empty treasury surely could not afford. In the spring of 1785 the Confederation government dispatched troops to clear out squatters. The officer in charge met resistance. A squatter leader, John Ross, announced that he did not believe the eviction notices came from Congress and "neither did he care from whom they came, for he was determined to hold his possession." The officer reporting continued, "And if I should destroy his house he would build six more in the course of a week." Who were these people who would defy the authority of the American government? Colonel Josiah Harmar, commanding officer at Pittsburgh, described the nature of the settlements: "Most of those engaged in this business are shiftless fellows from Pennsylvania and Virginia, though I have seen and conversed with a few who appear to be intelligent and honest in their purposes." In the end, the threat of the Indians rather than the American government restricted settlement north of the Ohio in the years immediately after the Revolution.[1]

At the same time that military detachments evicted squatters from the north bank of the Ohio, the Congress of the Confederation laid down administrative procedures under which the public lands would be surveyed and sold in an orderly fashion. The Ordinance of 1785 (and the land companies associated with it) and the Ordinance of 1787 concerned with government were the two instruments most directly responsible for the early development of the frontiers north of the Ohio River. The Land Ordinance, as it came to be called, laid down broad guidelines for the disposal of the rich lands that would send so many men and women across the mountains. It provided for the identification and preservation of mines, salt springs, salt licks, and mill seats. Of long-lasting importance was the reservation of section 16 in every township for the "maintenance of public schools within the said township." Two years later the framers of the Ordinance of 1787 elaborated on the purpose of this provision: "Religion, morality, and knowledge, being necessary to good government and the happiness of mankind, schools and the means of education shall forever be encouraged."[2] Schools, and churches too, were central to men's vision of the society they hoped to foster in the wilderness.

1. Ensign John Armstrong to Lt. Col. Josiah Harmar, April 12, 1785, in Western Reserve Historical Society, *Historical and Archeological Tracts*, 6 (1871): 3–4; Harmar to Gen. Henry Knox, June 15, 1785, in *ibid.*, 6.
2. The full text of the Ordinance of 1785 is printed in *TP*, 2: 12–18; its significance is discussed in Malcolm J. Rohrbough, *The Land Office Business: The Settlement and Administration of American Public Lands, 1789–1837* (New York, 1968), 8–9. The text of the Ordinance of 1787 is printed in *TP*, 2: 39–50.

The Ohio Company of Associates was the most important of the land companies influencing the settlement and institutional development of the Ohio country. This group of New England capitalists convinced Congress to strengthen the financial condition of the nation by exchanging certificates of indebtedness for western lands. Its initial contract with the national government called for the purchase of 1.5 million acres of the public domain at a price of $500,000, payable in depreciated public securities. After a vigorous advertising campaign stressing the fertility and proximity of its western lands, the company made plans to establish a colony. An advance party set out from Pittsburgh on April 2, 1788, and headed down the Ohio in a single boat. Four weeks later the *May-flower* (for so she was called) landed on the north bank of the Ohio to disembark the first legal American settlers in the Northwest Territory.

The directors of the company organized the new community to ensure the transmission of New England institutions to the western country. They laid out the town of Marietta, with reservations of land for church, school, a town common, and three-acre outlots for the proprietors. Like the towns of the seventeenth century, compactness was important, both for protection from Indians and the preservation of a sense of community. The directors eventually gave land to nonstockholders, for an increase in population seemed of paramount importance in the early years of the settlement. They also voted land grants to encourage the erection of a gristmill and windmill in the same communal spirit with which their New England ancestors had supported the church and the school. The settlers went to work in vigorous Yankee fashion, constructing log huts and cultivating the soil. With the settlement established, the immediate physical wants of the settlers satisfied, and reinforcements arriving in large numbers, the directors of the company found it necessary to make arangements for defense from external dangers, for the preservation of order within the colony, and for the more complex needs of a rising society and growing economy.[3]

Like most settlers on the trans-Appalachian frontier in the late eighteenth and early nineteenth centuries, pioneers in the Northwest Territory feared external dangers, a fear that was surely increased by the vastness of the great forest, the strength and reputation of the surround-

---

3. Archer Butler Hulbert, ed., *The Records of the Original Proceedings of the Ohio Company* (2 vols., Marietta, 1917), 1: 46. One account of the early settlements is John May, *The Western Journals of John May*, ed. Dwight L. Smith (Cincinnati, 1961).

ing Indian tribes, and the knowledge of their long-standing alliance with the British. Leaders of the company reacted accordingly. From its start the Ohio Company settlement at Marietta was an armed camp. The first need was for a militia. Regulations soon appeared, and rosters were drawn up. "Officers named to command the militia—guard to be mounted every evening—all the males more than 15 years old to appear under arms every Sabbath," wrote John May, an associate of the Ohio Company. Thus did the New Englanders compromise their observance of the Sabbath in order better to preserve themselves. The company was also mindful of internal order. The directors named themselves a "Board of Police . . . for the regulation of the settlement" and issued a code to govern the conduct of individual settlers. These regulations gave extraordinary powers to the police officers, requiring, among other things, that new arrivals in the settlement register their names with the authorities within twenty-four hours of their landing. The code also restricted the movement of settlers outside the limits of the town.[4]

The instrument that would provide structure of government for American settlement north of the Ohio was the Ordinance of 1787, or the Northwest Ordinance, as it came to be called. The proposal of this ordinance led to much debate between those who wished to rule the peoples west of the mountains as England had ruled her colonies and those who wished to grant wide latitude to frontier peoples to manage their own affairs. The end product was a compromise. In its final form the ordinance provided for orderly government, a court system, and the creation of a body of law suitable to the needs of the territory, all leading gradually with the passage of time and growth of population to greater local autonomy and eventual statehood. The structure of law and courts provided by the ordinance was based on English common law, as modified by colonial practice, and ensured that the institutional structure of the Northwest Territory would be a familiar one. ·

At the center of the new government provided by the ordinance was

4. May, *Western Journals*, 54; Hulbert, ed., *Records of the Ohio Company*, 1: 44–77. A description of the first Ohio Company court, convened at Marietta on September 2, 1788, is "The First Court in Ohio," *Weekly Chronicle*, March 29, 1842, in the Lyman C. Draper Collections, 19 CC 40–41, SHSW. Other settlement groups north of the Ohio—the Symmes Purchase between the Great and Little Miami Rivers; the Virginia Military Tract, between the Miami and Little Scioto; and the Seven Ranges, opposite the Pennsylvania line—had minimal institutional structure prior to the operation of the Northwest Ordinance.

an appointed governor with large-scale powers (some would have said dictatorial) to fit the large-scale needs of the new territory. In the range of his authority and independence the governor of the territory was closer to a monarch or a colonial governor than most Americans emerging from a revolutionary experience would have liked to admit. He was the chief executive in a government without legislative representation (at least in its initial stages) and the commander of the militia. In consultation with three appointed judges, he formulated, published, and enforced the laws of the new territory. Thus the chief executive united in one officer the powers later apportioned between the executive and legislative branches of government. The governor also had great power in the area of civil affairs. He could lay off counties and townships and appoint all appropriate magistrates and civil officers. The full measure of this authority rested with the governor only until the election of a territorial legislature (to be organized when the district had five thousand free adult males), after which he shared it with the Assembly. No legislature convened in the Northwest Territory until 1799, however, and the work of the governor in formulating the legal, political, economic, military, and even social life of the new district was of central importance for a full decade. Those who disliked his actions might complain, and eventually many did so, but the governor had office, authority, and the power of appointment.[5]

The Northwest Ordinance provided for other appointed officers to assist the governor. A secretary performed several administrative duties, mostly those of record keeper and correspondent with Congress and the executive. In the governor's absence from the territory, the secretary exercised all the powers of the chief executive. Three judges were also among the first appointments. In addition to collaborating with the governor in making the laws of the territory, the judges rode circuit and carried the law they had helped formulate to the remote areas of the territory. All five executive officers received freehold estates while in office, a reminder of the colonial period in which governors coming from England received a stake in the New World.

The first governor under the new ordinance was Arthur St. Clair, a native of Scotland who lived in the Ligonier Valley in western Pennsylvania. St. Clair's record of public service was extensive, including active duty in the French and Indian war and several local and county offices.

5. On the origin and provisions of the Ordinance of 1787, see Jack Ericson Eblen, *The First and Second United States Empires* (Pittsburgh, 1968), ch. 1.

During the American Revolution he rose to the rank of major-general, served on Washington's staff, and acquired much experience in the midst of no little adversity. He entered Congress in 1785 and was elected its president in 1787. Governor St. Clair came to the Northwest Territory at the age of fifty-four, mature in experience and achievement, blessed with good health and a strong constitution, confident that he was equal to the tasks before him and to the expectations of the territory's citizens.

After a leisurely trip from his Pennsylvania estate, the governor-designate embarked from Pittsburgh for the voyage down the Ohio River. On July 15, 1788, escorted by the officers of the garrison at Fort Washington, St. Clair crossed the Muskingum to the village of Marietta laid out a few months before. "This is the birthday of the western world," John May recorded in his journal; "At eleven his Excellency Governor St. Clair arriv'd at the garrison. His landing was announced by the discharge of 14 Cannon, and all rejoiced at his coming." St. Clair walked up the shore to the huzzas of a large crowd and the volleys of the ranked militia and the garrison's artillery. On a spot of elevated ground the governor met Winthrop Sargent, the new secretary of the territory, and two of the three territorial judges, Samuel H. Parsons and James M. Varnum. Sargent read aloud the Northwest Ordinance and the commissions of the five officers of the territory. The assembled citizens then presented the governor with a declaration of their pleasure at the institution of government. "When thus far removed from the country, that gave us birth, from our friends and from the influence of the government of any state," they declared, "we esteem it one of the greatest blessings, that we can have civil government established among us, which is the only foundation for the enjoyment of life, of liberty and of property." St. Clair responded with a broad-ranging address that revealed much about the man and the principles under which he intended to govern.

> A good government, well administered, is the first of blessings to a people. Every thing desirable in life is thereby secured to them, and from the operation of wholesome and equal laws the passions of men are restrained within due bounds; their actions receive a proper direction; the virtues are cultivated, and the beautiful fabric of civilized life is reared and brought to perfection.[6]

6. May, *Western Journals*, 63; Inhabitants on the Muskingum to Governor St. Clair, July 16, 1788, in *TP*, 2: 132; Arthur St. Clair, *The St. Clair Papers*, ed. William Henry Smith (2 vols., Cincinnati, 1882) 2: 54. The third judge, John Cleves Symmes, had not yet arrived at Marietta.

The inhabitants rejoiced at the governor's presence and his vision of the future. He was the personification of the concern of the national government for the people settled north and west of the Ohio. He would use his great authority in their interest—to solve their many problems, to encourage economic growth for which private strength was insufficient, to pacify the Indians with threats of official reprisal, to bring order and stability to the most remote western frontier.

Arthur St. Clair provided whatever assistance government could offer to American settlers in their struggle for survival north of the Ohio. His problems and solutions invite comparison with the experiences south of the Ohio during the previous decade. St. Clair had the attention (if not always the support) of the general government and the authority of the Ordinance of 1787 behind him. But the general government was in the midst of a transition to a new constitution, and it could not offer much physical assistance to an enterprise so distant. By contrast, Kentucky and Tennessee had the support of county governments established by the older states of Virginia and North Carolina. These state governments were not always attentive to the needs of a frontier people, and they were, in effect, absentee custodians. Distance and the nature of county government, however, combined to ensure the new settlements a substantial degree of independence. St. Clair's government in the Northwest Territory, on the other hand, had the capacity to provide institutions of government on call and in quantities to satisfy the needs of the most remote frontier settlements, but with power concentrated in the hands of a single individual. The authority of the governor (although presumably resident in the territory) outweighed whatever liberal provisions might be found in the Northwest Ordinance. At the same time, his work in providing the support of government for the distant frontiers of the Old Northwest was without precedent and untried. Initially, at least, it was not clear that the Ordinance of 1787 and its first governor would provide more assistance and better government than Kentucky and Tennessee received from Virginia and North Carolina, respectively.

Other differences from the earlier frontier experiences were equally striking. Except for Nashville—which grew rapidly to a sizable settlement—most of the Kentucky and Tennessee settlements lay close to one another, moving out from stations, then up and down the watercourses.

By contrast, St. Clair had to discharge his responsibilities over a vast area that stretched from the intersection of the Ohio with the Pennsylvania line down the great river in a sometimes south but always westerly direction to its junction with the Mississippi. To the north, his authority ran to the vast forests that ringed the Great Lakes waterway. Within the Kentucky and Tennessee settlements lived a largely homogeneous population, firmly rooted in the tradition of Anglo-American law and government—where any form of law and government was acknowledged at all—and generally Protestant in religious affiliation. The Northwest Territory, however, included long-established French settlements at Vincennes, Kaskaskia, and Cahokia, with their own institutions and allegiance to Roman Catholicism and French civilization.

Two pressing problems dominated Arthur St. Clair's first years as governor of the Northwest Territory. To begin with, he had to reach accord with the several Indian tribes of the region. This was a task constantly made more difficult by the growing American immigration to the Northwest and its obvious threat to Indian lands. On his trip down the Ohio, the governor wrote:

> Our settlements are extending themselves so fast on every quarter where they can be extended— Our pretentions to the country they [the Indians] inhabit has been made known to them in so unequivocal a manner, and the consequences are so certain and so dreadful to them, that there is little probability of there ever being any cordiality between us— The idea of being ultimately obliged to abandon their country rankles in their minds.[7]

St. Clair opened negotiations with several of the tribes of the Old Northwest, but behind diplomacy lay the ultimate question of military strength. The Indians were not strong militarily in the European sense, but their strategy of sporadic raids against frontier settlements was very effective. In negotiations and military activities in the Northwest, several tribes also received counsel and logistical support from the British in Canada. Indian tactics and numbers, British arms and ammunition were nicely balanced against the newly independent, decentralized American government, superior in manpower but weak in military preparedness, financially uncertain, and hard pressed to bring its strength to bear in the Ohio Valley wilderness.

7. St. Clair to Sec. at War, July 5, 1788 in *TP*, 2: 119.

St. Clair also had to establish civil government; he had to lay off counties and set up county government, appoint suitable local officials, and draft and publish a code of laws for the territory. All had to be accomplished as soon as possible in order to provide a structure within which civil and economic order might evolve. If the wilderness of the Northwest Territory was to move to "the beautiful fabric of civilized life," St. Clair thought that it would do so only within a framework of law. The passions, energies, and ambitions of men would be controlled and directed toward acceptable ends and the sanctity of private property recognized. Although he was bound to act in consultation with his judges, Arthur St. Clair was the most important single figure in the creation of the new laws. Within six months of his arrival, he had drawn up the legal code that was an outline of the society he intended to create.

In view of the overriding concern with physical security, it was inevitable that the first law of the territory should establish a militia. All male inhabitants from sixteen to fifty years of age were organized into military units. The law held that the regular assembling of the community was conducive to "health, civilization, and morality." St. Clair might call the militia to active service at his discretion. Fines were imposed for absence from "parade"; refusal to appear on order of the commander-in-chief brought a fine for the first offense, court martial for the second. The procedure for a court martial was described in detail, as befitted a man with St. Clair's extensive military experience. Armaments and equipment, to be provided by the individual soldier, were also specified: "A musket and bayonet, or rifle, cartridge box and pouch, or powder horn and bullet pouch, with forty rounds of cartridges, or one pound of powder and four pounds of lead, priming wire and brush and six flints." Most of the male populace had firearms. Indeed, in future years several laws would regulate their use in and around the settlements. St. Clair took his military duties seriously, and he and Sargent ordered out the militia on a continuing basis for such diverse duties as fighting Indians, constructing roads, putting down riots, and evicting squatters.[8]

The governor next established a court system that included everything from the justice of the peace to General Court of the Territory. As a former county office holder in Bedford County (Pennsylvania), St. Clair knew the structure and far-reaching influence of the county courts.

8. Theodore Calvin Pease, ed., *The Laws of the Northwest Territory, 1788–1800* (Springfield, 1925), 1–4; Eblen, *The First and Second United States Empires*, 81–85.

Their decentralized nature, with large numbers of prominent local officials, would be admirably suited to the vast spaces of the Northwest Territory. Among St. Clair's powers was the authority to lay off counties, and this he proceeded to do on July 27, 1788, within three weeks of his arrival at Marietta. He called the first new county Washington in honor of his commander-in-chief. It was a princely domain, extending from the Pennsylvania boundary west to the Scioto and from the Ohio River north to Lake Erie. The court system that served it was much like that of Kentucky and Tennessee. The law of August 23, 1788, established the office of justice of the peace at the county level, "appointed and commissioned" by the governor. From three to five justices constituted the "courts of the general quarter sessions of the peace." The powers of the court, which met quarterly, were broad: to "hear, determine and sentence, according to the course of common law, all crimes and misdemeanors, of whatever nature or kind . . . the punishment whereof doth not extend to life, limb, imprisonment for more than one year, or forfeiture of goods and chattels, or lands and tenements to the government of the territory." Individual justices might deal with minor crimes at any time and impose fines up to three dollars and costs. The governor also commissioned justices to serve as a county court of common pleas, which met twice yearly, to hear suits "of a civil nature, real, personal and mixed, according to the constitution and laws of the territory." Individual judges might hear cases of small debts and contracts to the sum of five dollars. The Code of 1788 also established a probate court to "take the proof of last wills and testaments and to grant letters testamentary and letters of administration" relative to the settlement of estates. A judge of probate, in conjunction with two justices from the court of common pleas in the same county, sat as a court of probate four times annually. Over this network of courts was the General Court of the territory composed of the territorial judges.[9]

The country court system had large powers, a complex administrative structure, and few physical facilities. The courts might issue subpoenas, warrants, and writs of several different kinds. As early as 1792, a special law described in detail the forms used in civil cases, for instance, and the semiliterate officials in distant frontier counties received examples of summons, replevins, executions, and other legal forms. Within a decade

9. Pease, ed., *The Laws of the Northwest Territory*, 4–10. The first part of the Ordinance of 1787 was a temporary law of probate. See *TP*, 2: 39–40.

county clerks in the distant parts of the Northwest Territory carefully transcribed Latin phrases familiar in the inns of Westminster. County officials on the American frontier knew little Latin, but they knew much of property. Where one was necessary to serve the other, they found a way. Facilities for confining criminals or suspects were rare or nonexistent. Construction of jails had to be funded by local taxpayers, and if there was anything frontier citizens worried about more than the Indians, it was the tax rate. It was far cheaper to force suspects (as potential disturbers of the peace) to post bond for their good behavior, at least until the next session of the county court, than to imprison them pending trial. There was much in the law about "recognizances," or bonds posted to ensure proper conduct. The judges might call upon any person in the county to post a recognizance without making any specific charge against him. Procedures for certifying recognizances were, accordingly, described in detail, with special attention to forfeitures. In 1792 laws provided for the construction of public buildings in each county, including a courthouse, jail ("for the reception and confinement of debtors and criminals well secured by timber iron bars grates bolts and locks"), pillory, whipping posts, and stocks. Counties might levy taxes for their construction.[10]

Within a month of the establishment of county courts, St. Clair appointed officeholders for Washington County. The number of offices was large, testifying to a court system more complete and detailed than that of the rudimentary governments of the early trans-Appalachian region. There were officers of the militia (captains, lieutenants, ensigns, and an adjutant), five justices of the peace, a clerk of court, sheriff of the county, and judge of probate (one of the justices of the peace). Some men had more than one office; three of the justices of the quarter sessions court also served as the court of common pleas. One man, Return Jonathan Meigs, held the offices of recorder of deeds, clerk of the orphans court, and prothonotary to the court of common pleas. When St. Clair had finished the work of organization and appointment, he wrote to the secretary of Congress with satisfaction: "The Government has been put in motion—a County erected by the name of Washington, Courts insti-

10. Pease, ed., *The Laws of the Northwest Territory*, 93–102, 77–79; the quotation is from p. 77.

tuted, and the Officers necessary for the Administration of Justice appointed, and so far every thing goes well."[11]

The section on crimes and punishments was the longest and most detailed part of the Code of 1788. It enumerated the crimes feared on the trans-Appalachian frontier: treason (always at the head of the list), murder, manslaughter (not to be confused with taking a life in self-defense), arson, burglary, robbery, "Riots and unlawful Assemblies" (defined as three or more people gathered together for an "unlawful act"), perjury, larceny, forgery, assault and battery, and "usurpation" (exercising authority in the territory without proper authorization). Punishments, presumably apportioned to fit the crime, included death (for treason and murder), public flogging, confinement in the stocks, and fines. Conviction for unlawful assembly, for example, carried a fine of sixteen dollars; for burglary, security for good behavior and a public whipping up to thirty-nine stripes. Prison sentences were rare, reflecting both the scarcity of jails and the reluctance of the public to support prisoners for long periods.

Governor St. Clair also intended to establish a moral society, a world in which property would be acquired by people of right principle and training, or, at the very least, people constrained by such principles. The code condemned crimes of moral turpitude. Among these were acts of disobedience on the part of children and servants. The law provided that "if any children or servants shall contrary to the obedience due to their parents or masters, resist or refuse to obey their lawful commands . . . it shall be lawful for such justice to send him or them so offending, to the gaol or house of correction, there to remain until he or they shall humble themselves to the said parents, or masters satisfaction." To strike a parent or master brought punishment of up to ten stripes. Drunkenness carried a fine of "five dimes" for the first offense and one dollar thereafter, or one hour in the stocks. "Improper and Profane Language," defined as "idle, vain and obscene conversation, profane cursing and swearing," was a punishable offense, as "repugnant to every moral sentiment, subversive of every civil obligation, inconsistent with the or-

11. Journal of the Executive Proceedings in the Territory Northwest of the River Ohio, in *TP*, 3: 278–89; St. Clair to Chas. Thomson, Sept. 2, 1788, in *ibid.*, 2: 152. A complete account of the organization of the territory is Chester Jacob Attig, "The Institutional History of the Northwestern Territory, 1787–1802" (Ph.D., Chicago, 1921), ch. 3.

naments of a polished life, and abhorrent to the principles of the most
benevolent religion." A clause in the law preserved the Sabbath for
religious observance, a practice "greatly conducive to civilization as well
as morality and piety." In 1790 St. Clair outlawed gambling, declaring
void any contracts to pay money won "at cards, dice-tables, tennis-
bowls, or other games." Tavern keepers could not keep "any billiard,
faro, E.O. hazard, or other gaming tables," by which money or property
might be "betted, won or lost."[12] The transgressions named were those
associated with a frontier society; the values supported were those of an
established society, perhaps even a gentry class.

This elaborate structure of courts provided lucrative employment for
lawyers and officeholders. Lawyers had a large business, mostly in civil
cases concerned with land and petty debts. Business expanded with the
increase in population, the growing number of commercial enterprises,
and the continuing addition of more laws to the territorial code. James
Backus, the first sheriff at Marietta, wrote, "The emoluments of this
business are trifling, yet there is more law business here than might be
expected from the newness of the place . . . it consists chiefly of suits
commenced on old debts against transient persons that resort here."[13] As
in Kentucky and Tennessee, merchants were among the principal users
of the court system. Officeholders profited in proportion to the growth
of the courts. A law passed in 1792 enumerated acts for which a fee
could be charged, ranging from five cents to the judge of common pleas
for swearing in a witness to one dollar for the judge of probate for a final
decree. In addition, there were other fees for the judges and clerks of the
General Court, the coroner, constable, sheriff, grand jurors, commissioners of assessment and so forth.[14] The scramble for offices increased
in like proportion, along with the power of those who controlled appointments.

The creation of this large structure of government and law coincided
with a growth of population. A single county was soon no longer sufficient. St. Clair, accordingly, created others: Hamilton County in 1790,
including the settlements around the Great and Little Miami Rivers and

12. Pease, ed., *The Laws of the Northwest Territory*, 13–21, 31.
13. Quoted in Josephine E. Phillips, "James Backus: Citizen of Marietta, 1788–1791,"
    OAHQ, 45 (1936): 163. Note that the law of 1792 permitted parties in litigation to
    manage their own cases.
14. Pease, ed., *The Laws of the Northwest Territory*, 102–16.

the village of Cincinnati, to which St. Clair moved the government of the territory in 1790; Knox County, laid off by Acting Governor Winthrop Sargent in 1790, encompassing the settlements at Vincennes on the Wabash, and extending from the Great Miami on the east to the junction of the Illinois and Chicago rivers, north to Canada; and, St. Clair County, organized in 1790 and embracing the French settlements in the Illinois country. As the structure of government and a court system extended over the Northwest Territory, St. Clair and his judges, sitting as the legislature, expanded the scope of local government. Legislation enacted in 1790 provided for the subdivision of counties into townships and the appointment (by the courts of general quarter sessions of the peace) of constables, overseers of the poor, and clerks of the townships. Among the duties of the overseer of the poor were to watch the vagrants "likely to become chargeable to the township for which he is appointed overseer, and also to take notice of all the poor and distressed families and persons residing in his proper township, and enquire into the means by which they are supported and maintained." The responsibilities of the clerk included maintenance of a brand book for distinguishing horses, cattle, hogs, and other livestock in the township; he also kept a book of estrays, to record the livestock found in the township. The township became, in addition, the administrative center of road construction and maintenance. In response to a petition from twelve citizens, supervisors and overseers at the township level would lay out a road. For assistance, they would call on every male inhabitant over sixteen years of age, each to work no more than ten days a year under the direction of the township supervisor "with such utensils and tools as may be ordered him."[15]

This government and court system did not always work smoothly. Distances in the wilderness were vast, and communications poor. The scanty population of the frontier areas moved out to the wilderness in search of land, and there were many small and scattered settlements, especially after 1795. It was difficult to disseminate a uniform body of law throughout such a broad area, much less to convene a court in one spot and meet the needs of a widely dispersed populace. The presence of

15. Journal of the Executive Proceedings, 294–95, 301–303; Pease, ed., *The Laws of the Northwest Territory*, 37–41, 74–77. Eblen notes the importance of local autonomy, which he lays to the prolonged absences of St. Clair from the territory. *The First and Second United States Empires*, 74–77.

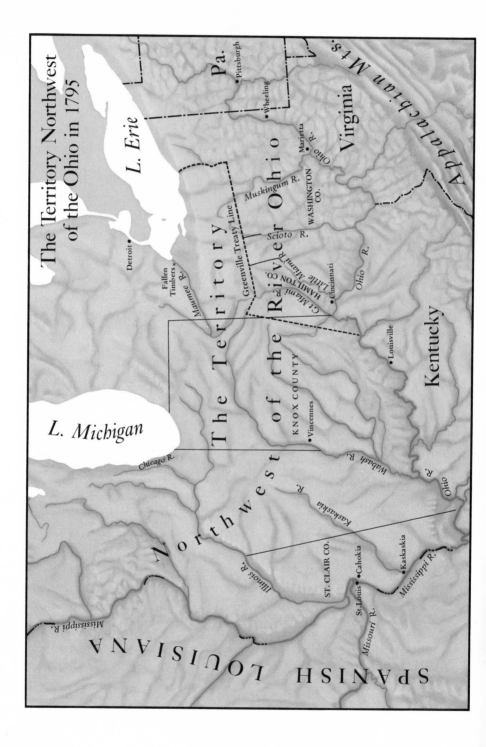

The Territory Northwest of the Ohio in 1795

L. Erie

L. Michigan

Pa.

Pittsburgh

Wheeling

Virginia

Appalachian Mts.

Detroit

Fallen Timbers ×

Maumee R.

The Territory

Greenville Treaty Line

Muskingum R.

Marietta

Ohio R.

WASHINGTON CO.

Scioto R.

Little Miami R.

Gt. Miami R.

HAMILTON CO.

Cincinnati

Ohio R.

Louisville

Kentucky

of the River Ohio

Northwest of the

KNOX COUNTY

Vincennes

Chicago R.

Wabash R.

Kaskaskia R.

Illinois R.

ST. CLAIR CO.

Ohio R.

Kaskaskia

Cahokia

St. Louis

Missouri R.

Mississippi R.

SPANISH LOUISIANA

Mississippi R.

hostile Indians in large numbers and the undeclared wars of this seven-year period tended to belie the order that the legal code was designed to give. "Civil Law is an admirable institution any where except on a frontier situated in the center of an Indian Country and in a time of War," Major Hamtramck wrote to Henry Knox from the Ohio frontier in the spring of 1792.[16] "An Indian country at war" was a phrase that might have described Kentucky in the 1770's, Tennessee in the early 1780's, and the Northwest Territory for the early 1790's—in short, much of the trans-Appalachian region for the years 1775 to 1795. Delays in the construction of courthouses and jails added to the informality of legal institutions in this period. Without regular courts and a satisfactory means of confining transient prisoners, justice was sporadic, often summary, and sometimes brutal. Courts were scheduled regularly but convened infrequently, and often the principal parties or witnesses failed to appear, making justice long-delayed, tiring, and expensive.[17]

An alien people far removed from the center of authority complicated the task of spreading government and law across the reach of this land. To the west and north of the Ohio lay ancient French settlements dating from the seventeenth century: Vincennes on the Wabash River; Kaskaskia and Cahokia in the Illinois country; and Detroit at the junction of Lakes Huron and Erie. All were French in origin and long settled when the Americans appeared from across the mountains; all suggested the vast dimensions of the French empire in the New World. These villages originated as fur-trading posts. In the early years ownership of land was unimportant. Much of it was farmed in common, and, for those interested in private holdings, land was everywhere, people were few, and central authority distant. The French inhabitants in the remote villages of the Northwest largely ignored the international negotiations that made them English in 1763. The objectives of the British government with respect to the fur trade did not differ appreciably from those of the French. And like the French, the English attempted only to maintain some sort of effective civil order in the villages; they left the details to the inhabitants themselves, knowing that a higher authority remained to impose solutions which could not be worked out at the local level. These French communities passed under American authority in 1783. With the

16. Major Hamtramck to Knox, March 31, 1792, in *TP*, 2: 381.
17. Attig, "The Institutional History of the Northwestern Territory," 145–58, discusses the problems of the court system.

complete neglect by the new American government and the ineffectual attempts of the Virginians to make good their claims to the region, the force of government vanished, and the villages lapsed into a condition of anarchy. At the same time, the French settlers began to be concerned about the ownership of their lands. In spite of persistent reassurances that their rights would be safeguarded, *les habitants* declined to present their land claims before the American courts. They were also reluctant to give any testimony in the land courts, and especially to testify against one another. As a result, the lands claimed by the French settlers remained unpatented and their status uncertain. Differences in language and legal institutions made it difficult for them to understand the Americans and to accept the new government. The judicial system of the Northwest Ordinance was never effective in the Illinois country. Local loyalties remained the strongest force in the French settlements, and the inhabitants struggled to retain their lands and their cultural heritage in the face of the oncoming American tide. By ignoring material progress as a standard, they kept intact their heritage but incurred the contempt of the ambitious, aggressive Americans. These problems of distance and cultural diversity added to Arthur St. Clair's burden. He never found satisfactory solutions to them.[18]

In the summer of 1795 Governor St. Clair and his judges completed the legal code of the Northwest Territory. The Code of 1795 was a summary of all laws in effect at that time, with some additional regulations touching on questions of dower, divorce, orphans, and asserting the formal adoption of the common law. The acceptance of the common law—confirmed in subsequent legislation in 1802 and 1805—placed the Northwest Territory directly in the Anglo-American legal tradition that ran from English courts through the Anglo-American colonies across the mountains into Kentucky and Tennessee.[19] What had emerged in the

18. May Allison, "Conditions in the Illinois Country, 1787–1800" (M.A., Illinois, 1907), chs. 1–4, 6.
19. The Northwest Ordinance gave judges common law jurisdiction and guaranteed "judicial proceedings according to the course of common law." See William B. Hamilton, "The Transmission of English Law to the Frontier of America," *SAQ*, 67 (1968): 249–50. Lawyers and judges debated the force of the common law in Ohio for a number of years, and Judge Benjamin Tappan handed down a decision that the Ordinance of 1787 brought the common law to what was later the state of Ohio. Note William T. Utter, "Ohio and the English Common Law," *MVHR*, 16 (1929–30): 321–33.

first seven years was a structure of government and courts well suited to a frontier people, for it could be expanded and new units of government and courts created at will down to township level; a society secured from external and internal threats, with provisions for tax collection, public buildings, the poor, orphans, and record keeping; and careful regulations for the acquisition and protection of property, with suitable forms and even provision for licensing lawyers. St. Clair had provided justices and justice of the peace courts to meet the immediate demands of a decentralized frontier world; the adoption of the common law laid down an institutional foundation for the future. The legal code that Governor St. Clair fashioned in such detail over seven years became the basis for subsequent legal codes in other territories of the Northwest. His was an enduring institutional legacy.[20]

The early economy of the Northwest Territory involved a combination of agricultural self-sufficiency and primitive trade. Commerical agriculture developed slowly. The settlements remained small, surrounded by Indian tribes that intimidated possible expansion to the interior. Outlets to market lay in several directions: a trade with the Indians; commercial transactions up the Ohio to Pittsburgh and downriver to Spanish New Orleans; or a commerce within the settlements of the territory, especially with newcomers. These possibilities proved inadequate, either individually or in combination. A state of constant hostility reduced the Indian trade, and Indians were never as interested in agricultural products as they were in the manufactured goods that came across the mountains. The return for frontier agricultural staples sent upriver to Pittsburgh did not justify the expense of transporting them such a distance against the current. The New Orleans market was remote and subject to a host of navigational hazards and diplomatic uncertainties. The Ohio country produced little agricultural surplus and engaged in little commerce until after 1795.[21]

All this is not to say that the early pioneers did not have their commercial needs. They did. Goods and tools from the East were required.

20. Eblen, *The First and Second United States Empires*, ch. 4, esp. pp. 109–10.
21. Robert Leslie Jones, "Ohio Agriculture in History," *OHQ*, 65 (1956): 229–58. An excellent article on early Ohio agriculture and its commerce is Frank P. Goodwin, "Building a Commercial System," *OAHQ*, 16 (1907): 316–39.

To meet this need, stores and merchants appeared on the scene almost as soon as farmers. We have a detailed account of the experiences of one early merchant in the journals of Colonel John May, an associate of the Ohio Company. In the summer of 1789 May journeyed on company business from Boston to the Ohio River Valley. On the basis of his trip to Marietta the previous spring, he decided to bring a supply of eastern goods for sale to the growing numbers of settlers along the Ohio. After great effort, and no little expense, May finally succeeded in moving his merchandise from Baltimore to the Monongahela. Five wagons transported five tons of shoes, iron shovels, clover seed, and cheese, wrapped in small packages for retail sale. The new merchant took a quick trip down the Ohio to spy out a suitable place of business and immediately discovered that stores and merchandise covered the western country, or so it seemed. Louisville and other likely river towns in Kentucky had more merchants than they could possibly support. The citizens of May's own Marietta were "poor and proud," not an attractive combination for a man with only a few months' credit. So May chose Wheeling, a village across the river in western Virginia that served the settlers of the Northwest Territory. He rented half a store and set himself up as a merchant.

May's new mercantile establishment immediately became a center of local interest. "There are mighty numbers of old and young women men and Boys collected here today brim full of interogations but totally Voyd of Money," he recorded; "They have asked me ten thousand Questions . . . the whole of this day Laborious work brought about Three Dollars and half." His experience demonstrates the limited life of that little frontier settlement, where people without funds flocked to a new store to handle the merchandise, interrogate the storekeeper, gossip, seek credit, and simply pass the time. Few came to buy, for they had nothing to buy with. May soon decided to accept skins and peltry, and later ginseng, in order to facilitate business; unless he did, his prospective customers would come empty handed. For a summer the Boston investor turned frontier merchant struggled to cater to his sometimes shy and always pitifully poor clientele, carefully watched his merchandise, and evicted those too noisy or rapacious. He worked from sunrise to sunset and into the evening. He wrote in his journal at night, his lamp attracting swarms of Ohio Valley insects. He worried constantly about his investment. Would he sell out the stock of goods? How much would it cost to transport peltry and ginseng to Baltimore? Had the price of ginseng fallen during the summer? At the end of the season, May sold the rest of his stock to one of the other merchants in Wheeling, packed his pelts and ginseng, and transported them by horse train to Baltimore. He left no record whether or not he made a profit, but he never tried again.[22]

For the first half dozen years of its legal settlement, the Northwest Territory lived in a state of military siege. The war against the Indians delayed the effective operation of the new court system and, indeed, affected every aspect of life in the Northwest Territory. It disrupted communication and interfered with orderly government; it retarded immigration and expansion to the interior; it brought with it physical destruction, suffering, and hardship. But it also stimulated the economy. This long war, like others before and since, encouraged the federal government to expand its authority, and nowhere was its influence more strongly felt than in the economic sphere. Into this military struggle the new American government poured a portion of its limited resources, determined to recapture international respect lost in earlier Indian victories. To this end, the government built roads, recruited and supported an army in the field for much of the period, and engaged in constant negotiations with the Indians. The presence of large numbers of troops fed at government expense meant that quantities of local corn, grain, horses, cattle, and hogs found a cash market and those pioneers with teams and wagons could rent them to the army for a good price.

Hostilities north of the Ohio began in earnest after 1788, when growing American settlements created demands for land cessions from the Native Americans in the Ohio Valley. The Indians resisted both the pressure to negotiate and the military forces sent against them. They won two dramatic military victories: against forces led by General Josiah Harmar (1790) and, later, over Governor St. Clair himself (1791). St. Clair lost more than six hundred men. It was this military disaster that persuaded the national government to take more vigorous steps, for the deterioration of its position in the Ohio Valley now embarrassed America's diplomatic posture in a time of extended negotiations with European nations. President George Washington appointed General Anthony Wayne as commander-in-chief and made available both troops and supplies. After two years of training—he had noted the results of cam-

22. May, *Western Journals*, 139, 134.

paigning with untrained militia—Wayne advanced slowly toward the Indian centers of strength in the Northwest. He won a decisive victory in August 1794 at Fallen Timbers near the rapids of the Maumee River. Wayne then called a peace conference where he dictated terms. The Treaty of Greenville (August 1795) ensured the survival and expansion of the American settlements north of the Ohio.[23]

The struggle of the first settlers of the Northwest Territory to establish institutions of an educational and religious nature was much like that of Kentucky and Tennessee. It was carried on by small numbers of people living in physical isolation and interrupted by sporadic Indian wars. Opportunities for religion and education reflected, in part, the growing distinctions in wealth and social position. Those with money and place clearly had advantages, especially if they lived in the river towns. In the countryside religious and educational activities were haphazard and unstructured, falling back again on the individual family and testifying to its importance. An exception were the several French villages on the Wabash and in the Illinois country, where the sense of community was strong and enhanced by a generation of self-sufficiency and commitment to the church as a center of life. But everywhere else northwest of the Ohio problems of isolation were intensified for women, who often lacked men's drive for economic success and excitement over the challenge of the wilderness and did not have occasion to travel and meet others for business purposes. The social needs of children were largely ignored. Schools were virtually unknown, at least up to 1795. The provision in the Ordinance of 1785 setting aside one section of land in each township for the maintenance of schools lay unused. Young enquiring minds lived in a closed world, shut off from books and ideas as the panoply of the great forest shut out the sun.

Thomas Ewing was one of those who grew up on the isolated rural frontier of the Northwest Territory. In the absence of local schools, his ambitious father sent him away to an academy, and young Ewing re-

23. A good general account of the Indian wars is Reginald Horsman, *The Frontier in the Formative Years, 1783–1815* (New York, 1970), 39–49. On the army as an early market for commodities and services, see Randolph C. Downes, "Trade in Frontier Ohio," *MVHR*, 16 (1929–30): 477–79. Downes notes that heavy immigration replaced the demands of the army for goods and services after 1795.

turned to read Virgil's *Aeneid* (presumably in translation) to the laborers employed on his father's farm. He made frequent trips to the mill, as did the other boys of his age, but while they wrestled and skylarked, he passed his time in reading. Books became a passion for him. When a few neighbors pooled funds to purchase books for a private circulating library, Ewing "contributed ten Raccoon skins—being all my hoarded wealth." At last the long-awaited volumes arrived, and, examining the sixty or seventy books on the cabin floor, he wrote, "It seemed to me like an almost unbounded intellectual treasure—the library of the Vatican and all other libraries of which I had read were trifles,—playthings— compared with it." Ewing went on to college, was admitted to the bar, and became a United States senator from the state of Ohio. A few of his contemporaries acquired some competence in reading and writing; most of them received no formal education and spent their lives on the land.[24]

In the Ohio Valley, as elsewhere on the early trans-Appalachian frontier, a continuing cycle of labor dictated the quality of life for its people. For the men the regular duties were backbreaking labor of clearing, planting, and harvesting. For children, limited schooling, hard labor on the farm, and a work-oriented youth left them tired as adults and painfully shy in social situations. A life in the woods on the early trans-Appalachian frontier conferred few social skills. On one occasion when Thomas Ewing returned from the mill, he hitched a ride on a flatboat headed down the river. On the flat was a family with a daughter Ewing found very attractive. But this future senator from Ohio, having spent most of his life in the isolation of the frontier, was at a loss how to approach her. He became painfully conscious of his rustic manners and dress. "My hands were chapped and black with toil . . . so that I hardly dared to offer them to help her out of the boat," he remembered, "and I took due care to hide them in her presence."[25]

The need for security and stability determined the direction of institutional development in the Old Northwest. Of greatest necessity was the creation of government, a court system, and a code of law. The Ordinance of 1787 responded to this need; the vigorous (if opinionated) leadership of Governor Arthur St. Clair provided chapter and verse. Few men in American life have wielded such far-reaching power. St. Clair

24. Thomas Ewing, "The Autobiography of Thomas Ewing," ed. Clement L. Martzolff, *OAHQ*, 22 (1913): 150–51.
25. Ewing, "Autobiography," 155.

was a man with a vision of the society that he wished to create, an orderly world where moral men and women prospered. For him, the frontier was an unpleasant and transitory condition, one fraught with dangers from an unstable and sometimes disorderly population. He did everything possible to protect society from such dangers. When Congress questioned the constitutionality of some of the territory's laws, the governor replied to the effect that unconstitutional laws were better than no laws at all and that to have gone without laws would have produced "a state of anarchy."[26] Under St. Clair's direction, county government and the county court system spread over the territory's widely scattered settlements. County bureaucrats, along with the militia and courts, gradually exerted a strong influence on the life of the individual settlers, even in remote regions. The government and the court system of the counties dealt with the most pressing needs of a frontier community: land, economic development, taxes, property, and civil order. Such institutions were often quite independent of higher authority. Distances from the territorial capital and the courts of appeal and the importance of local issues in a decentralized society meant that their decisions were virtually final.

The Northwest Territory had a structure of government and a legal code almost too complex for the small numbers of people it contained. Yet the Ordinance of 1787 and its institutional direction under Arthur St. Clair established a framework within which orderly development might take place in the future. A stroke of the governor's pen (later the legislature's) conferred government. A series of commissions with the same signature created a corps of officeholders. This system might be expanded indefinitely to keep pace with a westward moving population, and it spread over the Territory Northwest of the Ohio and, eventually, over much of the nation west of the Appalachians. In this sense, the institutions identified in the Northwest Ordinance and created by St. Clair and his judges were admirably designed to meet the needs of expanding people. With peace in 1795, the new wave of population to the Ohio Valley found that government had preceded it. Later in the decade St. Clair would be attacked as arbitrary and dictatorial; by the standards of the later period, he was. For the first settlers and the early experiences in the period from 1788 and 1795, however, his institution building was

26. Journal of the Governors and Judges, 1795, ESR, Ohio, p. 5.

eminently suited to the requirements of a people still dominated by the drive for security and stability. They needed protection from enemies within and without and hoped to see the visible force and authority of government. St. Clair gave them this force. What emerged worked in fits and starts: successfully for the compact settlements and urban areas along the Ohio; erratically in the sparsely settled areas inland; rarely in the remote and ancient settlements of the French. However sporadic, this form of government, mixed with the success of American arms in the field of battle, assured the survival and orderly development of these first settlements. In the period after 1795, as a consequence of peace at Greenville and the stable government provided by the government under the ordinance, large-scale immigration took place to the Territory Northwest of the Ohio. A new stage in its development had begun.

II

The Widening Frontier
1795–1815

From 1795 to 1815 the frontier of the trans-Appalachian West expanded in numbers, in geography, and in terms of new forces that influenced its development. The population of 150,000 west of the mountains in 1795 grew to more than one million by the federal census of 1810. Americans moved in increasing numbers into the Ohio Valley and along the Great Lakes at the intersections of the great rivers; up the valleys of the Whitewater, Wabash, Kaskaskia, Illinois, Missouri, Arkansas, Red, Yazoo, and Alabama; along the banks of the Mississippi in the Deep South; into the great savannahs and swamps of the newly organized Orleans Territory. They moved everywhere the numerous and powerful Indian tribes would allow and some places where they would not. Those already on the land—whether French, Spanish, or Native American—felt the impress of Anglo-American institutions and saw their own threatened. Only in long-settled portions of the Louisiana Purchase were the French sufficiently numerous and culturally strong to resist the advance of common law and the county court system. This expansion and the varieties of the frontier experience that flowed from it were dominant features of these twenty years.

This portion of the story opens on a world of primeval nature; it closes with the increasing frequency of small settlements that represent the harbingers of American civilization. The widening of the frontier brought the pioneer into contact with a vast panorama of rich and varied vegetation. Only a few tracks and cleared fields of maize testified to the lengthy and often continued occupation of the Indian tribes. The first settlers had to come to terms with the vast physical presence of nature, for they came not to admire it but to live in it. They had to clear the land, construct shelters, raise crops, create a defense against dangers from several quarters, and provide for the immediate needs of themselves and their families. At the same time, as a part of this early process, they sought institutions that would ensure security and lay the basis for the economic advantages that they presumed would accompany settlement and development. In this they drew upon the long experience of others in frontier areas from the early seventeenth century on and, more recently, the experiences of the new settlements in Kentucky, Tennessee, and the Northwest Territory. These places had survived and grown with the ancient and tried institutions of the militia and county government. The Northwest Territory was similar to Kentucky and Tennessee in institutional framework, although authority rested with the federal government rather than the states. An agricultural society that was familiar to frontier people developed along with the fertile lands that would make an agricultural people prosper. At the same time, the county emerged as the dominant political unit and a center of administrative decision making, law, and services.

Of the new forces that influenced the trans-Appalachian frontier, the most significant was the authority of the federal government. The new Constitution adopted in 1789 had provided for a stronger central government, but this government asserted its strength only gradually. With a series of military and diplomatic triumphs in the mid-1790's, it gained respect and confidence. Among those areas of increasing federal influence after 1795, two were paramount. The first was in the control of institutions of government through the Ordinance of 1787. The Northwest Ordinance had laid down a system of government that provided for the gradual development of a territory into a state. Between 1795 and 1815 the territorial system spread over the expanding frontier west of the Appalachians and accompanied the provisions of the Land Ordinance of 1785, which had given the federal government control over the organization, administration, and distribution of the public domain. Where the provisions of the Land Ordinance proved inadequate, too general, or inappropriate, Congress and the executive made laws governing the distribution of land, a matter of great importance to frontier people.

Foreign affairs was a second arena in which the influence of the federal government was dominant. From 1795 to 1815 the destiny of the trans-Appalachian frontier became intertwined with a larger world. Control over matters of state rested with the national government. The year 1795 marked a turning point, for military and diplomatic victories combined to alleviate the threat from the Indian tribes of the Northwest and to ensure an open Mississippi River for transporting the surplus commodities of the frontier to the world. General Anthony Wayne's victory at Fallen Timbers in 1794 and the large land cession at the Treaty of Greenville the next year removed the Indian danger to the Ohio settlements (as well as to much of the Kentucky and Tennessee regions) and freed a portion of the Northwest Territory for American occupation. The same year John Jay's Treaty with Great Britain provided for the evacuation of the Northwest posts, and Thomas Pinckney's diplomatic success in Madrid opened the Mississippi River to trade and established the right of deposit for American goods at New Orleans. The diplomatic triumphs of Wayne, Jay, and Pinckney were in part a response to the growing American presence and the commercial importance of American settlements in the trans-Appalachian West. Then, in 1803, Thomas Jefferson overcame his constitutional scruples and arranged for the purchase of Louisiana, which the accidents of an unhappy war had convinced Napoleon to sell. The result was a thunderstroke in the history of diplomacy and the American frontier. This single act changed the scope of the frontier beyond recognition and confirmed the decisive influence of the federal government in the destinies of people west of the mountains. The Mississippi River—trade lifeline of the frontier people—now lay safely within the boundaries of an expanding nation, and Americans west of the mountains moved to take advantage of Europe's distress. At the same time that trade expanded, the question of neutral rights at sea became a matter of national concern, for Americans sought to preserve their non-belligerency status and continue a prosperous commerce with all belligerents. The War of 1812 was a final demonstration of the degree to which the frontier of the trans-Appalachian West had become intertwined with the affairs of the nation.

4

Diversity
in Economic Development

Between 1795 and 1815 the dominant feature in the economic development of the trans-Appalachian frontier was the Ohio-Missouri-Missis-
sippi river trade axis. This broad continental water highway, connecting
Pittsburgh—by way of Louisville and Cincinnati—and St. Louis with
Natchez and New Orleans, was the main channel of trade and the route
of immigrants. The pioneers settled along the banks of the great rivers
and their many tributaries. Within this trade and settlement pattern, the
widespread expansion of the trans-Appalachian frontier was accompanied by a diversity of economic development. Furs and lead flowed
downriver from St. Louis and Upper Louisiana. Commercial agriculture
emerged in the Ohio Valley, where farmers grew increasing quantities of
corn, wheat, and livestock for market. Cotton cultivation appeared in
new settlements on the southern frontier. All testified to a maturing and
increasingly complex economy.

Throughout most of the western country agriculture lay at the center
of economic life. An unchanging rhythm governed the world of the pioneer agriculturist. In the spring, movement and immigration; in the winter, fencing, building, and repairing tools. Above all, the cycle was imposed by nature: plow, plant, cultivate, harvest, and preserve. The
addition of animals made it necessary to round up, brand, and butcher.
Immigrants came to the land with the required agricultural skills; they
knew how to clear, break ground, manage livestock, and construct buildings and improvements. They knew how to preserve food for winter;

93

they made their clothes in the home. These early agriculturists grew a variety of crops, principally corn. Their earliest surplus was often live-stock, and it was from the sale of cattle or hogs to new immigrants or at a nearby market that the pioneers obtained the funds to pay for their lands and to purchase a few necessities in a rare visit to a store. Schools and churches, like store goods, were luxuries. A few gravitated to the rising urban centers of commerce and services, but most of the pioneers only occasionally profited from the social and cultural institutions that developed in the towns.[1]

In the economic variations that went along with this widespread expansion from 1795 to 1815, three levels of agricultural enterprise can be seen: subsistence agriculture, surplus agriculture, and staple crop agriculture. Subsistence agriculture came first. It was a condition associated with new settlement and isolation, characterized by a mixed farming-hunting economy, with corn as a basic frontier crop, livestock pastured in the woods, and a garden. The family consumed the immediate products of the field and forest; there was little or no surplus, and a lack of transportation facilities may have ruled out export of a marketable crop in any case. Subsistence agriculture was the universal experience for the bulk of frontier peoples, at least initially. But within the framework of subsistence, the economic experiences of the first pioneers varied widely. Some pioneers came as part of a large community; others alone. Some came with livestock, tools, and money; others had nothing but the clothes on their backs and a little corn.

Hosea Smith was a solitary pioneer with ready money. In the spring of 1810 he moved from Kentucky to Knox County (Indiana) and purchased two hundred acres "with a Considerable Improvement with a crop in the ground." Smith wrote of his location, "In this Neighborhood there is land aplenty not Entered and the richest I ever beheld and as for stock it is one of the finest places that is to be found." He was surprised to find so few people and so much excellent land available for two dollars an acre, or land with improvements for three dollars. He wrote in a letter to his father of prospects for new immigrants, "I am satisfied they might better themselves if they had not one Dollar after getting hear." Smith advised his relatives to bring only the necessities, "tho any light tools is verry servisable as they come high, bed and clothing servisable to

1. Robert Leslie Jones, "Ohio Agriculture in History," *OHQ*, 65 (1956): 229-38.

bring." A crosscut saw was among the most useful items on the frontier, he continued, and "a new blade might be put in the bottom of a cart or waggon." He emphasized that those who came to the western country for its cheap fertile lands "must expect to meet with some hardship and expense." In the course of the summer and the next spring he noted with increasing frequency the large numbers of new immigrants headed to the West from all parts of the country. Their destinations varied, "some to Plattoker [Patoka, a small tributary of the White], some over the Wabash on the Donation, some on busroe settlement and abundance on the new purchase, and a number over the Mississippi and some up the Missory to St. Louis and different parts." Like scouts in the vanguard of an advancing army, land agents "from New England, Maryland, Pennsylvania, NY, Va, SC, Ga, Ohio, Ky States, as well from many others" preceded the immigrant families.[2]

Joseph Hayes had neither capital nor friends. His first job was in a salt manufactory near Lawrenceburg (Indiana), on the edge of the Ohio line. The year was 1802; the wage, fifty cents a day. The appearance of western Virginia salt on the frontier of the Old Northwest ended the salt industry in Indiana. Hayes married and flatboated for two years. In 1809 he bought land. With his wife and a new child he settled down to the life of a subsistence farmer. He described planting the first crop in these terms:

> The first field of corn I planted for myself was about 10 acres I kind of scratched it over with the plow. I then fixed a little crib on the plow so that we placed our first child I furrowed out and my wife dropped the corn. Then when near noon she would take the Child and go to the home and get dinner.—While she would be getting dinner—I took the hoe and would cover the corn. We continued this way—with the child riding on the plow alternately until we finished our ten acres.

The swarms of birds that filled the sky and the forest animals that still inhabited the woods took about one-third of the crop; Hayes got the remaining two-thirds. With autumn came the pressure of harvest and then a modest social life built around corn huskings. When winter was

2. Hosea Smith to his father, June 14, Oct. 13, 1810; June 5, 1814; Smith to his brother, Nov. 14, 1810 (two letters of the same date); Oct. 22, 1813; Smith to his father-in-law, Nov. 27, 1813, Hosea Smith Letters, 1810–14, IHS. According to Smith, the War of 1812 scarcely slowed immigration. Smith's reference to the Donation is to a tract comprising more than 100,000 acres on both sides of the Wabash that had been set aside under acts of Congress in 1788 and 1791 but was now open for settlement.

on the land, people made clothes, repaired tools, and planned for spring. Soon the cycle began again.[3]

Even in a land of such natural abundance, those with little or nothing found things difficult. The early history of Thomas Morrison is a study in hardship and perseverance and demonstrates the mixed economic functions already present in the Ohio Valley frontier by the turn of the century. Orphaned at an early age, Morrison grew up near Rising Sun (Indiana), on the edge of the Greenville Treaty cession. He attended school for perhaps six months. At the age of fourteen he planted five acres of corn on the public domain but soon left the land to work in a mill. In 1809 he went to Dayton and took work as a builder. He was landless, but small villages such as Dayton made it possible for him to find employment as a tradesman. Morrison wrote his account with an intensity that characterized the struggle he waged for survival. No mention of social activity or leisure punctuates its pages. His objects in life were shelter for the night, the next meal, basic economic sufficiency.[4]

Similar cycles of movement and labor governed early economic life on the southern frontier. In the Tombigbee River region—the far eastern part of the Mississippi Territory—the early settlers squatted on the land, made a clearing, cultivated corn, and grazed some livestock. The accounts of these first pioneers give the impression of the vastness of the wilderness, the tiny clearings of the settlers, and the profusion of nature all around. The Ramsey family were among these early settlers. Born in North Carolina, resident of Georgia for several years, the elder Ramsey knew life in the woods well. His son remembered, "In the fall of 1807 or thereabouts, Father hearing that a fine country was ahead and that it was to be found in the New Territory, that the United States had just acquired from the Choctaw Indians, in what is now South Eastern Mississippi . . . determined to move to it; so as soon as he could arrange for the trip, packed up and started." The caravan of three horses, one for the "bedding clothing, camp equipage &c," a second for his wife, and a third for the two young boys, marched to the "land of promise" through Indian country. The elder Ramsey walked. The destination was a tract on the Chickasawhay River, about fifty miles from Ft. St. Stephen (later St.

---

3. Joseph Hayes, "Life," ISL.
4. "A History of Thomas Morrison," ISL. A similar experience is the story of Thomas Rogers, "Reminiscences of a Pioneer," ed. Clement Martzolff, *OAHQ*, 19 (1910): 190–227.

Stephens). The family arrived on February 21, 1808, with an estate of "three horses, what baggage they had brought, the negro girl Dinah and twenty-one (21.00) dollars in cash."

What followed was a period of "Hard Times . . . Bread and meat, milk and butter, were the constant bill of fare," Preparation and planting came in the Anglo-American frontier tradition of nearly two centuries, and the Indian before that. The Ramseys cut the cane and burned it "so that the clearing would be in good order for planting." They planted corn and cotton "by making holes at proper distance, depositing the seed covering with the same earth taken out in making the whole." In order to clothe his family, Ramsey bought a spinning wheel, a pair of cotton cards, and a loom. Sitting around the fire at night, everyone ginned the cotton with a hand gin, "generally operated by the smaller or younger members of the family." Ramsey commented, "With these facilities; rough and unhandy as they were, Mother not only clothed the family, but made a surplus for market, which Father in the fall of that year carried to Mobile and sold for $2.50 per yeard." The small cotton crop was a portent of the future, for this staple spread rapidly through the Tombigbee region. The Ramseys stayed only a year, sold the improvements, and moved farther down the river. The son wrote that his father

> appeared to take up the idea, that improving new places and selling them out, to other new comers (and there were many) was better for him; more money in it; than to remain at one place and make large improvements and thereby accumulate money sufficient to buy, or enter him a permanent home. The country was then new and lands fertile; the range for stock good; bottom or river lands covered with solid cane brakes, easy to clear water and health good. It appears that could he have been contented to have remained there permanently with his energy and economy he might have done well.[5]

Louisiana offered a panorama of economic experiences. In a sense, the new land was a composite of the trans-Appalachian frontier: small settlements and villages, where descendants of the French colonists practiced subsistence agriculture as they had for generations; large-scale plantation agriculture directed to the production of a staple crop for sale on a world market; the rising influence of western commerce transforming a town into a great port. When the Americans came to Louisiana, as they did in

5. A. C. Ramsey, "A Sketch of the Life and Times of Rev. A. C. Ramsey . . . ," ADAH.

large numbers after 1803, they found a prosperous country. Interspersed among swamps, bayous, and innumerable watercourses were fertile lands. The forty thousand people of Louisiana had spread themselves over a wide area by this time. Great sugar and indigo plantations lined the Mississippi River on both sides, from New Orleans to Baton Rouge. Other important agricultural settlements centered around Opelousas, Natchitoches near the Red River, and the Attakapas country. In 1803 Thomas Nicholls described the Attakapas lands, the site of his new home, as "wide prairies, covered, as far as the eye could reach, with cattle and game of every description." Daniel Clark wrote the same year of the Attakapas and Opelousas areas, "Both these Posts having extensive & rich Plains have within the few years past attracted a great number of Emigrants from the other parts of the Country on account of the trouble & Expence of clearing and being unnecessary while there was a sufficiency of Timber for all the purposes of the Planter."[6]

In contrast to the plains and prairies of the interior, where corn and livestock were the major concern, in the bottomlands along the Mississippi agriculturists cultivated cotton and sugarcane. The Tensas Basin was one such area. The occupation and economic development of the Concordia and Rapides districts took place about the turn of the century. Farther to the west of the great river, settlers moved into the rich bayou lands. Martha Philips Martin, who came to Bayou Teche as a bride in 1811, remembered the stillness of the new country. "After leaving the Mississippi passing through Bayous & Lakes many places looked as never a boat had ever been before," she wrote. "Alligators were so numerous it was great sport shooting them in every direction." Soon after the Martins settled, "many families from Kentucky Tennessee & Mississippi came & purchased having plenty made quite a favorable change in our Bayou." The plantations on Bayou Teche and Bayou La Fourche were like those on the Mississippi, directed principally to growing sugarcane and, after 1803, to cotton.[7]

With all the talk of people, crops, and expansion, most of the land was empty. From the Tensas region north to the New Madrid outpost lay

6. Thomas C. Nicholls, "Reminiscences," LSU; Daniel Clark to James Madison, Aug. 20, 1803, in *TP*, 9: 14. On the diversity of Louisiana's land and people, see George Dargo, *Jefferson's Louisiana: Politics and the Clash of Legal Traditions* (Cambridge, 1975), 3–11.
7. Yvonne Phillips, "Settlement Succession in the Tensas Basin" (Ph.D., Louisiana State, 1952), ch. 2; Martha Philips Martin, "Memoirs," McIver Family Collection, TSLA.

three hundred miles of mangrove swamps, canebrakes, and heavy forests, unchanged, and most of it untrod, by white settlers. Upper Louisiana—as it was called—had little economic activity of a commercial nature. The fur trade and lead mining formed the staples of the economy in what would later become the territory of Louisiana-Missouri. Both were the work of a small, transient group of specialists, and their labors had brought a degree of prosperity to St. Louis.

A few St. Louis families dominated the political, social, and commercial affairs of the region. The Chouteaus were the best known and most influential. The wealth and estates of these leading Creole families contrasted with the illiteracy, subsistence, and even poverty in the countryside and villages. Upper Louisiana was strangely medieval in its sharp differences between noble and peasant. In this area the world of commerce—especially in agriculture—had not yet appeared, for in the several small French villages *les habitants* practiced self-sufficient agriculture in the tradition of their ancestors. Colonel Francis Jackson of Kentucky, who visited Upper Louisiana in 1800, found himself importuned by agriculturists who wished to sell their holdings. When he answered that he had no money and inquired of one man what he would take for his farm, a "dutchman" replied, "horses, cows, every ting." The change of government in 1803 reinforced the French tendency toward self-sufficiency, for the Americans threatened to call into question all land titles. In the face of the aggressive Americans and their institutions, the ancient French inhabitants—except for the leading St. Louis families, who intended to profit from new opportunities for leadership—banded together in order to preserve their cultural heritage.[8]

The transition to commercial agriculture, the second level of economic development, was often gradual. Commercial agriculture depended on trade routes and a market. Jacob Burnet wrote of the Ohio Valley at the turn of the century, "It was of no importance to the farmer, that his fields, with careful cultivation, would yield from 50 to 100 bushels of corn per acre, when a fourth part of the quantity would answer his purpose, there being no market for a surplus."[9] The purchase of Louisiana,

8. Lyman C. Draper Collections, 15 CC 8, SHSW; Harvey Wish, "The French of Old Missouri (1804–1821): A Study in Assimilation," *M-A*, 23 (1941): 175–82.
9. Jacob Burnet, *Notes on the Early Settlement of the North-Western Territory* (Cincinnati, 1847), 399.

however, opened the Ohio-Mississippi trade route to New Orleans, and a dependable market appeared downriver for corn, beef, pork, flour, grain, and other products of the western country. The volume of this trade expanded enormously, in proportion to the growing population and the new fertile lands constantly being placed under cultivation. The rapid growth of western commerce brought a measure of wealth to those western areas settled long enough to produce a surplus for export, and it offered to the more remote and recently settled backcountry frontiers the prospect of a future market. A wealthy and more leisured class of people emerged, for commercial agriculture sharpened economic distinctions. Surplus crops also meant a more advanced economic system, with large-scale transportation and storage facilities, a complex of credit, and economic arrangements with the eastern cities and sometimes with Europe. A host of commercial brokers performed these services in New Orleans. In the Ohio Valley the most important commercial center was Cincinnati, which controlled the trade of the Miami River Valley and eventually much of the Ohio. Capitalists, former army officers, real estate dealers, various men united by energy and ambition began to enter the business of commerce, which, if it were not new, was practiced on a scale not heretofore seen on the trans-Appalachian frontier.[10]

Joseph Hough, a merchant of the Miami River Valley with headquarters at Cincinnati, participated in the growing trade brought about by the rise of commercial agriculture. He began his commercial operations in 1806, purchasing eastern goods in Philadelphia and laboriously transporting them across the mountains to Pittsburgh. In Pittsburgh, Hough purchased a flatboat and moved the cargo downriver to his warehouse in Cincinnati. He then sent his goods to several stores at interior villages, where the storekeepers offered "fresh eastern goods" to their customers. Frontier farm families bartered growing agricultural surpluses and home manufactures for ammunition, pots, kettles, dishes, pans, nails, and other metalwork. The storekeeper took these commodities (he was without much alternative), and the process reversed itself. In the autumn and early winter quantities of pork, corn, and whiskey went downstream to Hough's Cincinnati warehouse. Then began the race to reach the New Orleans market before the endless parade of barges and

10. John G. Clark, *New Orleans, 1718–1812: An Economic History* (Baton Rouge, 1970), 302–11; Frank P. Goodwin, "The Development of the Miami Country," *OAHQ*, 18 (1909): 484–503.

flatboats from the Ohio Valley glutted the wharves in the Crescent City and reduced prices. Merchants of modest means went with their own boats; the larger entrepreneur employed assistants. Having sold the produce of the Ohio Valley in New Orleans, the merchant went to the East—New York, Philadelphia, or Baltimore—to settle his accounts and obtain credit for a new shipment of goods. The cycle had begun again. Thus the frontier surplus of the Ohio Valley gradually brought a degree of prosperity to the farmer and the village storekeeper (if he could collect his debts), and, provided that nothing disturbed the orderly flow of goods and their profitable sale, might bring a modest fortune to the Cincinnati merchants and the traders in New Orleans and Philadelphia.[11]

Merchants in long-settled areas, like John Coffee of Nashville, also served distant frontiers in several ways. Coffee's wide range of commercial and manufacturing enterprises stretched from the Mississippi Territory to the Illinois country. In 1798 he began to ship salt from the Illinois salines downriver. Coffee branched out into the slave trade between Nashville and Natchez and, gradually, into the large-scale shipment of corn, pork, saltpeter, cotton, tobacco, and other agricultural produce down the river to New Orleans. Eventually he had as many as five boats engaged in the river trade. By 1801 Coffee's commodity trade was so large that he built a store in Nashville to accommodate his business. He acquired interest in a cotton gin, boatyard, tavern, and racetrack—a cross-section of Nashville businesses. In addition to managing his growing enterprises, Coffee was a surveyor and land locator who continued to style himself a "planter."[12]

The introduction of commercial agriculture brought about a more complex economic relationship among the peoples west of the mountains and between them and their creditors to the East. Currency of many kinds circulated in the West: American dollars, French livres, British pounds, New York currency, and small quantities of United States bank notes. Most of all, money was scarce. In 1800 Governor Arthur St. Clair of the Northwest Territory wrote that the taxes levied in Knox County exceeded the specie in circulation in the county. "Money is extremely

11. R. Pierce Beaver, "Joseph Hough, An Early Miami Merchant," *OAHQ*, 45 (1936): 37–45. The experiences of an early Indiana merchant may be examined in the Samuel Vance Papers, IHS.

12. Gordon T. Chappell, "The Life and Activities of John Coffee" (Ph.D., Vanderbilt, 1941), ch. 2; Joseph Davis Applewhite, "Early Trade and Navigation on the Cumberland River" (M.A., Vanderbilt, 1940), ch. 2.

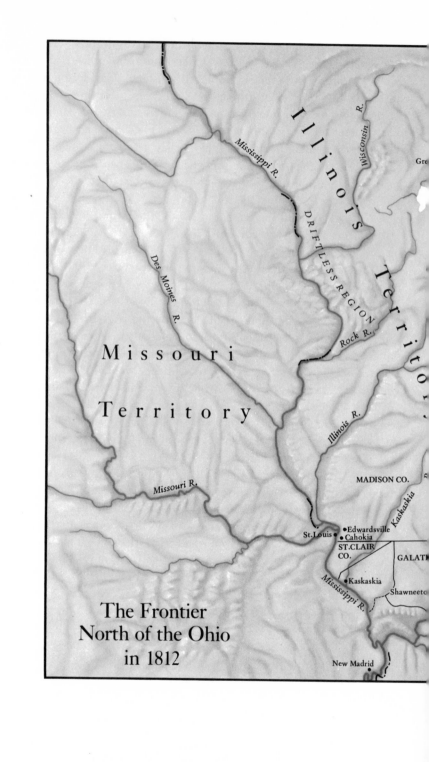

The Frontier
North of the Ohio
in 1812

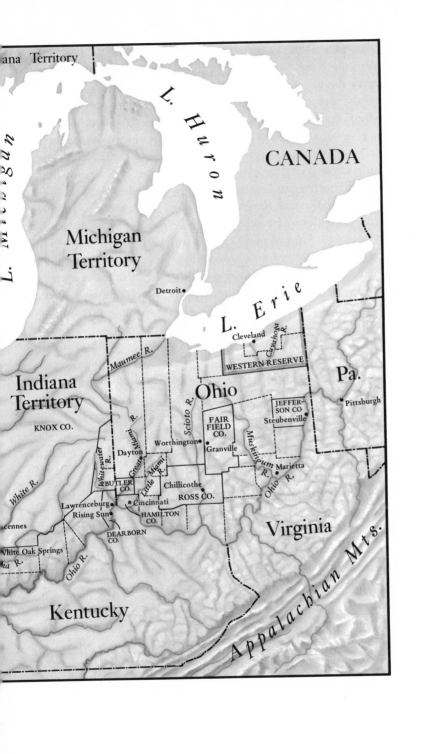

scarce in this part of the country," commented a correspondent of the *Scioto Gazette* about the Scioto River Valley. It is little wonder that the tax collectors found it almost impossible to make collections. Almost anything in the western country could be paid for in services or produce, such as wheat, corn, or more finished products like lard and flour. Furs always had value; whiskey was acceptable. For the most part, trade depended on a growing system of credit. Distances, small population, and the widely scattered nature of the settlements worked against the establishment of effective banking facilities. As late as 1808–10, the media of exchange in the Western Reserve of Ohio were land, cattle, and notes of indebtedness, under which the signee undertook to pay within a specified period of time. Unpaid notes carried interest. This was by far the most common form of commercial credit.[13]

Manufacturing enterprises developed with trade. In the tradition of the earliest trans-Appalachian frontier, the first processing took place in flourmills, gristmills, and sawmills. Mills themselves graduated in complexity and expense from hand driven to horse driven to waterpower, but at every level they offered an opportunity for great profit. Distilleries and tanneries also became significant industries. Salt manufacture was important for the export trade, as were lumber and lead in some places. Other manufacturing enterprises ranged from home-woven worsteds and tanned animal skins to large-scale industry like pork packing. With these early manufactories appeared a number of skilled and service occupations, among them blacksmithing, barrel making, and the building trades. Early industries in Jefferson County (Ohio) included broadcloth weaving and fulling, whiskey distilling, shipbuilding, and rope, iron, candle, and paper making.[14]

Thomas Worthington was an early industrial entrepreneur on the Ohio Valley frontier. A transplanted Virginian, Worthington became a landed aristocrat near Chillicothe (Ohio) on the Scioto River. He also promoted home industry. His land purchases included attractive mill

13. Arthur St. Clair to William Henry Harrison, Feb. 17, 1800, in *TP*, 7: 5; Chillicothe *Scioto Gazette*, Aug. 22, 1800; Memorial of Harrison County Citizens, Feb. 3, 1809, in *TP*, 7: 632–35; Sam'l Huntington to Alfred Kelley, May 24, 1816, Charles E. Rice Collection, OHS.

14. Jeanette Tobey, "Economic Life in Indiana, 1800–1816" (M.A., Butler, 1948), chs. 5, 7, 8, and conclusion, is an excellent analysis of early Indiana commercial activities. On early Jefferson County, see W. H. Hunter, comp., "The Pathfinders of Jefferson County," *OAHQ*, 6 (1898): 232–37.

sites, and by the turn of the century he had built three mills and leased them out for a rent in kind. In 1810 he began construction of an industrial establishment in Chillicothe that included a rope walk and a cloth mill. The mill wove flax, cotton, and wool; the finished products included linsey, cassimere, and flannel cloth. In order to assure a ready supply of wool, Worthington went into the sheep business on a large scale; he also grew some of the flax. He purchased additional supplies of flax from other Ross County farmers and imported cotton from the South, an early example of trade running up the Mississippi River. In 1817 Worthington's investments in machinery had reached $7,200, a large sum in the agricultural Scioto River Valley.[15]

The frontier had a long tradition of government interference in economic affairs. Following the example of the colonies, early county government often regulated the prices of taverns, ferries, and gristmills. It also supervised market operations, weights and measures, and even set the price of bread.[16] The national government now became a powerful influence in another way, for its relations with the belligerents in Europe directly affected the economy of the Ohio and Mississippi valleys. In the years from 1795 to 1815 economic and political considerations combined to sweep parts of the trans-Appalachian frontier forward to a condition of simultaneous prosperity and dependence. Prosperity came with the demand for American agricultural products—the very commodities that the West produced in abundance—stimulated by a general European war. Accompanying this prosperity was an increasing dependence on European trade and the attempts of the American government to remain neutral and, at the same time, to protect American rights on the high seas. The trade appeared and expanded in response to the success of American diplomats, and so government became a powerful force in the life of the western commercial economy. The embargo of 1807 emphasized the dependence and vulnerability of the West. With a signature President Jefferson crippled American trade with Europe, and there fol-

---

15. Alfred B. Sears, "Thomas Worthington, Pioneer Businessman of the Old Northwest," *OAHQ*, 58 (1949): 69–79. The census of 1810 was the first to list data on manufacturing.

16. Pierre de la Vergne, "Early Economic Life in Louisiana, 1804–1824 (An Historical Dialogue)," *LHQ*, 26 (1943): 915–36, stresses the powers of the City Council of New Orleans and the legislature to control economic life. On the impact of Anglo-American institutions on the City Council, see Clark, *New Orleans*, 280–87.

lowed years of falling commodity prices and growing economic distress in the western country.[17]

The third stage in the agricultural development of the frontier was the cultivation and marketing of staple agricultural commodities, including tobacco, rice, sugarcane, indigo, and especially cotton. All were associated with the frontier South. Although cotton culture emerged in its most complete form after 1815, its beginnings were already discernible in the period under consideration. With the introduction of the cotton gin, which made it possible to separate the fiber from the seed with little time or expense, cotton became an economic force unlike any other agricultural crop since tobacco in seventeenth-century Virginia. The rise of cotton to a position of such significance was also made possible by other technological innovations—the continued refinement of the steam engine and the invention of weaving machines for the large-scale manufacture of cotton cloth in the middle of the seventeenth century—and by the development of new strains of cotton especially suited to the American South. At the same time, American diplomatic successes opened the way for the movement of cotton downriver to New Orleans and subsequently to the ports of England, and so the slave plantations of the frontier South were tied to the squalid mill towns of the English Midlands.

The search of the southern agricultural frontier for a cash crop had ended. Any agriculturist in the American Southwest whose lands lay within reasonable distance of a navigable stream (cotton bales weighed about four hundred pounds) could find a cash market. He also found himself a part of a world economy, in which his fortunes were inexorably intertwined with the state of belligerency in Europe, the diplomatic maneuverings of the American government, the merchants in New Orleans who advanced him credit and marketed his product, the New England shipowners who transported his commodity to Europe, and the factory hands and industrial entrepreneurs of England. The isolation of the cotton frontier faded under such circumstances, bringing affluence

17. George Rogers Taylor, "Prices in the Mississippi Valley preceding the War of 1812," *Journal of Economic and Business History*, 3 (1930–31): 157–63, notes the falling prices of agricultural commodities, which began about 1805, and continued until the opening of the War of 1812.

but also compromising Thomas Jefferson's concept of the independent yeoman farmer.[18]

Mississippi became an early center of cotton cultivation on the frontier. John Hutchins's father arrived in what would become the Mississippi Territory in 1774. His accounts describe the world of Natchez and the Mississippi frontier before steam, white pillars, and crinolines. "For several years we were almost without bread, or milk, or both," he wrote. "Fortunately the country was well supplied with wild game." The little settlement of fifteen families lived in fear of Indians, Spanish officials, and thieves. Each member of the Hutchins family worked at several chores, the women in spinning, weaving, and the "household business"; the men in the fields and in the woods. As the family gradually opened up the land, corn replaced meat as the staple of the diet. Then Hutchins began to grow cotton, but without much prospect of a market. Separating the seeds from fiber was an onerous task. At first "if we went to visit a neighbor the ladies would fill their aprons with cotton to amuse themselves on the road picking out the seed." The cotton gin transformed all this. The younger Hutchins left to start his own plantation, with one milch cow, one ox, a few pigs and some poultry, a small pot for cooking, and a double cabin. With the help of two slaves and an old English soldier, Hutchins planted fifteen acres of cotton. "We were content," he wrote. But the cotton crop grew larger and larger. Hutchins saved his cotton for three years before he took it to a gin. Prices were high, and he prospered. By 1807 he had built his own mill and gin.[19]

The Natchez District—the term as generally used included rural areas around Natchez as well as the town itself—was one of the first of a series of noncontiguous agricultural frontiers that appeared after 1795 and exhibited many of the characteristics associated with cotton culture. The second settlement of the Natchez bluff and its surrounding agricultural lands—an Indian attack wiped out the first in 1729—dated from the 1770's. The people who immigrated there included a large band of En-

18. L. C. Gray, *History of Agriculture in the Southern United States to 1860* (2 vols., Washington, 1933), 2: 680–89. A brilliant introduction to the frontier cotton South is W. J. Cash, *The Mind of the South* (New York, 1941), ch. 1.

19. John Hutchins, "Memoirs," TSLA. Important general accounts of early Natchez and Mississippi are William Baskerville Hamilton, "American Beginnings in the Old Southwest: The Mississippi Phase" (Ph.D., Duke, 1937), ch. 2; and Nell Angela Heidelberg, "The Frontier in Mississippi" (M.A., Louisiana State, 1940), ch. 3.

glish loyalists who sought to escape the upheaval of the American Revolution. Others with an eye to attractive lands and a mild climate joined them. A variety of forces came together to spur the economic growth of this frontier. Under the scientific and economic direction of men such as Sir William Dunbar, the agriculturists of the area searched for a staple export crop for the better part of a generation. The success of tobacco depended wholly on the Spanish government's support; indigo was a costly failure. Cotton arrived at a fortunate moment. The first Whitney gin appeared in the Natchez District in 1795, and thereafter the number of gins and presses increased rapidly, especially after the turn of the century. As early as 1800, Narsworthy Hunter, a leading Natchez citizen, could write that "cotton is at present the staple of the Territory, and is cultivated with singular advantage to the planter." He continued, "We get a quarter of a dollar per lb. for clean cotton, and an active planter will make from five to eight hundred wt. to a hand: and as I conceive we have as many black as white inhabitants, we cannot make much less than three million pounds of merchantable cotton, equal to 750,000 dollars." By 1802 the larger planters had gins and ginned the crops of the smaller operators (for a fee), very much in the fashion of the gristmills in Kentucky and Tennessee twenty years earlier. Transportation facilities were a necessary part of cotton culture, and Thomas Fenton wrote, "Blest as we are with the benefit of Navigation, every creek of any size is Navigable ¾ of the year a Distance of fifteen or twenty miles from the Mississippi which affords almost every Planter Navigation to his Door." Cotton and its cultivation dominated every aspect of life and laid the economic foundation of a prosperous society.[20]

The cultivation of cotton also spread to other remote areas west of the Appalachians, changing the shape of frontier economic development in the South. When the federal government opened the region at the Great Bend of the Tennessee River (later organized into Madison County), Georgia and Tennessee planters, with cash and slaves, were among the first immigrants. They had come to raise cotton, and commercial agriculture rapidly superseded subsistence agriculture. It was firmly established

20. Hamilton, "American Beginnings in the Old Southwest," ch. 3; William B. Hamilton, "The Southwestern Frontier, 1795–1817: An Essay in Social History," *JSH*, 10 (1944): 389–403, is a brief discussion of the rise of this special society. The quotations are from Narsworthy Hunter to W. C. C. Claiborne, Feb. 4, 1800, in *TP*, 5: 101; and Thomas Fenton to Gideon Granger, June 27, 1802, in *ibid.*, 155.

in Madison County by 1809. Crops from northeastern Mississippi Territory moved by the Tennessee River to the Mississippi and thence south
to New Orleans, giving a reliable if distant access to market. By the turn
of the century cotton cultivation in portions of Tennessee had also become a larger-scale commercial enterprise.[21]

In the decade from the purchase of Louisiana to the opening of the
War of 1812, the Louisiana backcountry expanded in ever-widening circles, to the north, west, and south of the great port of New Orleans.
Population flowed outward, along the twisting watercourses, up the rich
river valleys to the interior of the continent, and along the banks of the
wide and silent bayous. The agricultural potential of the land matched
the prospects of the port that would market its produce. Staple commodities provided the basis of this expansion and prosperity, and the French
(and, increasingly, the Americans) of Louisiana began the large-scale cultivation of cotton. The French planters had experimented with cotton
toward the end of the eighteenth century, and soon thereafter cotton culture spread along the Mississippi River as far north as Baton Rouge. Cotton also moved slowly inland, where the rich alluvial soil and ready
transportation of this region offset the dangers of flood, disease, and
isolation. The Opelousas and Attakapas regions contributed to this economic expansion, both in terms of new settlements and the rise of commercial agriculture, as grazing on the open prairies gradually gave way to
intensive cultivation of cotton. "During our stay in Louisiana we raised
Cotton Sugar Corn & Rice which all grew to perfection," wrote Martha
Philips Martin of Bayou Teche, "finding a market in New Orleans for all
we could make."[22] Rapides Parish and the valley of the Red River also
experienced rapid immigration. In 1803 John Sibley of Natchitoches estimated that the Red River already had twenty-four or twenty-five cotton gins and contributed some three thousand bales of cotton to the exports of the region. Other commodities destined for market included a
large quantity of tobacco, furs ("Calculated to be equal in Am^t to the
Cotton"), and 7,300 horses. Sibley estimated that over one hundred
sugar plantations already lined the Red River. Many more appeared in

21. Frances Cabaniss Roberts, "Background and Formative Period in the Great Bend and
Madison County" (Ph.D., Alabama, 1956), ch. 8; Gray, *History of Agriculture*, 2: 688;
Harriette Simpson Arnow, "The Pioneer Farmer and His Crops in the Cumberland
Region," *THQ*, 19 (1960): 301.
22. Martin, "Memoirs"; Gray, *History of Agriculture*, 2: 687–88.

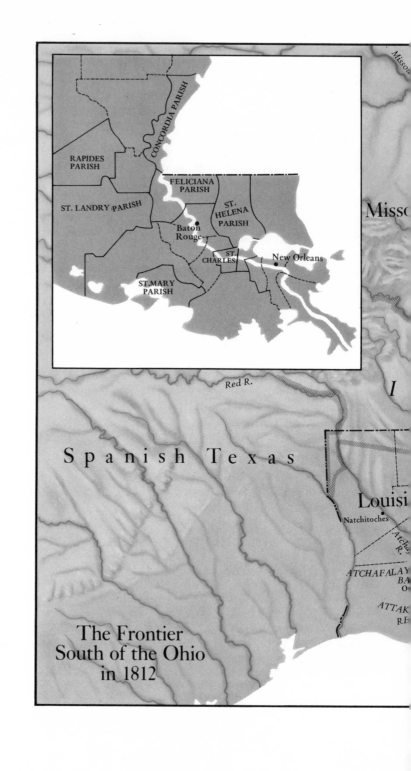

RAPIDES
PARISH

CONCORDIA PARISH

ST. LANDRY PARISH

FELICIANA
PARISH

ST.
HELENA
PARISH

Baton
Rouge

ST.
CHARLES

New Orleans

ST.MARY
PARISH

Misso

Red R.

Spanish Texas

I

Louisi

Natchitoches

Atcha
R.

ATCHAFALAY
BA
O

ATTAK
RE

Misso

The Frontier
South of the Ohio
in 1812

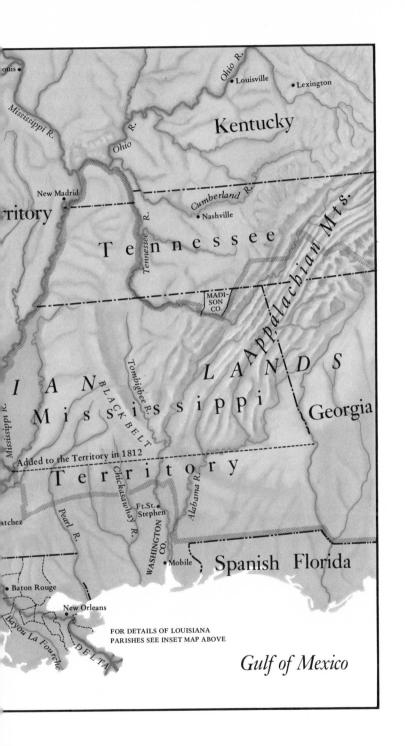

ouis •

Ohio R.

• Louisville

• Lexington

Mississippi R.

Kentucky

R.

Ohio

New Madrid
•

Cumberland R.

ritory

Tennessee R.

• Nashville

T e n n e s s e e

Appalachian Mts.

MADI-
SON
CO.

L A N D S

I A N

Tombigbee R.

BLACK BELT

M i s s i s s i p p i

Georgia

Mississippi R.

Added to the Territory in 1812

T e r r i t o r y

Chickasawhay R.

Pearl R.

Ft.St.•
Stephen

Alabama R.

atchez

WASHINGTON
CO.

• Baton Rouge

• Mobile

Spanish Florida

New Orleans

Bayou La Fourche

D E L T A

FOR DETAILS OF LOUISIANA
PARISHES SEE INSET MAP ABOVE

Gulf of Mexico

the next ten years, when large numbers of immigrants came to Rapides Parish. Agricultural commodities for export—increasingly cotton—went overland to the Red and downriver to New Orleans.[23]

The frontier of the South in the period 1795 to 1815 produced a new kind of frontiersman: the large-scale agriculturist who moved into remote areas with slave labor in search for cheaper and more fertile lands on which to grow a staple crop. John Palfrey, a planter in St. Mary Parish, was one of these. His career demonstrates the new prosperity and dependence experienced by frontiersmen in these years. In 1810 Palfrey bought nine hundred acres of land in the Attakapas country, "500 of which is Prairie & fit for immediate cultivation, the remaining 400 is woodland & has excellent timber & cypress which is very useful." He wrote optimistically about his prospects, "This prairie country is extremely well calculated for new beginnings without much capital as a great proportion is ready for the plow without any clearing." The Attakapas region had older settlements ("the Parish is tolerably well settled & the society good"), with a predominantly grazing economy. Palfrey joined a new group of entrepreneurs who intended to use the prairie lands for cotton culture. He noted the new frontier experience in these terms: "An acquaintance of mine commenced a new establishment in that neighborhood about the 1st April last with about 15 negroes & his present crop promises to give him from 50 to 60 bales cotton besides a sufficient quantity of corn & other provisions." Palfrey also planted cotton. He purchased nineteen slaves (for which he paid $7,750) and put them to preparing the ground for cotton cultivation. In his first year (1811) Palfrey's slave labor force planted fifty acres of cotton and another fifty in corn. Although "my commencement was on the 10th of April on an entire new piece of ground without buildings fence or any improvements whatsoever," he wrote, the crop was good. Palfrey continued, "I have now 30,000#s cotton picked & have every expectation of picking 20,000#s more which in my opinion is doing very well when the lateness of the season in which I began to work is taken into view." The rise of cotton and sugar as export crops made this prosperity a common experience in the period from the purchase of Louisiana to the outbreak of the War of 1812.

23. John Sibley to Claiborne, Oct. 10, 1803, in *TP*, 9: 75; G. P. Whittington, "Rapides Parish, Louisiana," *LHQ*, 16 (1933): 255, 429; William B. Knipmeyer, "Settlement Succession in Eastern French Louisiana" (Ph.D., Louisiana State, 1956), 27.

The success of staple crop agriculture rested on credit as well as cotton. Palfrey was constantly in debt. He maintained his children in private schools in the North, and the notes on his slaves always pressed him. Jefferson's embargo and the second war against England changed John Palfrey from a frontier cotton planter to a frontier subsistence farmer much like those a generation earlier in Kentucky and Tennessee. Cotton fell to a fraction of its prewar price, and commerce became uncertain. Although Palfrey remained on the plantation, he could not meet his financial obligations. In the fall of 1812 he traded "7 of my table cloths (which were useless to me here) for 2 Cows 8 yearling Calves all gentle. One large spinning wheel & an order on a person to whom I was indebted for 20 Dollars.—so that once more we have plenty of milk & I think I have made an excellent bargain." Two years later the Attakapas planter turned to the manufacture of salt, for which he found a ready market at a good price. Palfrey survived the war, despite the disappearance of money, the loss of some of his slaves on defaulted notes, and the outright sale of at least one other. His was the story of a large-scale agricultural enterprise on the Louisiana frontier, financed by credit and directed solely at the production of cotton for export. It is also a study of the vulnerability of the planter to the policies of the federal government.[24]

The many frontiers that emerged from 1795 to 1815 came to include many varieties of economic experiences. Within the South, cotton culture became a vigorous force, even in the remote settlements. The acquisition of Louisiana Territory in 1803 added names like Attakapas, Atchafalaya, and Bayou Teche to the lexicon of the American frontier. At the head of all these regions lay the port of New Orleans, a cross-section of the western world and the western country. In the style of road building in the Roman Empire, the watercourses of the West all led to New Orleans. Its presence dominated commerce almost everywhere west of the Appalachians. Supported by a vast and growing hinterland already undergoing a transition to staple crop agriculture, an increasing market

24. John Palfrey to Mark Pichard, Oct. 11, 1810; Palfrey to R. D. Shepherd, Nov. 5, 1811; Palfrey to William Simpson, Dec. 17, 1811; March 25, 1812; Palfrey to his son Henry, March 30, 1813; Jan. 2, 1814; March 22, 1815; Palfrey to Thomas Harmon, Oct. 9, 1815, William T. Palfrey Papers, LSU.

for cotton and sugar staples, and the demands created by a general European war, New Orleans threw off the trappings of a colonial frontier village and assumed the posture of a world port. The physical appearance of the village remained ramshackle and the climate unhealthy, but a large population poured into the city to take advantage of commercial opportunities. By 1810 probably something on the order of a quarter of the population of the Louisiana Purchase lived in New Orleans and its immediate environs. Along its streets walked a polyglot of the American frontier, old New Orleans, and the commercial world: here frontier boatmen from the Ohio Valley, merchants from Nashville, fur traders from the upper Mississippi and St. Louis, and planters from Natchez and the Louisiana hinterland rubbed shoulders with Creole commission merchants, Haitian refugees from revolution, and ship crews representing the commercial nations of the western world. Corporate organizations appeared to deal with the problems of banking, insurance, water, and navigation. Staples from upriver arrived between November and April, and during these months the city (for so it was becoming) was the center of commercial life in the trans-Appalachian frontier.

North of the Ohio there was no dominant port and no dominant agricultural commodity, but a wide variety of economic circumstances, conditions, and ventures. Cincinnati would not become a commercial center of the same regional significance as New Orleans until after the War of 1812. Agriculture remained a universal economic activity, the more so in the distant settlements. Yet substantial trade had developed with the bustling activities of merchants in small towns, the rise to prominence of several river towns along the Ohio, and the appearance of manufacturing enterprises in several places in the Ohio Valley by 1815. Across the broad range of a thousand miles from East to West and another similar distance from North to South, the frontier was active and vigorous. The beginnings were small, but they were real. The future seemed limited only by the machinations of the British in foreign affairs and the Indians at home. The War of 1812 would contrive to remove these obstacles by the beginning of 1815.

5

Government and Law
on the New Frontiers

Between 1795 and 1815 government and law expanded with people over the frontiers west of the Appalachians. Government came at several levels: the territory, state, county, and township, all providing yet another example of the diversity of the frontier experience. On the largest scale, government was the territory. By the turn of the century the territorial system conceived under the Northwest Ordinance was no longer in the experimental stage. Thereafter the extension of government into the frontiers was simply the extension of the Northwest Ordinance over the lands of the trans-Appalachian West. In the first decade of the nineteenth century, Congress subdivided the Northwest Territory into the territories of Indiana (1800), Michigan (1805), and Illinois (1809). To the south, it organized the Mississippi Territory (1798) to meet the needs of the prosperous Natchez District. The purchase of Louisiana in 1803 made necessary some form of government west of the Mississippi. After a series of steps to accustom an alien people to the democratic principles of the American Republic, Congress divided Louisiana into two parts, organizing the territory of Orleans (1804) on lines conforming largely to the Northwest Ordinance. The remainder it called the District of Louisiana and placed under the jurisdiction of Indiana Territory and Governor William Henry Harrison, who subdivided it into administrative units and appointed a military commandant to preside over each. Louisiana-Missouri became a separate territory in 1812. Aside from a few further subdivisions (Alabama from Mississippi, Arkansas from Missouri,

Iowa and Wisconsin from Michigan) and a new acquisition (Florida), Congress had provided territorial organization sufficient to accommodate settlement on the trans-Appalachian frontier until 1850. Government now came to the wilderness before people, and it helped to prepare for and to accelerate the arrival of settlers. Even in the most remote stretches of the frontier, government had the capacity to become an infinitely complex and complicated mechanism. The completeness of in its structure and forms contrasted with the incomplete societies it served.

Behind the proliferation of territories lay practical considerations of distance, politics, and the expanding needs of the larger numbers of settlers west of the mountains. In this period the emphasis in government passed from physical security to growth and economic development. Government at the state and territorial level performed a wide range of services for people on the frontier. Among the most important were managing relations with the Indian tribes. Negotiations with Indian tribes were always directed to the cession of more Indian land. In these twenty years treaty making was a major activity of government, and one in which it was notably successful if not exactly scrupulous about tactics or sensitive to the needs of the Native Americans. As the War of 1812 approached, relations with the Indians were more frequently of a military nature. In addition to protection, frontier people demanded the building of roads at federal expense (invariably on the grounds of national defense), and every energetic territorial governor did much to foster road construction. In one of his first official acts, Governor William Hull divided the Michigan Territory into seven road districts and appointed a supervisor for each. Mail was one of the first services sought by new settlers, for communication and commercial enterprise. The newspapers that appeared with the weekly mail delivery were the basis of the frontier press, and the failure of the mails produced universal complaints. In a sense, the growth of a territory might be measured by the expansion of its roads and mail services.[1]

The energy and strength of the territorial government reached to the edge of the frontier unevenly. As in the earlier period, the organized militia continued to give form to the largely unorganized and widely scattered settlements. The law demanded that all adult males join under

1. John Leslie Tevebaugh, "Frontier Mail: Illinois, 1800–1830" (M.A., Illinois, 1952), describes the expansion of post offices and post roads in one trans-Appalachian territory/state.

common direction. The militia was an appropriate medium, for the frontier population, with its temporary camps, resembled a large military encampment. The functions of the militia were varied: it supervised elections, conducted censes, apportioned and collected taxes. Everywhere, with the territorial governor as commander-in-chief, it served to centralize authority. The militia system reached from the governor by way of a prescribed pattern of command down to the most remote townships. In his difficult assignment to organize and, at the same time, reassure the citizens of the new Louisiana Purchase, Governor William C. C. Claiborne regarded the militia as one of the most important instruments at his disposal, especially for the maintenance of civil order. A rotating company patrolled the streets of New Orleans every night with the instructions "to contribute to the Security of New Orleans; to the safety of the property of the Inhabitants; and to aid the civil authority in the preservation of good order."[2] Throughout the trans-Appalachian frontier the militia continued to serve important social and political functions as well. Muster days, the company monthly, and the battalion, held on a quarterly basis to coincide with the county court, became focal points of social and economic life. High rank in the militia was an avenue to and a sign of political preferment. Although European travellers might scoff, military ranks among officers became permanent titles to be worn with pride throughout a long civil life.

The concept of government varied from place to place and time to time, but whether as a force to order society, or to provide services, or both, leaders in Washington, entrepreneurs in the new territories, and most of the citizens on the frontier wanted organized government by the beginning of the nineteenth century. People who ventured out into the western country worried about the unstructured nature of this new world. Threats of disorder came in many forms and from many directions. The potentially turbulent nature of the population and the extreme isolation of some settlements seemed to invite rule by force. Observers described the Tombigbee frontier as potentially violent; the villages in the Illinois country were uneasy about their distances from the authority of government. Rough transient elements in the frontier population included the

2. Order to the Commanding Officer of the Militia Guard, Jan. 30, 1806, in *TP*, 9: 596–97.

fur traders and lead miners of Missouri and St. Louis and the riverboat-men everywhere from Shawneetown (Illinois) to Natchez. The focus of this apprehension was violence—against persons and property. Of the Natchez District in 1800, one resident wrote, "Murder & Manslaughter are now the common topicks of the day." In addition there were periodic duels over questions of honor, especially in the longer settled areas of Kentucky, Mississippi, and Louisiana. Dueling was not indigenous to the frontier but came from the most aristocratic societies to the east of the mountains, especially those associated with the seaboard South. That these affairs frequently involved people of wealth and established social connection suggests a kind of class distinction about this kind of vio-lence, namely that brawling and destruction of property belonged to the lower classes, conflict over honor was the province of the upper elements of society.[3]

Finally, frontier violence took the form of brutality of master toward slave, and, with it, the growing concern in many places over the possibil-ity of slave insurrection. For a frontier society was not synonymous with a free society. From the beginning of the first trans-Appalachian settle-ments in 1775, law and custom recognized the institution of slavery. It had greatly expanded in numbers and area by the turn of the century, especially in those places associated with production of staple agricul-tural products. The presence of large and growing numbers of slaves produced a variety of institutions to protect the white population. These included a set of rigorous laws to control the black population, slave and free, the organization of the militia and its use for patrols, and the brutal suppression of any activity that could be construed as a slave insurrec-tion.

Nowhere was a concern over possible slave insurrections greater than in the wealthy and cultured Natchez District, which had entered into a period of prosperity founded on the cultivation of a staple crop with slave labor. The number of blacks increased accordingly. By 1800 the population of the district was half black; thereafter, blacks grew in numbers more rapidly than whites. The uneasiness in Natchez was the start of a growing concern over the presence of a slave population on the frontier that troubled settlers for the next half century. People wor-

3. H. Denison to Dr. Hillsman, Oct. 30, 1800, Miscellaneous Collections, TSLA. On un-settled conditions in the Mississippi Territory, see Robert V. Haynes, "Law Enforce-ment in Frontier Mississippi," *JMH*, 22 (1960): 27–42.

ried that the confused period which attended the rise of new institutions and the subduing of a wilderness or hinterland (in the case of Natchez) would mean a loosening of legal and social shackles that bound the black family as firmly as metal ones.

The most significant government for the largest number of people on the trans-Appalachian frontier was at the county level. With the expansion of the territorial system across the land went the establishment of new counties. The county court of general quarter sessions or the county board of commissioners (renamed and elective in Ohio under the state constitution) dominated local affairs. The county courts spent much of their time and energy providing such institutions and services for their citizens as jails, courthouses, the care of paupers, and the registration of stock markings. County courts also exercised much control over the local economy, granting licenses and special monopoly privileges and setting rates for a wide variety of economic activities from taverns to ferries and mills. In addition to the commissioners, the county bureaucracy generally included a treasurer, auditor, recorder, coroner, sheriff, and clerk of court. It cost money to support such a bureaucracy (for these positions could not all be supported by fees) and to make such improvements as were needed. To finance its public buildings, the county had the power to levy a tax, and as the needs for services and expenses grew, so did the time spent in apportioning and collecting revenue. This process introduced a new echelon of civil functionaries: appraisers, collectors, and listers. The tax collector was, in the tradition of the American Revolution, an unpopular figure, and few seem to have sought the position. The first county court of Knox County (Indiana) nominated eighteen men over four years to the post of tax collector before collecting any revenue from county levies.[4]

An examination of the sources of county income and items of expenditure in three different counties from three separate territories—Ohio, Indiana, and Illinois—in the Old Northwest for about the same period illustrates differences and similarities in county government on the frontier. Butler County (Ohio) lay in the southwest corner of the new

4. George Purcell, "Collecting Taxes in Indiana Territory, 1797–1802," *IMH*, 40 (1944): 363.

state, just north of Hamilton County and Cincinnati. In 1804 the income and expenditures of the county looked like this:

Credit		Debit	
property taxes	$ 770.13	listers of townships	$ 102.75
ferry tax	1.00	Jas. Dunn & John Green,	36.34
licensing of taverns	50.00	assoc judges	
-do-retailers	60.00	Jas. Dunn, return of lands in 1803	6.25
dividend of state tax	186.00	sheriff and clerk of common pleas	40.00
1803 tax not collected	68.13	atty prosecuting pleas of state	80.00
		associate judges fee	100.00
		grand jury fees	100.00
		judge of election fees	30.00
		support of paupers	75.00
		wolf and panther scalps	50.00
		listers, for completing lists of land	25.00
		Board of Comm, fees, clerk,	100.00
		stationary	
		collectors and county treas	70.00
		commissions	
		outstanding orders, unsatisfied	100.00
		delinquencies & contingencies	219.92
	$1,135.26		$1,135.26

The board of commissioners spent much of its time providing for its income, discussing valuations, and collecting the taxes. The state supplied some assistance from tax funds, in this case $186. The construction, repair, and maintenance of public buildings was a major expense obligation. Although not provided for in the annual budget for 1804, every county had to erect a courthouse and jail. This obligation might be met through an appeal to the citizens, especially those with a vested interest in the location of the county seat. That the citizens of a village should be prepared to underwrite the construction of public buildings was an underlying assumption of frontier government. If the citizens were unwilling to pay the costs, the commissioners would move the seat of government elsewhere. In this case a number of Butler County citizens pledged "money, whiskey, or grain" toward the erection of the necessary public buildings in the village of Hamilton, the county seat; others contributed "stones, lime, brick, timber, mechanical work, labor, or hauling, or any kind of country produce which can or may be exchanged for cash." [5]

5. *A History and Biographical Cyclopaedia of Butler County, Ohio* (Cincinnati, 1882), 44. A comparison with the budget for Jefferson County (Steubenville the county seat) from June 12, 1805, to June 4, 1806, shows the same categories of expense. The Jefferson

The income and expenditures of counties farther to the west provide a view of a different frontier. In 1790 Winthrop Sargent organized Knox County, the first county in what was later to become the Indiana Territory. It stretched from Canada to the Ohio, from the Great Miami on the east to St. Clair County and the Illinois River on the west. The court of common pleas met in session late the same year, and it gradually assumed administrative direction of the county. The taxes levied in March 1807, while the county was a part of the Indiana Territory, produced these figures:

Credit

houses, lots, land, buildings	$ 163.50
108 slaves @ $1	108.00
1395 horses @ 50¢	697.50
2136 neat cattle @ 10¢	213.60
179 single men @ $1	179.00
18 stud horses	43.00
ferries assessed	24.00
	$1,428.60

The total assessment in Knox and Butler counties was about the same; the sources of income were quite different. In a region where people and animals, however scarce, were more common than economic improvements, the county levied taxes accordingly. Almost half the tax income came from a levy on horses. Another sizable item was the tax on slaves, who presumably antedated the provisions of the Northwest Ordinance forbidding slavery or involuntary servitude. Although organized in 1790, not until 1808 did the county contract for a public building, and the courthouse was not completed and occupied until July 1813.[6]

Still farther to the west, the government of Madison County (Illinois) provided few services for a scattered population. The county, organized

County budget totalled $2,784.20. See Steubenville *Western Herald*, Aug. 29, 1807. The expenditures for Franklin County (Scioto River Valley, with the county seat at Chillicothe) are listed on an annual basis from 1804 to 1811, in the Worthington *Western Intelligencer*, Sept. 18, 1811. The Franklin County budget included annual items for roads, the courthouse (1805 and thereafter), and the "gaol" (1806 and thereafter). Every historian who writes on the trans-Appalachian frontier—or any frontier for that matter—has to come to terms with county histories. Almost every county mentioned in this study has a county history—some have more than one—and they form a useful source of information, not so much for their description or analysis as in their occasional printing of documentary materials from the courthouse records.

6. *History of Knox and Daviess County, Indiana* (Chicago, 1886), 159, 176–77.

in 1812, lay across the Mississippi River from St. Louis. The earliest official indication of government was a court of common pleas, meeting for
the first time in April 1813. The proceedings of the court were filled
with concern over roads and licensing taverns and ferries and setting
prices for their services. In 1814 William Ottwell built a jail in Edwardsville. The judges of the court viewed the structure, pronounced it satisfactory, and paid Ottwell $194 for his work. The territory laid a tax on
lands, dividing them into three classes (river bottomlands, other located
lands, and unlocated lands). The court levied county taxes along much
the same lines as those found in Knox County: single men, $1.00; each
slave, $1.00; horses, mule, or ass at 50 each; stud horses at the season's
rate; ferries from $1.00 to $3.00. The tax lists have not survived, but the
total collections were $426.84½. The small population—there were 161
men subject to road labor in the county—and the few services provided
for the county's citizens suggest scattered settlements and a primitive
economic development. The exact figures are:

Credit		*Debit*	
Thos Kirkpatrick, tavern lic.	$ 6.50	Isom Gillham, services, $75.00; attending election of 1812, two criminal cases, &c., &c.	$ 96.22½
Abraham Prickett, merchant lic.	15.00		
Sam'l G. Mooss [probably Morse], -do-	15.00	Josias Randle, clerk & sundries	115.53¾
		John G. Lofton, judge of probate 21 days	42.00
Squire Davidson, three fines	2.50		
Court, fine of Jas Green	1.00	Geo Caldwell, judge, listing property for taxation	32.00
Tax-levy of 1813	426.84½		
		Jacob Whiteside, 5 days Judge of Common Pleas	10.00
		Wm Rabb, 4 days, -do-	8.00
	$466.84½		$303.76¼
		surplus	$163.08¼

We would like to know something more specific about the three fines
levied by Squire Davidson, presumably a justice of the peace. What
were they for? Judging by the sum of $2.50, the usual frontier offences
were involved: disorderly conduct, contempt of court, failure to turn out
for work on the public roads, livestock not properly fenced or marked.
Probably they were not too serious.[7]

---

7. *History of Madison County, Illinois* (Edwardsville, 1882), 119–23.

If government provided a framework of regulations for orderly conduct, the authority of law and the courts forced public acceptance of these rules. The extension of law to the trans-Appalachian frontier from 1795 to 1815 may be examined in two parts: the creation and publication of a code of law by the first territorial officers and the establishment of the territorial or state court, and the organization and operation of the county court system, the basic unit of justice on the frontier. The activities of Winthrop Sargent, appointed governor of the Mississippi Territory following his service as secretary of the Northwest Territory, provide an excellent example of the work of a territorial governor in framing a code of law. Sargent's empire stretched from the prosperous, sophisticated world of Natchez across three hundred miles of wilderness to the wretched settlements on the Tombigbee. For this region Sargent sought to fashion an effective and consistent set of laws. He first adopted the English common law for the Mississippi Territory. Sir William Blackstone and Lord Mansfield became the authorities cited by lawyers before the bar. The territorial judges drew their inspiration—insofar as their decisions could be called inspirational—from the same sources. Local circumstances forced the modification and simplification of some English forms, but the courts accepted the general principles of the applicability of the common law, along with the English principle of equity. Thus, Governor Sargent by fiat implanted the institutions of the Anglo-American legal tradition. The Natchez gentry vigorously supported an effective legal system, for it gave stability and promoted commerce in an increasingly commercial society.[8]

The law of the territory was specific and detailed. Winthrop Sargent formed it in consultation with his territorial judges, Peter Bryan Bruin and Daniel Tilden. The third judge, Thomas Rodney, did not arrive

8. Thomas Rodney, *Anglo-American Law on the Frontier: Thomas Rodney & His Territorial Cases*, ed. William Baskerville Hamilton (Durham, 1953), 117–32. Much of what we know about early law in the Mississippi Territory is derived from the decisions and correspondence of Thomas Rodney, one of the first territorial judges. Rodney was a soldier in the Revolutionary War and a minor Delaware politician with strong Jeffersonian principles. Jefferson appointed him to the Mississippi court in 1803. Rodney's decisions have been edited by Hamilton, whose perceptive introduction is especially useful to students of the American frontier. A general discussion, centered on Rodney, is Clarence E. Carter, "The Transit of Law to the Frontier: A Review Article," *JMH*, 16 (1954): 183–92.

until 1803. Neither Bruin nor Tilden had legal training and were clearly subordinate to Sargent in the drawing up of the first legal code. Published in the early months of 1799, the forty-six sections of Sargent's Code (as it came to be called) covered nearly every aspect of personal conduct and commercial affairs in the territory. One of its most important provisions dealt with local courts. The code established the general quarter sessions of the peace, to meet quarterly for three days of sessions. These courts dealt with minor misdemeanors—minimal punishment offenses—committed in the counties. A justice of the peace sitting as judge presided over the court, with great powers to assist him in keeping the peace, including the authority to imprison for an indefinite period. A parallel court, the court of common pleas, heard cases concerned with civil, personal, or real causes. The governor designated "a competent number" of citizens as justices of the court of common pleas, three of whom constituted a court. The code established a probate court to handle wills and testaments, as well as the poor, minors, and lunatics. Cases from the courts of common pleas and the general quarter sessions could be appealed to the territorial supreme court, which met yearly in each county. The supreme court also tried cases of a more serious nature, such as official misconduct and felonies. In addition Sargent's Code dealt in detail with crimes and punishments. Perjury, treason, and arson were among the most significant crimes, along with murder, mutilation, robbery, and burglary. Punishments were severe. The code provided for whipping posts and pillories in each county, as well as a jail. The governor also had great authority over aliens, who had to post bonds as a guarantee of good behavior and to report to the governor on a regular basis. They could be deported on almost any charge. Sargent's Code underwent substantial modifications after 1803, but the basic common law foundation remained undisturbed.[9]

Under Sargent's Code and other legal codes on the trans-Appalachian frontier, the privileges and responsibilities of the common law applied solely to the white population. Yet some black Mississippians in bondage took advantage of the code and its court system to seek their freedom in the courts. Thomas Rodney recorded several such suits and his reactions

9. John Remley Wunder, "The Mississippi Territory's First Experience with American Legal Institutions: Sargent's Code, Its Adoption and Abolition, 1798–1803" (M.A., Iowa, 1970), 28–34; William N. Ethridge, "An Introduction to Sargent's Code of the Mississippi Territory (1799–1800)," *AJLH*, 11 (1967): 148–51.

to them. Abraham Jones, or Samson, sued for his freedom for fifteen years, always without success. Even more striking was the case of Sue, a black woman of Indian ancestry, who sought freedom through the courts under a Virginia statute that freed Indians. She brought suit in Virginia, where the court found in her favor. By the time the judgment was handed down, however, her master had already taken her (and her family) from Virginia to South Carolina (1788), thence to Georgia (1800), and finally to Mississippi Territory. Here Sue once more commenced her suit, on behalf of herself and her children. She failed. The judges recognized the complexities of the case, but in the final analysis, they judged property rights more powerful than human rights. Thomas Rodney's court condemned her and her children to another two generations of slavery. That Sue persevered so far and that the court permitted her to do so, and with representation by some of Mississippi Territory's established white lawyers, suggest that in this period, at least, black men and women had access to the courts for redress.[10]

Three hundred miles to the east of the center of government and commerce at Natchez lay the Tombigbee settlements, an administrative part of the Mississippi Territory. According to reports, eastern Mississippi consisted of a restless, transient population that included fugitives from justice. Governor Winthrop Sargent recognized the existence of these far-off settlements with the creation of Washington County in 1800. Distances made it impossible for a court structure centered in Natchez to function effectively in Washington County, so Sargent laid off a separate judicial district. The new judge of the Washington judicial district, Harry Toulmin, an English immigrant, had been, in turn, a Unitarian minister, educator, and public official in Kentucky. More to the point, he emerges from the legal records as a man of character and integrity. Although his judicial circuit was smaller in size, his duties were far more difficult than those of his colleagues in the western part of the territory. During the early years of his magistracy, Toulmin found himself opposed by a variety of factions, and his experience suggests that the laws of the territory could not be enforced without the support of its citizens. Law in the Natchez region functioned effectively because it was a reflection of the values of the dominant commercial element and so had the approbation of powerful men. Toulmin had values different from those

10. This account follows Rodney, *Anglo-American Law on the Frontier,* 145–49.

prevalent in the region he served. As befitted the nature of his duties and new situation, he interpreted the law in a different fashion and with different ground rules. He did much to codify the law and function of the courts. His digest of the territorial laws, published in 1807 and incorporating most of the changes made in Sargent's Code, helped to establish a uniform law throughout the region. He followed this with his *Magistrate's Assistant*, a practical guide for justices of the peace in the Mississippi Territory. The annexation of West Florida in 1810 complicated his judicial world; so did Mobile and newly created counties shortly thereafter. But Toulmin remained a leader in the struggle to establish legal institutions in the eastern part of the Mississippi Territory, where he used his authority to foster respect for the law and the courts.[11]

The most important of the local courts was the justice of the peace court. It was certainly the most widely known to individual frontiersmen. The office had been an important one in seventeenth-century England and was transported to the colonies. Its significance increased with the dispersal of the population, as people moved farther from the settled areas and access to higher courts. In the colonies justices were often men of wealth and influence, but west of the Appalachians the office gradually became elective (without property requirements) and a fee system transformed the honorary nature of the office. The duties of the justice of the peace west of the mountains pertained primarily to civil cases involving small sums. Only rarely did the justice venture into areas of peace enforcement or criminal cases. The justice court was designed to provide convenient and cheap justice without long trials and recourse to lawyers. The courts were informal; the justices expedited the cases wherever possible. In addition to serving as arbiter in cases for small sums specified by law (say twenty dollars), justices of the peace checked stray livestock and performed marriages. In their availability, their informal nature, and their significance for frontier people, they resembled the courts of the first trans-Appalachian frontier of the previous generation.[12]

11. Robert V. Haynes, "Early Washington County, Alabama," *AR*, 18 (1965): 190–200. On Toulmin's different interpretation of the law, see William B. Hamilton, "The Transmission of English Law to the Frontier of America," *SAQ*, 67 (1968): 243–54. Hamilton's article is an excellent account of the spread of the commow law across the trans-Appalachian frontier. Note also his discussion of other kinds of English law, pp. 246–47.

12. James Griffith Harris, "The Justice of the Peace in Missouri, 1800–1845" (M.A., Missouri, 1948), esp. 54–89, is an admirable study of the justice courts generally and Mis-

In spite of the formal titles, the courts were often informal. At the local level, where justice courts were the basic instruments of law, the judge (or justice) was generally a man without formal legal training, but, it was hoped, an individual of much common sense and strong integrity. A judge had to be prepared to hold court at any time, under all sorts of physical conditions, and to protect himself from the unexpected. At the first session of the Dearborn County (Indiana) Court a recalcitrant witness, tired of being admonished to speak to the subject, seized a board and swung at the judge's head. The judge warded off the blow with his arm, which was broken in the process. All present, especially the judge, agreed that the act was in contempt of court. The judge ordered the witness jailed, but there was no jail, so the guilty party was bound hand and foot and "laid along the ground and a section of worm fence was built up over him, the lower rail just touching his neck." Here he was left for several hours to ponder his intemperate action. Contempt of court also took milder forms. An 1808 session of the Miami County (Ohio) Court was held in a room over a tavern. When the noise from the lower floor became too loud, the judge summoned two boisterous men and fined them for contempt. One of the victims addressed the court with some bitterness: "Judge Dunlevy, I knew you when you were so poor you had to lie in bed until your wife washed your breeches."[13]

The court of common pleas dealt with civil cases involving citizens of the same county. Three justices sat as a court of common pleas, although in some cases one was sufficient to hold the court. It was generally assumed that they would come from different sections of the county and that at least one of the three would be a lawyer. Quarter session courts, of equal rank and presided over by the same men, had jurisdiction over petty crimes and misdemeanors, such as assault and drunkenness. Sometimes the justices of the court also served as county commissioners and so conducted the administrative as well as judicial business of the county; where this custom did not prevail, the justices chose the commissioners. Justices also named fence viewers and recommended those who needed licenses, such as tavern keepers. In short, the justices of the counties combined the functions of government and the law, and the court structure tended to focus authority in the hands of a few.

---

souri in particular. Harris notes that the importance of the justice courts declined in the 1830's with rising property values and the increasing influence of lawyers.

13. *History of Dearborn, Ohio and Switzerland Counties, Indiana* (Chicago, 1885), 114; *Miami County, Ohio* (n.p., 1880), 279.

Within the basic framework of the territorial system were broad differences in law and governmental structure. The most striking variations were in the Louisiana Purchase. The problem was not how to familiarize a population with government—for the people of Louisiana had much experience with government under the French and Spanish—but rather how to impose the American system of government in such a way that it would rest comfortably on an alien people and, at the same time, presumably point toward the democratic forms described in the Northwest Ordinance. The French and Spanish officials had governed a society, as one American wrote in 1803, "accustomed to arbitrary prompt decisions."[14] The governor of Spanish Louisiana (the direct representative of the king), the intendant (in charge of the treasury), and the cabildo (a town council for New Orleans that advised on public good and served as a court of appeals) guided the affairs of the entire colony. Laws and ordinances in Spanish Louisiana covered a wide range, regulating the construction of bridges and roads (the road network in the Louisiana Territory was better than in most American territories) and levees to control high water; inspecting produce offered for sale and fixing prices; and providing swift trial for those charged and brutal punishment for convicted offenders. Throughout the colony, the *Code Noir* gave form and permanence to the institution of Negro slavery.

Along with this highly centralized government went a relaxed and easy-going way of life that amazed and even outraged the Americans. Governor Claiborne thought the people of Louisiana wealthy and generally honest but "uninformed, indolent, luxurious—in a word, illy fitted to be useful citizens of the Republic."[15] Claiborne's comment points to the innumerable differences between the Creoles and the Americans. The *ancienne population* did not rejoice in the change of government and remained reluctant to accept the presence of the Americans. This reluctance took forms varying from indifference to the ceremonies marking the transfer of ownership to downright hostility at the examination of land titles in the light of Anglo-American legal principles. The separate settlements of Creoles and Americans in the countryside and also in the cities of St. Louis and New Orleans intensified the divisions along ethnic lines. Conflicts appeared over basic cultural, political, and legal institutions. Not the least of these was the question of the legal code.[16]

14. Benjamin Morgan to Chandler Price, Aug. 7, 1803, in *TP*, 9: 7.
15. William C. C. Claiborne to Thomas Jefferson, Jan. 16, 1804, in *TP*, 9: 161.
16. Differences in temperament, style, and institutions run far deeper than can be con-

The settlements on the west side of the Mississippi River had legal codes based on the civil law of Spain and France. When the United States purchased Louisiana, it found an established legal system, with both civil and ecclesiastical courts. The basis was civil law, a legal system that functioned with speed and rested on the judgment of individual officials. Trial by jury was unknown; appeal was rare; litigation was minimal; and lawyers, accordingly, few in number. The transition to American legal institutions proved difficult in the face of a long-standing system, a large indigenous population, and a reluctance to abandon a European heritage in favor of the encroaching American civilization. American officials agreed that the legal system had to be changed gradually. "In the course of my efforts to introduce the American System of Jurisprudence into the ceded Territory, I experienced many difficulties, and excited some dissatisfaction among the People," wrote Governor Claiborne. In the same letter he identified many of the principal points of difference: "I fear the trial by Jury, the introduction of oral testimony, the Admission of Attorneys &c will illy comport with the former habits of the People, and that the Court, (as I have been) will be accused by the designing few, of making injurious innovations on the Spanish Law." Louisiana gradually became a part of the American territorial system, but the civil law foundations of Spain and France remained. The Legal Code of 1805 affirmed the principles of civil law as the dominant legal system within the territory of Orleans.[17]

Local government from the Old Northwest to the Mississippi Territory was much alike, especially in the county and township structure and the duties apportioned to various units of government. In Louisiana (Orleans Territory), however, local government was significantly different, for the institutions at the local level were the parish government and the police jury. Parish was another name for county. The French government had subdivided colonial Louisiana into ecclesiastical districts, a tribute to the importance of the Catholic Church and the parish priest—the church had its own instruments of authority, including

---

veyed in this brief description. Students of institutions in Louisiana should consult George Dargo, *Jefferson's Louisiana: Politics and the Clash of Legal Traditions* (Cambridge, 1975), 9–11, 23–25; and Harvey Wish, "The French of Old Missouri (1804–1821): A Study in Assimilation," *M-A*, 23 (1941): 167–89.

17. Claiborne to James Madison, Oct. 29, 1804, in *TP*, 9: 317. On the conflict between common and civil law, see Dargo, *Jefferson's Louisiana*, chs. 5 and 6; and Elizabeth Gaspar Brown, "Legal Systems in Conflict: Orleans Territory, 1804–1812," *AJLH*, 1 (1967): 35–75.

courts—in the life of the colony. The territory's Legislative Council originally divided Orleans Territory into twelve counties in 1805, but the
unit of government proved too large to meet the needs of local popula-
tions, and the parish remained the basic unit of administration. In 1807
the council supplemented the county by the division of the territory into
nineteen parishes. The parish had the usual county officers: sheriff,
coroner, clerk, and justices of the peace, all under the control of the
police jury. Another act of the same year, "relative to roads, levees, and
the police of cattle," contained the early roots of the police jury system.
The name referred to the committee of twelve citizens who dealt with
administrative and judicial problems of the parish. The judge and the
police jury served as an administrative grand jury, identifying problems
and setting up the administrative machinery to deal with them. The
police jury had some judicial functions, but its primary concern lay in its
administrative capacity. Law, practice, and custom gradually conferred
great powers on judge and jury.[18]

The case of St. Helena Parish illustrates the variety of administrative
functions performed by the police jury. The police jury of the parish
came into existence in 1813 under the direction of the judge of the
parish, Shepherd Brown. As its first official act, the police jury adopted
a set of regulations for the conduct of business ("no member shall be permitted to speak in the settings of the Jury without rising from his seat").
The jury then appointed administrative officers, a clerk ($2.00 per day
and $.12½ per hundred words transcribed), three appraisers, and a con-
stable for each justice of the peace district. In the subsequent meetings
several committees presented reports on the principal problems of the
parish: licensing, fees, and prices; strays and wild cattle; the condition of
roads and bridges. Under a provision in the license law, the jury regulated the charges of tavern keepers. It assessed billiard tables at the rate
of $20 annually. In the important matter of mills, "All millers attending
water mills in this Parish shall keep good order in their respective mills
by giving every man his proper turn, keeping lawful measures and
keep'g his mill in good order." The jury set compensation for millers at

18. Robert Dabney Calhoun, "Origin and Early Development of County-Parish Government in Louisiana, 1805–1845," *LHQ*, 18 (1935): 61–65, 93, 118–20, 153–57. Initially,
the parish judge, the dominant figure in local government, chose the police jurors. An
act of the state of Louisiana, passed in 1813, divided parishes into wards, and voters
chose representatives from each to serve as the police jury.

no more than one-eighth the flour ground. A committee of the police jury also fixed the annual tax structure: free white males over twenty-one assessed $1.00; masters to pay $.25 for each slave over ten years of age; horses or mules three years and older, $.12½ each; and stud horses should be taxed "the amount he stands for by the season." The jury needed fourteen articles to describe "the manner of proceedings with strays and wild cattle and also to regulate the structure and heighth of fences." The construction and upkeep of roads, bridges, and causeways required even more detail. Finally questions about ferries (licensing, fees, and continuity of service) and fines for delinquents had to be resolved, and administrative machinery to supervise all this business had to be set up. After four days of continuous sessions, the jurors adjourned with the solemn declaration that their actions were now the laws of St. Helena Parish.[19]

In Concordia Parish, government and the court system began with the appointment of James Williams as parish judge. With the advice of "the majority of the Magistrates," Williams directed that the court meet in the residence of William Nicholls "until permanently established according to law." The court first convened in 1805. In its first term Judge Williams licensed attorneys and appointed Charles Morgan "Cryer for the Court and Constable." The court also ordered the clerk to take "into his custody the records and papers relative thereto from the Civil Commandant." Over the next six terms, in two years, the court administered such necessary matters as licenses, roads, ferries, and provisions for orphans. Beginning in 1807 slave patrols made their rounds twice a week. In addition to its administrative duties, the court occupied its time in civil suits. There was a good deal of litigation, and the court established procedures to be followed. Most of the suits concerned property, and in the tradition of frontier courts to the north and east, justice was slow. The court continued numerous cases in the absence of one or both of the parties to the suits, or their lawyers, or the witnesses. A number of defendants left the parish permanently. Many judgments

19. Walter Pritchard, ed., "Minutes of the Police Jury of St. Helena Parish, August 16–19, 1813," *LHQ*, 23 (1940): 405–27. Other examples of the operation of the police jury are in St. Charles Parish, Police Jury Minutes, 1811–17; and St. Landry Parish, Police Jury Minutes, 1811–19, LSU. Parishes and counties existed side by side until 1845 when counties went out of existence and parishes emerged as the only unit of Louisiana local government.

came by default, and probably with little or no material advantage to the victor, for there was no one to collect from. Most of these cases dealt with sums of less than two hundred dollars. Because of the nature of the economy of the day—with little circulating medium, much credit, and notes of indebtedness that passed from hand to hand—it was difficult to establish who owed what, much less who owed what to whom. But this did not prevent citizens from pursuing legal redress, and for small sums.[20]

This second generation—those who shared the frontier experience from 1795 to 1815—was an active one. It created several frontiers in as many places. It helped make and then put into operation several codes of law. It assisted in the rise of several societies. And it did all these things and more despite the need to absorb new frontiers west of the Mississippi acquired in the Louisiana Purchase of 1803 and the growing uneasiness about a war that finally broke out in 1812. Contrasts and contradictions characterized this second generation on the trans-Appalachian frontier: the sophisticated and worldly vied with the rustic and primitive; the large-scale wealth of Natchez was set against the violent, materialistic lawlessness of the Tombigbee settlements; the ramshackle, dingy, unkempt appearance of New Orleans belied its energy and vigorous growth; the orderly fields and thriving villages along the Ohio did not suggest that only a few miles inland were the isolated clearings of subsistence farmers; a vast body of law and an elaborate court system could not prevent the delayed and uneven justice that so often characterized the frontier, justice that could not always protect the property all asked it to or prevent the violence all deplored but few would take action against.

For the most part, the essential characteristic that united the societies that emerged in this twenty years was newness, newness not in the sense of unique but of unfinished. There was a rawness about these societies that marked them as being in the process of change. Collectively, this

---

20. See, for example, the case of *Wray* v. *Donaughoo*, April Term, 1806, "Minutes of the County Court of Concordia, 1805–1807," Concordia Parish Collections, 1794–1896, folder 1, LSU. On the affairs of the parish court in general, also note Robert Dabney Calhoun, "A History of Concordia Parish, Louisiana," *LHQ*, 15 (1932): 225–29, 440–41, 428–32.

second generation of pioneers knew how to do much. From the previous generations and with generous assistance from the Native Americans, they knew a great deal about agriculture, and if they knew little as yet about how to preserve the land, they knew much about the land itself and how to make it respond to their desires for larger crops. From their own experiences and the first generation of trans-Appalachian frontiersmen—some of whom had gone to these newer frontiers—they knew about institution building. At bottom, however, this world remained raw and unformed. It was a child of great physical and economic potential whose ambitions reached beyond its physical capacity to control its movements or its words. The world around was still too big, distances too vast, and obstacles too great. The wilderness had not mastered the frontiersman, but it kept him from creating finished societies—at least immediately. What emerged was a society with extensive laws and great economic promise, but unable as yet to develop or manage such gifts. The full realization of this potential would come with the next generation.

6

Many Societies
from Similar Institutions

Between 1795 and 1815 several societies emerged on the trans-Appalachian frontier, as individuals and groups living west of the mountains found a common past, shared values, similar goals, in short, a sense of identity, one with another. These societies might be grouped into three broad divisions. The first was characterized by a prosperous commercial economy and a degree of leisure and introspection. Some of these societies were in urban centers, others in long-settled agricultural communities. A second group included those societies joined by special characteristics of their members, specifically cultural traits, sometimes immigrant communities. The most easily identifiable were transplanted New England communities in the Old Northwest and the several small French villages in the upper Mississippi Valley. Beyond these homogeneous groupings was a universal frontier society, of the kind described by so many visitors to the western country. It was generally rural, isolated, and largely self-sufficient.

In this second generation on the trans-Appalachian frontier, the number of urban centers increased, and urbanization (in its many forms, large and small) became an important force in the life west of the mountains. Peoples with diverse skills came together in a single place to sell and trade their goods and services with an agriculatural hinterland. The urban society transcended geography, for it prospered in the Ohio River and lower Mississippi River valleys alike, and indeed everywhere in the West. At the same time, urban centers varied enormously—in size, character, and degree of maturity. Some towns like Louisville and Lexington belonged to the first generation of settlement and had already achieved permanence and prosperity on the trans-Appalachian frontiers. Others, such as Cincinnati and Natchez, began about 1795 a period of growth built on the commodity trade that would make them significant commercial centers. The Louisiana Purchase of 1803 introduced new and contrasting urban centers like New Orleans and St. Louis. By 1815 several towns on the trans-Appalachian frontier had achieved a level of economic development that gave them common attitudes and values. A closer look at three of these will show some of their similarities as well as their differences.

In the years immediately after 1795 the Natchez District moved from prosperity to affluence, and a high level of society emerged based on cotton culture and Negro slavery. Not all those who lived and worked in the Natchez District felt this shared sense of identity or common character. The increasingly large number of black slaves in Natchez lay outside this emerging society, as did the transient boatmen and collective undesirables found "under the hill." But a number of wealthy and articulate leaders gave voice to a common sense of purpose and shared values in the Natchez District. By the turn of the century, wealth had been translated into material possessions, and Natchez imported quantities of European luxury goods. The intense interest in property that characterized the district was occasionally transcended, and its leaders in 1803 founded the Mississippi Society for the Acquirement and Dissemination of Useful Knowledge. These men intended to go beyond the boundaries of the district, the Mississippi Territory, and even the nation to correspond with similar European societies. The same year a group of energetic and ambitious citizens established Jefferson College. Natchez had by this time a wealthy and materialistic society, with intellectual and economic interests that spanned the Atlantic, social activities and entertainment that met the needs of all ages, and an outlook on institutions that was strictly Anglo-American; all these accomplishments were based on the cultivation of cotton by slave labor.[1]

1. Facets of Natchez society are analyzed in William Baskerville Hamilton, "American Beginnings in the Old Southwest: The Mississippi Phase" (Ph.D., Duke, 1937), ch. 4; Hamilton, "The Southwestern Frontier, 1795–1817: An Essay in Social History," *JSH*,

New Orleans had the same air of economic prosperity, but the two societies of New Orleans and Natchez also offered striking contrasts: the latter was predominantly agriculatural, the former dependent upon trade; the latter strongly exhibited rural values, while the former was already in the process of acquiring urban values; the latter expressed an interest in several forms of social, educational, and intellectual life; economic gain more narrowly dominated the former. Finally, Natchez was a relatively homogeneous society built around staple crop agriculture; New Orleans was a potpourri of peoples on the trans-Appalachian frontier, brought together in the search for wealth through commerce.

There was no mistaking the rise of New Orleans to a position of commercial pre-eminence. Founded in 1718 as an anchor of the great French empire in the New World, New Orleans grew up with the fur trade. The cultivation of the staples of the South combined with the settlement of the backcountry brought growth and prosperity to the port city. An urban society matured in like proportion, more interested in commercial than intellectual pursuits. This was the city that the Americans took possession of in 1803, and the large influx of Americans diluted the heretofore French character of the city and, in a sense, produced two urban societies. The two national cultures did not mix easily, and, where brought together, cultural, economic, and sometimes physical conflict resulted. James Sterrett wrote in 1804 of "the great enmity existing between the Creoles & the English & Americans several fights & Challenges—there are some of both sides in jail." A clever woman identified the contrasts in character between the French and the Americans for Governor William C. C. Claiborne at an evening soiree. In response to the governor's charge that she did not favor the American as much as the French character, she replied

> that in many respects, the *former* was more amiable, than the *latter* Character; the French love with more Ardour; but the Americans with more constancy; the French make affectionate Husbands; but the

---

10 (1944): 389–403; Hamilton and William D. McCain, eds., "Wealth in the Natchez Region," *JMH*, 10 (1948): 290–316. An excellent description of the district as a whole is Chales S. Sydnor, *A Gentleman of the Old Natchez Region: Benjamin L. C. Wailes* (Durham, 1938). A list of the members of the Mississippi Society for the Acquirement and Dissemination of Useful Knowledge appears in the Natchez *Mississippi Herald*, Oct. 19, 1804. A fascinating manuscript account of social life in Natchez (1805–06) is Eliza Chotard Gould, "Autobiography," ADAH.

Americans are the best Father's; the French love their Country; but the Americans are attached to their Government; the French act from feeling; But the Americans consult their Judg'ment—to conclude—the French evidence much bravery and Enthusiasm; but the Americans display most firmness & preseverance.

Claiborne responded that "she justly appreciated the American Character," but the young lady continued in a less happy vein: "You Americans will all take another Bottle." The governor was so stunned by this observation that he could make no reply, and the lady added, "You I observe, cannot deny it." Claiborne concluded his account with the comment, "Her goodness however was such, as to admit that there were some exceptions."[2]

Urban societies came in varying degrees of completeness. The village of St. Louis had an economy and society far more limited than either Natchez or New Orleans. Colonel Francis Jackson of Kentucky, who visited St. Louis in 1800, thought the place physically mean and its people unpleasant. He found only two individuals in the town who spoke English, a free black and an American entrepreneur who was building a tavern adjacent to the ferry. St. Louis had its long-established French families who served as the economic and social leaders of the region. With the sale of Louisiana to the United States, aggressive Americans came to the district. One observer described the newcomers as "vile wretches" and "illiterate-semy-savages." Territorial Secretary Frederick Bates saw every element in the rapidly growing population of town and territory, "the *wise* and *foolish;* the *honest man* and the *knave;* the *Slanderer* and the *Slandered,* sometimes meet as in other countries—." St. Louis prospered and grew, but the presence of the lead mines, the continued importance of the fur trade, and the thriving business of supplying army posts hampered the emergence of a distinctive urban society like that of Natchez and New Orleans, based on commerce and services to an agricultural hinterland.[3]

2. James Sterrett to Nathaniel Evans, Oct. 22, 1804, James Sterrett Letters, 1802–10, Nathaniel Evans and Family Papers, box 17, Merritt M. Shilg Memorial Collection, LSU; William C. C. Claiborne to Albert Gallatin, Aug. 11, 1806, in *TP*, 9: 680. On the consumption of alcohol, also see Sterrett to Evans, Oct. 23, 1804, Sterrett Letters.
3. Lyman C. Draper Collections, 15 CC 7–9, SHSW; Frederick Bates, *The Life and Times of Frederick Bates,* ed. Thomas M. Marshall (2 vols., St. Louis, 1926), 1: 113–14; Richard C. Wade, *The Urban Frontier: The Rise of Western Cities, 1790–1830* (Cambridge, 1959), 59–64.

Societies with clearly defined characteristics also emerged in rural areas. Some were wealthy and worldly, such as the longer-settled agricultural regions of the Ohio Valley, especially in the river valleys of the Muskingum, Scioto, and the Great and Little Miamis. The same was true of the cotton-growing region around Natchez, and up and down the Mississippi River from south of New Orleans to Baton Rouge and inland. The rural areas were more placid than the river towns, with their vigorous commercial life, but no less affluent. Thomas Nicholls, whose father was civil commandant of Attakapas Parish (Louisiana), described the life there as one of "primitive simplicity." He especially remembered the pleasant Creole families of the neighborhood, who sent "little delicacies which the season & Country afforded, such as wild Ducks, game of every description, a fine quarter of Mutton, &c." The population in the Attakapas country was mostly French, and through the quiet years after the turn of the century "the young amused themselves with dancing and love-making; the old with cards and conversation." This leisured world extended to the east bank of the river, where the Felicianas were an economically prosperous and socially unified society by 1814. No less an authority on societies than Thomas Bolling Robertson, congressman and future governor of Louisiana, declared that the planters of St. Helena Parish were "wealthy & well informed and their hospitality & politeness reminded me constantly of our best Virginia Country circles."[4]

Observers in the western country noted that affluence and leisure did not dilute the focus on money. This was true of the Ohio River towns; it was true in the Southwest, where the institution of slavery mixed with cotton culture offered great opportunities for profit. None was more aware of the possibility of financial gain than a settled and prosperous society, whether in Virginia or New Orleans. In such an environment, marriage often served as a profitable form of economic alliance. The early fur trader had married the daughter of the most influential Indian chief to ensure a continuous supply of furs. Of Lieutenant Newman's projected marriage in New Orleans in 1804, James Sterrett wrote, "The Old Man . . . had made Some money—gives young Newman 7.000 D[rs]—the youthful Bride is blind in an eye—but she's extremely Sharp with the one God has left her— She discovered that Newman is a handsome genteel young man & that he is the first *papt* the question." An-

4. Thomas C. Nicholls, "Reminiscences," LSU; Thomas Bolling Robertson letter, June 3, 1814, Thomas Bolling Robertson Letters, Walter Prichard Collection, folder 12, LSU.

other marriage, where love was the primary concern, seemed to Sterrett impractical, even foolish: "She is 25 years old & very handsome—but no Money at interest, nor lands, houses, or bank Stock—*love all* powerful love." When Thomas Bolling Robertson travelled to the rural Feliciana parishes in 1814, he found the same values there. "The last day of my stay among them we have a pretty large party of ladies at Welches, among them a Miss Barrow pretty enough & rich and a great favorite with R[obinson]," he commented. "Their attachment is said to be reciprocal but hard hearted & avaricious parents heaven help them mar their happiness."[5]

Along with the appearance of staple commodities on the southern frontier came the rise of a particular kind of production unit associated with the cultivation of the great staple crops. For the first Anglo-American settlers in the New World, the word "plantation" was synonymous with farm, and the "planter" was simply a farmer. By the late eighteenth and early nineteenth centuries, the term "plantation" had come to be associated with an agricultural unit of substantial size, the use of slave labor, the cultivation of staples such as cotton, rice, or sugar-cane, and a certain social standing or pretension on the part of the owner. The early settlers carried the concept of a plantation society across the mountains into the trans-Appalachian frontier, where in this as other things they wished to re-create the values of colonial Tidewater. The plantation was a vigorous force in some areas southwest of the Appalachians before 1815. Cotton cultivation offered to the newest frontiers the potential for wealth and economic independence. Imported luxuries, tutors, European finery, music, and crystal chandeliers might appear in an enlarged dogtrot cabin, surrounded by a series of cotton fields that stretched to the edge of a great wilderness. Encouraged by the eager merchants of New Orleans and Mobile, the new settlers purchased luxuries with the first successful cotton crop. For the entrepreneur with land, slave labor, and access to water transportation, cotton offered the opportunity to indulge in the trappings of European luxury in spite of the isolation of the American frontier.

The plantation was more than a large-scale economic unit. It was also a self-contained society for its people, black and white. Within the larger institutional framework of the state or territory, county, township, and

5. Sterrett to Evans, May 12, 1804; June 10, 1809, Sterrett Letters; Robertson letter, June 3, 1814, Robertson Letters, Prichard Collection, folder 12.

town, the plantation was the focus of life for many. In a period when distances and primitive communication slowed institutional development, the plantation provided its own institutions to direct all aspects of life. Economic enterprise, social order, religion, education, and social intercourse were all centered in the plantation. Public education and religion came slowly to the South, their arrival often retarded, even in those areas long settled, by the independence and isolation of the plantation agricultural unit. Life in the South came to revolve around the plantation rather than around the village. In some areas of the southern frontier, the plantation was the village.[6]

Small communities were a second kind of society on the trans-Appalachian frontier. The family (or families) frequently served as the focal point of this society. Many pioneers moved to and across the frontier in family groups, for the family was a natural concentration of strength in economic enterprise and a source of support for physical protection. In a manner reminiscent of an earlier age, ties of kinship and marriage served as guarantees of mutual safety and support. And so men and women migrated in company with others with whom they had formed such ties. Intermarriage and other kinship interests united the ten families who settled at White Oak Springs in the White River Valley (Indiana), for example. The first White Oak settlers were only the advance party of a larger migration of immigrants from the Albemarle shores of North Carolina to the White River Valley. Other kinds of common values and identities united pioneers. Some groups of Whitewater River Valley settlers were known by their geographic origins, e.g., the Carolina settlements, the Kentucky settlements, and others, in a sense celebrating their common past.[7]

One variation of the small community on the trans-Appalachian frontier was the highly organized group that deliberately moved and settled in such a way as to preserve its identity. In the Old Northwest such

6. A brilliant introduction to the South, cotton, the plantation, and the new society created there is W. J. Cash, *The Mind of the South* (New York, 1941), 1–21. Note also William Faulkner's fictional treatment of Thomas Sutpen's construction of his plantation in *Absalom, Absalom!*
7. Margaret Story Jean and Aline Jean Treanor, "The First Families of White Oak Springs, 1810–1817," *IMH*, 36 (1940): 232; Chelsea L. Lawlis, "Settlement of the Whitewater Valley, 1790–1810," *IMH*, 43 (1947): 27–29.

communities often had New England origins. Because of a group allegiance, established institutional framework, and accepted leadership, these groups were less dependent upon economic prosperity and outside forces. The village of Granville (Ohio) was such a community. A Connecticut group organized itself into a stock company prior to its departure for the Ohio Valley. The officers and directors of the company carried with them a mandate to re-create the same kind of society as that existing in the old home, with special reference to religious, educational, and cultural institutions. A committee viewed and later purchased land in Fairfield County (Ohio), and another committee then supervised immigration to the new promised land. After extended negotiation with the commissioners of Fairfield County, the Granville settlement assumed political control of a township, and so the community integrated itself into the county without loss of identity. With the election of its own justices of the peace, local government was in the hands of friends. At almost the same time that township government came into existence, a late arrival brought with him (in addition to a long saw blade for the mill) several boxes of books which formed the basis of a village public library. The Connecticut settlement had now been re-established down to the very books its members read and approved.[8]

The Connecticut Western Reserve in northeastern Ohio was a large area of settlement that attracted like-minded peoples. The reserve had its origins in the many land schemes of the 1790's, when the state of Connecticut sold its reservation in the west to the Connecticut Land Company. In 1796 a surveying party under Moses Cleaveland laid out at the mouth of the Cuyahoga River a town that would bear his name. The settlement grew slowly (it reached perhaps one thousand in 1800), but after the turn of the century larger numbers of New Englanders came. Jonathan Hale was one of these. The first Hale in the New World, Captain Samuel Hale, was living in the Hartford Valley in 1635; by the beginning of the nineteenth century, Hales had lived in the vicinity of Glastonbury (Connecticut) for five generations. Family roots ran deep, but economic considerations were also strong. Jonathan's father left only a small estate to be divided among seven children. A married man with three young children himself, Jonathan determined to seek a more advantageous life in New Connecticut. He traded his property and land in

8. William T. Utter, *Granville: The Story of an Ohio Village* (Granville, 1956), 64–67.

Connecticut (about one hundred acres) with Thomas Bull, a hard-
pressed shareholder in the Connecticut Land Company, for five hundred
acres of wilderness in Township 3 Range 12 of the Connecticut Western
Reserve. Jonathan Hale's migration west in 1810 was only the first step
in the gathering of an extended family in the Connecticut Western Reserve. Jonathan's brother-in-law, Jason Hammond, purchased an adjacent tract and joined him the same year. At almost the same time,
Jonathan's cousin and brother-in-law Elijah Hale and his family moved
to Bath Township (Portage County) just down the road. The war against
England slowed immigration, but it began again in 1815, when Jason
Hammond's well-to-do brother Calvin immigrated from Boston to the
Western Reserve. Other settlers had similar strong family ties and support in the vicinity of their undeveloped farms. Although they were not
necessarily more prosperous than individual settlers in the western
county in an economic sense, those on this new frontier of the Connecticut Western Reserve had family ties, shared New England values, and a
sense of continuity.[9]

The French villages in Louisiana, Illinois, and Missouri formed another series of separate societies. Here, people lived in isolated communities, where little changed from generation to generation. The villages
were worlds unto themselves, with their own peculiar modes of dress,
the exclusive use of the French language (often in a dialect almost incomprehensible to Europeans), allegiance to the Catholic Church, and
communal cultivation of the fields. Almost all of these settlements dated
from the eighteenth century, when they were established to serve the
great fur-trading enterprises of the French and later English nations. The
immigration of the Americans in large numbers coincided with the decline of the fur trade and rising interest in agriculture and landownership. Yet the sense of community and shared life style remained.
These French settlements continued to be quiet, pleasant, agreeable,
calm, and orderly. They presented few examples of wealth or want. The
necessities of life were plentiful; most of the inhabitants sought little
more. Agriculture was largely self-sufficient. Among themselves, the
French enjoyed a vigorous social life. In the small villages like Vincennes, cards, billiards, and dancing helped to pass the long winter days

9. John J. Horton, *The Jonathan Hale Farm: A Chronicle of the Cuyahoga Valley*, Western Reserve Historical Society, Publication 116 (Cleveland, 1961), chs. 4–6.

and nights. Visits and social activities of various kinds filled this world of shared values.[10]

The arrival of the noisy and aggressive Americans directly challenged this old and quiet life. The villages at Vincennes, Kaskaskia, and Cahokia—strategically located for the fur trade—lay astride the tide of immigration to the western country. The French had little of the restless economic ambition and physical approach to the wilderness that characterized the Americans. *Les habitants* were in no hurry to accumulate real estate or even to establish ownership. For generations the land had always been there in abundance for those who wanted it. Few did. Those who took land often farmed without reference to the question of ownership. The arriving Americans had come to accumulate great estates founded on the doctrines of Sir William Blackstone that ownership of land may be conveyed forever on a slip of paper. It was only with great reluctance—and sometimes not at all—that the French presented their claims for approval in the American courts.

Yet differences between the French and the Americans were deeper than questions of landownership. In 1814 Thomas Bolling Robertson made a leisurely trip from Pittsburgh to New Orleans. In the course of this journey, he encountered several of the different societies that already existed in the western country. He addressed himself to the differences between the French and the Americans in these comments:

How strikingly different is the appearance of a French and American settlement the one presents small but badly managed fields but gardens abounding in vegetables salads and flowers and vines hanging in festoons over the doors & windows of their houses which, however essentially miserable exhibit a certain air of finery & frivolity—their poultry yards & pigeon boxes are well stocked the sides of their rooms hung around with flaring pictures and the floor covered with sleek cats & pet lap dogs On the other hand the American builds himself a coarse substantial Cabin surrounds it with a high fence to keep off his horses cows & hogs the chief objects of his care, despises all minor accommodations, and cultivates extensive fields, *belting* the largest trees, and giving additional gloom to the wilderness, instead of making it to blossom as the rose—if he does not fell or extirpate, he inflicts mortal wounds on the

10. Chester Jacob Attig, "The Institutional History of the Northwestern Territory, 1787–1802" (Ph.D., Chicago, 1921), 230–46; Malcolm Maurice Hodges, "A Social History of Vincennes and Knox County, Indiana, from the Beginning to 1860" (Ed.D., Ball State, 1968), 112–18. For the economic life of the French villages, see May Allison, "Conditions in the Illinois Country, 1787–1800" (M.A., Illinois, 1907), ch. 7.

gigantic oak poplar & Beech and leaves them standing as monuments of the devastating vigor of his arm— he hunts with large dogs the wild beasts of the forest or drags the mammoth catfish from the flood— the interior of his residence exhibits a stout and stirring wife healthy dirty children, rifles, shot pouches, & powder horns, earthen ware, bacon hanging in the chimney, & Iron pots & pans on the hearth—the one has too much of Civilization, the other too little—the one is pinched up, and fashioned, shewing the effects of Government, & of dense population, the other is wild & rough & rude as the roaming savage—the one has the playfulness of the Kitten with the sycophancy of the vine the other the gruffness of the bear with the sturdiness of the oak—[11]

The American's style of life was the wave of the future. He left his French counterpart far behind in the race for economic advantage and treated him with the contempt that progressive civilizations have always reserved for those who choose for whatever reason not to run the race for more material goods and services. In the face of this rising tide the French villages found it more and more difficult to retain their identity and way of life.

The largest numbers of people were in a third broad division, namely those alone on the remote rural frontiers of the western country, without wealth and accordingly with little leisure and no time for introspection. Most of these frontier people lived in isolated cabins. Economic motivations predominated; the emphasis was on economic sufficiency. The basic dwelling was the log cabin or lean-to. Servants were rare. Clothing and food were plain. Under such conditions, interest in the world beyond the horizon was minimal. Young people grew up shy and socially backward, the courting process was quick and to the point, and marriage speedily accomplished. The life cycle then began anew. The people on this frontier were without identity except in the broadest sense: rural, poor, and ignorant. David Hoover's memoir of life in the Indiana Territory at the turn of the century characterizes the dimensions of this limited world. He wrote, "I never had an opportunity of reading a newspaper, nor did I ever see a bank note, until after I was a man grown."[12]

11. Thomas Bolling Robertson, "Journal of a Tour down the Ohio and Mississippi," Robertson Letters, Prichard Collection, folder 12.

12. David Hoover, "Memoir," *IMH*, 2 (1906): 18. Edward Eggleston's novel, *The Hoosier Schoolmaster* (1871), which is set in Indiana in the 1840's, suggests that this sort of rural primitivism did not necessarily end with the frontier period.

For those who belonged to this broad group, the focus of society was the family. It was the only unit with which these people felt an identification. Of the activities that revolved around the family, the most important were associated with birth, marriage, and death. Upon these solemn or festive occasions, relatives or friends might come from distant points to assist in the celebration of the rites. These people lived close to birth and death. Another constant companion was work, and it is not surprising that these pioneers also used work as a form of social celebration. Joseph Hayes has left a description of a husking bee in Indiana Territory about 1810 that may serve as an example. "Corn-huskings, were kept up every night during corn gathering," he wrote. "The corn after being pulled from the stock & hauled is thrown into a pile often six feet high and about 200 feet in length. the owner provides himself with 2 or 3 gallons of Whiskey in a stone jugg, kills a pig or 2 or sheep, some dozen chickens or more." Neighbors came from miles around to make a frolic of hard labor.[13] People on the remote rural frontier of the western country were generally not concerned with the great issues of the day, or even with the question of what was going on in the territory. They worried about the basic necessities of life—food and shelter; they worried about themselves and their families.

Beyond the separate and distinct societies on the trans-Appalachian frontier grounded in shared values and an identity of interests were two institutions that transcended economic and geographic conditions. Of course, not all frontier people experienced either religion or education, but the two—especially religion—were present to a greater or lesser degree in almost all frontier societies, from the rising urban centers of the Ohio Valley to the remote French villages in the Mississippi Valley, from the tidy farms of the Hale clan in the Western Reserve of Ohio to the isolated cabins of people like the Ramseys in the remote parts of the Mississippi Territory. In general, this second generation of frontier people had the same religious and educational opportunities as their fathers and mothers, for like the secular world, religious denominations built on the institutional base established west of the mountains between 1775 and 1795.

Of the two, religion was by far the more significant and universal. It was a unifying element in a world that tended to divide and isolate peo-

13. Joseph Hayes, "Life," ISL.

ple by distance, the repetitive and unending nature of hard labor, and the consuming economic needs of the moment. Into this emotional vacuum came representatives of several religious denominations, bringing love, community, hope, and a purpose to life. They also brought stern judgment, inflexible standards of conduct, narrow-mindedness, and sometimes hatred. But whatever the message, religion brought people together. It transformed the lives of those it affected as dramatically as it had the Apostle Paul's on the road to Damascus. It was a great social and emotional experience that served to counter the drabness and sameness of frontier life. Religion followed hard on the heels of the first settlers and sometimes, like government, preceded them. In mobilizing their resources to meet the dramatic expansion of people after 1795, the several religious denominations relied on hundreds of devoted men and women, who worked without regard to the cost in the cause of organized religion on the trans-Appalachian frontier.

Representatives of institutional religion had been in the Mississippi Valley long before the arrival of the Americans. The earliest explorers of the Mississippi Valley had been French missionaries. Roman Catholic communities at Green Bay, Detroit, Vincennes, and throughout the Illinois country traced their founding to the eighteenth century. Those across the Mississippi River in the Louisiana Purchase were just as old and influential. All served as reminders of the great influence of French civilization in the Mississippi Valley long before the arrival of the Americans. By the beginning of the nineteenth century, Protestant denominations had penetrated the trans-Appalachian frontier as part of the advance of American settlement to the West. New Englanders brought the Congregational Church to Marietta, the surrounding Ohio Company lands, and then to the Connecticut Western Reserve. Several communities of Quakers, many of them antislavery, had already begun to settle in the Indiana Territory. The Methodists, drawing on their earlier experience on the frontiers of Kentucky and Tennessee and led by Bishop Francis Asbury, hastened to serve the new settlements. Asbury set up regular circuits in Ohio as early as 1798 to minister to Methodists who had crossed the mountains and sought to re-establish contact with the church; from there his circuit riders fanned out into Indiana Territory and other frontiers farther west. Within the first decade of the new century, Methodist circuit riders and Presbyterian missionaries had reached the Mississippi Territory. In the former Spanish and French possessions

of the Louisiana Purchase, the Catholic Church remained a dominant influence in temporal as well as spiritual affairs. It provided a familiar institutional base for these people, an anchor against the changes threatened by the impact of American occupation.[14]

Of the evangelical churches that vied for the souls of the pioneers in
the western country, the Methodists had the most experience and best
organization. The circuit rider was not an educated man in the formal
sense of the word, and his generally humble and rural background made
him eminently suitable to follow the track of new settlers. He had no
formal theological training but perfected his preaching skills by experience in the local church. He was a dedicated, hard-riding, earnest, sometimes stern man of God, armed with a Bible and a copy of the *Discipline*,
who combined several talents in fostering, expanding, and leading his
circuit. He had to be preacher, for it was the oral and not the written
word that inspired a frontier congregation; doctor, to minister to the
physical needs of a pioneer people; lawyer and sage, to adjudicate disputes within his Methodist "societies"—the many small congregations
that he visited on a regular basis; and policeman, to control the rowdy elements who tried to disturb his meetings. Allen Wiley's memoir of
1845–46 has left us descriptions of several of these early Methodist preachers. Samuel Parker, a man of great oratorical powers and bizarre appearance, served in the Indiana Territory as early as 1808.

> He was rather a tall, slim awkward man in appearance, with large blue
> eyes, with an enormous big Roman nose; and, when he preached, the
> inside of his upper lip protruded ungracefully. He had a long chin,
> which he used in the wintertime to hold up the blanket which he used
> for comfort; in the centre of which he had a hole cut and well bound, to
> prevent it from tearing, and which was just large enough to let his small
> head through, when he would hang the fore part of the bound hole on
> his chin, and bid defiance to wind and rain. If his bed covering, or
> frequently his pallet covering, was scant at quarterly meetings, his
> blanket assured him another valuable purpose for additional covering.[15]

14. Attig, "The Institutional History of the Northwestern Territory," 260–87. The writings on frontier religion for this period are extensive. Almost every state historical journal has several articles. The topic is also a popular one for theses and dissertations. A
good basic account is Reginald Horsman, *The Frontier in the Formative Years, 1783–1815*
(New York, 1970), 129–39, 212–13, 224–25.
15. Allen Wiley, "Methodism in Southeastern Indiana," *IMH*, 23 (1927): 164; T. Scott
Miyakawa, *Protestants and Pioneers: Individualism and Conformity on the American Frontier*
(Chicago, 1964), ch. 5.

The structure of the Methodist Church provided a sense of belonging for those who desired identification with a larger society. The local unit was the "class" and, above it, the "society," but the church also had circuits, and district and national (called "general") meetings. The expansion of the circuits and districts in response to the movement of population endowed the church like the Northwest Ordinance, with an infinite capacity to extend its doctrines and institutional structure into the distant wilderness. The message that the circuit rider brought to the distant reaches of the western country was the doctrine of free grace, and it also stressed individual salvation through good behavior and right conduct. Thus, doctrine provided a degree of freedom for those who wished it, and the organization gave a permanent institutional affiliation for those who wanted such a connection in the amorphous world of the frontier.[16]

The Baptist Church also appealed to frontier peoples. Known in the East for its vigorous opposition to established churches, in the decade of the 1790's the Baptists came in numbers to Kentucky and later Tennessee, and their influence spread north of the Ohio and, soon after the turn of the century, into the Mississippi Territory. The Baptists were a plain people, and their capacity to touch the frontier was, accordingly, large. Their churches exercised much independence, as befitted a denomination that struggled so long for freedom from established religion. Baptists formed themselves into church groups and, on a higher level, into associations. Many of the associations had written constitutions. Baptist preachers were almost entirely laymen and without formal training. The process of moving into the ministry was informal and, at the same time, personal. When an individual had a call from God to preach, he made it known to the congregation, to whom he delivered a "trial" sermon. The process of a public appearance on such an important and deeply felt matter must have been an agonizing experience for the untutored, shy, and inarticulate people of the frontier. Jacob Brewer, who moved with his father to Kentucky in 1786, described his decision to become a Baptist preacher in strongly personal terms. Months of prayer preceded his declaration. Finally the moment came.

16. William Warren Sweet, ed., *Religion on the American Frontier, 1783–1840* (4 vols., Chicago, 1931–46), vol. 4: *The Methodists*, chs. 3 and 4; Elizabeth K. Nottingham, *Methodism and the Frontier: Indiana Proving Ground* (New York, 1966), chs. 2, 3, and 4. Miyakawa argues that church members of all denominations on the frontier were part "of disciplined groups and an increasingly organized society." *Protestants and Pioneers*, 3.

I was trembling like a lief. I recollected the promise God gave me in the woods; as soon therfore as the congregation was dismissed. I steped up on a bench and gave out. "There will be preaching next sunday at Brother Wellborns." And jumped off the bench and made for the door, as I passed on, several persons asked me, "Who is to preach." I said, come and see. that week passed off verry slowly, and with much fear & trembling. . . . When I went to fill my appointment, I soon discovered that the Lord heard prayer. The lane was literally filled with horses, and the house with people. I trembled at the sight —but I retired behind a high bank— prostrated myself on my face and prayed to God to help me. Glory to God, he made good his promise to me in the woods. Yes, he did help, for if ever I was favored with the presence of the Holy one, surely he was with me at this time.

Brewer's sermon was so successful that the congregation licensed him to preach within the bounds of the church. After a day's work in the fields, he would "gather dry sticks, and read at night by fire light." "I made slow advances," he wrote, "Laboured incessantly on the farm all week and tryed to preach on sundays." Two years later the church licensed him in writing "to preach the gospel, whersoever God in his providence mite direct."[17]

The Baptists were suspicious of anything that suggested an established church, even a salaried minister. Instead, they felt, in the words of one congregation, "it is the duty of the church to give their minister a reasonable support" in order to relieve him of the need to struggle with the "affairs of this life." This support was not in the form of a salary but rather a subscription. In 1798, for example, the South Elkhorn (Kentucky) Baptist Church subscribed various commodities for the support of minister John Shackleford, including salt, corn, wheat, pork, flour, "beaf," sugar, tallow, and whiskey. A few men even contributed cash, ranging from six to twenty shillings.[18]

Two other major denominations, the Congregationalists and Presbyterians, also ministered to the needs of the advancing frontier. Missionary societies in the East, especially in New England, were vigorous

17. "Autobiography of Jacob Brewer," in Sweet, ed., *Religion on the American Frontier*, vol. 1: *The Baptists*, 202–04. Walter B. Posey, "The Frontier Baptist Ministry," East Tennessee Historical Society, *Publications*, 14 (1942): 3–10.

18. "Minutes of the Elkhorn Baptist Association," dated Kentucky, 1798, in Sweet, ed., *The Baptists*, 37. On the prominent place of black members in one Baptist Church in Tennessee, see the minutes of the Mill Creek Baptist Church, 1801–02, TSLA. On the Baptists generally, see Miyakawa, *Protestants and Pioneers*, ch. 4.

supporters of Congregational activities west of the mountains. The Connecticut Missionary Society (established 1798), for example, maintained an energetic program in the Western Reserve of Ohio. The predominantly New England settlements in the Ohio Company lands to the south petitioned for missionary support in 1799 in order to spread "religious instruction . . . among the multitudes of our brethren, dispersed in the wilderness, we may share in that munificence, which the more wealthy parts of the community have generously afforded for this purpose." Such was the recent nature of the settlements, the plea continued, that the settlers, "just beginning to clear their land, conceive themselves unable to spare a sufficiency from their necessary support, to pay for constant preaching." From the beginning of their New England settlements in the New World, the Congregationalists had employed an educated ministry. Consistent with their desire for trained ministers, the congregations on the trans-Appalachian frontier sought support from the East. This was perfectly satisfactory for the Ohio Land Company settlement and the Western Reserve, but it was not an approach to religion that appealed to large numbers of uneducated and poor frontier people throughout the western country. So the Congregationalists, with their emphasis on strict judgment and the sinful nature of man, their close official connection with the states of New England, their allegiance to the Federalist party, and their suspicion and even contempt for the uneducated masses of the frontier, were at a distinct disadvantage in carrying their spiritual message beyond the New England settlements.[19]

The Presbyterians also offered a structured, intellectual, professional church. With their emphasis on Calvinist theology and their doctrines of predestination and damnation, they offered little in the way of hope and release. The Presbyterians had contempt for the emotional optimism of the Methodists and regarded evangelical Christianity as pandering to the masses and doing violence to the word of God. The heirs of John Calvin forced the frontier to accept the gospel on Presbyterian terms or not at all. Presbyterians were present in substantial numbers on the frontiers of the Old Northwest and the South where there were large numbers of Scotch-Irish, who presumably found these doctrines familiar and acceptable. Beyond this group, the Presbyterians found their field a narrow one. They came to minister to the educated, but frontier people were

19. Sweet, ed., *Religion on the American Frontier*, vol. 3: *The Congregationalists*, 3–12, 44–45; Daniel Story and Rufus Putnam to Strong, May 22, 1799, in *ibid.*, 72.

largely without education. Their ministers were highly literate and professionally trained men who expected to be paid for their services, but frontier people were accustomed to amateurs who worked for little or nothing. When Presbyterian ministers supported a wide variety of reform movements, including temperance and education, frontier people resented them for what they regarded as criticism of their personal lives. Finally, the ministers talked of John Calvin and his doctrines, while the frontier people wanted a religious experience that emphasized hope and salvation. The match up was a poor one.[20]

In the last years of the eighteenth and early years of the nineteenth centuries, the western country experienced an outbreak of religious enthusiasm known as the Great Revival. The first large-scale manifestations of the revival appeared in Kentucky in 1798 and 1799, and from there it spread to Tennessee and north of the Ohio. The culmination of the movement, at least in terms of numbers, came in 1801, when an estimated twenty thousand people gathered at Cane Ridge (Kentucky) for an extended camp meeting. Revivals attracted hundreds of pioneer families from miles around. The organizers established large open-air campgrounds where they built several speaker's platforms. In the larger meetings it was not unusual to have six or eight preachers holding forth simultaneously, castigating the Devil and urging their listeners to repent. A typical schedule included three formal meetings a day, plus uncounted informal prayer meetings. An enthusiastic evening service might last until sunrise. The gatherings created controversy among the various denominations, and theological disputations among frontier preachers commanded the close attention of onlookers. The coming together of so many people, especially women and children, made the camp meeting the greatest social event of its day, and the emotional excesses provided additional excitement. Physical manifestations of the spirit were a feature of every meeting, and some were very violent. As the ministers shouted and the sinners writhed, the onlookers gaped and wondered about the conditions of their souls and whether they would soon suffer torment and anguish. At times the emotionalism moved beyond the control of the ministers. In the midst of such confusion, emotion, and violent outbursts, various kinds of misconduct invariably appeared. Gradually the founders of the movement became more and more reluctant to associate

20. L. C. Rudolph, *Hoosier Zion: Presbyterians in Early Indiana* (New Haven, 1963), 28–36; Miyakawa, *Protestants and Pioneers*, ch. 3.

themselves with the extremes of behavior encouraged in the name of God, and other denominations followed suit. The enthusiasm for the open-air revival faded about 1810, although a series of natural disasters (earthquakes, fires, and floods) in 1811 and 1812 produced another intense outburst of revivalism. The Baptists continued to hold long revival meetings for several years, but by 1815 the Great Revival had passed from the scene, replaced by more traditional forms of worship and salvation.[21]

The appearance of several different societies in this period did not produce a parallel range of educational experiences. Quite to the contrary, if anything, it only served to intensify the thrust for survival and to confirm book learning as a dispensable frill. The New England settlements probably offered more opportunities for education than others, and certainly the only example of public education. Only in settlements where New England traditions were strong did all children—or at least the children of church members—have the chance to attend a public school.

Marietta, Granville, and the Western Reserve (all in Ohio) supported public education in their own way. Writing from the Western Reserve in 1808, Abraham Scott, a missionary, noted that "the education of children in this country is considered and made an object of particular attention." Most of the towns employed teachers for the winter, and some even for the entire year. Scott thought most of the teachers qualified for their responsibilities, and he was "well pleased with their method of teaching, altho' not in every particular. In teaching children I find that in some schools they make use of novels and romances." Scott sternly condemned this practice, for everyone knew "from reason, observation and experience the danger of filling the youthful mind with vanities, and neglecting the means of forming a tast[e] for, and improving it with useful knowledge." He recommended reading the Scriptures instead. Scott's comments suggest the continuing tie between religion and education in these Congregational settlements.[22]

21. The literature on the Great Revival is extensive. An interpretive article is Donald G. Mathews, "The Second Great Awakening as an Organizing Process, 1780–1830: An Hypothesis," *American Quarterly*, 21 (1969): 23–43, which suggests that the Great Awakening was an organizing process and social reform movement in a time of national upheaval.

22. "Report of Abraham Scott, Missionary, Jan. 22, 1808," in Sweet, ed., *The Congregationalists*, 94–95. Attig, "The Institutional History of the Northwestern Territory," ch.

A more widespread educational institution on the frontier was the subscription school, with a curriculum fitted to the needs of the scholars of the day and to the capacity of the itinerant masters. "There were but little school in those days to educate the children perhaps two months during the year and that taught by subscription at so much per schollar," remembered Erastus Nevins of Parke County (Indiana). He continued: "To learn the alphabet was a tedious and slow one and spelling seemed to be one of the most important studies and must be recited three times a day." School facilities in the form of teachers or schoolhouses were scarce, almost "unknown" in the words of Ira Meater. When volunteer labor at last completed the long-awaited Parke County school, the building was only sixteen by twenty feet. Meater described school in session in these terms: "If you could weld together three frog ponds with denizens the size of a stove boiler down to a peanut, all doing their level best at noise, you would have a small specimen of our first 'Hoosier School.' " Amidst the dull and tedious routine of lessons, the youngsters enjoyed, now and then, the performance of a fiddler who entertained and then treated them with a jug of whiskey, or the first snowball fight of the winter. Meater's description of a Hoosier school suggests that it did not foster much learning, but many frontier families had no educational opportunities at all.[23]

Almost everywhere, education at all levels, like life on the frontier, was a matter of luck and economic status. Wealth in Natchez meant tutors and exposure to the gentle arts of books, imported luxury goods from Europe, music and the theater; wealth on the Tombigbee meant only more land and more slaves, for there was little else to buy in those isolated settlements. But, in most places, differences in education tended to reflect growing differences in wealth and leisure. Two notions about education prevailed everywhere on the trans-Appalachian frontier, from Louisville to New Orleans, from the Tombigbee to the Attakapas country to St. Louis: first, that education was private and for those who could afford it; and, second, that the federal government ought to support educational institutions, generally through a grant of land, and citizens of the western country constantly appealed for such support. Natchez and the

---

5, describes the miserable conditions for schooling throughout much of the Northwest Territory as late as 1802.
23. Erastus Nevins, "Reminiscences"; Ira Meater, "Early Reminiscences of Parke Co.," IHS. A similar account is A. C. Ramsey, "A Sketch of the Life and Times of Rev. A. C. Ramsey . . . ," 23, ADAH.

surrounding countryside established and maintained an institution of higher learning for several years, Jefferson College. The federal government contributed a section of land to its founding, but Jefferson College could hardly be described as reflecting a commitment to public education.[24] New Orleans had a variety of private academies, but their influence did not reach into the distant countryside. Wealthy planters supported a tutor on the plantation or sent their sons north for a classical education. The cost was high. John Palfrey, who moved to the Attakapas country in 1810 for better economic opportunities, was in constant need of money to support his children at northern schools. The situation along the Mississippi River in Rapides or Concordia parishes was much the same. Once more the dominant feature was the academy or the private tutor, both instruments that served only a small number of those settled there. The curriculum of the academy (or the tutor for that matter) was generally classical. Members of the leisured class displayed a fragmentary knowledge of Caesar, Cicero, and Virgil, for classics remained the base of education for gentlemen. The gentler arts, or "accomplishments," constituted education for women. Thomas Bolling Robertson described the Farrar sisters of the Mississippi Territory in these terms: "Rich as cream beautiful as God made them and sufficiently accomplished to read and write (write as well as I do) and play on the Guitar the sweet old ditty 'How imperfect is Expression.' " Robertson found the accomplishments of these fashionable ladies more than acceptable. He continued, "I wish I could fall in love with one of them and I am not sure that I shall not."[25]

Those less economically fortunate derived what information they could about the outside world from their parents. For most of the children on the trans-Appalachian frontier, the home was the dominant force in education. Education was not so much formal training from books as it was preparation for life, and, in this form, it serves to emphasize again the significance of the family on the frontier. If their parents were literate, the children might also achieve some degree of proficiency in reading and sums and would probably learn how to sign their names.

24. William B. Hamilton, "Jefferson College and Eduction in Mississippi, 1798–1817," *JMH*, 3 (1941): 259–76, is a complete account.
25. John Palfrey to Chew & Rolf, ca. 1812, William T. Palfrey Papers, LSU; Nell Angela Heidelberg, "The Frontier in Mississippi" (M.A., Louisiana State, 1940), ch. 8; G. P. Whittington, "Rapides Parish, Louisiana," *LHQ*, 17 (1934): 112–13; Robertson to his sister, Aug. 2, 1809, Robertson Letters, Prichard Collection, folder 11.

John Hutchins did a man's work in his father's cotton fields in Mississippi. At dusk he returned to the family cabin, where "I got my class board, which was shaved smooth and with a piece of charred wood for a pencil, the old man would teach me to write and cipher. Our light was a torch of dry canes." For some, instruction consisted simply of moral precepts offered for the conduct of life. The Reverend A. C. Ramsey, who grew up in eastern Mississippi near the Tombigbee settlements, absorbed this kind of education from his parents.

> The aim and object of this parental training was to fix in the young minds, such correct principles, as would lead to the adoption and cultivation of all those rules of moral and religious experience and practice, as would secure them against the evil tendencies of depraved nature; and the corruptions of evil society; and thereby be developed in an honorable stand in this to a useful citizenship among men; and worthy and useful members of the church of God.[26]

The condition of the world in which these frontier people found themselves and what they hoped to do in it determined their views about education. They hoped to educate their children in a practical way to meet what they felt were the needs of their station in life. Moral precepts formed the staple of education in the Ramsey family; how to walk across a drawing room and sing a song did the same for the Farrar sisters. These represented the sum total of educational experience and social preparation for two such groups. It suggests the ways in which education was a function of economic status, even on the frontier. Each individual sought a minimal capacity to meet the worlds he knew. The same thread united the chattering pupils in the schools of the Indiana Territory, with one difference: the act of attending school was a socializing experience in itself, and one in which not all children participated. In the world that stretched out before all these people, they feared the unknown. Not all the dangers were physical. Some were social. Solitary farmers, trained by long years of labor, were ill equipped to meet with or mix in society. They were only comfortable among their own kind. Little wonder they disliked educated ministers and others who put on "airs."

The social gap that separated the people on the frontier from the people at ease in an urban society may have been greater than their eco-

26. John Hutchins, "Memoirs," TSLA; A. C. Ramsey, "Sketch," 6.

nomic differences. W. J. Cash's self-made planter, with the big house, piano, and daughters trained by a Presbyterian parson was closer to the world of the log cabin than to Charleston society, which lay at the end of a long road, light-years away, as alien and remote as another planet. The only thing that the planter had in common with the Charleston aristocrats was money. It was not enough. As Cash reminds us, these self-made southern planters stood with one foot on the frontier as late as the outbreak of the Civil War. It took more than one generation to educate the people on the trans-Appalachian frontier, whatever their economic status. They could not escape the backwoods and its mark.[27]

27. Cash, *The Mind of the South*, 28–30. Cash's case would have been more persuasive with more specific reference to time and place. A poignant comment from a later frontier on the force of the frontier experience is the statement by Big Andrew in the frontispiece to Mari Sandoz, *Old Jules* (1935).

III

The First Great Migration
1815–30

Shortly after its confluence with the Miami River, the Ohio—"la belle Rivière" of the early French traders—turns sharply to the south and west. For almost three hundred miles it runs to its rendezvous with the Mississippi, whence the waters of the two great rivers flow another thousand miles in uninterrupted majesty to New Orleans, and eventually to the Gulf of Mexico. This was the route of the American empire. Upon the waters of these two rivers and their tributaries floated the panorama of the American frontier: the immigrants headed toward the dreams of the future, the agricultural products that represented the achievements of the past. In a sense, the people of the nation passed in review along these sovereign waterways. West of the Appalachians lay a great expanse of land, most of it drained by these two rivers and their tributaries. Despite the movement of people associated with the first and second generations of the trans-Appalachian frontier, most of this land was still empty in 1815. To the north, ice sheets had glaciated the land, smoothing some hills and raising others. As the pioneer moved inland from the watercourses, he moved from the familiar woodlands to the open prairies and level expanses that would become the settlement sites of the new generations. The vegetation ranged from hardwood forests to garlands of prairie flowers that bloomed profusely in the spring. To the south lay dense forests of pine and walls of thick tropical cane. Game was present in quantities to delight the most avid hunter: clouds of birds, including the passenger pigeon destined to pass from the scene within a single lifetime; the prairie chicken, grouse, and turkey; animal life ranged from smaller game such as squirrels and raccoons to deer, bear, and the bison. Fresh meat would play a prominent part in the diet of the first pioneers, as did the fish taken from the numerous streams. Much of the vast region was fertile; some sections came to be counted among the garden spots of the western world. Almost everywhere the land was well watered; in some spots it was almost too wet. Innumerable watercourses penetrated into this vast land. Some were enlarged creeks, flooded in the springtime, reduced to a trickle in the dry months. Others were major rivers, the Wabash, Illinois, Sangamon, Whitewater, Tennessee, Arkansas, Missouri, and Yazoo. All pointed the way to the interior. Indians had lived on these lands for a thousand years and changed them little. Now, within one generation, the American pioneer would transform them. The Great Migration had many of the qualities of a revolution: for the Native Americans thrust aside; for the pioneers who took the land and exploited it; for the land itself.

To this fertile and open land in the years immediately after 1815 came one of the great immigrations in the history of the western world. In numbers of people, land occupation, and impact on the nation, it far exceeded anything experienced on the early trans-Appalachian frontier. It conveyed a sense of motion, of movement, a kinetic energy that separated it from the earlier frontier experience. It was the frontier in motion. Westward expansion had entered its modern period; the mobile societies of the nineteenth century were in the process of replacing the motionless societies of the eighteenth. The bench mark was the year 1815. Perhaps this was the significant result of the War of 1812, that it arranged national and international affairs in such a way as to unleash the powerful forces of movement in the nation. A period of postwar readjustment followed, with the attendant economic and social upheaval. The threat of the Indian—vague and menacing still in the popular mind—had receded. The war with England was a military stalemate, but the conflict between the white and red occupants of the nation ended in decisive Indian defeats.

As it had been for generations past, land was the lure, and the flood of new settlers experienced the operation of a land system moving at last beyond the experimental stage, an administrative mechanism that could place vast quantities of public lands on the market. Military bounty lands for veterans in Illinois, Arkansas, and Michigan also attracted prospective settlers to the western country. Added to these inducements were prosperous times, rising prices for staple agricultural products (especially cotton), and a banking system that was almost as democratic as the dominant political philosophy of the day. From the Ohio and the Mississippi and their tributaries people disembarked and headed inland as far as their ambitions, inclinations, and supplies would take them. Their trade and contact with the outside world, especially in commerce, would continue to focus for several years on the great waterways. Thus, the impulse of the Great Migration after 1815 covered several hundred miles in breadth, brought together and intermingled streams of population from north and south of the Ohio, and began the further occupation of the trans-Appalachian frontier that would continue over another generation.

The impact of this great immigration was widespread. The movement of peoples, and American diplomacy, led to the organization of new territories, Arkansas and Florida in 1819. Governors and legislatures laid off much of the new country into counties after 1815. State government also had a powerful influence on the frontier experience. Entering the union at a steady pace—Indiana (1816), Mississippi (1817), Illinois (1818), Alabama (1819), and, after a quarrel of national proportions, Missouri (1821)—states became a common political unit of the frontier.

Who were these people who went west in such astonishing numbers? As befits a rush to take up land, most of them were farmers. From the accounts of those who participated and others who observed, large numbers moved together, tied by bonds of family, religion, or simply common interest. Many small settlements in the western country consisted of these agriculturists, living in sufficient proximity to lend one another a hand and to meet for social activities. Others were skilled in the trades of the time, blacksmithing, building, and milling, all grouped under the heading that people at the time referred to as "mechanicks." Still others were professionals, principally doctors and lawyers, who gravitated to the innumerable small towns that sprang up to serve the surrounding agricultural countryside.

This generation of frontier peoples was the first to experience steam and, more particularly, the steamboat. The sight of the steamboat rounding the long reach on the river, the distant wail of the whistle, and the tremor of excitement in the crowd became a striking feature of the trans-Appalachian frontier. The reactions of those who understood in more specific terms what steam meant to the economy and society were no less strong. But in spite of this dramatic—even revolutionary—development, the world was not transformed. At least not yet. The steamboat, the steam-driven cotton gin, and the steam-driven factory portended a revolution in the nature of this civilization that ran counter to the doctrines of Thomas Jefferson. These alien forces would triumph, but not at once. It was still the same old agricultural world that the newcomers found on the frontier from 1815 to 1830. In values and technology, things were not yet remade. Flatboats carried the bulk of the cargo downriver to market, as they had for two centuries. People moved, cultivated, and travelled at the speed of the horse. This was the world of the land, the draft animal, the doctrines of Jefferson, and an agricultural society. Nowhere was this truer than on the frontiers west of the Appalachian mountains. There were vast expanses, different peoples, and varying experiences, but the ways of doing things would be familiar to those of earlier frontier generations.

In their institutional development the pioneers who immigrated to the trans-Appalachian frontier after 1815 also owed much to preceding generations, which had marked out a wide range of institutions for meeting the challenge of the frontier. Indeed, the techniques for dealing with the frontier were much the same after 1815 as they had been in the two previous generations. Between 1775 and 1815 the pioneers had laid down the broad outlines of a world that emerged with increasing rapidity after the War of 1812. This early period was one of exploration and experimentation—in the land, in institutions, in societies. Men and women gradually structured the institutions of the new western country, guided in part by the ordinances of 1785 and 1787. This process was largely completed by 1815. After 1815 the institutional structure of the promised land had been defined, the fundamental decisions had been made and need only be applied in the newly occupied areas of the next generation.

The institutional structure of the western country after 1815 was increasingly orderly and cyclical. The exotic and sharply different elements of the former French societies faded; so did the economic uncertainties brought on by European diplomatic and military conflict and a para-military emphasis necessitated by the presence of the large numbers of hostile Indians. Gone also was the uncertainty of the American government about how to handle these problems. An all-consuming nationalism and confidence in American frontier virtues and strengths replaced military weakness, diplomatic delicacy, and niceties of conscience. For those concerned with institutional development, the hesitant experiments of the past, many of them carried on amidst difficulties of isolation and physical weakness, were over. In the years after 1815 the standardization of life on the frontier was a force as wide and deep as the heavy current of immigration that covered the spaces from the Muskingum to the Missouri, from the Arkansas to the Tombigbee. In an institutional sense, it was a dramatic change, comparable to the impact of steam on the movement of people and commodities. Supported by two generations of experience, the court, codes of law, government, militia, and churches brought structure to frontier life almost everywhere. In a sense, the search for order and form on the trans-Appalachian frontier was over.

The period after 1815 also produced a new kind of diversity in the frontier experience, in the many new frontiers, the older frontiers in transition, and the new people making new societies. Differences in levels of development were broad and sometimes very striking: consider, for example, the level of economic and political development in an Ohio River town and that of a cabin in a clearing forty miles inland. The differences in values, interests, and the quality of life were correspondingly broad. Some areas of the trans-Appalachian frontier had even passed through the frontier stage into a condition indistinguishable from the agricultural settlements east of the mountains. Thus the frontier west of the Appalachians came again to encompass several societies, at different stages of development.

People who went out to the wilderness across the mountains in 1815 and thereafter did not simply disappear from the current of national life. Quite to the contrary, they carried the force of the American nation west—its ideals, virtues and prejudices, strengths and weaknesses, and there they added to the power and authority of the rising colossus of North America. They made this part of the trans-Appalachian frontier thoroughly American. These were the pioneers who gave voice and provided motion to support John Quincy Adams's concept of a continental empire. Their children would reach the shores of the Pacific and their grandchildren settle and cultivate the Great Plains. These were the begetters of this great national movement.

7

Across the Old Northwest
and into Missouri

"Old America seems to be breaking up, and moving westward," wrote Morris Birkbeck as he observed the rush of settlement down the Ohio in the spring of 1817. "We are seldom out of sight, as we travel on this grand track towards the Ohio, of family groups behind, and before us, some with a view to a particular spot, close to a brother perhaps, or a friend who has gone before, and reported well of the country."[1] Birkbeck was witness to the first part of a great migration that would settle the remainder of the trans-Appalachian frontier within a generation. A dominant feature of this phenomenon was the numbers of people. The figures that they made on the land were striking, with heavier concentrations in the eastern territories like Ohio (see table 2).

This mass movement affected people, societies, and institutions in dif-

Table 2. Growth of the Old Northwest and Missouri, 1810–30

	1810	*1820*	*1830*
Ohio	230,760	581,434	937,903
Indiana	24,520	147,178	343,031
Illinois	12,282	55,211	157,445
Missouri	19,783	66,586	140,455

Source: *Historical Statistics of the United States, Colonial Times to 1957* (Washington, 1960), 13.

1. Morris Birkbeck, *Notes on a Journey in America from the Coasts of Virginia to the Territory of Illinois* (Philadelphia, 1817), 34.

fering ways. Societies became more determinedly agricultural, as the opening of the rich lands of the interior river valleys overwhelmed wilderness industries like the fur trade and salt manufacturing. Individual communities continued to move together and to retain their identities. The force of the Americans and the authority of their government surrounded and isolated individual pockets of cultural resistance like the French villages. These pioneers dealt with familiar institutions, devised and tested by the previous generations; yet even these exhibited occasional variations.[2]

The experiences of individuals were also broadly similar, but they were no less compelling for the mass nature of a frontier in motion. Behind the rush of people were thousands of individual decisions to move. The impulse to immigrate was basically economic. For the rich lands of the trans-Appalachian West families left the stony ridges of New England, the high rents of New York State, and even the lands settled by a previous frontier generation in the Ohio Valley. James B. Lewis's father, who returned from the war with a severe hand wound, departed Trumbull County (Ohio) after his third consecutive crop failure. Lewis wrote, "The whole country was a stench in our nostrils and we could taste it in our mouths." At the suggestion of the Methodist circuit rider, the Lewis family moved to Indiana.[3] Many immigrants were young, and some newly married, seeking their first opportunity. Others, who had been on the land before, sought a fresh start. All shared the desire for something new. Their hopes carried them to the remote and distant frontiers, where lands were most readily available and at little or no cost. With such household goods and agricultural tools as their finances permitted, and a few carefully preserved mementos of their past, they floated down the Ohio on all manner of rivercraft, moved overland by horse and wagon, or simply walked, a random and unending procession of pilgrims in search of a promised land.

What they found were rich lands and a pioneer life like that experienced by a previous generation. It was without amenities and frills. For

2. The most detailed account of the settlement north and west of the Ohio River after 1815 is R. Carlyle Buley, *The Old Northwest: Pioneer Period, 1815–1840* (2 vols., Indianapolis, 1950), vol. 1, ch. 1. On the great land sales that accompanied immigration, see Malcolm J. Rohrbough, *The Land Office Business: The Settlement and Administration of American Public Lands, 1789–1837* (New York, 1968), chs. 5 and 6.
3. "The Pioneers of Jefferson County—Reminiscences of James B. Lewis, Esq.," ISL.

most of the immigrants, this was a continuation of a condition that they had long known. Morris Birkbeck penetrated to the distant frontiers of the western country. He described these early frontier people in front of their cabins, standing awkwardly and self-consciously in their buckskin and linsey-woolsey: "The man, his pregnant wife, his eldest son, a tall half-naked youth, just initiated in the hunter's art, his three daughters, growing up into great rude girls, and squalling tribe of dirty brats of both sexes, are of one pale yellow, without the slightest tint of healthful bloom." Birkbeck might have been more tolerant, for these early pioneers experienced repeated bouts of the fever that robbed them of their color, strength, and sometimes their lives. The physical hardships of the first years on the new land dominated the pioneering experience. T. V. Denny wrote his brother from Indiana in 1818, "Well I can tell you, after a person has been here in the woods awhile he will learn to use economy in the strict sense of the word." The pioneering period was long remembered by those who experienced it. From the perspective of a lifetime on the land, Ira Meater of Parke County (Indiana) commented, "Life meant business in those days."[4]

Scenes of hardship and even want sometimes were noted by travellers in the western country. On his journeys across the Old Northwest in 1819, Richard Lee Mason saw many of the first inhabitants of this new country. He entered the new state of Indiana at New Albany ("a little village inhabited by Tavern keepers and mechanics") and pushed on to the northwest, cataloguing the poor houses and bad accommodations. Mason had a low opinion of Hoosiers and thought that Indiana's "Inhabitants generally possess a smaller share of politeness than any met with before." Yet he was touched by a rural scene outside of Paoli, the county seat of Orange County. It was early November in this sparsely settled frontier, and the nights were already cold, when he recounted this incident:

> In the midst of one of those long and thick pieces of woods we passed one of the most miserable huts ever seen. A log house built out of slabs without a nail. The pieces laid against a log pen such as pigs are commonly kept in, a dirt floor and no chimney. Indeed the covering would be a bad one in the heat of summer and unfortunately the weather at

4. Birkbeck, *Notes on a Journey in America*, 139; T. V. Denny to Christopher Denny, Jan. 24, 1818, T. V. Denny Letters, ISL; Ira Meater, "Early Reminiscences of Parke Co.," IHS.

this time is very severe for the season of the year. This small cabin contained a young and interesting female and her two shivering and almost starving children, all of whom were bare headed and their feet bare. There was a small bed, one blanket and a few potatoes. One cow and one pig (who appeared to share their misfortunes) completed the family except for the husband, who was absent in search of bread. Fortunately for the dear little children we had in our carriage some bread, cheese toddy, etc. which we divided with them with much heartfelt satisfaction. In this situation the woman was polite, smiled and appeared happy. She gave us water to drink, which had been refused to us, by persons on the road several times during the day.[5]

The mass immigration that characterized this frontier experience included individuals, some of them men of property and influence; families joined together for mutual protection and advantage; and whole communities of people who immigrated west together. Among the individuals of political and economic standing who came out to the frontier was Edward Coles. Born into a Virginia family of rank and influence, possessed of a superior education and the benefits of foreign travel, he was private secretary to James Madison for several years. Coles went north and west to escape the institution of slavery and to find good lands. He floated down the Ohio in 1819, disembarking at Louisville to continue the trip overland. He was enthusiastic about the lands of Illinois and wrote to Madison that men could not be expected to continue holding an acre of land in Virginia or even on the Miami River "when they can exchange it for 15 or 20 acres of equally good land on the Wabash, with the additional advantage of good range for their stock." But Coles initially found the Illinois countryside depressing: "So flat and marshy a country, present to the eye of a mountaineer no very pleasing prospect, either of comfort or of health." The Illinois prairies were wet, and Coles thought that they were "too level and too wet to afford good water, good health, good roads, or good any thing except most abundant crops of vegetation and of musketeers." He consoled himself that the settlement of the country would mean its clearing and eventual drainage. Coles purchased a large tract of fertile land in Madison County. As soon as his slaves arrived—he later freed them in accordance with his principles—he set them to work in building, clearing, and planting. The experiences of the first several months he recounted in a letter to James Madison.

5. Richard Lee Mason, "Journey from Philadelphia to Illinois and Missouri, 1819," ISHL.

On the 17 of May, the day after the arrival of my Negroes, I commenced ploughing up the Prairie, and splitting rails to fence it; and continued breaking prairie and planting corn until the first week in July. The consequence was that the corn was in some places 5 feet high, while in others it was not yet up. I have planted between 12 and 15 acres in corn for each horse I have worked. This I am sure you will consider good work, when you reflect how late I commenced, and that my horses were exhausted by a long and fatiguing journey; and that the Prairie was so rough & hard that it required my whole team to pull one plough. I am now employed in mowing hay from the prairie, and following it to seed wheat this autumn.[6]

In 1819 some seven or eight families formed a company to settle the "Horseshoe prairie" just below the later site of Noblesville, Hamilton County (Indiana). The leader of the enterprise was John Finch. Loaded in three wagons, the pioneers moved through seventy miles of wilderness to their new homes. On at least one occasion the party paused to construct a bridge over a swift stream. Once arrived, the settlers unloaded, pitched tents, and immediately went to work: "Some went to cutting logs for the cabin, some to hauling and others to making clapboards to cover the house with." Indians appeared and soon called on the settlers daily, to watch, smoke a pipe, or trade. Sickness began in September with the onset of the "ague" season. Times were hard before harvest, "Our provisions gave out and 60 or 70 miles to the settlement." Finch wrote about their food, "Conner had a little corn which he sold them at $1.00 per Bu. This they had to pound in a mortar, lift out the finest of it and use for bread and boil the coarser of it and eat it with milk, they called it samp." Some of the settlers died in the fall, but other families arrived, and the autumn harvest was sufficient. Over the winter a few enterprising men built a horse mill to grind the corn. More families appeared in the spring of 1820. The experiences of immigration and survival were over. The hard work had only begun. People married, bore children, died, and continued the natural phases of life; claims changed

6. Edward Coles to James Madison, July 20, 1819, Edward Coles Papers, CHS. On Coles's continuing opposition to slavery and its influence on his later political career, see Donald S. Spencer, "Edward Coles: Virginia Gentleman in Frontier Politics," *JISHS*, 61 (1968): 150–63. A sense of economic distinctions in frontier Illinois emerges in William Wilson's letter from Shawneetown: "It is true we have no slaves here, which is some inconvenience, but here as in every other country where slavery is not tolerated, there is a certain class of people who supply their places." Wilson to May Wilson, June 14, 1819, William Wilson Papers, ISHL.

hands, some settlers moved away, others arrived. The story of the Finches and their company was repeated over and over in the western country.[7]

Farther to the west, the TenBrook family moved toward Parke County. It was the fall of 1822. The TenBrooks had settled outside of Cincinnati in 1815 and decided to move on because of hard times. Andrew TenBrook wrote, "Sickness and doctor's bills and very low prices for corn and wheat made it impossible to make more than a poor living." The TenBrook party numbered twenty-seven in all, made up of three families, two teamsters, and three single men. Their stock included thirteen horses, twenty-one cows, two yoke of oxen, and four dogs. They travelled over roads in terrible condition—"turned around old logs and trees in every direction, and the progress was slow." The wagons and teams frequently mired in the sloughs, amidst a swarm of insects in the hot, sticky, midday air. The travellers went on for days, never seeing other settlers, pitching camp at night, where they ate "mush and rich warm milk." An axle broke—"there was neither wagon maker nor smith within fifty miles that we knew of"—and the immigrants repaired it by native ingenuity. In mid-autumn the party passed through Indianapolis, which Andrew TenBrook described as still largely unbroken wilderness, a single two-story house bravely suggesting future urban development. The most prominent residents were two Kentuckians "that had come to see the country and had a two horse wagon and a barrel of whiskey to sell out to pay their expenses." The TenBrook party "bought several gallons." Some nights later, at Greencastle, came the first frost. The next day the TenBrooks crossed into Parke County.

Jacob TenBrook, Andrew's uncle, had selected his farm site on a previous trip. He immediately built a cabin, as much for the corn as for his family, for the one hundred bushels he brought along had to last through the winter and to provide seed in the spring. Jacob, his brother John, and a hired hand turned to clearing the land. They worked through autumn of 1822 and into the winter. By spring they had cleared fifteen acres of small timber and split two hundred fence rails. As soon as winter broke, men began burning the logs and underbrush and putting up rail fences. Plowing and planting began on June 12—"one furrow every four feet and then step drop every three or four feet." The Ten-

7. John G. Finch, "Reminiscences," IHS.

Brooks also planted an acre each of potatoes and turnips. The harvest was good and the corn divided into three classes: best quality for bread, second quality for horses, damaged corn for cows. The nearest mill at Roseville was "so crowded with customers that there could not be a grist ground in less than a week at any time that winter," and the miller charged "more than one third for grinding." Jacob TenBrook soon found ways to grind corn at home.

The livestock prospered. The first spring brought seven new calves to supplement the herd of cows, and the TenBrook family "depended very much on the milk." The hogs purchased in the winter ran wild in the spring and summer, turning up at Christmas just in time for butchering. The first summer the women in the family made forty twelve-pound cheeses, which they sold at Rockville and Armieburg for about one dollar each. The TenBrooks, like other farmer immigrants, made quantities of sugar from the plentiful groves of sugar trees: "The first season we made three hundred and fifty pounds of sugar and ten gallons of molasses on the same ground that we were clearing for corn." Andrew Ten-Brook, who had title to the original farm sixty-six years later, remembered that the experience of settling was hard but rewarding. The fertility of the soil and the natural gifts of the land quickly supplied subsistence. "After the first year, I never saw any scarcety of provisions," he wrote. "The only complaint was that there was nobody to whome the supplies could be sold."[8]

Communities of people united by common values and a common destination also made the trip out to the trans-Appalachian frontier. Several were from New England. Daniel Brush's father was from Vermont, and he came west with a colony of Vermonters. In the spring of 1820, after a journey of more than two months, the colony settled in Greene County (Illinois), on a tract adjacent to the Illinois River. The elder Brush was enthusiastic over the site: "A prairie of the richest soil, stretched out about 4 miles in length, and one mile wide, extending from the timber

8. Andrew TenBrook, "From Lycoming County, Pennsylvania, to Parke County, Indiana: Recollection of Andrew TenBrook, 1786–1823," ed. Donald J. Carmony, *IMH*, 61 (1965): 17–29. Another account of life in early Parke County is Meater, "Early Reminiscences of Parke Co." On the abundance enjoyed through hard work and rich lands— "we have either beef, pork, or chickens on our table three times a day, both Indian and wheat bread to accompany every meal; all kinds of sauce, sweetening aplenty from our sugar orchards and beehives, and when blessed with a house-wife, we have always pickles and preserves"—see the Edwardsville *Spectator*, Feb. 15, 1820.

growing next the river . . . to the Bluffs . . . , complete with pure springs of cold water in abundance." After its establishment the colony became known as the "Yankee Settlement." Brush's father put up a sixteen-by-twenty-foot cabin and settled down to the business of breaking the prairie. The heavy plow required three spans of horses or three yoke of oxen. His son wrote of the experience:

> The "breaking up" consisted in turning over the sod which was matted with grass roots, & frequently a "red root" of one to three or four inches in thickness, very strong & hard to tear out, the strips turned over being say 15 to 20 inches, with a heavy plow with coulter for cutting the sod as deep as desired to run the plow, attached to the beam in advance of the share a small way— The work required a team of Horses or Oxen in proportion to the width and depth of the furrow to be cut—if horses were used three or more span—if oxen three or 4 yoke moved the plow. The strips turned over fitted evenly & snugly into the last displaced sod—so that when a piece of ground was "broken," the surface was as smooth & level as before the sod was turned upside down so that no grass was in sight but the severed roots appeared on top— The Corn was planted by striking an axe, say every 4 feet between the edges of the sods, and dropping kernels for a hill, 3 or 4 grains—and then by a tread of the foot pressing the sod again together. No weeds or grass sprang up on such ground the first year and the corn needed no attention with plow or hoe, and if got in early good crops were yielded—of corn and fodder.

In the spring flowers bloomed profusely, and later came wild berries. Into this natural paradise with its present beauty and its future promise came the sudden tragedy that the frontier often visited on its people. Brush's father suffered a stroke in early July 1821. Within three days he was dead, leaving a widow and four children, ages ten, eight, five, and two. No sooner had the family recovered from this shock and determined to remain in the West rather than return to Vermont than the autumn fevers prostrated all members. "Fever 'n ager was in every house," remembered Brush; "Not one in the settlement, I think, escaped." Others in the "Yankee Settlement" rallied around to assist their own. Care and food assisted the Brush family through illness and helped it to survive a first winter without the father. The Vermonters helped one another at every opportunity, and the colony gradually prospered. After a few years, Brush concluded, "Provisions in abundance, was the rule in that Yankee Settlement, and no one needed to go supperless or hungary to bed."[9]

Particular regions became identified in the popular imagination with the ultimate virtues of good lands—attractive vistas, fertile soil, pure water, native timber. A large agricultural tract up the Missouri River had this reputation. The Boon's Lick country (as it came to be called) lay on both sides of the river in a belt some sixty miles wide. The territorial legislature organized the area into Howard County in 1816, with the county seat at Franklin. Timothy Flint, missionary and writer from New England, described the circumstances surrounding the fame of Boon's Lick.

> From some cause, it happens that in the western and southern states, a tract of country gets a name, as being more desirable than any other. The imaginations of the multitudes that converse upon the subject, get kindled, and the plains of Mamre in old time, or the hills of the land of promise, were not more fertile in milk and honey, than are fashionable points of immigration. During the first, second, and third years of my residence here, the whole current of immigration set towards this country, Boon's Lick. . . . Boon's Lick was the common . . . point of union for the people. Ask one of them whither he was moving, and the answer was, "To Boon's Lick to be sure."

The Franklin *Missouri Intelligencer* set the tone for the rapidly growing region with a toast in the spring of 1819: "Boon's Lick—two years since, a wilderness; now, *rich in corn and cattle*." Tobacco, cotton, and flax supplemented these traditional frontier crops. Despite the disruptions of economic panic in 1819 and a changing channel of the Missouri River— which washed away the town of Franklin—growth continued. By 1823 the state legislature had laid off another eight counties in the Boon's Lick region.[10]

In the 1820's the country bordering the Sangamon River in Illinois received a similar acclaim. The movement to publicize the region began

9. Daniel Brush, "Autobiographical Memoir, 1813–1861," 19–24, ISHL.
10. Timothy Flint, *Recollections of the Last Ten Years in the Valley of the Mississippi* (Boston, 1826), 202–03, 52; Franklin *Missouri Intelligencer*, June 11, 1819; Jan. 28, Oct. 28, 1823; Rohrbough, *The Land Office Business*, 132–34. On the growth of the region, see Walter A. Schroeder, "Spread of Settlement in Howard County, Missouri, 1810–1859," *MHR*, 63 (1968): 1–24.

in the summer of 1819, when a correspondent wrote in the Edwardsville
Spectator of the attraction of "The Sangamo."

> The prairies are too large, but they are the richest and best kinds of
> prairies, the uplands as well as the bottoms. The timber is very large
> and lofty, and generally approaches the prairies with the fulness of the
> interior, without underwood or barrens. The country is well watered
> with large and small springs . . . the streams continue to hold the usual
> quantity of water during the dry season.

The Sangamo (as it was called) offered "some enchanting situations for
agriculture and habitation." The writer concluded that the number of
settlers in the region did not exceed three hundred families. Immigrants
rapidly swelled the number, and in 1821 the state legislature established
Sangamon County.[11]

Earlier experiences had laid down the lines of economic development,
the patterns of trade, and the routes to wealth for the pioneers who participated in the Great Migration. This new generation followed, by and
large, these guidelines. Even the poorest settlers had their hopes of ac-
cumulating great estates. William McCutcheon was one of those who
moved to the frontier almost without capital, but his ambitions were no
less real. He brought a strong constitution and a willingness to work.
Settling in Parke County (Indiana), he hired himself out for wages or
kind. Gradually he built an economic base. "If we have luck we will
soon have a nice start," he wrote to his father in 1830. "I hav had to
work out for all the wheat we got since we come hear and for a cow and
calf and other things or I wood been out of money before now wich keep
me back in giting my farm open." Still McCutcheon managed to cut
three thousand rails and put nine acres in corn and one-half acre in flax.
He also had two cows and two calves.

> I had got a nice stock of hogs but last winter when the snow was on the
> ground twelve of my best that I allowed to kill this fall got into my
> clearing where I was burning logs and brush and got all burnt to death
> but fore and they got so scorcht that they had done no good since—that
> instead of having poark to sell I will hardly have what will doo me.[12]

11. Edwardsville *Spectator*, July 10, 1819, reprinted in its entirety in the Brookville *Enquirer*, Sept. 10, 1819. This is a good example of how information was transmitted on
the frontier, where newspapers traditionally copied from one another.
12. William McCutcheon to his father, Aug. 13, 1830, William McCutcheon Letters, ISL.
Cf. another reaction in Charles Lamb's essay on roast pig.

Like other early settlers on even the most remote frontiers, Mc-Cutcheon sought something to sell. "The principal object pursued at this time, is to raise a crop of corn and a great number of hogs, which embraces almost entirely the whole surplus of the country," noted the editor of the Evansville *Gazette* in a comment that summarized the economy of the western country in this early period.[13] The buyers and the means of transportation were more varied. For the first half a dozen years incoming immigrants might provide a strong market for corn, meat, livestock to start their own herds—for almost all products. Eventually, however, production outstripped the capacity of new arrivals to absorb it, and given the widespread availability of land, every new immigrant was likely to be a producer within a few years. The way to a larger market was, initially at least, by water, to the small towns downstream, thence to the market ports on the Ohio and Mississippi or to New Orleans itself.

The steamboat was a potential revolution in the life of western commerce. Steam navigation had first appeared on the western waters with the voyage of the steamboat *New Orleans* from Pittsburgh to New Orleans in 1811. After the war other vessels and trips quickly established steam transportation on western rivers. The response was euphoric. "Who could or would have dared to conjecture, that in 1819, we would have witnessed the arrival of a steam-boat from Philadelphia and New York," exclaimed the editor of the *Missouri Gazette*. "Yet such is the case." In spite of the outward enthusiasm, the influence of steam navigation on the western waters spread slowly—at least for the first decade. Steamboats plied their trade along the major waters of the trans-Appalachian West, especially the Ohio, Mississippi, Kentucky, Tennessee, and later along the Tombigbee and Alabama, where their captains and owners found the safest passage, thickest settlements, and largest profits. They did not penetrate to the remote frontiers. Nor did they appear in large numbers. Seventeen steamboats engaged in western commerce in 1817. Three years later the figure had risen to sixty-nine, but this was a modest number to serve the more than two million people found west of the mountains by the census takers in 1820. Competition for service was, accordingly, intense and foreshadowed that for railroads half a century later. Not all communities succeeded. As late as 1824, for

13. Evansville *Gazette*, Jan. 21, 1824.

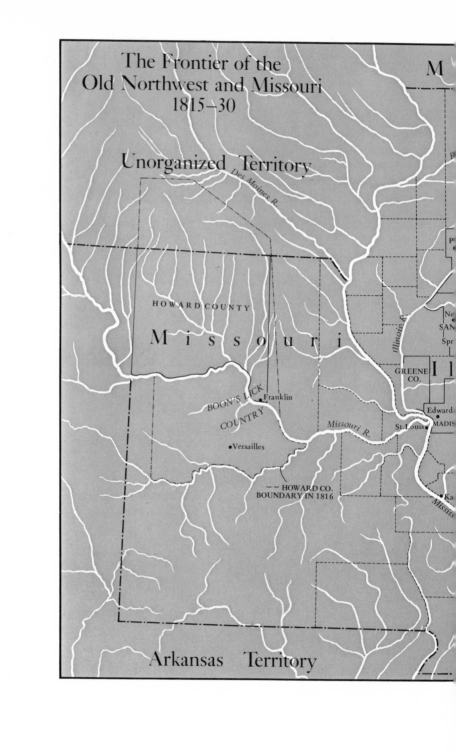

The Frontier of the
Old Northwest and Missouri
1815–30

M

Unorganized Territory

Des Moines R.

HOWARD COUNTY

Missouri

Illinois R.

GREENE
CO.

Ne
SAN
Spr

I 1

BOON'S LICK
COUNTRY

Franklin

Edward

MADIS

Missouri R.

St. Louis

•Versailles

– – HOWARD CO.
BOUNDARY IN 1816

Ka

Messes

Arkansas Territory

example, the refusal of steamboats to stop was a source of bitter complaint at Evansville (Indiana). With revived prosperity of the 1820's, steamboats expanded in numbers and geography. Enterprising captains ventured up distant rivers, and the arrival of the steamboat became a bench mark in the advance of the frontier: to Terre Haute in Indiana in 1823; Lafayette, 1826; Spencer, 1828; and to Peoria in Illinois in 1830.[14]

Much of the growing commerce of the frontier went downriver by flatboat and keelboat. These were suitable conveyances for people with small quantities of western produce and little capital. Some men flatboated for a living. Archibald Shaw's father floated produce on a flatboat from Switzerland County (Indiana) to New Orleans. Business was so good that he continued the voyages annually until 1820. Early settlers on the Lamotte Prairie in Crawford County (Illinois) built flatboats and sent them by way of the Wabash River to New Orleans. The principal crop was corn, but the flats also carried sides of bacon, honey, and butter. The venture was often a cooperative one, with several families joining together. On the return trip overland the pioneers would bring sugar, coffee, molasses, and endless stories of adventures from the outside world. The tributaries of the Ohio were also routes to the interior for ambitious traders with strong backs, or the means to employ strong backs, and up the streams went keelboats loaded with goods for the interior. As early as the spring of 1821 a keelboat reached the new town of Indianapolis on the White River, where it took off a load of corn. In the early 1820's perhaps as many as three thousand flatboats floated down the Ohio each year, a figure suggestive of the search for a cash market, the demand for agricultural produce in the South, and the rising importance of New Orleans as a world port.[15]

Facilities for transportation by land developed more slowly. Almost all so-called roads in the western country were poor and inadequately maintained by county supervisors. They were heavily used (this was one of the problems) by immigrants moving north away from the rivers. They were also used for communication, but not usually for the movement of bulk commodities, at least not where alternative water transportation was available. Politicians and editors, not to mention merchants and

14. St. Louis *Missouri Gazette*, May 19, 1819; Evansville *Gazette*, Feb. 11, 1824; George Rogers Taylor, *The Transportation Revolution, 1815–1860* (New York, 1951), 63–67.
15. Archibald Shaw, "Autobiography," ISL; Finch, "Reminiscences"; Francis S. Philbrick, *The Rise of the West, 1754–1830* (New York, 1965), 314–15.

farmers, talked constantly of the need for better roads. With the accelerated movement of population north, the need became more pressing. By 1830 pioneers had penetrated far into the interior of the Old Northwest and settled on lands distant from water transportation. The establishment of state capitals at Indianapolis and Springfield, both inland from the Ohio River, increased the necessity of better overland routes. Roads of a kind gradually connected the settlements on the White, Ohio, and Wabash rivers. Illinois lagged somewhat behind, although there were roads running Shawneetown–Kaskaskia–St. Louis and, later, a track from Vandalia to the Sangamon country.[16]

The commercial world of postwar America was more complex—even in the western country—than that of an earlier generation. It brought forth forms and occupations in proportion to its more complicated needs. Among the new economic enterprises that appeared were a large transportation industry, with boat builders, pilots, and a new waterfront world. Some of the most thriving of the auxiliaries were merchants. Like the multiplicity of frontier experiences, these came in various forms. Some were merchant capitalists, incipient bankers who borrowed and lent on a grand scale; others were middlemen in the rising agricultural trade from frontier to market; still another group was content to keep a store at the crossroads. All came in great numbers. When the English traveller Thomas Hulme passed through the village of Princeton (Indiana) in 1818, he was astounded by the large herds of hogs in the countryside and the large number of merchants in the town. "I was sorry to see very little doing in this town. They cannot *all* keep stores and taverns!" he wrote in his journal. "One of the storekeepers told me he does not sell more than ten thousand dollars value per annum: he ought, then, to manufacture something, and not spend nine-tenths of his time lolling with a segar in his mouth." According to reports, however, storekeeping was profitable. The larger numbers of people, the spread of commercial agriculture, and new transportation facilities gave an assurance of trade that John May, Lardner Clark, and other merchants of the previous generation lacked. From the beginning of settlement, the new pioneers bought something, and as their funds expanded with trade opportunities (and sometimes without), so did their appetites for "eastern goods."

16. Two studies of road construction with excellent maps are Nell Holland Ramey, "History of Early Roads in Illinois" (M.A., Illinois, 1948); and Virginia Lowell Mauck, "Population Movements in Northern Indiana before 1850" (M.A., Indiana, 1948).

Those with funds to invest acted on this opportunity. T. V. Denny wrote in 1818 that the immigrant to the western country could "make a good profit in a small store." John Reynolds, later governor of Illinois, used his profits from land speculations to buy two dry goods stores.[17]

Moses U. Payne of Versailles (Missouri) was one of the many small-town merchants. He traded with small agriculturists, and his business style reflected not so much his own desires as their condition. From time to time he received cash payments, but most of his sales were on credit. When (and if) his customers squared their accounts, it was largely in produce. In 1814, for example, Payne accepted in payment sewing thread, skins, bacon, flour, one shoat, beef, potatoes, turnips, meal, and wood. One affluent client left funds to the sum of $552 on deposit at the store, making Payne something of a banker. In general, the scope of his business was safe, small, and secure in spite of occasional nonpayments. His location in a town also provided him with certain creature comforts and the advantages of an urban society.[18]

Some ambitious merchants went out to the remote new villages. They trekked or poled up the Illinois, the upper Wabash, or into the Boon's Lick settlements. Elijah Iles went to the Sangamon country. In 1823, finding a stake in the ground to mark the site of a town named Springfield, he determined to exploit the region's commercial possibilities. Iles made arrangements for the construction of a storehouse "to be set near the stake, eighteen feet square, with sheds on the sides for shelter." He then set out for St. Louis, where he bought a large supply of goods. Chartering a boat, he shipped his cargo up the Illinois to the mouth of the Sangamon. "The boat was towed up the river by five men walking on shore and pulling a tow line about three hundred feet long," he wrote. The crew dumped Iles and his store of goods at the mouth of the Sangamon, in the middle of the wilderness, fifty miles from the site of Springfield. Iles left his goods stacked by the river: "As no one lived near, I had no fear of thieves." He walked through the marshy ground to

17. Thomas Hulme, "Journal of a Tour in the Western Countries of America . . . ," in Reuben Gold Thwaites, ed., *Early Western Travels, 1748–1846* (32 vols., Cleveland, 1904–07), 10: 46; T. V. Denny to Christopher Denny, Jan. 24, 1818, Denny Letters. Reynolds's career as entrepreneur is analyzed in Josephine L. Harper, "John Reynolds, 'The Old Ranger' of Illinois, 1788–1865" (Ph.D., Illinois, 1949), chs. 2 and 3.

18. Mary Alice Kennedy, "Business Career of Moses U. Payne, 1828–1870" (M.A., Missouri, 1944), 1–3. A general account with emphasis on a later period is Lewis E. Atherton, *The Frontier Merchant in Mid-America* (rev. ed., Columbia, Mo., 1971).

Springfield, where he hired wagons and teams to carry his twenty-five tons of cargo to the village. His was the first store in Springfield and probably one of the first buildings. In the first few years he was without competition and traded about as much with Indians as with settlers. He later wrote, "My customers were widely and thinly scattered over the territory," an area subsequently organized into fourteen counties. "Many had to come more than eighty miles to trade," he went on. "They were poor, and their purchases very light." The town of Springfield grew up around the store. Business increased rapidly with the growth of population, especially after the first land sales in 1823. Like other prosperous merchants, Iles bought land and, through careful management, developed a thriving farm. In his case, as others, merchants appeared together with or even before farmers.[19]

Large-scale entrepreneurs like Iles performed a number of services for their growing communities. They served as financial institutions on the frontier—combining the duties of storekeeper, exporter, and banker. Their contributions to the development of urban life were also noteworthy, especially in the areas of legal, governmental, religious, educational, and cultural affairs. Trade thrives on settled, stable conditions, and merchants worked energetically toward these ends. They often stayed on to grow up with the community and the surrounding countryside.

In addition to small-scale merchants in town and entrepreneurs on the edge of the newly settled lands there were traders even farther out on the frontier—beyond agriculture, at least initially. The Chouteaus of St. Louis belonged to this group, so did the Ewings of Ft. Wayne (Indiana). Locating at an important portage site between the Maumee and Wabash rivers, the Ewings directed their early trade to the surrounding Indian peoples. As the Indians began to depart in the mid-1820's, the Ewing brothers moved into a variety of other economic ventures: land purchases and speculation, livestock for sale to migrating Indian tribes, and transportation of goods and various services connected with the economic development of the region. With the arrival of the agricultural pioneers, the Ewings offered many of the services of bankers: credit and a circulating medium, loans for land purchases. As commission agents they were also

19. Elijah Iles, *Sketches of Early Life and Times in Kentucky Missouri and Illinois* (Springfield, 1863), 23–24. The nature of the business in the more prosperous period may be examined in Iles's General Merchandise Acct Book, no. 1: 1824–26, ISHL.

much in demand. To the extent that the area around Ft. Wayne could be said to have experienced economic development beyond subsistence agriculture in this period, the Ewings were a moving force behind it.[20]

With the increasing complexity of frontier economic life came a need for banks, and in the years after the war banks expanded out into the frontier almost as rapidly as people. In 1818, a generation removed from Marietta, Ohio had twenty-eight chartered banks to serve its large population and maturing economy. The legislature of the Indiana Territory chartered two banks in 1814—at Vincennes and Madison—and permitted two additional private banks of issue. A territorial law of 1815 even granted rights of note issue to individuals. In the period from 1816 to 1818 the Illinois legislature chartered banks at Shawneetown, Edwardsville, Kaskaskia, and Cairo. The territory of Missouri had an incorporated bank as early as 1813. This listing reflects only the beginning of western banking that expanded by leaps and bound up to 1819, and far more slowly and carefully in the 1820's. These banks shared certain basic characteristics. Generally they were in urban centers, and the sites of banks in Indiana, Illinois, and Missouri provide a catalogue of the most important towns in the territories and young states. Banks engaged in several economic activities to facilitate trade, including deposit, note issue, and note discount. The benefit to merchants was evident, and the spread of a banking system accompanied the spread of commercial agriculture. Speculative activities gradually dominated banking, and in the economic crisis of 1819 western banks failed disastrously. The sense of outrage left by this experience would emerge later in a warm response to the antibank views of Andrew Jackson.[21]

A massive influx of people to the frontiers of the trans-Appalachian West characterized the Great Migration. Individuals of different backgrounds, like John Finch, Edward Coles, and William McCutcheon,

20. Francis X. Brady, "W. G. and G. W. Ewing, Pioneer Mercantile Capitalists" (Ed. D., Ball State, 1965), esp. chs. 3 and 8. Bert Anson, "The Fur Traders in Northern Indiana, 1796–1850" (Ph.D., Indiana, 1953), 289–90, concludes that the merchant class of northern Indiana came from the ranks of the fur traders.

21. *Columbus Gazette*, March 20, 1818. A detailed discussion of banking, money, and finance in this period is Buley, *The Old Northwest*, vol. 1, ch. 8. Buley does not always make a distinction among the levels of economic development in the several territories and states of the Northwest. Also note Harry S. Gleick, "Banking in Early Missouri," *MHR*, 61 (1967): 427–43; 62 (1967): 30–44.

headed at different times for different places, but they were all part of the same movement. So, too, were extended families like the TenBrooks. Some, like Daniel Brush, came as part of larger communities, bound together by common values and a sense of mutual responsibility, a characteristic amply illustrated in the support Brush's family received when his father died. In their search for subsistence and shelter, all shared in the basic frontier experience that characterized the first frontiers of Kentucky and Tennessee: the need to clear, plant, harvest, and prepare shelter for winter remained. This cycle of the American agricultural frontier would continue onto the Great Plains and across to the Pacific Coast in the latter half of the nineteenth century. The economic experiences of these peoples were also similar: the search for a marketable commodity and for a route to market. The rise of commercial agriculture, even for small farmers, increased the significance of the Ohio and Mississippi rivers and their navigable tributaries and the importance of water transportation generally. This trade, in turn, enlarged the numbers of merchants and the roles they performed. These various peoples created varied societies, in different times, at different places, and at different stages of development.

The diversity of frontier life that emerged in this period contrasts sharply with the standardization of some aspects of institutional life, especially those concerned with government. From the intersection of the Ohio River and the Pennsylvania line to the Boon's Lick country, uniformity of government and law gave a continuity to frontier life. Some structure of government at the county, territorial, or state level was, by this time, universal. It was a strong and hardy pioneer who could penetrate sufficiently far into the wilderness in the 1820's to escape the reach of the county court, at least for more than a few months. The struggle over what kinds of institutions of government (and all that flows from them) to establish had taken place in an earlier generation. By 1815 it was largely over. Territorial government had successfully passed through the experimental stage and spread across the western country. Territorial or state legislatures created new counties on a regular basis. The struggle for office and the battle over the location of the county seat were an inevitable and continuing element in the frontier scene. County government stretched westward over the frontier like the rays from the rising sun—sometimes obscured by clouds or great forests, but always there. Sooner or later they would break through.

A focal point of the institutional structure of life in the western country continued to be the county court. These courts had been on the frontier of the trans-Appalachian West for more than a generation by 1815. They were universally accepted. They were also organized with great facility and speed. Even as Elijah Iles made arrangements for his store and goods and other settlers built their cabins, the Sangamon County Commissioners Court met for the first time. The initial terms dealt with matters of organization, especially the selection of a constable and clerk. Appointments and recommendations (to the governor for the office of justice of the peace) filled the pages of the court journal. The commissioners located the county seat at "a certain point in the prairie near John Kelly's field on the waters of Spring Creek at a stake marked ≠D . . . called and known by the name of Springfield." Much administrative business needed attention at the convening of the June term. The commissioners gave the job of building a jail to the lowest bidder— "Robert Hambleton at Eighty-four dollars, and seventy five cents"—to be completed by the first Monday in September. In response to the petition "of Sundry citizens of Sangamon County [who] pray for a public road runing," the court sent three commissioners, James Tewly, Stephen England, and Robert Pulliam, "to veu Said road and make report to the next term of this court." The court laid off election districts—or "precinks"—by natural boundaries (e.g., "opposite the mouth of Spring creek runing northern course between the waters of Fancy creek and Higgins Creek to the northern extream of the County including all west of Edwards old trace") and called for the election of militia officers. It also established townships and levied a tax to defray county expenses: "Horses, neat cattle wheel carriage stock in trade and distillery" to be assessed as taxable by the county assessor. By the end of 1821 the county government was established, staffed, and in operation. It now entered into a routine managing roads, orphans, county buildings, juries, and similar duties. All were necessary services to the citizens of the county, and the needs and solutions were largely the same throughout the frontier of the Old Northwest.[22]

22. Sangamon County, Commissioners Court, Record Book A, 1821–26, ISHL. A similar story is found in the Jefferson County, Commissioners Court, 1819, *ibid.* A different

The administrative structure of the county created a bureaucracy. People in growing counties needed expanded services, and the lengthening list of offices and duties brought to the fore a figure that, if not new, now appeared in larger numbers than ever before—the frontier bureaucrat. His work was not dramatic, but the citizens of his county—great and small—came to him or knew of him, and his signature and the seal of his many offices appears on thousands of documents. Amos Williams of Vermilion County (Illinois) was one such public figure. He came to Illinois in 1821 by way of Vincennes and Terre Haute and settled in Edgar County. There he surveyed and taught school—in Paris, the county seat, among other places. He also served as clerk of the county court. In 1826 he helped to organize Vermilion County and was among those who, the following year, laid out the county seat at Danville. In view of his experience in Edgar County and his prominence in early Vermilion County, Williams was a logical choice for the office of clerk of the commissioners court. Soon thereafter he became clerk of the circuit court, judge of probate court, postmaster, and county recorder. The official business of the county—with its innumerable transactions including everything from the issuing of birth certificates to the probate of wills—flowed through his hands. The documents that came across his desk needed his signature, and he collected the fees and perquisites due his many offices. In time that he could spare from official duties, Williams built a number of mills in the county. His career represents the rise of the county bureaucracy, and he had his counterpart in the many other counties organized in this period.[23]

Williams was also an example of the early frontier school teacher. Schools and schooling on the frontier functioned without large-scale institutional direction in these years. Education was still very much an individual or family enterprise. The "articles of agreement" between Williams and eleven subscribing parents read:

---

aspect of county affairs is the Greene County, Poor Book, 1824–26, also in *ibid.* An account of criminal proceedings is John Arnold, "Early History of Rush County Courts," IHS. A published account of the proceedings of the Fountain County (Indiana) circuit court (1826–30) is Harry L. McGurk, "A Pioneer Indiana County Circuit Court," *AJLH*, 15 (1971): 278–87.

23. A large quantity of materials relative to Amos Williams is in the Williams-Woodbury Collection, IHS-U. See especially "Danville at an Early Day," folder 149, and several examples of Williams's documents in folder 88.

That the said [Amos] Williams engages to teach a School in the town of Paris, Edgar County, Illinois, for the term of six months, (Saturdays excepted) at the rate of Five Dollars per scholar, one half of said sum to be paid in trade at cash prices; the other half to be paid in money.— School to commence on or before the first Monday of October next, if a sufficient number of Scholars can be had— The subscribers, on their part, engage to furnish a sufficient quantity of Firewood and keep the Schoolhouse in good repair during the above term.[24]

The early frontier societies seemed as loosely structured as the vast land over which they spread themselves. Judicial circuits were "like the young gentleman's whiskers, 'extensively laid out, but thinly settled.' " wrote Sandford Cox. Yet both land and societies came under direction from the growing institutional structure. The change was early evident in towns. Cox, who observed the transformation of Indiana's New Purchase—the large portion of central Indiana acquired from the Indians by treaty in 1818—saw "aristocracy" appear in Crawfordsville in the guise of "a new pair of silver plated spurs" and "a pair of curiously embroidered gloves." "Society is in a chaotic state," he wrote, "but the floating elements began to indicate some definite formation." Of the institutions that brought "definite formation" to the mass of pioneering humanity that was the Great Migration, Cox specifically cited law and the court system and religion and the organized church. His instincts were correct.[25]

From the first settlements some early frontier people were litigious. Petty debts and land business formed the favorite subjects for civil suits. Business from merchants alone could have supported the swarm of ambitious men who called themselves lawyers and came flocking to the new frontiers. A correspondent assured Ninian Edwards that suits brought by St. Louis merchants would maintain the lawyers in frontier Illinois. So lawyers came, began practice, settled in, and perhaps married advantageously.[26] One of the most important activities of the frontier lawyer was riding circuit with the judge, for the neophyte legal man must go

24. Articles of agreement dated Aug. 21, 1824, Williams-Woodbury Collection, folder 88.
25. Sandford C. Cox, *Recollections of the Early Settlement of the Wabash Valley* (Lafayette, Ind., 1860), 19.
26. Daniel Cook to Ninian Edwards, May 24, 1815, Ninian Edwards Papers, CHS. Although influential, lawyers were not universally admired. The editor of the *Indiana Gazette*, for example, accused them of placing their interests above those of the public. Corydon *Indiana Gazette*, July 17, 1819.

where cases were, and the itinerant nature of the job gave many the opportunity to test political ambitions. On court days the fledgling lawyers "mingled among the people in the court yard with an air of superiority, as they electioneered for seats in the next legislature." [27] So lawyers crisscrossed the wilderness, stopping in the ever-enlarging settlements to plead in court.

In spite of these young lawyers—and perhaps because of them—the judicial system was, in large part, the work of amateurs. Take the circuit court of Indiana as an example. The presiding judge, chosen by the legislature, was a man of legal pretension and training if not a great legal mind; the two associate judges, called "side judges," were elected by the people in each county and, by voting together, could overrule the presiding judge. This was "equity" and "local law" carried to its logical end, reaffirming that the common folk of the frontier knew as much or more about justice and equity under the law as anyone with formal legal training, especially someone from the East. The clerk of court was a local figure of importance who could presumably write a legible hand; sheriffs were chosen for strength of arm and voice. The most dramatic part of the public proceedings, however, was the young lawyer's "pleading" for his client. Oliver H. Smith has left an account of the judiciary system in early southeastern Indiana.

> All was silent as death, when the young "squire," afterward Judge Charles H. Test, arose and addressed the court: "If the court please—," He was here interrupted by Judge Mitchell from the bench, "Yes, we do please. Go to the bottom of the case, young man; the people have come in to hear the lawyers plead." The young Squire, encouraged by the kind response of the judge, proceeded to address the jury some three hours. [28]

The court was more than a judicial proceeding; it was a social-political-economic-cultural event. People came for miles around to enjoy society, witness the drama of the court, pass judgment on the learning of

---

27. Wendell Holmes Stephenson, "Amos Cane," *IMH*, 26 (1930): 182. A detailed account of lawyers practicing on the Cumberland River Circuit (Tennessee) is Daniel H. Calhoun, *Professional Lives in America: Structure and Aspiration, 1750–1850* (Cambridge, 1965), ch. 3. Howard Feigenbaum, "The Lawyer in Wisconsin, 1836–1860: A Profile," *WMH*, 55 (1971–72): 101, shows the high ratio of lawyers to the population for Wisconsin, Iowa, and Michigan in a later period.

28. Quoted in *History of Dearborn, Ohio and Switzerland Counties, Indiana* (Chicago, 1885), 115–16.

judge and bar, and consummate financial transactions. Court day was a kind of medieval market day with entertainment. The spectacle might be spontaneous and physical, in the case of the inevitable fistfight, or it might be official, in the case of the court proceedings.

Sandford Cox also wrote from the Indiana's New Purchase of the early presence of church in giving form to society. "The Baptists talk of building a small house for worship," he wrote. "The Rev. Hackaliah Vredenburg, of the Methodist denomination, preached here a few Sabbaths ago, and took incipient steps for the organization of a church, while the Presbyterians think strongly of building a college north-west of town, between Nathaniel Dunn's and the graveyard." [29] The same general observations might have been made about the trans-Appalachian frontier as a whole. The church was a vigorous force in giving form to frontier life. By this time, America's churches—principally the Protestant denominations—had prepared for the Great Migration. They spread over the frontier almost before the pioneer wagons were unloaded. If their reach and plans sometimes exceeded their financing and manpower, they nonetheless moved in an organized way to bring organized religion to the distant frontiers. Church officials and secular leaders alike believed that frontier people needed guidance on the path to law and the establishment of social order, especially in that earliest period when institutions were in the process of establishment.

Through the comment of the day runs the theme that the frontier represented great temptation for the young. The open-ended nature of the world, its opportunities to enjoy gratification in all sorts of glorious (and to some irresponsible) ways needed to be controlled. Yet the shaping institutions of church and school and the small-town standards for behavior were just in process of formation. Much attention had to be given to young people to keep them at work in a useful way, to keep them from straying to those pleasures so available on all sides, to instill in them the need to persevere like their parents, who were locked in a struggle with the land. Although temptations for idleness and enjoyment lay all around, the dangers were especially great when the subsistence period was passed. The more intangible drive toward estate building then replaced the immediate needs of shelter, food, and clothing. Young people, who were reluctant to work fourteen hours a day in the fields,

29. Cox, *Recollections of the Early Settlement of the Wabash Valley,* 16–17.

might not fully appreciate this new goal. By confirming traditional values of work and obedience, the church attempted to deal, in part, with this problem.[30]

Supporting the church in its emphasis on morality and social order were two satellite institutions, the Bible society and the Sabbath school. Both were associated with established denominations and urban areas. Bible societies appeared in conjunction with churches, ministered to the needs of adults, and had as their object the wide circulation of Bibles and other religious tracts. Sabbath schools focused on the young. Volunteer teachers guided the pupils (divided by age group) in the study of the Bible and the inculcation of moral behavior. The annual report of the Indianapolis Sabbath School noted, "The memories of many have been stored with large portions of hymns, catechism and scripture, and the knowledge of the school generally in the doctrines and precepts of the gospel greatly increased; and the seeds of religious instruction appears to have taken root in the conscience, spring up, and the field to be whitening for the harvest." Periodic public examinations or recitations might be held for the gratification of the parents. Both long- and short-range benefits accrued to the community from such institutions. Wrote one editor:

> We have heard it proclaimed that no Sabbath school scholar has ever been condemned at the bar as a criminal; we have heard of the genius that has been elicited, the tempers and habits that have been corrected, and may we not with confidence look forward to the most important mental and moral improvements with the rising generation, from the effects of this institution?[31]

The "religious character" of a community was important on the frontier, at least to a certain literate and influential class of people. The equation was direct and unmistakable: religion was morality and orderly behavior. "A few weeks ago our streets exhibited little else than intemperance and profanity," reflected an observer, "but now, so far has the scene changed that morality seems to predominate in every quarter, through the day, and at night the sounds of prayer, praise, and the

30. Hamlin Garland's *Boy Life on the Prairie* (1899), an autobiographical account of a childhood on a farm in northwest Iowa, describes the conflict between play and work. Garland recounts the joys of the prairie—horseback riding, fishing, swimming, hunting, or even hiking—and his bitter resentment at the seemingly endless repetitive field labor imposed on him, beginning at about the age of ten.

31. Indianapolis *Indiana Journal*, May 3, 1825; see also April 10, 1827. The Corydon *Indiana Gazette*, March 14, 1822, speaks of a Sunday school for "people of Color."

shouts of the new born souls cheer the evening shades."[32] The church's strengths in this respect were twofold. First was the power and strength of the Lord, and the individual's accountability to Him. "We believe that by nature we are fallen and depraved Cretures," read the Covenant of the Shale Creek Baptist Church in Bond County (Illinois). It continued, "We believe the joys of the righteous and the punishment of the wicked are Eternal." Second, the church itself acted as a check on individual misbehavior. Those who failed to attend meetings, for example, were guilty of "an offense and lay themselves liable to be reproved by the Church." Careful procedures for the mediation of disputes between and among members were also described. Throughout this period the church was a most effective device for promoting personal harmony in an atmosphere of strained relations and frequent resort to the courts.[33] With its structured hierarchy of officials and courts, the church exercised many of the functions of a government. In a region where the capacity of government to constrain behavior was sporadic, churches performed an especially important function. Most of the settlers in the period after 1815 felt that government should provide services such as protection from the Indians, roads, and mail. The church inherited the emphasis on personal conduct that had been so much a part of the early governments in Kentucky and Tennessee.

The organization and expanding influence of the church can be seen in the work of the Presbyterians. In the autumn of 1824 the Reverend Isaac Reed, minister to a church in Owen County (Indiana), received a call from the people of Edgar County (Illinois) to minister to the needs of Presbyterians there and to do missionary work under the sponsorship of the Connecticut Missionary Society. These settlers, in his words, "had been about two years there with their families, and no minister had yet found his way to their settlement." He described his enthusiastic reception in detail. For thirteen days Reed rode over the county, preaching, baptizing, burying, examining, organizing, ministering to the sick and elderly, and holding communion. At Big Raccoon Creek he found the beginnings of a church: "It was formed near three years ago, by a missionary of the General Assembly, but has no minister nor meeting

32. Corydon *Indiana Gazette*, July 31, 1819.
33. Shale Creek Baptist Church, Bond County, Minutes, 1818–1845, ISHL. A persuasive account of the influence of the circuit rider is Paul H. Boase, "Moral Policemen on the Ohio Frontier," *OHQ*, 68 (1959): 38–53.

house, nor meeting, except when a missionary comes along." At the New Hope meetinghouse, Reed preached a funeral sermon and the congregation promptly subscribed toward its publication. He organized a church at Paris, "the county seat of Edgar county, but is a very small place of about 8 cabins. It lies on the prairie." He ordained a ruling elder for each of the other churches he visited.[34]

The establishment of a church was an important milestone in the development of any community or town and was looked forward to with fervent expectation by lay promoters as well as ministers. The presence of religious institutions implied a sense of uplift and civilization that was especially gratifying to frontier areas. Their establishment was as important as the founding of a newspaper or the opening of a bank. In 1825 Rev. Reed journeyed to the infant town of Indianapolis, where he assisted in the installation of George Bush as minister of the Presbyterian Church. The editor of the *Indiana Journal* gave the event extensive coverage, for he viewed the ordination as a bench mark for Indianapolis and its citizens.

> This is understood to be the first Presbyterian Ordinance which has taken place in this state. And, when it is considered that but little more than three and a half years have elapsed since the first foot of land was sold in this or any adjoining county; and that, while other denominations exist in this town and are supplied with regular preaching, the Presbyterian Congregation has for more than a year and a half enjoyed the stated labours of a resident clergyman, and have erected a meeting house, and that a Sabbath School has been in operation here nearly two years, it is somewhat encouraging towards the future religious character of Indianapolis.[35]

With the strong influence of the church and its obvious importance to the western country, matters of doctrine now became increasingly significant. Differences of opinion between and even within denominations

34. Ira Allen, "Early Presbyterianism in East Central Illinois," *JISHS*, 9 (1916–17): 136–43. A similar experience in establishing a church is Franklin D. Scott, ed., "Minutes of the Session of the First Presbyterian Church in Morgan County, 1827–1830," *JISHS*, 18 (1925–26): 142–51. Reed's astonishment at the spiritual poverty of these people contrasts sharply with the account of a Methodist circuit rider, who ministered to scattered congregations on a regular basis. Note, for example, the career of Elihu Springer, as reflected in his letters and diary, ISHL.
35. Indianapolis *Indiana Journal*, March 8, 1825. The account states simply that "the Rev. Mr. Reed gave a suitable charge to the people." I have assumed that it is the same Rev. Reed who travelled through Edgar County.

were a continuing part of life on the new frontier after 1815. Men fought with great determination over abstract theological questions, for to them their salvation depended on such matters. It was no longer necessary simply to minister to the new settlements; the ministry must be doctrinally sound. To be a Methodist no longer sufficed: the new question was, What kind of Methodist? "For several years between 1810 and 1820," Allen Wiley later wrote,

> there was a most fierce and unpleasant controversy among Methodist preachers, concerning infant purity on the one hand, and innate depravity on the other. The preachers and people of the present day [1845] can form no estimation of the asperity of feeling and language which prevailed in those days of bitter waters, even among good men and able ministers. When I look back, it seems to me little less than a miracle that the church was not rent into a thousand fragments.[36]

The cold statistics of population, crops, and churches do not sufficiently convey either the force of numbers or the complete and total commitment of those who went to the frontier during the Great Migration. Behind every Fourth of July oration on the doctrines of growth and progress were individuals and families who took the land, placed it under cultivation, and had faith that this new experience (for all its uncertainties and mysteries) would be better than what they left behind. This generation of frontier peoples represented a high point of faith and self-confidence in the new nation and the new country west of the mountains. The second war for Independence was behind; the Civil War was not yet a cloud in the sky of limitless horizons. Expectations for the future knew no bounds. The land was good and plentiful. The institutions were as perfect as man could make them. Not even the financial crisis of 1819 could mar the basic optimism of the people. They were confident that hard work would make them independent freeholders, the ultimate de-

36. Allen Wiley, "Methodism in Southeastern Indiana," *IMH*, 23 (1927): 134. Wiley's accounts were originally published in the *Western Christian Advocate* in 1846. For the various aspects of religious institution building on the frontier in the period from 1815 to 1830, a basic starting point is Buley, *The Old Northwest*, vol. 2, ch. 14. Also note Leslie Gamblin Hill, "A Moral Crusade: The Influence of Protestantism on Frontier Society in Missouri," *MHR*, 45 (1950): 16–34. Among the best unpublished studies are Elmer Clarence Sandmeyer, "Methodism in Illinois before 1850" (M.A., Illinois, 1924); and Marion Lola Chapman, "The Establishment of Methodism in Central Illinois (1824–1840)" (M.A., Illinois, 1929).

sire of every agriculturist: to have and to hold land, forever, for himself
and his heirs. Little wonder that the virtues of political liberty and Jefferson's independent yeoman farmer held the center of the stage. Never
had the land been richer; never was there so much of it; never was the
future brighter.

8

The Flowering of
the Cotton Frontier

The Great Migration that began in 1815 was a national phenomenon, and the frontier south of the Ohio experienced the same rush of immigration that occurred to the north. Among the reasons for this movement were a postwar readjustment that impelled Americans to pull up roots and begin life anew elsewhere and the enlarged opportunities for commerical agriculture. Some forces were peculiar to the South. Two hundred years of tobacco culture had depleted the lands of the Upper South, especially in Virginia and the Carolinas. Military successes against the Indian tribes of the South in the recent war opened up vast tracts for American settlement, and the impulse to settle these new lands now sent the agriculturists of the Upper South to the frontier of the Southwest. They brought with them capital and a well-established social and economic system emphasizing staple crops, slave labor, and commercial agriculture. The frontier south of the Ohio—stretching from Louisville to New Orleans, from Alabama Territory to the distant reaches of the state of Louisiana—differed from that of the north. Within this vast area emerged a series of societies with great differences among them, and, at the same time, striking similarities.

In the nineteenth century, Americans lived closer to the land. They spoke and wrote about differences in land and climate and felt that these differences literally shaped people, societies, and institutions.[1] Land and

1. Southern literary figures from John Pendleton Kennedy to William Faulkner have emphasized the distinctive shape and texture of the land and the attachment of southerners

climate impressed upon the southern frontier two significant influences that shaped institutions, societies, and even people: cotton and slavery. Cotton was grown on some southern frontiers before 1812—most notably in the Natchez District, in Madison County on the Great Bend of the Tennessee, and in the river parishes in Louisiana. Conditions following the peace made its cultivation and marketing almost universal. The demands of the English mills seemed unlimited. The price of short staple cotton on the New Orleans market doubled within a year and reached nearly thirty cents a pound before 1819. New strains of cotton, more resistant to drought and disease, increased production. Cotton was not the only crop grown in the South after the war, but it became a standard of economic and social success. Slave labor admirably supplemented cotton cultivation. The institution of slavery, firmly established along the seaboard by tobacco culture in the seventeenth and rice in the eighteenth centuries, received new life from cotton and sugar in the nineteenth. The price of slaves rose accordingly, and the Great Migration to the Southwest after 1815 included white and black, moving side by side, the one coming to take the land, the other to work it in bondage. Both cotton and slavery were a part of the new frontier from the very beginning. They were as universal as the corn crop north of the Ohio. They also produced, almost from the first, a homogeneous and, at the same time, a sharply differentiated society: homogeneous in its interests, agricultural orientation, and the homeland of its immigrants; sharply divided by distinctions of wealth and quality of life evident almost from the earliest settlements and by the basic contrast between slavery and freedom.[2]

---

to it, as Faulkner did, for example, in "The Bear" in *Go Down Moses* (1942). In the 1930's a prominent literary movement of Southerners surfaced, and its declaration of principle, *I'll Take My Stand: The South and the Agrarian Tradition*, by Twelve Southerners (New York, 1930), was a restatement of the agrarian values associated with the South. W. J. Cash's *The Mind of the South* (New York, 1941), is an interpretation of the South that also emphasizes the land and its climate.

2. The South as a distinctive section has been a continuing theme from the beginning of serious attempts to describe and interpret America's past. It was perhaps first identified by Henry Adams in the introduction to his *History of the United States of America during the Administrations of Jefferson and Madison* (9 vols., New York, 1891–98). In recent times the most prominent interpreter of the southern experience is C. Vann Woodward, whose *Burden of Southern History* (Baton Rouge, 1960) is a capsule exposition of his views. John Hope Franklin's *Militant South* (Cambridge, 1956) emphasizes the violent aspects of southern life. The most recent scholarship has concentrated on slavery as a key to the history and character of the antebellum South.

Cotton needed more than improved strains and slave labor. It also required large quantities of land. In the period after 1815 the frontier South benefited from a government land system in full operation and ready to place vast tracts of land on the market. This it did, especially in 1817 and 1818. The efficiency of the government in surveying and selling the public domain assisted the spread of the cotton kingdom after 1815. Transportation facilities were also vital, for cotton bales were heavy. Thus the steamboat was the major means of transportation in the cotton South and the symbol of its prosperity. Docks appeared along the major southern watercourses, giving the frontier South the appearance of a tropical Venice. No town could hope to survive and grow without regular steamboat service. The arrival of the first steamboat was cause for rejoicing, with a holiday (at least one) and a dinner for the captain and crew, complete with solemn toasts to the prosperity of the region and the partnership between commerce and agriculture.

The Great Migration to the South made a different pattern on this frontier. North of the Ohio, the Indians were either gone or in process of removal, at least where they were adjacent to settlement. The stream of immigration resembled rising floodwaters moving up river valleys, lapping at the hills, sometimes flooding the lowland prairies, moving with watercourses—always tied to the configuration of the land. On the southern frontier the presence of large and powerful Indian tribes across the breadth of the region compartmentalized immigration. This is not to say that settlers respected Indian treaty rights, but in the face of Indian strength as represented by the Creeks and Cherokees in Alabama and the Choctaws in Mississippi, white pioneers moved into Indian country at considerable risk. Few men with capital to invest proposed to venture it under such circumstances, especially when large quantities of vacant and fertile land with good title were available elsewhere. The frontier of the South was not a continuing line constantly moving west under the impact of successive waves of new settlers but, before 1815, several widely separated centers of settlement: the Natchez region; eastern and central Tennessee around Knoxville and Nashville; Huntsville and Madison County in Alabama; the Mississippi and Red River valleys within Louisiana; and, to a somewhat lesser degree, the east Louisiana parishes and the settlements of the lower Tombigbee and Alabama rivers. The areas occupied in the period from 1815 to 1830 were also separated from one another and closely associated with Indian cessions: the Alabama Black

Belt, a crescent-shaped tract through the central part of the state, its urban center at Montgomery (acquired from the Indians at Andrew Jackson's Creek Cession in 1814); the west-central portion of Mississippi, from the river halfway across the state, centered in Jackson (Treaty of Doak's Stand in 1820); the western third of the state of Tennessee, with its economic center at Memphis, a northward extension of the cotton kingdom (Chickasaw Cession of 1818, also associated with Andrew Jackson).[3]

One other characteristic of the southern frontier was its vigorous interest in international affairs, or, to be more precise, affairs that directly affected the South. There were several. The seizure of the port of Mobile in 1812 was an important event for the American settlers on the Alabama and Tombigbee rivers. Its retention after the war—the only lasting territorial conquest of the War of 1812—gave central Alabama a direct access to the sea. Activities along the Florida boundary and the eventual purchase of Florida from Spain in 1819 played a significant part in the settlement and economic growth of the South. Aside from the potential of the land, the disappearance of foreign influence among the several Indian tribes—remarked upon by all those concerned with the frontier—was an important preliminary step to Indian removal. Interest in expansion later found expression in Texas, reaching a high level of intensity at the periods of revolution (1835–36) and annexation (1844–45).

The remarkable speed of immigration, the large numbers of people involved from 1815 to 1820, and the slow but steady pace for the next decade brought together varieties of people to settle the new frontiers, people differing in wealth and social status, but united by interest in agriculture. The increase in population, its expansion over new lands, and the economic force of staple crops (especially cotton) involved varied geographic areas of the frontier South. This was the flowering of the cotton frontier.

The Treaty of Ghent put people in motion to the Southwest by the spring of 1815, and a year later immigration had reached flood tide,

3. The relationship between the land system, Indian cessions, and transportation on the southern frontier after 1815 is examined in Malcolm J. Rohrbough, *The Land Office Business: The Settlement and Administration of American Public Lands, 1789–1837* (New York, 1968), chs. 5 and 6.

especially to the Alabama country. A North Carolina planter described the force of this impulse to move in these terms:

> The *Alabama Feaver* rages here with great violence and has *carried off* vast numbers of our Citizens. I am apprehensive, if it continues to spread as it has done, it will almost depopulate the country. There is no question that this *feaver* is contagious . . . for as soon as one neighbour visits another who has just returned from the Alabama he immediately discovers the same symptoms which are exhibited by the person who has seen the allureing Alabama. Some of our oldest and most wealthy men are offering their possessions for sale and desirous of removing to this new country.[4]

New lands were the object of immigrants, young and old, affluent and poor, especially those tracts seized from the Indians in 1814 and 1816. They surpassed anything ever seen before in richness, fertility, and quantity, or so it was said. Robert Woods wrote to John Hale in 1817 about the agricultural potential of the Alabama Territory. It had "the greatest prospect of corn and cotton I ever saw," he boasted. "Why will you stay in franklin and work them poor stony ridges when one half of the labor and one third of the ground heare will bring you more and not a stone nor hill in the way."[5] It was a sentiment echoed in numerous letters from the New Country to the Old.

The movement of people in the South assumed a form, a direction, even a force, that would in time make the Southwest more South than West. The immigration to western Tennessee, central Mississippi, and backlands of Louisiana and Alabama involved more than the opening of new lands. It involved the transmission—virtually intact—of a civilization, a set of values, and an economic and social system. It was, in short, the conveyance of the plantation system from Virginia, the Carolinas, and coastal Georgia to Mississippi, Alabama, and western Tennessee. Well-to-do planters of the Upper South sold their holdings, often lands worn thin by generations of tobacco croppings and poor management, and moved to the rich, black, cane-covered lands on the frontier. Not everyone who came was a planter, of course, but many were. And the planter class was a symbol of a new frontier society. It set the economic

4. James Graham to Thomas Ruffin, Nov. 9, 1817, in Ruffin, *The Papers of Thomas Ruffin*, ed. J. G. de Roulhac Hamilton (4 vols., Raleigh, 1918–20), 1: 198.
5. Robert Woods to John Hale, June 11, 1817, Bensen Family Papers, LSU. Woods eventually settled in Perry County (Alabama), one of the most attractive agricultural sites in the new purchase.

and social tone of the newly occupied areas. Large-scale cultivation of cotton with slave labor, open-handed hospitality, a genteel education for the children, perhaps winters in Charleston, Mobile, or even Saratoga, these were the aspirations of the time. They were to become, in large part, the goals of the new frontier of the Southwest.

The Taits of Georgia were among the prosperous families who immigrated to eastern Mississippi (the Alabama Territory after 1817). Charles Tait was a political and legal figure of the first rank, who served as judge of the superior court for the western district of Georgia (1803–09) and as United States senator for Georgia (1809–19). His brother, James Tait, a planter, was the first to move. He wrote Charles in 1817 of the exodus, "Thus you perceive the present inhabitants are moving off [to the Alabama Territory]. I hope to follow in the autumn of next year and that you will bring up the rear the year after." James Tait intended to take with him to the Alabama Territory three slaves, "whom together with some young men I shall get in that country, will I hope, make corn enough for my family the next year." He moved early the following year. The slaves constructed a shelter for the Tait family and immediately began to prepare the land for cultivation. Although Charles Tait remained in Washington, D.C., ties between the brothers remained strong. James wrote to Charles in February 1818:

> I am lost to reflect on the vast differences that exist between your situation and my own. I in my humble cabin on cane creek, entirely alone, in a wilderness, write these few lines to one who is in the centre of every thing that is the result of a well organized and dense population. You engaged in the noble business of legislating for a great nation, I in the obscure one of preparing a few acres for the cultivation of indian corn.[6]

Yet James Tait's letter pointed up not so much the contrast between the two scenes as the connection. The people who made up the Great Migration to the Southwest after 1815 were, many of them, joined to the political, economic, and social elite of the Upper South by ties of kinship, and soon by similar interests. In 1819 Charles Tait left Georgia to become a planter and federal judge in Monroe County (Alabama). He transferred his wealth and prestige to his newly adopted state; he also

6. James Tait to Charles Tait, Nov. 10, Dec. 15, 1817; Feb. 7, 1818, Charles Tait and Family Papers, ADAH.

left behind a host of influential friends, whose good offices might be
called upon for the benefit of the new state of Alabama.[7]

The career of Israel Pickens is another case in point. Pickens was a
North Carolinian who served three terms in Congress. He found the at-
tractions of Alabama compelling, and to his father-in-law, Major William
B. Lenoir, he confided "my intention to take a route next summer westward & southwardly. I am perfectly convinced it will be in my interest
as at presently circumstanced to move somewhere in the new country."
In his baggage he carried a commission as register of the land office at St.
Stephens, tangible evidence of his influence with officials in Washington.
Pickens wrote enthusiastically of the lands in Alabama: "My place of
farming is on a large canebrake tract in the sunflower bend of the Tom-
beckbe River, 18 miles below St. Stephens, the largest body of high rich
& unbroken bottom land I have heard of in either of these rivers." He
bought heavily at the land sales. Other planter capitalists like him did
the same. Newcomers like the Taits and the Pickenses—people of economic and social substance—engaged in spirited competition for Alabama land. The volume of sales and prices reached unheard-of levels in
1818 and 1819.[8]

The speed with which cotton might catapult the frontiersman of the
Southwest into the world of commercial agriculture was a striking feature of the postwar cotton frontier. The acceleration of the frontier experience was built around large tracts of fertile lands, slave labor, and a
ready market for cotton. No sooner had slaves raised shelter for black
and white families and put the first corn crop in the ground than they
began extensive clearing of the virgin lands. In the five weeks between
mid-December and January, Israel Pickens's hands cleared one hundred
acres. Pickens so reported to Lenoir, adding, "Nothing remains to com-
pleat the clearing than to set fire to the cut cane which leaves the whole
an ash bed."[9] The next spring the crop of the large-scale frontier planter

7. John Perry Cochran, "James Asbury Tait and His Plantations" (M.A., Alabama, 1951),
   notes that on August 6, 1819, Charles and James Tait purchased at the St. Stephens
   land office 10,247.15 acres of land (pp. 9–15), of which they subsequently sold very
   little. James Asbury was the son of Charles. Charles Hill Moffat, "The Life of Charles
   Tait" (Ph.D., Vanderbilt, 1946), ch. 4, also emphasizes group migration.
8. Israel Pickens to William B. Lenoir, July 29, 1816, Israel Pickens Papers, ADAH;
   Pickens to Lenoir, Jan. 12, 1819, William B. Lenoir Papers, Special Collections, UT.
   On the presence of men of means at the sales of public lands in Alabama Territory, see
   Rohrbough, *The Land Office Business*, 118–22.
9. Pickens to Lenoir, Jan. 18, 1819, Pickens Papers.

was not corn but cotton. The staple might even be planted in the first growing season. That autumn, wagons which the year before had carried the planter and his extended family to the frontier carried baled cotton to the nearest watercourse, where it was floated downstream to market. A man who stood in a wilderness fewer than twelve months ago now stood at a dock watching his crop load out for the English factory towns. The frontiersman was already a part of a commercial economy. The incentive to cultivate cotton was high. In the postwar years short staple cotton fetched record-breaking prices in all the South's Atlantic seaports; it was the most valuable agricultural staple of the day. The planter returned with the luxury commodities that the prosperous times entitled him to and eager merchants insisted that he take. Cotton made it possible for a man to hang a crystal chandelier in his frontier log cabin. Most likely he resisted the temptation, opting instead for more slaves, new lands, and a bit of finery for his wife.

The cotton frontier of the Southwest was not composed solely of plantation squires and their slaves. There were also thousands of small-scale farmers who came to work the land. They grew corn and cotton and raised herds of cattle. Sometimes they had a few slaves; often they did not. When they did, they probably worked in the fields alongside their blacks. They could generally be found in the hillier portions of the cotton frontier—farther from the rich, expensive lands of the valleys and more distant from the seaboard markets. Pleading for preference in purchasing by pre-emption, some early Alabama settlers of Montgomery County described themselves as having "settled our selves in the poor Broken & remote parts of the Alabama Territory Montgomery County being generally of the poorer Class we doubted Success in Settling in the richer Soil below."[10] Some members of this group were making the upward transition to the economic and social status of a plantation society. Others were simply holding their own. These smaller farmers could be found almost everywhere on the cotton frontier—from Natchez on the Mississippi to Montgomery on the Alabama. These were not people who had failed. Accounts emphasize their wide-ranging talents, intelligence, and integrity. An early chronicler wrote of the early development of St. Clair County (Alabama), located in what he called "the best lands in the mountainous region of the state." "In its early history we

10. Petition to Congress by the Inhabitants of Montgomery County, Dec. 29, 1817, in *TP*, 18: 225.

had but few stores, and schools and churches were of slow growth," he recounted. William Cather spoke of the small farmers in glowing terms. People worked the soil with a fierce independence, and their wants were few and practical. Agriculture was commercial: "The products of the country were carried in wagons to Tuscaloose and Wetumpka, or on flat boats down the Coosa River." The farmers of St. Clair County did not capture the imagination like the planter civilization, but they were an important part of the cotton frontier.[11]

A third group lived a transient life by hunting, fishing, and trading on a more sparsely settled land where a claim and a few improvements could be purchased for little. The over-riding characteristic of this frontier was its transitory and unstructured nature. What dominated life was not so much the reality of the current situation as the vision of the next one. The best water, the most luxuriant grasses, the riches soil, the fattest and most abundant game lay just across the next ridge or river. What seemed to distinguish these transients from the planters was not ability—for some of the accounts suggest people of great talents—but the high value placed on endless independence, far removed from association with institutions of permanence and responsibility for conforming to and maintaining them. These people penetrated into the woods and clearings before the surveyors, often trespassing on Indian land; later, after survey and sale, they retreated up the valleys into the hills. They were not especially articulate or verbal, but the surviving records show substantial numbers of people in the backcountry of the Carolinas, Georgia, and Tennessee, drifting south and west to the newly opened lands of Alabama and Mississippi.

The Lincecum family were of these people. Gideon Lincecum and his father embodied the pioneer spirit and its transition to a more institution-oriented world, all in one family and in the space of a few years. Gideon Lincecum was born in a log cabin on the Georgia frontier in 1793. His mother was just sixteen. Gideon's father was a border transient who moved every two or three years to a new situation, "being naturally of a restless disposition," in the words of his son. Gideon later wrote, "My father loved a border life." The principal family crops were

11. "A Brief Historical Sketch of St. Clair County," William H. Cather Collection, ADAH. These small-scale farmers and graziers are the focus of Frank L. Owsley, "The Pattern of Migration and Settlement on the Southern Frontier," *JSH*, 11 (1945): 147–76.

children and corn. The Lincecums also grew cotton, which brought a high price at any market, and cotton crops financed their migrations. Gideon grew up a free spirit in the woods, except at cotton harvesting time, when, he remembered, "everyone that could pick five pounds a day was forced into the cotton fields." He was untouched by religion. He entered his first schoolhouse at the age of fourteen, to discover that he had missed some things in life: "I began in the alphabet. There were some very small boys, seven years old, who could read." Gideon attacked learning with the same vigorous determination with which he tracked a deer in the woods, and, blessed with aptitude, he progressed. At the end of five months (when his father moved again), "I could read, the master said, 'very well,' could write a pretty fair hand by a copy, had progressed in the arithmetic to the double root of three, and had committed Webster's spelling book entirely to memory, besides many pieces of poetry which the teacher gave me for night lessons." It was a substantial frontier education, and all done in one season. Gideon graduated to a man's world of work. He carried the chain for a surveyor, clerked in a store, served as county tax collector, and, as his principal occupation, farmed with his father.

In 1815 Gideon Lincecum, age twenty-two, a man grown and recently married, as fully educated as the frontier allowed, experienced the postwar restlessness that moved so many. He described the state of his preparation for the Great Migration in these terms: "I was as strong as two common men and could do anything from cutting and splitting fence rails to fine cabinet work. And in mercantile action was familiar with all the duties from the lumber house to the counting room. I could mix drugs and practice medicine as far as it was known in the interior of the country in those days." His crop was good and cotton already $.31½ a pound, "but I became restless and did not feel like staying in that country until the crop could be gathered." His father also felt the urge to be on the move once more. "The Alabama, Black Warrior, Tombeckbee, and Chattahoochee countries had all been acquired by conquest," Gideon later wrote, "and I was determined to seek a home in the wilderness." After a year on the Ocmulgee, where Gideon taught school and farmed, the Lincecums—father, son, and extended families—moved again. Gideon commented of the prospect, "I had been reared to a belief and faith in the pleasure of frequent change of country, and I looked upon the long journey, through the wilderness, with much pleasure." In the spring of 1818 the caravan rolled into Tuscaloosa (Alabama), "at that time a small log cabin village; but people from Tennessee were arriving daily, and in the course of that year it grew to be a considerable town." A year there and his father discovered a wilder, less settled country on the upper Tombigbee. "His description of the dark, heavy forests, the wide thick canebrakes, and the clear running river, full of fish put me into a perfect transport," recalled the son. Since no road ran through this perfect wilderness, a certain amount of cutting and construction was necessary, especially at the river banks. After twelve days the Lincecums crossed the Tombigbee and settled near the future site of Columbus (Mississippi), where Gideon remarked, in the frontier tradition, that "we felt ourselves fully competent for the emergency."

It was in Columbus that Gideon began his gradual transition to a more permanent life style, built around the economic and social advantages offered by the institutions of the day. Initially he built a house for his family. Then he turned to the forest. Gradually he reduced the canebrakes that pressed almost up to the door of the cabin and planted a crop of corn. His only agricultural tool was "a sharp stick." No sooner was the house up and the corn in the ground than he began to cast about for other opportunities. The most attractive was the government's road—in reality a track—from Nashville to Natchez. Where it crossed the Tombigbee, Gideon saw the prospect of a town and trade. He purchased trade goods, "in three days had knocked up a pretty good shanty," and opened a store. Most of his early customers were Indians, who "had heard of the arrival of a great supply of nice new goods and plenty of liquors, and they flocked in by hundreds." Gideon had no scruples about selling whiskey to the Indians; he sold them anything they could pay for. This isolated portion of the new state of Mississippi was slow in organizing: "We were there 18 months before we saw an officer of any kind." Eventually the legislature laid out Monroe County. Gideon was a leader in organizing the new county. He wrote of his role:

> I first appointed four other country justices and a county clerk, called a meeting, organized a county court and proceeded to appoint and commission the rest of the county officers. Everybody wanted office; and I found it a very difficult duty to get through with. I finally succeeded; and then turned my attention to surveying the town, and regulating all the school lands in the county. I also had to superintend the erection of two—male and female—academies. . . .
> Holding the courts, appointing the officers, surveying the town lots,

appointing and regulating school commissioners at town, and all the other school sections in the county, procuring teachers, engaging workmen for the academies and opening the mail six times a week, consumed so much of my time, that my own business was badly neglected.

Gideon formed a partnership with a Choctaw that gave him a large share of the lucrative Indian trade. While his business prospered—initially at least—the Lincecums were in poor health. Fevers of various kinds forced Gideon to move to "the hill country" above Cotton Gin Port, where he recovered. At the same time, his mercantile business suffered. After a short tour with a "company of ball players in the Cherokee Nation," Gideon went into the practice of medicine and drugs. At last he prospered, for many who came to the country in the Great Migration found it as unhealthy as he had in earlier years. This sickness, which had so plagued the Lincecum family, became the basis of his prosperity.[12]

Gideon Lincecum's story was another part of the Great Migration into the new cotton frontier. He was a border transient who loved the free and easy life of the wilderness. The men of the Lincecum family were hunters, traders, merchants, entrepreneurs, artisans, and farmers. They were skillful with tools and in the woods. Yet Gideon was not indifferent to money; he spent much time and effort on all sorts of money-making schemes. He saw the need for institutions and led in organizing Monroe County, with its county court and school system. He even helped to lay out the town. He moved back to Columbus—at considerable risk to his health—in order that his six children might have an opportunity to attend the schools that he organized. In these interests and achievements, Gideon differed from his father. Whether the change represents a new kind of frontier people participating in the economy of the Great Migration and the creation of a new society, or simply differences between individuals, is not clear. What we do know is that in spite of his wanderings, Gideon was anxious to seize the economic advantage of the new cotton frontier and to participate, at least in part, in the greater opportunities that it afforded.

The increase of population, its movement over new lands, and the economic force of new staple crops took place throughout the frontier

---

12. This account is based on Gideon Lincecum, "Autobiography of Gideon Lincecum," *Publications of the Mississippi Historical Society*, 8 (1904): 443–519; the long quotation is from pp. 474–75.

South, but the figures for Alabama in particular stand out (see table 3). The lands of Andrew Jackson's Indian cessions (1814 and 1816), opening up the central two-thirds of Alabama, were especially attractive for the cultivation of cotton, and circumstances came together in the right proportion to promote their settlement and cultivation. The first areas taken up were the river valleys—especially the Alabama, Cahaba, Coosa, and Tallapoosa—where rich soil might be found in combination with water transportation. The high percentage of slaves in the river valley counties as early as 1818 testifies to the establishment of staple crop agriculture within a few years of their settlement. Immigrants rapidly occupied and

Table 3. Growth of the Southwest, 1810–30

	1810	1820	1830
Alabama	9,046	127,901	309,527
Mississippi	31,306	75,448	130,621
Louisiana	76,556	153,407	215,739
Tennessee	261,727	422,823	681,904

Source: *Historical Statistics of the United States, Colonial Times to 1957* (Washington, 1960), 13.

placed under cultivation the Tennessee River counties. Land seekers considered the hillier portions less desirable and overlooked, too, the poorly drained black prairies that would later become known as the Black Belt. Settlements in eastern Mississippi also concentrated around the rivers, east and west. Steamboats reached Columbus on the upper Tombigbee soon after 1821, and the village became a center for the cotton trade. In the western part of the state search for cotton lands carried people east from Natchez to the piney woods and north to the Indian cession lines.[13]

In the decade of the 1820's the cotton cultivation of postwar America

13. Thomas P. Abernethy, *The Formative Period in Alabama, 1815–1828* (Montgomery, 1922), ch. 7. A general discussion of the Great Migration may be found in Abernethy, *The South in the New Nation, 1789–1819* (Baton Rouge, 1961), ch. 16. Nell Angela Heidelberg, "The Frontier in Mississippi" (M.A., Louisiana State, 1940), ch. 5, is superior to, but less accessible than, Charles D. Lowery, "The Great Migration to the Mississippi Territory, 1789–1819," *JMH*, 30 (1968): 173–92.

firmly consolidated its position as a dominant force in the life of the southern frontier. Part of this development lay in the continued occupation and cultivation—albeit at a slower rate—of those areas in central Alabama opened immediately after the war. This was, in short, a repetition of previous patterns of settlement and cultivation and marketing, now associated with new areas. The most important of these was the Black Belt of Alabama with its extension into Mississippi. The first settlers had ignored the wet, flatlands in favor of wooded river valleys. Stretching across the center of the state from Montgomery County in a south and westerly direction to the Choctaw Indian reservation on the Mississippi boundary, the Black Belt filled rapidly in the 1820's. It presented a number of new problems, such as how to drain and cultivate the thick black clay, and it raised the issue of internal improvements to move the heavy crops of cotton to market. Cotton cultivation reached its height in the Black Belt. The region absorbed capital and slave labor and, in turn, began producing cotton in large quantities. Like other agricultural areas of Alabama and Mississippi, land, slaves, and especially cotton became the dominant topics of the day.

The cotton frontier included several other parts of the South. Cotton exercised a powerful influence in the settlement and economic development of western Tennessee. Geography and cycles of settlement divided the state of Tennessee into three distinct regions: the mountains and valleys of the east, centered at Knoxville; the fertile limestone lands of the center, with an economic and social focal point at Nashville; the western third of the state, occupied by Indian tribes and without white inhabitants as late as 1815. The Chickasaw Cession of 1818 opened most of western Tennessee to settlement. The population of the Western District (as it came to be called) grew rapidly. In 1820 it was probably about twenty-five hundred people; by 1830, close to one hundred thousand. Between 1819 and 1823 the legislature laid off fourteen new counties to mark this influx of people. The Western District was long dependent upon water transportation, with the Tennessee River and its tributaries to the east and the Mississippi River and its tributaries to the west providing avenues for immigration and commerce. The pioneering experience was typical in its struggles and isolation, but relatively short. The first important urban center was Jackson (county seat of Madison County), laid out in 1822. At the sale of the town's lots, the record showed that "Joseph Lynn was allowed $20.00 for whiskey furnished to

The Frontier of the
Cotton Kingdom, 1815–30

Louis

Illinois

Indiana

•Louisville   •Lexington

Kentucky

Cumberland R.

WEAK-
LEY
CO.

•Nashville

CARROLL
CO.

Tennessee

Knoxville•

Jackson
•
MADISON

•Memphis

MADISON CO.
•Huntsville
•Madison

Decatur•

CHEROKEE

CHICKASAW

MONROE•

LOWNDES•
•Columbus

Black Warrior R.

ST.
CLAIR

Coosa R.

CHOCKTAW

•Tuscaloosa

Cahaba R.

CREEK

Talapoosa R.

Georgia

Mississippi

Tombigbee R.

PERRY
CO.

Wetumpka•

BLACK

•Montgomery
•
•Cahaba
MONTGOMERY
CO.

Jackson•

BELT

•St.Stephens

Alabama R.

MONROE

Alabama

tchez

•Blakeley
Mobile•

Florida Territory

Pearl R.

•New Orleans

Gulf of Mexico

TERREBONE
PARISH

▬▬▬▬▬▬▬ Borders of Indian Reservations
------------------ Borders of Indian Cessions
                    of 1814 and 1816

encourage bidding."[14] Agriculture was the center of economic activity. Initially corn was the basic crop, but the settlers soon turned to cotton.

The rapid occupation and growth of the cotton frontier produced a strong demand for the services provided by organized government. Whereas after the passage of the Ordinance of 1787, government (in form, at least) appeared promptly and, in the period immediately after 1815, often preceded settlement in the Old Northwest, the movement of people in the South threatened temporarily to outdistance any formal structure of government. Two forces made the question of government in Alabama pressing. The first was the enormous influx of population in the period from 1815 to 1820; the second, the decision to form a separate territory of the lands that lay in eastern Mississippi, necessitating the organization of a territorial government and innumerable new counties at precisely this period of heavy population pressure. In early 1818 the new governor of the Alabama Territory, William Bibb, wrote that in three weeks he would appoint four hundred officeholders in thirteen new counties. In some cases the governor simply sent blank commissions to the county courts in the new counties and asked some responsible official to fill in the names of suitable appointees. Officials could not organize government at the territorial or county levels rapidly enough to meet the needs of the incoming population. County militias were in a state of disarray as a result of the tumultuous and transient population. Private military organizations appeared in a manner reminiscent of early Kentucky and Tennessee. Mail service was also inadequate to the extent that at least one town, Cahaba, established a mail service financed by private subscription. A delay in the organization of the judicial district for North Alabama distressed citizens "throughout the six populous Counties," who wrote of their unhappiness that "the operation of courts of Justice have been suspended in this district for more than seven months" with the result that "creditors are unable to enforce the payment of their debts."[15]

14. Samuel Cole Williams, *Beginnings of West Tennessee, in the Land of the Chickasaws, 1541–1841* (Johnson City, 1930), 136–37, 140, 176–79, 202–04.
15. William Bibb to John Quincy Adams, Feb. 16, 1818, in *TP*, 18: 256–57; Offer of a Miltia Company, April 22, 1818, in *ibid.*, 310–11; Alexander Pope to Josiah Meigs, Sept. 3, 1819, in *ibid.*, 691; David Moore and others to John Quincy Adams, May 28, 1819, in *ibid.*, 636.

The formative period of the cotton frontier, with its highly competitive land sales, occupation of new lands, and organization of several counties, led to a widespread and continuous search for office, and at the same time, constant complaints about officeholders and the inadequacy of their performance. The new society needed mail service, roads, county courts, and all with dispatch. So men who had won out in the contest for office found themselves harshly criticized for not instantly meeting these needs—by those trying to circumvent the law and prevented from doing so, by those who felt themselves victimized by mistakes, by those who were themselves disappointed officer seekers. One correspondent wrote Alabama's governor from Tuscaloosa, a newly organized county seat in the Black Belt, "The state of society in this section of Country is such that few persons in public office, can avoid censure, however correct their conduct may be." The rapidity of the settlement process and the development of large-scale commercial agriculture focused the need for institutions like government and its auxiliary functions. Initially, at least, government was inadequate to meet these pressing needs.[16]

The new frontiers of the cotton South created unheard-of opportunities for wealth—at least for a frontier society. Wealth came in many forms: a new house with white columns and a piano, cotton receipts from the local gin and notes from a New Orleans factor, or perhaps simply land, slaves, and cash. But whatever the form, hand in hand with wealth came the need to protect it. In his opening address to the newly convened Alabama legislature, Governor Bibb affirmed that "the rights of persons and property are carefully protected."[17] The fluid frontier condition quickly gave way to a static society interested in preserving the status quo. The foremost allies of those interested in an orderly society and protection of property were the legal system and the county court. In an earlier frontier, groups of men had gathered to give order and direction to a new society. They did so largely through the strength of their own arms and public opinion. Centralized authority—at least in any form capable of bringing force to bear—was virtually unknown. By the time of the Great Migration after 1815, state and territorial governments were well established (except for the special case of Alabama), and

---

16. James O. Crump to Governor Bibb, July 28, 1818, in *TP*, 18: 386.
17. Journal of the Legislative Council, 1818, ESR, Alabama, p. 6.

central authority a strong and ever-present force. To be sure, it was rarely used. Still, it was there, in the form of the militia, federal courts, and, if necessary, the federal government itself. If social, cultural, and intellectual institutions were still in the process of development—as they were in many places in the frontier South—the same could not be said with respect to law, the court system, and institutions bearing on property.[18]

County government functioned similarly throughout the cotton frontier, as exemplified in three different areas with different histories: Alabama, reclaimed from a wilderness since the end of the war; western Tennessee, heir to a long frontier experience dating back to the first trans-Appalachian frontier; Louisiana, with its diversity of cultures and institutions. Perry County (Alabama), organized in 1819, had been settled after the war. The activities of its county court, however, are indistinguishable from those of the older counties. Officeholders appeared with the organization of the county and the five-man orphans court directed the county's affairs. Its most important duties dealt with the development of a county road system. The court also concerned itself with two ferries over the Cahaba River, regulation of prices, and licensing ministers. Like other frontier communities at this time, the first industrial activity was the construction of two mills (saw and grist), quickly followed by a cotton gin. Indeed the gin had become as necessary to this economy and civilization as the gristmill was on the first trans-Appalachian frontier two generations earlier.[19]

Unlike Alabama, Tennessee was a well-organized state by the time of the Great Migration to its western lands. Carroll and Weakley were typical new counties in the Western District. In their deliberations, judgments, and the scope of issues considered, the county courts were much like the courts of an earlier generation of frontier counties. The basic difference was in the volume of business related to economic matters. The county courts concerned themselves largely with administrative (recording) and economic affairs, and specifically probate of estates, taxes, and the recording of deeds of "bargain and sale." That the court also paid

18. Clanton Williams, "Conservatism in Old Montgomery, 1817–1861," *AR*, 10 (1957): 99–102; Bernard Cresap, "The Muscle Shoals Frontier: Early Society and Culture in Lauderdale County," *AR*, 9 (1956): 190–211.
19. Weymouth T. Jordan, "Early Ante-Bellum Marion, Alabama: A Black Belt Town," *AHQ*, 5 (1943): 14–19. Leonard Calvert Cooke, "The Development of the Road System of Alabama" (M.A., Alabama, 1935), is a detailed study.

wolf bounties testifies to its location on the edge of settlement. The most time-consuming problem was the roads. The court was constantly occupied with appointing people to view, mark, lay out, and maintain roads. Several officeholders formulated and carried out the laws of the county. In addition to justices of the peace, the roster included a county clerk, county treasurer, trustee, coroner, constable (for each militia company), and solicitor general, who presented the government case in court. Trials for assault and battery were rare, and, in the case of a conviction, the fine was generally $.12½ and costs. The less fortunate received attention and even some support. In one case, the county paid the medical fees ("medicine and attendance") for an "Inphant child" whose father was deceased. The court still bound out orphans under an apprenticeship system.[20]

The structure of state government carried into the frontier areas a system of federal and state courts. The first immigrants arrived in the area of Madison County (Tennessee) in 1818 or 1819; the legislature organized the county in 1821. At regular intervals thereafter, the authority of the state came to Madison County in the form of the Eighth Circuit Court. Some of the business was administrative, such as the certifying of sales of land and slaves. The docket always contained a number of appeals from the county courts. A grand jury met to examine the state of local affairs. In one case, it returned a presentment against a man and woman for living in adultery. The moral condition was not, however, the dominant concern; property was. Most of the cases before the court concerned debt, petty larceny, or divorce. Most of the divorce cases were uncontested, since one or another party failed to appear. The sums involved in the higher courts were larger than those at stake in the county courts, often several hundred dollars. Punishment for criminal convictions was still largely physical. Squire Dawson was presumably a man of some importance. Yet, on his conviction for "pettit larceny," the court sentenced him to "be taken from this place to the common whiping post there to receive twenty lashes well laid on his bar back, and that he be rendered infamous, and that he then be imprisoned one hour, and that he make his peace with the state by the payment of one cent."[21]

20. Carroll County, County Court, Minute Books, 1826–33, pp. 1–10, UT; Weakley County, First Minute Book, 1827–35, pp. 1–12, *ibid.*
21. Madison County, Circuit Court, Minute Book No. I, 1821–28, UT. The elected judge, Joshua Haskell, had to take an oath that he had not violated the state's antidueling law of 1819.

The police juries in Louisiana conducted similar business—roads, mail service, recording functions—as the county courts of the cotton frontier east of the Mississippi River. Like the county courts, the police juries also created road districts and appointed overseers. Instructions for road maintenance were sometimes very detailed. Drainage ditches that crossed public roads had to be bridged. There were continuing complaints about the conditions of the roads, especially those leading to market.[22] Where the parish lay on a waterway such as a river or bayou, the police jury put special emphasis on keeping the waterway clear for open access. Where waterways abounded, ferries were important and had to be licensed. There was also a continuing interest in livestock, especially its proper identification. Avoyelles Parish had a communal livestock drive, and each citizen of the parish "should contribute according to the number of horses, cattle, in furnishing one man consecutively for each eighty heads, for the purpose of bringing them out of the swamps." Parishes established slave patrols and supervised their rounds. They levied taxes according the the value of land. Taxes on taverns, grog shops, and billiard tables were universal. The police jury also kept a wary eye on the morals of the parish citizenry. The Avoyelles Parish Jury pronounced that "great injury to the Citizens of the parish and to the general police thereof has been found to arrive from the use of Billiard Tables" and placed a tax of three hundred dollars on each table. Avoyelles also controlled undesirable transients by a law which specified that "all persons found working on the banks of Bayous, Rivers, and in by-places shall be subject to be prosecuted . . . provided they do not give a satisfactory account of the manner in which they obtained Subsistence."[23]

With its many forms of wealth and its unending quest for stability, the cotton frontier was made to order for lawyers, who branched out from the practice of law into land speculation, banking, and other forms of economic enterprise. From Alabama Territory, Israel Pickens catalogued the economic affairs of one planter-lawyer on the new cotton frontier: "My [land] office though troublesome is a convenient matter in point of revenue. . . . The whole compensation is about $3000 per annum—the

22. Alexandria *Louisiana Herald*, July 29, 1820; Jan. 21, 1825.
23. Terrebonne Parish, Police Jury Minutes, April 6–Nov. 1, 1822; Lafayette Parish, Police Jury Minutes, June 3–Sept. 9, 1823; Avoyelles Parish, Police Jury Minutes, June 5, 1821–Aug. 31, 1822, LSU.

small sallary as president of the [Tombigbee] Bank, & my few Courts yield some thing in addition, so that with a little contrivance, & land trade, I am scuppling along." All of these enterprises were, of course, in addition to Pickens's principal occupation as a planter. John Williams Walker of Alabama was politician, jurist, and land speculator. Charles Tait was a planter who also served as a judge. Most of the leading lawyers of the day still styled themselves "planters." Men such as these dominated the statehood convention in Alabama—Walker was its presiding officer—and it is not surprising that the constitutions of these states reflected the political principles and legal ingenuity of some of the South's foremost lawyers.[24]

The cotton frontier also gave rise to several early industries. There were numerous sites for dams, which were used for cotton gins, sawmills, gristmills, flour mills, and wool carding, cotton spinning, and weaving factories. Even infant industries, however, required an integration of several elements—labor force, capital, and markets—that taxed the capacity of this early frontier world. The first cotton factories of Madison County (Alabama) manufactured yarn that settlers wove and knitted at home. The exchange was at the barter level. When Horatio Jones, one of the early entrepreneurs in northern Alabama, located on the Flint River, he arranged for a carpenter to construct a factory and dam of wood for $813 on credit. It was an appropriate start for an economic enterprise that would depend much on credit in the years to come. Jones had the support of the local populace, who backed him with loans, supplies, and accepted his notes. To spin his cotton yarn, Jones hired slave girls. He exchanged spun yarn for seed cotton or baled ginned cotton. His commission was ten percent. Little cash changed hands. Jones sold his yarn in the towns of Huntsville, Madison, and Decatur, and even did some business as far away as Lexington (Kentucky). The delicate economic balance that depended on the goodwill of his neighbors vanished with his untimely death in 1825.[25]

24. Pickens to Lenoir, July 10, 1819, Pickens Papers; Hugh C. Bailey, *John Williams Walker: A Study in the Political, Social and Cultural Life of the Old Southwest* (University, Ala., 1964), 95–96, 169. A case study of a lawyer who immigrated to Alabama from Vermont in 1816 is William H. Brantley, Jr., "Henry Hitchcock of Mobile, 1816–1839," *AR*, 5 (1952): 3–39.
25. In this account, I have relied on James William Bragg, "Frontier Entrepreneurs of Madison County, Alabama: The Bell Factory Enterprise, 1819–1842" (M.A., Alabama, 1958). This is an excellent thesis, characterized by imaginative use of manu-

In this same period, the rapid transition from subsistence to commercial economy called for larger and more complex financial arrangements. Banks soon appeared on the cotton frontier, as early as 1818 in Alabama. Initially founders designed them to provide loans for purchases of public lands, but the international cotton market, of which the region was soon a part, created other needs. The planter in central Alabama or Mississippi had financial transactions with one or more merchants in New Orleans or Mobile. He or his agent sold his cotton in Liverpool or New York, from whence came receipts and notes. From the cities of the North and Europe came the goods and luxuries that he purchased, and sometimes he bought foodstuffs from the Ohio Valley. Remittances to and from all these areas had to be provided for. Merchants took on expanded duties as factors. Banks had additional functions to perform, and while the economic panic in 1819 showed the weakness of banks, it did nothing to eliminate their usefulness. Banks became a political issue as well as the institution of a more complex economy. Struggles ensued over their chartering and management. In short, frontier communities found themselves embroiled in the banking issue and in need of banks, or at least some of the services that banks could provide. This concentration of economic authority in banks ran parallel to the rise of the cotton frontier after 1815, with its ever-enlarging assets of lands and slaves.[26]

In trying to assess the quality of life and the kind of civilization that emerged on the new cotton frontier, one must bear in mind the need to get behind later stereotypes. Although cotton as a market crop dominated this frontier experience, for many planters the returns in these first years were modest—a house of logs or wood sawed on the plantation, minimal social activity, maximum time in the fields. Nor was the social and economic force of cotton agriculture uniformly established. Large numbers of small, independent farmers and more traditional frontiersmen like Gideon Lincecum existed side by side with planters, and in a style of living that was not much different. This was a frontier of abun-

---

script sources. Another aspect of manufacturing enterprise is discussed in John A. Eisterhold, "Lumber and Trade in the Lower Mississippi Valley and New Orleans, 1800–1860," *LH*, 13 (1972): 72–76.

26. See, for example, William H. Brantley, *Banking in Alabama, 1816–1860* (2 vols., Birmingham, 1961), 1: 3–51.

dance—with game, fish, trade, with the wilderness still standing tall in many places—and abundant potential.

The large slave population did not share in the generally high expectation of the cotton frontier. But perhaps this silent mass of people—more than thirty percent of the population in many counties—also had a sense of expectation. Did hacking a plantation out of a wilderness provide greater freedom and opportunity than cultivating endless fields of cotton? Did the felling of trees and the raising of shelter—the more unstructured life of the formative period—provide expectations for the future that died in the heat of endless annual growing seasons? The records are silent on this subject. The black men and women in bondage on the frontier left few accounts. Yet their presence lies everywhere over the cotton frontier—in the advertisements for runaways that dominate the local papers, in the concern of local government for patrols and their effectiveness, in the occasional rumor of a rebellion. Information is always indirect, but it is there. And in a sense, of course, it was this vast, silent, omnipresent labor force that made the cotton frontier a frontier of high expectations. The expectations were based, at least in part, on the projected work that the slave would do over a lifetime of bondage.[27]

In at least one sense, this frontier was much like that experienced by the earlier generation of the Kentucky and Ohio Valley settlers. It was a frontier of activity. People were still engaged in subduing the wilderness and in turning it to their own benefit. Or, in the case of people like Gideon Lincecum, they remained in the wilderness and enjoyed it. The net effect was the same. These were not introspective people. They had no doubt about where they wished to go, what they wished to do, or the world they hoped to create. The gentle arts were as low on the priority list of this frontier as any other. Religion could be more easily experienced than in the earlier generations, for the organized churches had prepared to minister to the needs of the frontier. Generally speaking, people wanted a religion that met social needs (especially for women and children), emphasized the teachings of the Bible as a basis for salvation, and preserved the good order of society.

Schooling reflected the diversification of the cotton frontier. For the majority of school-aged children there were no facilities. Schooling was

27. A useful statistical compilation of the numbers of blacks in selected counties on the trans-Appalachian frontier is James Edward Davis, "Demographic Characteristics of the American Frontier, 1800–1840" (Ph.D., Michigan, 1971), ch. 5.

available on a subscription basis to those who contracted with a teacher. The school Gideon Lincecum entered at the age of fourteen was run by an itinerant teacher with a family, who "made up a school, which was to be kept in a little old log cabin, a mile and a half from our home. Father entered my sister, brother and me as day scholars at the rate of $7.00 each per annum." The school day ran "from an hour by sun in the morning to an hour by sun in the evening." The term lasted five months. Scholars recited on a first-come, first-served basis, and between recitations children studied their lessons aloud. The schoolroom was always a torrent of noise. Gideon later taught school, and the character of his class was probably representative of the frontier: "There were forty-five pupils—fifteen grown young men, five of them married, five grown young ladies, and boys and girls of all sizes and ages to make up the forty-five. All entered for the full term." The curriculum was "reading, writing, and arithmetic." [28]

At the other end of the educational (and economic) scale were the large number of private academies. These emphasized a classical education and social niceties, especially for young ladies. Such educational institutions were especially common in towns, where a concentration of population might ensure a clientele. Miss Campbell's school for young ladies in Mobile provided a traditional curriculum and a genteel educational philosophy:

> the Instruction of Young Ladies in Reading, Writing, Grammar, arithematic, Geography, the first principles of Astronomy, natural and civil history, composition, drawing and music, with embroidery, map work, satin-work, marking, and various other branches of useful ornamental Needle-Work.
>
> The principal advantages of this Institution will consist in providing Young Ladies with a liberal and solid education—in drawing the attention of such pursuits as are lasting and useful as well as elegant and ornamental—in substituting the more important acquirements of the mind in lieu of the frivolous pursuits which engage the time and talents of the majority of the rising generation. [29]

For the dominant white population, the cotton frontier was generally a frontier of abundance, security, and high expectation. Everything was available in quantities to sustain life. Even at its lowest price in 1825 and

28. Lincecum, "Autobiography," 455–56, 459.
29. Blakeley *Sun*, Feb. 2, 1819.

1826 cotton sustained hopes for the future. Such expectations sometimes led to a strong interest in the quality of life. Thus, as early as 1820, Charles Tait could identify the split personality of the new cotton frontier. Of a friend, he wrote, "He wants to plant 200 acres. He will I dare say get rich, but what is this miserable task without consideration; without refined society; without intellectual pleasures.—But some will say give me the Pudding and you may have the empty praise."[30] Tait had been in Alabama for three crucial years, during which it had passed through the territorial period into statehood. Nowhere was the force of the cotton frontier more powerful. The vision of culture and an elegant society was large and real, but it had not yet replaced the search for economic gratification.

The cotton frontier was several societies in pursuit of a single agricultural staple, cotton. A planter society put its stamp on institutions and was served by the courts, lawyers, law codes, slave codes, patrols, and banks, but this is not to say that the interests of this group diverged from other less affluent agriculturalists. The central themes everywhere were land, slaves, and cotton. The leaders of the South at the time celebrated an allegiance to the land since echoed by later southern writers and politicians. And the land meant cotton. The cotton frontier carried the prospect of great wealth and offered a vision of the same kind of bonanza that would later drive dusty men across deserts and into impenetrable mountains. The difference was the permanence of the land and the rising acceptance of land as a social force. The land was always there. If the frontier experience for two generations from 1815 to 1850 was one of expectations and high spirits, none were higher than in the South after 1815. This instinct for land provided the basis for the legend that "cotton was king" and confidently led those who devoutly believed this into their own exercise in nation building. Here was the beginning, often in modest circumstances, but a beginning nonetheless. So amidst the enduring forces of land and cotton we find much diversity: large-scale planters like the Taits and the Pickenses; small agriculturists like Robert Woods; wandering border entrepreneurs like Lincecum. All gave the South a distinctive flavor. All were present at the flowering of the cotton frontier.

30. Charles Tait to John Williams Walker, Jan. 5, 1820, John Williams Walker Papers, ADAH.

IV

The Enduring Frontiers

The Great Migration that began in 1815 was a frontier experience of high expectation: of landownership, not tenancy; of wealth, not subsistence; of security, not uncertainty. It was the immigration of a confident people, buoyed by success in war, secure from the Indian, moving forward to take up the promised land. In the midst of these rapid and dramatic changes three widely separated geographic areas remained outside the range of movement and economic prosperity. These were the Michigan peninsulas, organized as a territory in 1805; Florida, with settlements dating from the middle of the sixteenth century, purchased from Spain in 1819, and created a territory in 1821; and the broad expanse between Louisiana and Missouri organized as Arkansas Territory in 1819. Theirs were experiences removed from the mainstream of development in the western country after 1815. Their remoteness, plus the slow pace of growth, gave the frontier condition a lasting character. These were, in truth, enduring frontiers.

In spite of their diverse geography, the three territories shared many similar characteristics. One was isolation. The frontier experience of the postwar years came to be associated with a contiguously linked agricultural frontier that moved across the land from east to west in a series of waves. The mass immigration of people after 1815 submerged the several islands of existing settlement. Much wilderness remained, however, and the vastness of the land was still a powerful influence in many places, specifically the new political creations of Michigan, Arkansas, and

Florida. Here the early frontier experience of Kentucky and the North-west Territory was repeated. The frontier condition always implied a degree of physical isolation, but few frontiers were as remote as these three territories. Facilities for communication and transportation were central needs of these areas, for only through tapping the mainstreams of immigration and the dominant routes of trade could these distant territories become part of the expanding western country. But the new steam navigation spread across the frontier unevenly, and steam transportation was least available in areas that required it most.

Another shared aspect of the enduring frontiers was their continuing association with the American Indian. Since the first settlements in Kentucky in 1775, relations with the Indians had been a central concern. The War of 1812 seemed to resolve the Indian question, and a decline of concern over the Indian was a characteristic of the Great Migration after 1815. The Indian remained a dominant force on the enduring frontiers, however, his power enhanced by the scattered nature of the American settlements and their limited resources. Indian affairs were an important topic of official correspondence and added to the demands made on the federal government. Michigan was especially sensitive on this point because of her recent war experience. Florida's population was too small in numbers and influence to demand and enforce the removal of her resident Indians. Arkansas actually became the object of Indian immigration for tribes displaced from east of the Mississippi.

The demands imposed by isolation, transportation and communication requirements, and Indians were increasingly transmitted to the federal government. This circumstance emphasized once again the importance of political boundaries on the frontier. The frontier condition knew only natural boundaries, but the meeting of these demands lay in the force of government, and government had precise boundaries. A region with organized government was in a position to ameliorate the problems of its citizens. In the Great Migration of the postwar years the numbers and energy of sheer mass immigration tended to dilute the significance of the national government throughout much of the western country. But on the enduring frontiers of Michigan, Florida, and Arkansas, the United States government remained the paramount force in solving the many problems associated with the frontier condition. It was a contradiction of the changing and varying frontier scene that the more distant and remote the frontier, the more it came to depend on a central authority. To government at all levels went a constant stream of appeals for assistance, and, as the needs became larger, they were passed upward. To the county government went requests for roads, bridges, and maintenance for both; to the territory, petitions for assistance in supporting schools and in constructing public buildings, like jails and courthouses; to the federal government, appeals for road networks to connect the remote settlements of the territory and to prepare for new immigrants, demands for the removal of the Indians and for improvements in rivers and harbors, and complaints about the mail service.

A principal outgrowth of this dependent condition was the enlarged importance of the machinery of government in the territories. Officeholders were the intermediaries who passed on the numerous requests for assistance drawn up by the citizens of the territory. This condition had the effect of centralizing authority in the hands of a few. The growth of the territory depended much on the energy and vision of the governor, who was also the center of patronage and appointments. The territorial delegate, too, exercised great authority because of his presence in Washington, where he was responsible for presenting the pleas of the territory for assistance. The press was essential to give a sense of identity and to promote the image of the territory in the outside world, but there was seldom support for more than one territorial paper. Only with official patronage in the form of contracts to print laws and the proceedings of the territorial legislature could an editor, often his own printer, survive. So the editor joined that select group of men who directed the destinies of the territory. In view of the concentration of authority, it is not surprising that the territories became the centers of political disputes in the late 1820's. Political factions appeared, fought, dissolved, reformed, and continued the struggle for preferment at every level and at every opportunity. The search for appointment was as avid and unceasing as in any part of the Republic, the more so on the enduring frontiers where opportunities for economic advancement seemed fewer.

Institutional forms expanded across the western country after 1815, and the enduring frontiers had their share. The territorial legislatures of Michigan, Florida, and Arkansas filled their journals with solemn deliberations and laws—many laws, in fact laws that the territory scarcely yet required. The legislatures laid off counties, and the governor appointed officials to preside over virtually uninhabited wilderness. In these new counties officeholders almost outnumbered other citizens. Perhaps these counties assisted a few distant people; perhaps they were only to make jobs for officeholders. In any case, county making outstripped settlement. Officeholders, court systems, and a legal structure expanded across hundreds of miles of trackless forest, prairie, and swamp. The experience of the enduring frontiers showed that institutions and institutional development spread over these areas regardless of population and even need. In providing for rapid institutional development, the people on the enduring frontiers followed the example of the mainstream of the Great Migration.

9

Michigan:
The Great Lakes Frontier

Michigan had a long settlement experience. Founded in 1701 to serve the fur trade, Detroit became a British possession under the Treaty of Paris in 1763 and, after prolonged negotiations, American in 1796. The region's routine organization as Michigan Territory in 1805 little affected its character as a French fur-trading post. Nothing in its heretofore largely placid existence—not even Pontiac's uprising—prepared it for the War of 1812. Its strategic location on the Great Lakes and its proximity to British Canada made Michigan—especially the area around Detroit— the cockpit of that conflict. Nowhere on the continent did the armies (by frontier standards, at least, they were armies) march and countermarch with such regularity. Nowhere was physical devastation so complete as in the crescent of land around the western end of Lake Erie. Nowhere was the war fought with so much personal vindictiveness, fueled by the decision of both sides to use Indian allies. The troops who had lived off the countryside physically devastated the land; energetic army commanders stripped it by their endless requisitions; the Indians who had been used as auxiliaries in a war they little understood plundered what remained. The war disrupted the fur trade and left many of the territory's people in a condition close to starvation.[1]

The people of Michigan survived, but the infant territory (infant in

---

1. On the condition of Michigan at the close of the war, see Judge Augustus B. Woodward to James Monroe, March 5, 1815, in *TP*, 10: 513.

population, not in age or size) faced formidable problems, some natural and others self-inflicted. Of the natural obstacles, the foremost was location. The traveller William Darby commented, "Detroit, politically and commercially, is separated by an expanse of water, and by an uncultivated waste, from the other part of the United States, and remains, together with the little community in its environs, an isolated moral mass, having few sympathies in common, and but a slight tie of interest to unite it to the sovereignty of which it forms a part."[2] This condition became the more obvious after 1815 as population poured down the Ohio and into other parts of the Old Northwest, but not into Michigan. Michigan's vast area—extending from Lake Erie to the Mississippi River—lay far to the north of the natural immigration route down the Ohio River. To the southeast, at the mouth of the Maumee River, the well-known Black Swamp isolated the territory from the state of Ohio. In 1815 no road connected Michigan with the growing American settlements to the south. Lines of communication, such as they were, ran through the Great Lakes to western New York State.

Michigan emerged from the war with its government a dictatorship. Military needs had been paramount throughout the war; the territory was almost continually in a state of crisis; decisions in the form of military orders were the logical—some would have said the only—way to meet such exigencies. For the next fifteen years Michigan provided a case study in the power of one man to shape a frontier and its society. The future of the territory rested in the hands of its governor, Lewis Cass. He was a most fortunate choice. Like Arthur St. Clair of the Northwest Territory in an earlier generation, Cass was a strong nationalist who believed in the authority of government to deal with a wide range of problems; like William Henry Harrison of Indiana, Cass was young and ambitious. Lewis Cass was a general when he became governor of the territory in 1813. His was a military rule and, after 1815, in many ways a military reconstruction. His leadership as civil executive was strong and energetic in accordance with his military experience. Indeed, he thought of Michigan's needs in a military framework: supplies for the hungry and indigent, force and negotiation in proper proportion to deal

2. William Darby, *A Tour from the City of New York, to Detroit* (New York, 1819), 188.

with the Indian presence, a watchful correctness in relations with the nearby English whom he suspected of dark designs, roads to Ohio and the interior of the territory and ships on the Great Lakes to open communication with the rest of the nation, the survey and sale of the public lands. Cass set about rebuilding the territory, and military considerations entered forcefully into decisions. The object of his plans would be large-scale immigration of American agriculturists to settle and cultivate the lands, to provide a ready source of military strength, and to make Michigan truly American in the sense in which Cass understood the term.

The governor immediately made himself the principal spokesman for the territory, and, as such, he issued innumerable public pronouncements on the physical attractions of Michigan and the virtue of its citizens. In 1817 Cass persuaded John P. Sheldon to establish a newspaper, and the Detroit *Gazette* carried out this role for the territory. The governor actively campaigned for the rapid survey of Michigan's public lands and their immediate sale, for he felt that only such sales would bring the agricultural population that the territory so desperately needed. Cass constantly negotiated with the Indians. Among the results of his labors were two major treaties: the Treaty of Saginaw (1819), which extinguished Indian claims to the east central portion of the territory, and the Chicago Treaty (1821), which did the same for the western portion of the Lower Peninsula south of the Grand River. At the same time, Cass used the Indian presence to keep garrisons of federal troops stationed in the territory, where they provided a welcome economic stimulus. He also employed the troops to construct roads, arguing that this work was necessary to the national defense.

Of Cass's activities, none was more important than the struggle for effective transportation and communication. Michigan's small population was widely dispersed. Most of the people lay around Detroit in an arc south to the Raisin River, but other smaller settlements were at Mackinac in the far north; at Green Bay, on the far side of Lake Michigan; at Prairie du Chien, at the intersection of the Wisconsin and Mississippi rivers. The task of providing regular communication with these distant parts in order to carry on the business of government was enormous. Cass discovered this himself in 1820, when he took his first tour of the distant reaches of the territory. He was gone three months and covered five thousand miles, mostly in a canoe. The vigorous efforts of Cass, the support of the Congress, and the work of the army constructed a road from Detroit to the Ohio line, finally linking Michigan to the Union in 1827. Cass completed Michigan's road network with the Territorial Road from Detroit to St. Joseph on Lake Michigan by way of the Kalamazoo Valley (begun in 1829) and the so-called Chicago Road (completed in 1832) from Detroit to Chicago, which opened up central Michigan for the land rush of the 1830's.[3]

The postwar revolution of transportation on the trans-Appalachian frontier was not on land but on water, and its principal agent was steam. On August 27, 1818, the steamship *Walk-in-the-Water*, some forty-four hours out of Buffalo, anchored in Detroit harbor. The age of steam had come to Michigan and with it, presumably, the transformation of the territory.[4] But if the revolution was at hand, it was destined to be a gradual, not a precipitous, change. Inland from Detroit harbor the birchbark canoe remained the means of travel; on the lakes it was the durham boat. In 1820, when sixty-nine steamboats served the rivers of the western country, only one served the frontier of the Great Lakes. The season for navigating the Great Lakes was a short one, the risks high, and the good ship *Walk-in-the-Water* remained alone. There was no sudden proliferation of steam navigation on the lakes. In late 1821 a heavy storm beached this sole harbinger of the modern world. A new ship, the *Superior*, was ready by the next season with *Walk-in-the-Water*'s salvaged engine, but she also sailed alone.[5]

Governor Cass vigorously promoted the economic development of the territory, which meant the transition from a fur-trading economy to agriculture and, as rapidly as possible, to commercial agriculture. As economic life began anew in 1815, the French *anciens habitants* were almost the only farmers. The territory needed aggressive economic activity, and

3. Lewis Cass to John C. Calhoun, Oct. 21, 1820, in *TP*, 11: 65–69, is an account of the governor's trip. On road construction in Michigan Territory, see R. Carlyle Buley, *The Old Northwest: Pioneer Period, 1815–1840* (2 vols., Indianapolis, 1950), 1: 456–58. An excellent example of the influence of an important road on the settlement patterns is a map "Showing the influence of Chicago road on settlement in Branch Co.," in George Newman Fuller, *Economic and Social Beginnings of Michigan: A Study of the Settlement of the Lower Peninsula during the Territorial Period, 1805–1837* (Lansing, 1916), lxii.
4. Ecstatic welcomes of the vessel are in the Detroit *Gazette*, Aug. 14, 28, 1818.
5. Floyd R. Dain, *Every House a Frontier: Detroit's Economic Progress, 1815–1825* (Detroit, 1956), 34–40. On the western steamboat, see George Rogers Taylor, *The Transportation Revolution, 1815–1860* (New York, 1951), 63–67.

Michigan's public officials had little sympathy for the passive, communal life style of the French. In Cass's view the French farmers were as indolent as their fur-trading ancestors, and their agriculture lacked a scientific basis. Cass concluded, "Until therefore a radical change shall have taken place in the manners & customs of the people of this Territory, or until a migration into it shall have changed the character of its population and added to its moral strength and physical resources, we shall have a number of indigent helpless people."[6] The Americans at last arrived, but they were slow to bring about the agricultural transformation of the territory. They cleared and cultivated, but they also traded, trapped, hunted, and, in short, made no rapid changes in the economic patterns of Michigan. In early 1818 the *Gazette* described the economic condition of the territory in these terms: "Agriculture, that true and invariable source of wealth, exempt from destructibility, has been altogether neglected. We have a town with (comparatively) no country —a very considerable trade, and instead of exporting country produce, we import almost the whole of our provisions." "The prosperity of the territory depends on the exertion of agriculturalists," the *Gazette* charged, and a few years later observed that "there are not TWELVE good *practical farmers* in the territory." This condition was not for want of interest. Rarely has a pioneering agricultural population received more attention from the press. The *Gazette* filled its columns with advice of a theoretical and practical nature, charges of indolence, and the vision of a prosperous future. Commenting on the arrival in 1821 of three hundred barrels of produce from Ohio for sale on commission, the editor noted, "There is not a farmer in the territory that ever had sufficient enterprise to cultivate any article for exportation, although we have thousands of acres of the best hemp land in the world."[7] The territory's first agricultural exports—two hundred barrels of flour shipped to New York City in 1827—were celebrated as a triumph. The grain was sown, harvested, and milled in Michigan, and the flour packed in barrels of local manufac-

---

6. Cass to Calhoun, May 31, 1816, in *TP*, 10: 643. The governor could reverse these views on the appropriate occasion. In 1825, when urging General Lafayette to locate his township of land in Michigan Territory, Cass emphasized the territory's French heritage and referred happily to "this ancient seat of French enterprize." Message of the Governor, Jan. 18, 1825, in Journal of the Legislative Council, 1824–35, ESR, Michigan, p. 13.

7. Detroit *Gazette*, March 13, Aug. 14, Dec. 4, 1818; May 11, 1821.

ture, all, wrote the *Michigan Sentinel,* "evidence of the great change that has taken place in this section of the country within a few years past."[8]

A characteristic of the enduring frontiers was the prominence of a few small urban centers. People in insufficient numbers to push settlement into the countryside huddled around the few towns that served as the focus of all aspects of life. Detroit is a case in point. The fur trade had established its commercial role. In 1817 the city had "upwards of thirty commercial houses, some of them doing business on an extensive scale." But large-scale commercial prosperity required agriculture, and the "boundless wilderness" stretched on all sides to within two miles of the town. Could this land be "converted into a farm and manufacturing country, Detroit might challenge competition for extent of commerce and nature advantages with any of the rising cities of the West." In the years immediately after the war, agriculture produced no export crops, and manufacturing was no more advanced. In 1821 the *Gazette* castigated the economic enterprise of the territory with the declaration that not three families could make clothes, no carding machines or fulling mills could be found within a hundred miles of Detroit, and the whole territory did not contain even five looms.[9]

The territory of Michigan imported much of what it ate and everything it wore and used for business. Prices, reflecting transportation costs, were high. Manufactures in 1819 included "a small quantity of leather" shipped to Montreal, to supplement exports of furs and maple sugar. To these were added, on occasion, shipments of fish and fruit. Commercial activities continued to center on the fur trade. As late as 1821, the *Gazette* testified that furs were the only commodity that might be profitably exported to the East. On the eve of the opening of the Erie Canal, this pattern had changed little. An observer put together a "guess" for exports of the 1825 season: furs, $700,000; fish, $20,000; lumber, $7,500; indian sugar, $3,000; pot & pearl ashes, $8,000; for a total of $738,500.[10]

As private enterprises struggled forward, the business of government remained a focus of another kind of economic activity. Whereas those territories that benefited from the Great Migration became states,

<hr/>

8. Monroe *Michigan Sentinel,* June 23, 1827. A description of a prosperous farm at Dexter in 1828 is contained in the diary of Munnis Kenny, July 31, 1828, MHC.
9. Detroit *Gazette,* March 13, 1818; May 11, 1821.
10. Detroit *Gazette,* July 30, 1819; June 1, 1821; Aug. 30, 1825.

Michigan remained a territory, and political power remained concentrated in the hands of a few appointed officials. Federal officeholders, especially the governor, controlled patronage and influence. They represented a territorial elite and dominated political, economic, and social development. In truth, the range was even narrower, for Governor Cass was a figure of inordinate importance. Dependence on the federal government and its principal representative was almost complete. Expressions of discontent were, for the most part, muted. Of the national election of 1828, the *Sentinel* commented that whoever won, the territory must "cling to the Administration. The Territory is slave to an 'absentee aristocracy.' "[11]

County government also occupied a significant place in the lives of Michigan's citizens. In this, as in everything else, the initiative lay with the governor. At the close of the war, Cass quickly laid out lakefront counties: Monroe (1817), Macomb (1818), and St. Clair (1820). In 1820 he organized Oakland, the first truly interior county. Some counties had specialized problems associated with their locations. Mackinac (or Michilimackinac), Brown, and Crawford counties, set off in 1818, lay north and west of Lake Michigan, and the county seats of Mackinac, Green Bay, and Prairie du Chien contained scarcely enough people to fill the offices. The costs of such basic services of government as courts, roads, and mail were high. Because of the many services provided by counties, and always in search of ways to stimulate the peopling of the territory, Cass believed it wise to lay off counties in advance of settlement. He did so energetically, organizing some counties that were almost empty. With great distances, primitive communication, and a few people, government at the township level came to exercise considerable influence. The township was the basic administrative unit for the construction and maintenance of roads, and each township had a supervisor of roads and highways. Townships also had constables for preserving the peace. Township organization sometimes preceded county government, and some of the early townships were, accordingly, very large.[12]

11. Monroe *Michigan Sentinel*, Dec. 6, 1828. The identity, numbers, and order of an earlier version of the territorial "Establishment" may be examined in the funderal procession of Lt. John Brooks. Detroit *Gazette*, Nov. 7, 1817.
12. Daniel Strange, "Pioneer Days in Eaton County," *MHM*, 7 (1923): 12; Fuller, *Economic and Social Beginnings of Michigan*, 270. The journal of the board of supervisors of Oakland County for 1827 to 1844 (MHC) discloses nothing beyond the usual run of subjects that concerned county government everywhere in the Northwest in this period.

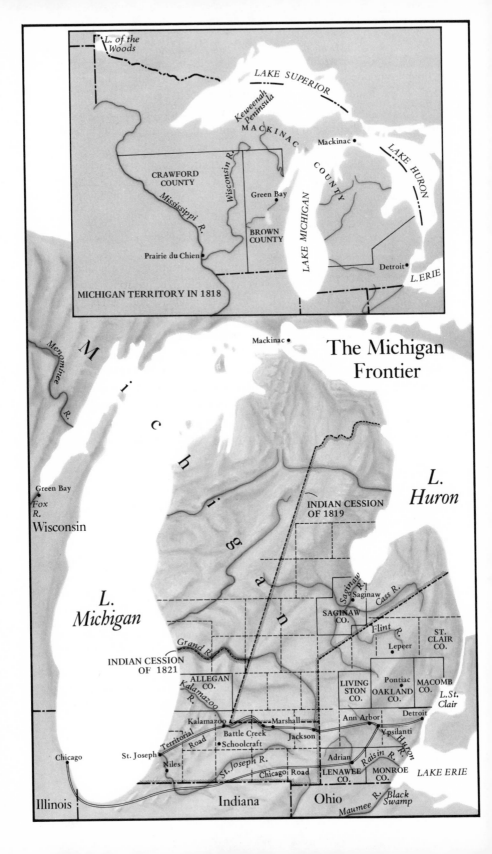

MICHIGAN TERRITORY IN 1818

L. of the Woods
LAKE SUPERIOR
Keweenah Peninsula
MACKINAC COUNTY
Mackinac
LAKE HURON
CRAWFORD COUNTY
Wisconsin R.
Green Bay
Mississippi R.
LAKE MICHIGAN
BROWN COUNTY
Prairie du Chien
Detroit
L. ERIE

The Michigan Frontier

Menominee R.
M
Mackinac
c
L. Huron
Green Bay
Fox R.
Wisconsin
INDIAN CESSION OF 1819
i
g
a
Saginaw R.
Cass R.
Saginaw
SAGINAW CO.
L. Michigan
Flint R.
Lepeer
ST. CLAIR CO.
INDIAN CESSION OF 1821
Grand R.
ALLEGAN CO.
Kalamazoo R.
LIVING STON CO.
Pontiac
OAKLAND CO.
MACOMB CO.
L. St. Clair
Kalamazoo
Marshall
Ann Arbor
Detroit
Territorial Road
Battle Creek
Schoolcraft
Jackson
Ypsilanti
Chicago
St. Joseph
Huron R.
Niles
St. Joseph R.
Chicago Road
Adrian
Raisin R.
LENAWEE CO.
MONROE CO.
LAKE ERIE
Illinois
Indiana
Ohio
Maumee R.
Black Swamp

Governor Cass recommended much legislation to meet the needs of the territory, and the Legislative Council responded with laws to meet almost every contingency. Cass's message to the new Legislative Council in 1823 showed the range of issues with which he concerned himself. He asked for more effective local government at the township level, reform of the militia and courts, more attention to road construction, an educational system, and that some provisioñ be made for the poor. The council entered upon its duties with the utmost energy, as evidenced by the extent of its legislation on a wide variety of subjects. Legislation for the session of 1827, for example, filled 354 printed pages. Laws on a multitude of subjects—indeed on almost every subject—were introduced, debated, passed, signed, and placed on the books.[13] Towns supplemented these with their own ordinances. This large and growing body of law was then rewritten. As early as 1824, Governor Cass commented that the legal system was being "altered too frequently and with too much facility." The condition of the law in 1826 called forth this description: "It is literally a cobweb, through which a snail may crawl, or creep around, and there is none to say *who*."[14] In short, by 1830 Michigan Territory was no colony of isolated simple frontier people, living by the tenets of natural law and under conditions that required little or no formal law or its apparatus. Quite to the contrary, Michigan Territory had legislation as complete and detailed as far more populous and prosperous territories and states.

The modest population of Michigan also enjoyed an extensive court system. In 1820 the governor and judges appointed a county court to serve as an appellate court for decisions of the justices of the peace and with original jurisdiction in civil cases up to one thousand dollars and criminal cases not involving capital punishment. Such wide latitude was eminently suitable to the dispersed nature of Michigan's population. But justice was not as rapid and impartial as the territory's citizens wished. The problems of appealing a decision—or carrying an original suit for that matter—from Green Bay to Detroit were almost insurmountable. The principals—lawyers and witnesses—would leave as the ice went off the rivers and with luck might be back in the north country before the first hard freeze the following autumn. Of course, if justice miscarried or was delayed, another trip would be necessary, or a winter spent in De-

13. Alec R. Gilpin, *The Territory of Michigan, 1805–1837* (East Lansing, 1970), 105.
14. Journal of the Legislative Council, p. 13; Monroe *Michigan Sentinel*, Jan. 27, 1826.

troit. One tangible response to complaints from people in the north
country was the creation by Congress in 1823 of a judge with powers of
the General Court for the western counties of Mackinac, Brown, and
Crawford. The new judge, James Duane Doty, was a meticulous jurist
in a remote wilderness and later a territorial executive of great skill.[15]

In 1818 the Detroit *Gazette* called Michigan a "newly organised and
rising society."[16] Probably no one could foresee at the time how gradual
that rise would be. In the ten years after the war not even the determined executive leadership of Lewis Cass could accelerate the painfully
slow growth of Michigan Territory. Signs of economic maturity began
to appear in the late 1820's: the export of flour, which showed a significant advance in agriculture and processing, and the completion of a road
network across the territory from Lake Erie to Lake Michigan. The
greatest impetus to growth and accelerated immigration was the opening
of the Erie Canal in 1825. This shallow ditch across upper New York
State brought about an economic transformation of the upper Great
Lakes, uniting the fertile but undeveloped lands of Michigan Territory
to the great export markets of the East Coast, principally New York
City. Michigan now joined the rising western economy. Immigration
rose in quantum leaps. Larger numbers of steamboats appeared on the
Great Lakes, five new ships for the 1825–26 season alone. Detroit became an important port of entry. Governor Cass laid off new counties
across the southern part of the territory in response to people in motion.
New towns sprang up in the western part of the territory: Niles, St.
Joseph, and Jackson. New agricultural areas to the west like the St.
Joseph River country acquired reputations as garden spots. By the end of
the decade, assisted by the Erie Canal and the imminent completion of
her western roads, Michigan was on the verge of enormous physical expansion and accompanying economic prosperity.[17]

15. On Doty as a frontier politician and entrepreneur, see Alice E. Smith, *James Duane
Doty: Frontier Promoter* (Madison, 1954); on Doty's judicial work, see Doty, "Judge
James Doty's Notes of Trial and Opinions: 1823–1832," ed. Elizabeth G. Brown,
AJLH, 9 (1965): 17–40, 156–66, 216–33, 350–62. An indication of Doty's orderly way
of conducting judicial business is his "Rules of the Circuit Court of the United States
for the Counties of Mackinaw Brown and Crawford, passed by J D Doty," printed in
the Detroit *Gazette*, Sept. 24, 1824.
16. Detroit *Gazette*, Oct. 2, 1818.
17. Fuller, *Economic and Social Beginnings of Michigan*, 56n.; Buley, *The Old Northwest*,
2: 80–86.

In the generation after the opening of the Erie Canal, an agricultural people occupied the southern part of the peninsula from Lake Erie to Lake Michigan, took the land, placed it under cultivation, and propelled Michigan into the front rank of expansion and prosperity. This growing agricultural frontier was the result of forces felt throughout the Northwest: the opening of the Erie Canal, which benefited Michigan in a very direct way; liberal land policies; and a general feeling of prosperity that produced large-scale investments in public lands, town sites, and banking ventures. In the 1840's an influx of foreign immigrants came to Michigan. New economic ventures also appeared, as mining and lumbering supplemented agriculture. Settlement gradually expanded north up the peninsula. Accompanying growth and expansion was the rise of several important urban centers, which appeared as a necessary concomitant to agricultural development, providing goods, services, and markets for the settling countryside.

Over the course of this new generation, Michigan's immigrants had two distinct settlement experiences derived from the condition of the nation as a whole: the first, lasting from 1825 to about 1840, was a period of motion, prosperity, optimism, easy credit, good markets, and the profound confidence in the future that was associated with the political movement known as Jacksonian Democracy. Banks appeared in every village. Railroads were on every lip and the ambition of every promoter. A railroad line across the peninsula from Lake Erie to Lake Michigan would have an impact like that of the Erie Canal, or so it was said, over and over. By 1836 promoters had drawn up elaborate plans for no fewer than five railroad projects involving the port town of Monroe alone. The bright hopes for the future faded in the wake of the panic of 1837 and the depression that followed. Population growth slowed. Cash markets vanished. The northward movement and sense of progress that was so much a part of the Michigan frontier of the early and mid-1830's ceased. As elsewhere in the trans-Appalachian West and the nation as a whole, the depression was severe and long lasting. Yet the decade of the 1840's gradually emerged as a time of subdued expansion. Grain exports became a major factor in Michigan's economy, with Detroit and St. Joseph as the principal ports on Lake Erie and Lake Michigan, respectively. The rise of the grain trade owed much to railroad construction, and the state of Michigan entered vigorously into the business of state-owned, state-financed internal improvements. The thirty miles of railroad line com-

pleted from Detroit to Ypsilanti in 1836 was extended to Ann Arbor in
1840, Kalamazoo in 1843, and to the shores of Lake Michigan at St.
Joseph in 1849. The state also planned and built other lines in the 1840's,
responding to larger numbers, increased production, and the economic
forces associated with them.[18] The growth of Michigan's population
displays these cycles of isolation, prosperity, depression, and recovery
(see table 4).

Table 4. Growth of the Old Northwest, 1820–50

	1820	*1830*	*1840*	*1850*
Michigan	8,896	31,639	212,267	397,654
Illinois	55,211	157,445	476,183	851,470
Indiana	147,178	343,031	685,866	988,416
Ohio	581,434	937,903	1,519,467	1,980,329

Source: *Historical Statistics of the United States, Colonial Times to 1957* (Washington, 1960), 13. The population of Michigan in
1820 includes the territory as then constituted.

The people who participated in Michigan's first settlement experience—characterized by movement and optimism—left many accounts of
happy frontier memories. They moved in a world of rising expectations
and within a firm institutional framework already in operation. Kingsley
Scott Bingham was one of this group. In 1833 he immigrated to what
would become Livingston County. Like many others, Bingham entered
the territory at Detroit. His object was land, and he quickly departed the
city for his errand in the wilderness. Bingham left his family in Ann
Arbor and followed the Huron River north to an attractive site where he
purchased two parcels of land. For a farm of two hundred acres, eighty
fenced and six acres already in wheat, watered by a branch of the
Huron, with excellent lowland and meadow, Bingham paid $650. He
also bought 240 acres of government land located on the Territorial Road
between Ann Arbor and Pontiac, for which he presumably paid the
minimum price. Gathering his family on the way, he returned to Detroit
to pick up the goods that he had shipped by steamboat and to purchase
supplies. He bought "a good timber wagon," a yoke of oxen, "some groceries, hardware and farming utensils and started for our farm." His

18. Monroe *Michigan Sentinel*, Oct. 25, 1834; June 4, 1836. Robert J. Parks, *Democracy's
Railroads: Public Enterprise in Jacksonian Michigan* (Port Washington, 1972), chs. 5–7,
analyzes the complicated story of Michigan's railroad planning and construction with
special attention to public ownership. On the rise of Michigan's grain trade in a larger
context, see John G. Clark, *The Grain Trade in the Old Northwest* (Urbana, 1966), chs. 3
and 4, esp. pp. 75–84.

purchases and those of others like him laid the foundation for urban development in Michigan. Ann Arbor, Jackson, Marshall, Kalamazoo, Battle Creek, and especially Detroit became outfitting points for immigrants. Bingham hastened back to the land and went to work. "We
moved in with a family living near us and in less than 4 weeks from the
time we left home, we were at work on our own land," he continued.
With the assistance of a hired man, he put up a log house, built of
"seasoned lumber" from Ann Arbor. The first year he planted only half
an acre of the traditional frontier crop of corn, but two acres of potatoes
and two acres of turnips. The staple crop for market was wheat.
Bingham hoped to plant thirty acres in wheat the first year, thus already
pursuing the new commercial agriculture of the Michigan frontier. The
nearest "permanent market"—as he called it—was Detroit. The grain
trade across the Great Lakes had made itself felt in the hinterland, and
its presence in southern Michigan did much to explain the energy behind
proposed railroad construction.[19]

Immigrant markets and cash crops aside, the demands of the land
were constant: break new ground, improve the old, fence the land, construct outbuildings. In this sense, the farmer of Michigan Territory followed the patterns of the first frontier peoples of Kentucky and Tennessee. The Scots immigrant, W. Forbes, wrote of the chores at all seasons
of the year. In the winter, for example, he would rise at seven and cut
wood and rails and draw them to the house on a sled; or, if the weather
was exceptionally bad, he would work in the carpenter shop or weave
baskets. In the spring and summer he rose two hours earlier, did chores,
then went to the fields at seven, where he remained until sunset. Forbes
thought the beauties of his situation and the promise of the future more
than compensated for his hard labor. Here is his description of a summer
day:

> Mornings and evenings delicious sitting out of doors in the shady side
> of the house or trees at breakfast or supper eating melons in (middle) of
> the day not a cloud, pure blue skye. light & heat. Cattle breaking away

19. This account is based largely on Bingham to family, July 1, 1833, Kingsley Scott
Bingham Papers, MHC. Reference was also made to Ebenezer Laken Brown, "The
Beginning of Schoolcraft"; W. Forbes Collection; William Watts to parents, Nov. 9,
1836, William Watts Letters; Dennis Family Papers, all in MHC; and William Now-
lin, "The Bark-Covered House, or Pioneer Life in Michigan," *MPHC*, 4 (1881):
480–541. On the grain trade, see Thomas D. Odle, "The American Grain Trade of the
Great Lakes, 1825–1873" (Ph.D., Michigan, 1951), chs. 1 and 3.

to get into the deep shaddow of trees or into the river to cool themselves—drinking water by the gallon which distills from you in large
drops in a few minutes—dress shirt and trousers and straw hat, this
never lasts 3 or 4 days until it is succeeded by a thunder shower falling
in torrents for 1 hour and all is fair and cool and fresh again.

So wrote a pioneer transplanted from Peterhead (Scotland) to Allegan
County. With what wonder the family left behind in that cold, inhospitable agricultural land must have read his reports of the warm summers
and the fertility of Michigan. He called the growth of his crops "a rapidity that staggers the belief of those accustomed to the slow growth of
colder climate."[20] The sensations Forbes described were experienced by
the optimistic on the frontier, those who were healthy and whose expectations were buoyed by the new land and the bright future.

After 1830 large numbers of New Englanders, New Yorkers, and
Pennsylvanians came to the Michigan frontier. Many of them were hard
working, ambitious, orderly, and literate. Among these were the Chandlers, Elizabeth Margaret and her brother Thomas, who immigrated to
Michigan Territory in 1830. The Chandlers were Quakers from Philadelphia. They settled in a Friends community near Adrian (Lenawee
County), preferring the quality of its society to the faster-growing section in the west around St. Joseph. Thomas bought an eighty-acre tract
and hired a carpenter to build a log cabin. Elizabeth wrote to their relatives that the finished dwelling was twenty by twenty-six feet, one and
one-half stories high, with two doors and four windows. Thomas was
from the city, but he soon rejoiced in his growing physical strength,
becoming more and more the acquisitive pioneer. In short, he worked
and prospered. Elizabeth wrote of his world: "Brother seems so happy
and satisfied that I could scarcely be otherwise if I were disposed to be.
He is now independent of the world and master of a fine farm, which
requires only industry to insure him a regular competence . . . and
there is some comfort, too, in our expecting the roughest part of our undertaking to come first." Thomas raised corn, wheat, and tended a growing herd of livestock. In 1832 he bought another lot with valuable timber
and bottomland. "He does dearly love the business of farming, and
seems very happy in his situation," confided his sister to their relatives.

What of his sister? Elizabeth sat by a "favorite window" and wrote.

20. W. Forbes to James Forbes, Peterhead, Scotland, April 10, 1835, Forbes Collection.

She described the beauty of the countryside and the delights of the seasons as they succeeded one another: sleighing in the winter; sugaring and brilliant fires in the oak openings in the spring; her garden and flowers in the summer; harvesting, threshing, and bright colors in the autumn. She also described the new society of which she was a part. In dress, the plain people of Lenawee County "might be seated down in any of the Philadelphia meetings on first day without their being known from their dress to be strangers." In manners, too, they were genteel. The society with which she identified included a number of active women who cooked, quilted, sewed, and attended to chores around the house. But they also did much more. They read and wrote, and vigorously studied and argued the principal issues of the day. Elizabeth was an avid reader and expressed herself on such diverse questions as the coming of the railroad and the abolition movement. She read every issue of William Lloyd Garrison's *Liberator* and strongly approved. With people like Elizabeth Chandler in the 1830's, the crude society of the early frontier had clearly passed, at least in some parts of Michigan. The society that emerged was much like the society that people had left behind, even in Philadelphia.[21]

Not all the immigrants to Michigan came with the money of a Bingham, the exuberance of a Forbes, or the intellectual qualities of a Chandler. Nor did all new arrivals live in such happy and prosperous times. Many came to the frontier with nothing but a strong constitution, and when the financial crisis of 1837 ended good times and the full-scale depression descended in 1839—one of the longest and most severe in the American economic experience—they stayed and fought it out. They had no choice. Lovira Hart and his family were among those who experienced the changed atmosphere of the 1840's. They endured hard times, isolation, and personal tragedy to a high degree. In 1836, at the age of twenty-eight, Lovira Hart moved from Livingston County (New York) to what would become Tuscola County (Michigan), where he settled on the Cass River. The next year, he brought out his wife Hannah Emeline,

21. The Elizabeth Margaret Chandler Papers (MHC), a collection of fifty-five letters, are among the most detailed and extensive collections dealing with the lives of literate and perceptive people on the frontier. They are also filled with what women did, or could reasonably expect to do. This account is taken from the Chandler Papers, with particular reference to the following letters: Sept. 8, Oct. 10, Dec. 23, 1830; May 30, June 28, 1831; Feb. 12, March 27, June 20, Dec. 13, 1832; Jan. 27, March 9, May 28, 1834.

two young daughters, and his mother. From the accounts that remain, it seems Hart knew little about some aspects of pioneer life. He never owned firearms, and his daughter later wrote that he only fired a gun once in his lifetime. The family had one trap in which they caught a large timber wolf, but too late to collect the bounty. Hart was a farmer. He wanted the security of landownership, and he wanted to make himself part of a society of like-minded people. To this end, he lavished much attention on his own little settlement—which came to include his brother and brother-in-law—and he maintained close ties with his relatives in New York State, talking of visits and urging them to move to Michigan. Unfortunately, he immigrated at the height of a boom period that soon faded into depression.

When the Hart family arrived at their tract of land in March 1837, the snow was still deep on the ground. Hart transported the family goods and supplies to the site by sleigh. With the coming of spring, he built a cabin, planted crops, and tried to cut a road. He wrote of his hard work, "Weary man has enough to do to bake his own Johnnycakes—especially if he has no help." In the spring of 1838 the Hart family made "100 pounds of sugar, 10 gallons of molasses, and a barrel of vinegar." Hart planted the usual crops: oats, potatoes, rutabagas, corn, and a large vegetable garden. His livestock consisted of only one cow and three pigs. The harvests were adequate to support the family and produced a small surplus. That winter Hart went to Flint with the ox team and sold some corn and wheat. He bought two kettles. The next year he planted flax for home use, and he and the bound boy, Ebin, fenced the cultivated fields. Hart needed a barn to protect his grain, but his wife wrote that "I don se much prospect of having a barn verry Soon." The pattern of economic subsistence persisted. Hart cleared more land and cultivated larger crops, but little surplus remained, prices were low, and the market distant.

Hart discovered the fundamental economic fact that the prosperity of the frontier depended on the territory, the trans-Appalachian region, and the nation as a whole. The crash of land speculations, town site schemes, and banks in distant parts affected his frontier farm. In the spring of 1838 he wrote, "The times are distressing hard in Michigan, the banks are breaking down by the dozens. All branches of trade is monopolized, opression and extortion is the order of the day. Conscience and humanity are strangers here." He needed nails, salt, and the services of a carpenter, a blacksmith, and a shoemaker, and he wrote, "This makes it hard for those that have everything to buy and nothing to sell, but I hope the times will be better soon." He continued, "If they are not, I hope our rulers will all turn into pillars (not of salt but gold and silver)." To supplement a meager diet, the Hart family tried to catch fish in the Cass. They were not successful. The annual return of the fields kept them alive, but "the luxuries of life we shall have to dispense with in a great measure." The struggle continued, but the price for agricultural produce fell as the family's production increased. By the winter of 1839–40 Lovira Hart had his farm in good operation. He was producing plenty of fodder—"my rutabagas were pretty good for the season three hundred and fifty bushels from an acre which makes us comfortable in the fodder line"—but he could not afford to buy more stock. The family cow had gone dry, "but cattle are so dear and money so scarce that I can not buy any we need another cow verry much the children want milk." As for prospects of trade: "There is no cash market at Flint for produce of any kind wheat will fetch 5 shillings in goods corn, 4, oats, 2." The family had enough to eat and clothes and shoes for the winter, but nothing more. That fall Hart and four friends expressed their discontent by travelling the thirty miles to Lapeer to cast votes for the Whig party. The trip there and back took three days.

Hart and his community welcomed an institutional framework that would convey a sense of security in the wilderness and, at the same time, provide them with many services that they so greatly needed. Michigan's new state government proved as energetic as its territorial predecessor in laying off counties. Among the by-products of county government was one that struck at every frontier family—taxes. In 1838 Hart noted that no taxes had been levied, but he expected that the settlement in his area would be attached to Saginaw County. "We shall Organize as soon as we can and then taxes will come thick and heavy," he wrote. In the spring Hart walked to Lapeer and talked to Judge Hotchkiss "about the taxes," which were "seventy-two cents town and county tax and two dollars and fifty cents road tax for every 80 acres." He objected to the road tax, for his settlement "lay outside the township." Hart and other settlers petitioned the legislature but to an unrecorded effect. When he returned to Lapeer the following year, he learned that state and road taxes on the section he owned jointly with his father-in-law came to $60.11. He asked that the road commissioners lay out roads, in order that he might work out the road tax. That summer Hart faced another road tax of twenty-four dollars for 1839, but he could report, "We have made some improvement on the roads in this district." Although the economy worsened, taxes fell due regularly—to be paid for in hard money and hard labor. Hart reflected that he never got a suitable return for his taxes, and the need to deal with government cost him valuable time in travelling to Lapeer, the seat of local government.

The one service of government and use for his tax money that Hart valued was road construction, and not simply because it provided a way to work off taxes. Roads were a necessity. With crops and the family's health, roads formed a staple of Hart's early correspondence. Roads were the avenue to the all too remote outside world for people and agricultural surplus, and the routes by which new visitors and settlers could reach the Harts. In his second winter in Michigan, Hart spent much time "cutting" roads—from the house to the southeast corner of the section, to the river, to Harrisons (two miles, he reported). Of his experiences, Hart wrote, "It costs a great deal of time to make poor roads in this country." The road commissioners laid out some better roads, and Hart and others worked off their taxes in laboring on them. In the winter transportation by sled continued to be widely used. In the summer and fall Hart hauled his grain and corn by wagon over terrible roads to a mill in Saginaw, eighteen miles away. Whenever possible, he floated his commodities down the Cass River.

The importance of roads was only one symbol of the isolation felt by all members of the family. In the beginning the land seemed beautiful and the opportunities limitless, the wild animals were not to be feared, and, all together, the new place "begins to seem like holm here." Emeline Hart's brave words did not last. Economic depression settled over the land and brought an abrupt halt to immigration. "You rote that I must keep up good courage and hope for the best," she wrote to her family two years later. "I try to my courage gets pretty lonsome times I have not been out of the Settlement since I first came in it." Even the taciturn Lovira Hart longed for society. He once wrote, "If we can see no prospect of our having neighbors soon we shall decamp for some central place where we can have the benefit of school and the society of good neighbors.'" In spite of such talk, he never moved. But he did urge his father-in-law to sell his land (bought for a speculation in happier times) to someone who would settle on it. Once he traded two half-quarters to people who planned to move onto them. "I did it for the sake of getting some neighbors and I think I shall not lose in the bargain," he admitted.

The 1840's also brought several personal reverses to the Hart family. Their health was a constant worry, ever a topic of discussion in their letters. All members of the family suffered at intervals from the "ague." Emeline Hart was often ill; "nervous weakness," she called it. She gave birth to a third daughter in January 1839. The flies were bad in the summertime, and the mosquitoes made life miserable for the children. A daughter Emmergine had a serious speech impediment. In the fall of 1840 Ebin went berserk and attacked Lovira Hart. "Lovira could not manage him I run to Mr. Davis the men came half a dozen of them bound him," wrote Emeline. "Oh it is a trial to us in a trouble that you don't know anything of I am affraid he never will get over it." Through the fall, Ebin remained tied to a bed in the house. In the summer of 1841 Emeline Hart died in childbirth, leaving a daughter born prematurely. Lovira Hart now had to provide for his four daughters, one of them an infant, and his aged mother. Some time in the next few years he returned to the East with his oldest daughter Jannette and left her with her grandparents. The remaining children of the family turned to and did the work—as best they could.

To the labors of opening a farm amidst physical and economic isolation, and in continuing periods of depression, Lovira Hart had the added responsibility of raising a family alone. Of his children, he wrote, "I should like to have the oldest ones where they can go to school. They are running wild in the woods, poor little things." Not until 1845, four years after his wife's death, did the children attend a formal school, and then only for two months over the winter with the prospect of another term in the summer. "We have a good teacher and the Children learn well as would be expected," he wrote. "They lack for books our Schooling comes high." In spite of the gradual return of economic prosperity, the prospect of neighbors, and the opening of a school, Hart sometimes expressed bitterness over the hardships of life on the frontier. In 1845, after he had been on the land for eight years, Hart wrote, "But why complain I expect neither Sympathy nor assistance I have got into the woods and cannot get out, but must make the best of it now past Errors can not be remedied and myself and family must suffer the consequences."

Hart constantly longed for some sort of society in the form of neigh-

bors, roads to reach them, perhaps even a town. He called his little settlement Cassville, and it had three families in the spring of 1837. A year
later, he wrote, "Mr. Perry has got his blacksmith shop arunning so we
now have a shoemaker and blacksmith and two carpenters in the settlement." By 1845 "the town," now named Tuscola, had thirteen families.
Next year, "Our settlement now numbers 23 families. The land on the
River is all taken to Bridgeport." The arrival of immigrants and the
growth of the town was a signal that the economic depression had at last
ended. Among the new arrivals was a colony of Germans. Seven German families—complete with pastor, two church bells, and a schoolteacher—moved into Hart's vicinity in 1845. They were the advance
guard of what would be a large foreign immigration over the next decade. Hart liked the Germans. They were "intelligent," had money, and
many spoke good English. The Germans soon had a grist mill and sawmill in operation five miles down the Cass River from Hart's farm. At
last, he concluded, "this part of the state is fast settling." By this time
what Hart called "the lumbar business" had become economically significant, and lumbermen received higher wages for day labor than farmers.
In 1852 Lovira Hart built a new house, a symbol of his economic success. It had, according to one of his daughters, "a kitchen or cook room
with a stove in it, a dining room with a fireplace, a parlor with a stove,
and three bedrooms below and plenty of room upstairs, a new wood-
house, and a room for Pa to keep his tools and work in when it is bad
weather." It stood on Hart's Corners as a monument to fifteen years of
unremitting labor and human sacrifice. Hart had long promoted schools,
and, as part of this interest, he gave his old house to be used as a
schoolhouse. Hart wrote to his oldest daughter in New York and urged
her to come for a visit: "Remember that life is short and what we have to
do must be done quickly." Perhaps he recalled the long-deferred expectations of his first wife, Hannah Emeline.

Years of physical labor and economic hardship left their mark on
Lovira Hart. Among the stories told about him when he was an old man
was an encounter between him and his daughter as she worked in her
flower beds. He told her she might better be doing something worth-
while. She answered him, "But father don't they look pretty?" "Yes," he
replied; "They look pretty all right, but I think a hill of nice potatoes
would look prettier." It was said of Hart that "he seemed to be a very

stern old man in his later years." It was a comment by those who had not shared in his struggles on Michigan's enduring frontier.[22]

Two new economic frontiers now appeared in Michigan: copper mining and lumbering, still in early forms. Rumors of valuable minerals had swirled around Michigan since the days of the fur trade carried men vast distances into remote settings. These stories became reality in the 1840's on the Keweenah Peninsula, a finger of land projecting into Lake Superior from the Upper Peninsula. The land itself was as desolate and distant as any visited by an American mineral rush. The peninsula, accessible only by sea, consisted of scrub forests amid rock outcroppings and was subject to violent winter weather. Here, in the 1840's, the prospect of copper drew young men in search of mineral wealth. Mining techniques—social and economic—were still in their infancy. With a supply of blasting powder and with or without a government permit, men dug and blasted for copper. They found some, enough to sustain expectations, but little to suggest the great mining enterprise that would appear in the last half of the century and make Michigan's mines a determining factor in the world price of copper. Yet, as early as 1847, Michigan led the nation in copper production. Individual economic return, however, was fragmentary, and physical conditions were primitive and harsh. The society that emerged was rough and rude. Strictly speaking, there was no society as people on the agricultural frontier understood the term. Miners were transients; they were not institution builders. They wanted only enough structure to provide for the resolution of disputes in a very remote and unregulated world. Beyond this, they preferred to think of their stay as temporary. But they forecast the large-scale mining frontier that would engage so much of the mountain West in the last half of the nineteenth century.[23]

22. This account is based on the Lovira Hart Collection (MHC) of twenty-four letters from Hart to his wife's relatives in New York State, covering the period from 1837 to 1853. It relies especially on the following letters: April 1, 1837; Feb. 25, April 8, July 1, 1838; Feb. 10, June 7, Dec. 1, 1839; Sept. 5, 1840; July 5, Aug. 4, 1841; Aug. 24, 1845; Nov. 22, 1846; May 9, 1847; May 5, 1850; Feb. 8, 1853.
23. Mark E. Neithercut, "The Development of the Portage Lake Mining District" (B.A. [honors], Michigan, 1974), chs. 1 and 2. Three useful accounts are diaries by Cornelius G. Shaw and William W. Spaulding and the anonymous "Recollections and Reminiscences of Early Life on Lake Superior," all in MHC.

Lumbering had a more widespread influence. The combination of vast pine forests belonging to an absentee landlord and an expanding population in search of building materials created an industry that added a new dimension to Michigan's frontier experience. The search for good pine began as early as 1820–21 at a Pontiac sawmill in Oakland County. The lumber business steadily expanded through the 1820's and experienced a surge in the following decade with the rising demand of a growing population and the settlement of the more northern counties. Early lumbering provided seasonal winter employment for idle agriculturists. Men worked in small units to spy out the best pineries, always trying to keep their discoveries secret until the trees could be cut and hauled away. The first and most obvious target was government land, which stood without public defender. Enterprising bands of men picked over large portions of the public domain for choice stands of pine. Lumbering in its early stages did not require much knowledge or equipment: the axe, saw, team of horses or oxen, and a strong back. Men felled trees and dragged logs through the snowy woods to a mill—sometimes for sale, sometimes for personal use.

A raw material plentiful as the woods itself and a ready market led to the widespread construction of sawmills. In Michigan, the sawmill became especially important with the introduction of steam, which roughly coincided with the large-scale expansion of the lumbering industry. The first raft of sawed lumber floated down the Flint River in the winter of 1832–33, to be hauled on sleds to market. Saginaw had a sawmill as early as 1834, and a big sawmill in 1836–37. At about the same time, or perhaps a year earlier, entrepreneurs built a large steam sawmill in Ann Arbor. In response to the market created by the great immigration of the 1830's, lumber had become big business. The new immigrants—like the Germans upriver and downriver from Lovira Hart—built sawmills immediately. The center of the industry was the northern counties, where the great florests lay on land less attractive for agriculture, and a growing number of sawmills met the demands of an agricultural population to the south.[24] The degree of interest, competition, and rising stakes were a harbinger of the lumbering frontiers that appeared in the next generation

24. Carl Addison Leech, "Sharon Hollow: Story of an Early Mulay Sawmill of Michigan," *MHM*, 17 (1933): 377–92. An important article about the varieties of Michigan's frontier experience is Willis F. Dunbar, "Frontiersmanship in Michigan," *MH*, 50 (1966): esp. 100–04.

in Michigan, Wisconsin, and, somewhat later still, in the Pacific Northwest.

Leadership and location dominated Michigan's frontier experiences up to 1850. Governor Cass provided the first in a period when the territory's location placed it outside the mainstream of frontier development. Cass's leadership was much like that provided by territorial governors before the War of 1812; Michigan's condition much like these earlier frontiers. The two factors that carried Michigan beyond this early stage were steam navigation and the Erie Canal. Suddenly, within the space of a few years, the Great Lakes became the thoroughfare to the West. Location now brought growth and prosperity. So the territory prospered in the 1830's under a mass immigration that gave diversity to the frontier experiences. Beyond the impact of technology and the new frontiers of mining and lumber lay the land. Michigan's was still predominantly an agrarian world, and, as such, it was one with the rest of the frontier. By 1850 its enduring frontier experience was behind (if not always forgotten), and the state of Michigan was one with the Old Northwest.

10

Florida:
A Sectional Frontier

When John Quincy Adams and Don Luis de Onís signed the treaty of cession in 1819, Florida resembled a typical Spanish frontier: a few scattered military outposts with missionary churches, surrounded by thousands of square miles of wilderness. Imprints of people on the land were few. Geography was a strong influence. The rivers of East Florida emptied into the Atlantic Ocean; those of West Florida into the Gulf of Mexico. The land was also a powerful physical presence, with twelve hundred miles of coastline, new flora and fauna, and an interior of swamps and pine barrens emphasizing the tropical nature of this new American frontier. Aside from forts and churches, only half a dozen government buildings and several place-names testified to two hundred and fifty years of Spanish occupation. In its American phase, Florida matured as a study in frontier sectionalism, with widely separated areas, each associated with an urban center, struggling not only against the forces of geography and climate but also against each other.

More than on the trans-Appalachian frontier, Florida's people lived in and around cities and towns. In part, this was the legacy of Spain's colonial system, which emphasized a capital city as the center of economic, political, and social life. When population grew, as in the case of Louisiana, expansion to the hinterland took place. But Florida's numbers remained small, the land too vast, and physical expansion slow. The territory had no dominant geographic feature comparable to the Mississippi River to encourage settlement patterns. The Spanish had divided the province into East and West Florida, each with a capital city—St. Augustine in the East, Pensacola in the West—and the two cities served as lasting monuments to the Spanish colonial empire and, incidentally, to the sectional nature of the territory. Nearly four hundred miles of wilderness separated the two administrative, economic, and social centers. A man travelling light might make the trip overland in twenty days. Few did. So the towns turned to the sea for their contact with the outside world, initially to Cuba and to other Spanish colonies in the Far Southwest. Later, as the American settlements pushed down from the north, St. Augustine and Pensacola made contact with Georgia and Alabama respectively, not with each other.

Florida was not a new frontier. Settlement at St. Augustine dated from 1565. To the extent that the Spanish legacy of two and a half centuries influenced the Americans, it was through the towns. When the Americans came to Florida, both St. Augustine and Pensacola had well established city governments. These were the centers of institutional life. Most of Florida's people were Spanish in 1821, but a colony of Minorcan Islanders also lived around St. Augustine, as well as groups of runaway slaves and Indians. The attendants listed at an offical ceremony at St. Augustine in 1821 display the diversity of peoples in Florida. They included, among others, the justices (American); the mayor, aldermen, and officers of the "City" (a mixture of English and Spanish surnames); officers of the American army and navy; the French consul for South Carolina; "the late mayor, and officers of the late government" (all Spanish); and fifty Choctaw Indians.[1]

The organization of America's new possession and the transition to American institutions began with military rule. Andrew Jackson was the Caesar. Jackson appeared in Florida on two dramatic occasions: the first as military invader, the second as civil ruler. His commission as governor gave him authority comparable to that exercised by "the Governor and Captain General and Intendant of Cuba."[2] Jackson was hardly the logical choice for the governorship by training or temperament. His achievements were military; he was not noted for his tact in dealing with people. He had no use for the Spanish and did little or nothing to reassure Florida's Spanish population, which departed in large numbers for Cuba

---

1. St. Augustine *Florida Gazette*, Sept. 1, 1821.
2. The commission is dated March 10, 1821, in *TP*, 22: 10.

and the Indies. In other respects, however, Andrew Jackson was a most suitable selection. He was the best-known general officer in the armed forces, and his victory over the British at New Orleans was probably the greatest yet won by an American commander. The law reducing the American military establishment made his retirement necessary, however, and the governorship was a suitable—and at the same time not too arduous—office to ease his departure.

Jackson took formal possession of Florida on July 10, 1821, with a proclamation that continued in force "all laws and municipal regulations, which were in existence at the cessation of the late government." He retained such Spanish forms as the alcalde and cabildo, to which he added the basic American frontier institutions of the county—Escambia in West Florida and St. Johns in the East—and its auxiliary, the county court, which functioned with an amalgamation of Spanish and American law. The governor also issued ordinances for the operation of county government, including detailed procedures and the fees to be charged by officials.[3] Each with a city corporation and a county court, the widely separated parts of Florida went their separate ways, East Florida under the direction of Acting Governor William G. D. Worthington, who carried out the general's ordinances in St. Augustine. The extension of customs and the mail service completed Florida's transition to American rule. A government established and as many of his friends rewarded as possible, Jackson resigned in November 1821.

Congress established Florida Territory along the lines laid down by the Ordinance of 1787. By this act Congress made a basic decision: Florida would be one territory. At the same time, the organic act confirmed Florida's sectional nature by dividing judicial authority between two superior courts, one for East Florida to meet at St. Augustine, the other for West Florida to convene at Pensacola. The new governor of Florida was William Pope Duval, a Virginian who had spent much of his life in Kentucky, where he was a lawyer, an officer in the Rangers (1812), and a congressman (1813–15). In 1821 President James Monroe had appointed him the first judge for East Florida and, soon thereafter, governor of the new territory. Duval spent much of his first term in office in Kentucky, where he tended to his own affairs and for which

---

3. Jackson's proclamation is in *TP*, 22: 110; see also St. Augustine *Florida Gazette*, Sept. 1, 1821, which printed the ordinances in English and Spanish.

sojourns Floridians subjected him to vigorous criticism. His family did not move to Florida until December 1825, three and one-half years after he took the oath of office. Duval was an amiable man who sought the role of statesman and compromiser rather than advocate in a territory splintered into sections. He felt that Florida's development would be slow, and he was not inclined to hurry. In every way, he was a contrast to Lewis Cass of Michigan.[4]

The activities of Andrew Jackson in organizing Florida for transition to American rule, the Congress of the United States in establishing a territorial government, and William P. Duval in his first years as governor set a trend that would grow stronger with the passage of time. Florida was to become American in the sense in which people understood the term in the 1820's. The rejoicing of the editor of the *Florida Gazette* at the time of government organization set the tone for the arrival of American law and justice. "*Liberty of the Press*, and *Trial by Jury*, have taken up their abode in the fine land of Citron and Orange Groves!" he exclaimed. "The sons of WASHINGTON will vindicate the goodness of the Creator, in showing that man can be great and free, though within the influence of the torrid zone, and fanned by breezes and shaded by bowers of a tropical clime."[5] Americans exhibited much less care and concern for the Spanish in Florida than they had for the French in Louisiana in 1803. In the generation since the purchase of Louisiana, the Americans had fought a war to preserve their institutions and, in the process, acquired much self-confidence and a strong streak of nationalism. American officials in Florida showed little regard for the rights and privileges of the Spanish population and their institutions—guaranteed to them under the treaty of cession—and virtually none after the first few months. Where Jackson noticed the Spanish people, it was to emphasize the procedures under which they might become American citizens. American law and legal institutions rapidly replaced the Spanish. The machinery of justice also passed into American hands. The lawyers were increasingly American, and, with the exception of some of the city magistrates, so were the judges. Although most of the claimants were Spanish, the mechanism for handling land claims rested with American officials. After the first few months newspapers no longer printed laws in Spanish. As early as

4. James Owen Knauss, "William Pope DuVal, Pioneer and State Builder," *FHQ*, 11 (1933): 95–139, is a general history of Florida, for Duval was active from 1822 to 1849.
5. St. Augustine *Florida Gazette*, Sept. 15, 1821.

December 1821, the Grand Jury for East Florida objected to "the inconvenience to which this Province is subjected, in the establishment and Continuation of the Spanish Laws." In 1829 the Legislative Council removed this source of complaint when it repealed all laws and ordinances in the territory prior to July 22, 1822, thus ending any Spanish influence.[6]

The government of territorial Florida went into operation in midsummer 1822. Some of the peculiar problems associated with the territory came into focus in attempts to convene the Legislative Council. Duval called the first session to meet in Pensacola, seat of the governor's residence. One member of the council from St. Augustine died in a shipwreck on the way. Two others arrived safely, having endured a hazardous sea voyage of fifty-nine days. Soon after deliberations began, an epidemic of yellow fever broke out and took the life of the president of the council, Dr. John C. Bronaugh. The survivors hastily adjourned, to meet the following year at St. Augustine. This time the Pensacola delegation was en route twenty-eight days overland. The hazards of travel had become a dominant topic of discussion for this important body. At its second gathering the Legislative Council agreed to select a central site for a territorial capital. Two commissioners (one each from East and West) chose a ridge of land between the Suwannee and Ochlockonee rivers. The Indians called it Tallahassee, and the name survived. Governor Duval made the selection official, and in November 1824 the council met in a log cabin on the site. Tallahassee was more frontier town than territorial capital, at least for several years. On a visit to Florida in 1827, the New England sage Ralph Waldo Emerson passed through the town and wrote of it, "Tallahassee a grotesque place, selected three years since as a suitable spot for the Capital of the territory, and since that day rapidly settled by public officers, land speculators and desperadoes."[7] Whatever the character of the people, the town and the surrounding countryside settled rapidly. The founding of Tallahassee, halfway between the major towns of St. Augustine and Pensacola, intensified the sectional division of the territory. The rapid rise to political, economic, and social prominence of Middle Florida changed the even balance of population and influence. The section had fertile lands unencumbered

6. Presentment of the Grand Jury of East Florida, Dec. 6, 1821, in *TP*, 22: 295; Pensacola *Gazette*, Nov. 21, 1829, in Journal of the Legislative Council, 1822–38, ESR, Florida.
7. Quoted in Knauss, "William Pope DuVal," 127.

by litigation over private claims, and Tallahassee was the seat of government. As Middle Florida began to outdistance the other sections in population and prosperity, East Florida and West Florida shifted their suspicious glances from one another to the center of the territory.

The people of Florida sought to solve their problems of isolation from each other and from the rest of the nation and to deal with the usual frontier problems by appeals to Congress. Unfortunately, sectional conflict immediately emerged around preferment from the federal government, which was the source of so many gifts and bounties for the enduring frontiers. In any case, whatever the divisions, petitions, resolutions, and memorials flowed to Washington in an unending stream. With a congressional appropriation and the assistance of the United States Army, officials eventually constructed a road between St. Augustine and Pensacola. Open in 1826, it was little more than a track where travellers made their way single file on horseback. The interest in roads far exceeded concern about sea transportation and water routes, reflecting a desire to bind the territory together and to foster commercial development through agriculture.[8] Another issue that demanded federal intervention was the question of private land claims. Both the Spanish and English had made several large grants of land. In 1822 Congress established two boards—everything in Florida was done in pairs—to resolve the claims. The cases dragged on for several years, followed in some instances by appeals to the courts. The contest over land claims had a great impact and almost certainly slowed the occupation of lands and subsequent economic development of East and West Florida. This circumstance gave an advantage to Middle Florida, where the federal government could give good title.[9]

Health was an ever-present problem in territorial Florida. A tropical climate meant tropical disease. Observers most frequently mentioned a widespread recurring fever (probably malaria) and a disease identified only as the "black vomit." The fever season ran from August through October, when those in a position to do so left the coastal towns for the countryside. Authorities spent much time on the question of public

8. Mark F. Boyd, "The First American Road in Florida: Pensacola–St. Augustine Highway, 1824," *FHQ*, 14 (1935–36): 73–106, 139–92. A general discussion is Alice Whitman, "Transportation in Territorial Florida," *FHQ*, 17 (1938): 25–53.
9. Sidney Walter Martin, "The Public Domain in Territorial Florida," *JSH*, 10 (1944): 174–87.

health, and the focus of their concern was the city, where the concentrations of people intensified the impact of disease. One of Andrew Jackson's first ordinances established a board of health for St. Augustine, adopted rigorous regulations for the quarantining of foreign ships and their crews, and provided for the appointment of a resident physician and a health officer. The city of Pensacola also passed wide-ranging ordinances for health and sanitation, with special reference to the disposal of dead animals and fish, for an outbreak of disease was customarily associated with noxious odors.[10] In spite of these provisions, epidemics continued, for example, at St. Augustine in 1821 and Pensacola in 1822. In 1826 St. Augustine passed a special ordinance to provide for searching incoming ships for "malignant, pestilential, or contagious disease" and made the captain of the vessel subject to suit in the local courts for violations. In Pensacola the master of an incoming vessel had to anchor in the quarantine grounds and there "submit to such search, cleansing and purifying as the boarding health official shall direct," and all this "at the expense of the vessel." Those who offered public accommodation were required to submit a list of their lodgers each week, and every householder (public and private) had to report any sickness within twelve hours under penalty of a ten-dollar fine for each offense. Deaths also had to be reported within twelve hours, and "a detailed account of the deaths" would be published each week.[11]

Florida's economy reflected the sectional nature of her settlements. At the time of government organization in 1821, the St. Augustine *Florida Gazette* hoped that coffee, orange and citrus trees, olives, indigo, mulberry, sugarcane, and cotton would be cultivated in the new territory.[12] Of these, cotton became the most significant and profitable. The arriving Americans established a plantation economy in Middle Florida, and the economy and society of this section came to resemble those of other cotton frontiers. In 1827 the first steamboat appeared on the Apalachicola River; in early 1828 a steamboat reached Columbus (Georgia) at the falls of the Chattahoochee. Merchants found business handling the expanding trade of upriver planters. Cotton exports from Apalachicola rose from 317 bales in 1828 to 51,673 bales in 1836. As early as 1830, Apalachicola

10. St. Augustine *Florida Gazette*, Sept. 1, 1821; Pensacola *Floridian*, Sept. 1, 1821; Pensacola *Gazette*, Oct. 16, 1824.
11. St. Augustine *East Florida Herald*, Oct. 3, 1826; Pensacola *Floridian*, July 5, 1823.
12. St. Augustine *Florida Gazette*, Aug. 4, 1821.

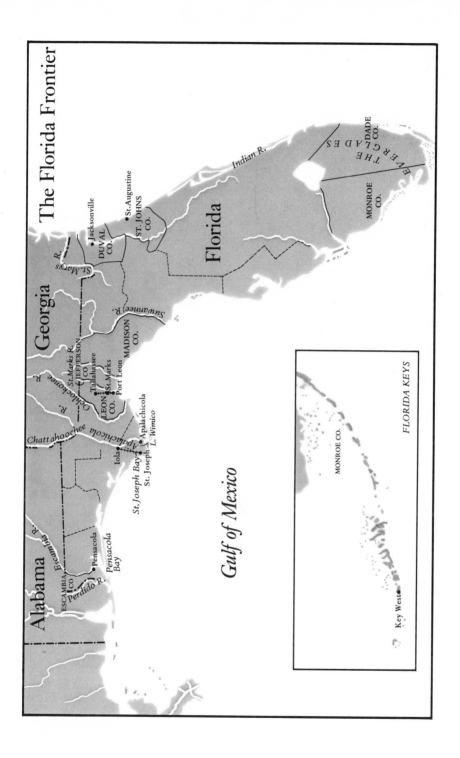

The Florida Frontier

had surpassed Pensacola as the most important Gulf port in Florida, and Middle Florida, settled within the last half-dozen years, had almost half the territory's population.[13]

Economic development in East and West was slow. Self-styled planters cultivated rice and corn to the south and west of Pensacola, but the soil was more suitable to livestock grazing. The dominant feature of West Florida was the forest, and lumber became its largest crop. The several sawmills that appeared late in the 1820's on the inland waterways testify to the growth of this form of enterprise.[14] Pensacola had a fine harbor but a sparsely settled and sterile hinterland, without a large river system to draw on. It never became a significant commercial port; it did not even have a pier. The United States Navy early used the harbor at Pensacola (where disease sometimes took a frightful toll) and, in 1830, announced plans to build a full-scale naval yard facility. St. Augustine was the center of an infant citrus industry and had visions of a growing tourist trade. Both developed slowly. Like other Florida towns, St. Augustine had few manufacturers. A St. Augustine editor remarked in 1823 that "the most common articles of domestic use can neither be made or mended here." The generalization applied to Florida as a whole.[15]

Four hundred miles to the south lay Key West and a flourishing salvage industry. The continuous commercial traffic of the Gulf flowed through a strait of water eighty miles wide between Key West and Havana. Here dangerous reefs and sudden storms provided opportunities for a thriving business in crippled ships and abandoned cargoes. At the time the United States took possession of Florida, this business involved fifty to sixty vessels and perhaps as many as five hundred seamen. In response to a demand from Key West, territorial acts of 1823 and 1825 gave preference to American salvagers and laid down rules for salvage operations. The organization of a superior court for southern Florida in 1828 gradually transformed salvaging into an orderly eco-

13. Harry P. Owens, "Apalachicola before 1861" (Ph.D., Florida State, 1966), is a detailed study; the figures of cotton exports are from pp. 87, 88n. The population of Middle Florida in 1830 was 15,777; of the territory as a whole, 34,725. See Abstract of Census of Population, 1831, in *TP*, 24: 505–06.

14. Horatio S. Dexter Correspondence, James David Glunt Papers, PKY; Pensacola *Gazette*, Aug. 27, 1825; John A. Eisterhold, "Lumber and Trade in Pensacola and West Florida, 1800–1860," *FHQ*, 51 (1973): 267–80.

15. St. Augustine *East Florida Herald*, May 3, 1823.

nomic enterprise. Key West experienced recurrent seasonal attacks of yellow fever. The United States Navy established a base there in 1823, but such was the cost in lives from fever that it was occupied only in the winter and spring. Key West was the only part of Florida to depend for its livelihood on the sea.[16]

In its forms of government, court, and law, the Florida Territory conformed to the patterns found on the trans-Appalachian frontier. The incoming American population—which became dominant in numbers and influence in the 1820's—brought the values of the Deep South. The purposes of government seemed to be the preservation of order, the performance of useful services, and the protection of property. "Here, in this age, there is no community of goods," wrote one observer. "Each person claims a separate and district right to property, and expects that the laws and administration of justice will secure to him the enjoyment of it." Florida's court system and laws were largely concerned with property and its security: dower, rights of widows, wills, execution and executors, attachments, and divorce. The law prescribed vigorous punishment for crimes against property. For stealing horses or cattle, for example, penalties ranged to a maximum fine of five hundred dollars, two hundred lashes, double damages, and permanent disqualification from voting, giving testimony, or holding office. By contrast, crimes against persons were less severely punished. Convictions for assault and battery brought fines of only a few cents. That such violations of the law often involved leading citizens in the community probably had much to do with leniency.[17]

Interest in an orderly society was high, intensified by the unstructured and transient nature of the frontier. The first frontier people were all transients. This early stage of settlement, a kind of sorting out process, saw the influx of numbers of people who lived off the land, spied out the main chance, and tested the region for signs of future economic opportunity. Some stayed; others moved on. Yet distinctions soon became apparent among those who stayed. Some participated in the formation of

16. Dorothy Dodd, "The Wrecking Business on the Florida Reef, 1822–60," *FHQ*, 22 (1944): 171–99.
17. St. Augustine *East Florida Herald*, April 12, Jan. 11, 1823; Samuel Pasco, "Jefferson County, Florida, 1827–1910," *FHQ*, 7 (1928): 139–46. Pasco comments that for assault, juries were "lenient in their penalties, fines of six and a quarter or twelve and a half cents, sometimes a dollar with the costs of prosecution, were often imposed on offenders" (p. 146).

an increasingly structured society, centered around property ownership and estate building, with respect for hard work and the rewards due it. In this fashion, one part of a recently arrived mobile population was now permanent, with vested interests in property rights and growing political power. These people now joined together to cast a suspicious glance at the portion of the population that had not joined them in this forward thrust. Florida Territory's agreeable climate and bounties of nature made it attractive for those still living off the land and undecided on their directions, but they were increasingly at the mercy of their more directed fellow frontiersmen. So the report of a grand jury attacked "the great number of vagrants, that are now going at large through the county, and who have no visible means of support the most pernicious consequences may result to society, unless a law is passed authorizing the infliction of a punishment upon them." Pensacola passed a local ordinance against vagrants as early as 1821, specifying that "all able bodied persons, who have no known or visible means of making a support, in an honest way, shall be deemed and taken to be vagrants" and fined five dollars upon conviction. For a second offense, the convicted vagrant might be set to work "for the benefit of the city" for up to two months.[18]

Grievances against "vagrants" had a querulous air about them, traditional complaints against traditional adversaries, public nuisances rather than public dangers. The universal concern about Florida's black population hit a different note: concern about a real and present danger. The Americans who immigrated into Florida after 1821 brought slaves. The municipalities of St. Augustine and Pensacola immediately established slave patrols with orders "to disperse all assemblages of Negroes, and apprehend any slaves which they may find without the enclosure of their owner or employer, without a written ticket allowing such absence, and place them in jail, to be punished as one of the council may direct, not exceeding fifteen lashes, nor less than five."[19] In 1827 the territory adopted an act that discouraged the immigration of free blacks to the territory by providing for their arrest after thirty days and requiring the posting of a bond of two hundred dollars to guarantee a court appearance and a surety of five hundred dollars as a guarantee to leave the territory.

18. St. Augustine *East Florida Herald*, Dec. 20, 1823; Pensacola *Floridian*, Sept. 1, 1821. For vagrants in Michigan at the same period, see Detroit *Gazette*, May 29, Sept. 25, 1818; Nov. 23, 1821.

19. St. Augustine *Florida Gazette*, Sept. 8, 1821; see also Pensacola *Floridian*, Sept. 1, 1821.

This process might be repeated indefinitely. Grand juries constantly investigated the activities of slaves, especially those who lived in towns. In 1827, for example, the Grand Jury of Escambia County charged that "Balls and Assemblies of Negroes," along with "gambling houses and tippling shops," threatened to bring about "the ruin of the Slaves, and consequent great injury of their owners." The executive was equally vigilant, calling on a regular basis for better laws "for the good government and subordination of our slave community." After all, Acting Governor William M. McCarty noted later that year, "It cannot be unknown to you that a large proportion of the slaves who are brought to the South, are sold by their more Northern owners as a punishment for their crimes." Floridians must be alert and guard against any "dangerous leniency."[20]

Florida's black population raised issues beyond slave control. Spanish Florida had a free black population, and the terms of the Treaty of 1819 entitled the free blacks in Florida to the same rights and privileges as those given other former Spanish subjects. The guaranteeing of these "rights," however meager, did not fit with the South's growing belief that free blacks were dangerous to a well-ordered slave society. In Florida restrictions on slaves were gradually expanded to include free blacks as well. In May 1823 a handwritten petition from "various free men of color" declared that they had been denied the privileges of citizens by the city of St. Augustine, including the right to walk the streets or to "assemble for amusement" after 9 P.M.[21] In 1824 the city of St. Augustine levied a special tax on "free Persons of Colour," three dollars for males ages eighteen to fifty, half that sum for females. This time the free blacks resisted in court. James Clarke, "a free man of colour," argued that the tax was illegal because it was not collected for any "specific object" and also because "a discriminatory tax was unconstitutional." The superior court agreed and threw out the tax. The issue of a free black population was especially pressing in Middle Florida, where the slave population expanded rapidly with the rise of the plantation economy. In 1826 Leon County taxed free black men, ages eighteen to fifty, at the rate of five dollars per annum; the poll tax on white males of

20. Pensacola *Gazette*, March 16, May 18, Dec. 28, 1827, in Journal of the Legislative Council.
21. Petition of May 31, 1823, in Journal of the Legislative Council.

similar ages was fifty cents.[22] The Pensacola *Gazette* objected to the discriminatory levy and used the occasion to attack the Legislative Council's "persecuting and proscriptive course against free persons of colour. They have certain natural and constitutional rights, and those who were in Florida prior to the change of Government, also have rights secured by Treaty." Resistance through courts at law and the consciences of editors gradually ceased, and the discriminatory tax and registration became a common device for limiting the rights of Florida's free black population.[23]

The laws and court system of the Florida Territory were like those of other American frontiers, at once elaborate and transitory. The lawmaking mania which seems to prevail throughout the United States, is not less remarkable in Florida than elsewhere," commented the Pensacola *Floridian*.[24] The many and changing laws, the complexity of the court structure, and the widespread litigation over land claims that dragged on without resolution lent an uncertain air to this aspect of institutional development in the Florida Territory. From the perspective of almost a decade of experience with the American judicial system, the *Florida Herald* summed up the situation with the comment that the judiciary system of the territory, "which should at once have been placed upon a permanent footing, has been sported with more than any thing else." The editor concluded of the legal system, "For these eight years past this territory may be compared to a vessel in a gale of wind with her sails shivered to pieces." The prosperous years of the 1830's intensified the impulse to make new laws and revise the old. In 1834 a compilation of the territorial code ran to nearly four hundred pages. By 1840 the statute books contained more than one thousand laws.[25]

"There is nothing which more strongly marks the progress of civilization in a country, than a well regulated judiciary," declared the St. Augustine *Herald*. Well regulated or not, Florida had an elaborate judicial system. The act organizing the judiciary in 1822 established two su-

---

22. St. Augustine *East Florida Herald*, Oct. 30, Nov. 20, 1824; Tallahassee *Florida Intelligencer*, Sept. 1, 1826.

23. Pensacola *Gazette*, May 18, 1827; Memorial Referred Jan. 28, 1833, in *TP*, 24: 800–02.

24. Pensacola *Floridian*, Aug. 9, 1823.

25. St. Augustine *Florida Herald*, Sept. 30, 1829; Feb. 27, 1840. On the multitude of legal occasions in territorial life, the complicated nature of the legal mechanisms early established, and the widespread use of lawyers, see the John Faulk Correspondence, Glunt Papers.

perior courts in recognition of the traditional division of the territory into East and West. These courts remained functional for the entire territorial period. In 1824 Congress added a third court district for Middle Florida (defined as the area between the Suwannee and Apalachicola rivers) and, four years later, a fourth for southern Florida to serve the large number of cases flowing out of the salvage business at Key West. Of all the territories, only Florida had superior courts that met in every county. The multiplicity of the courts conformed to the sectional nature of the territory. It was also expensive. By 1836 the cost of maintaining the judiciary in Florida Territory exceeded thirty thousand dollars a year, higher than for any other territory.[26]

The grand jury was a prominent part of the legal apparatus in Florida. It was not an expression of public opinion, but a group "selected by one individual," meeting in secret, not responsible for its actions, and permitting no defense by those it censured. Yet grand juries convened at regular intervals to consider the state of the county. The matters discussed were the most important problems facing the community: roads, bridges, schools, protection from the Indians, the need for a courthouse and jail. It was a rare grand jury report that did not remind its county citizens and representatives in government of these needs. Other considerations revolved around the special requirements of a particular community. The Duval County Grand Jury (1834) supported railroads and attacked nullification and "incompetent" magistrates. The Grand Jury of the town of Apalachicola condemned "the practice of profanely swearing in common conversation"; the Grand Jury of Madison and Jefferson Counties decried "the practice of trading with negroes by the keepers of the various tippling shops established throughout the country"; and Leon County attacked the increasing "number of establishments, familiarly known as doggerys, the tendency of which is, to impede the cultivation of morals, and in many instances, to corrupt our slave population."[27]

Florida Territory presents an interesting study in the problem of taxation on the frontier. "The people of the territory must expect to pay taxes too, or how will the country be improved," commented the *Herald*

26. St. Augustine *East Florida Herald*, April 12, 1823; Joseph M. White to William Wilson, Feb. 16, 1836, in *TP*, 25: 234. Charles D. Farris, "The Courts of Territorial Florida," *FHQ*, 19 (1941): 346–67, is a complete study.

27. Pensacola *Gazette*, May 20, 1837; St. Augustine *Florida Herald*, Jan. 9, 1834; Tallahassee *Floridian and Advocate*, June 2, 1831; June 5, 1832; Nov. 21, 1840.

in 1823. "How are *roads to be opened, jails* and *bridges* built—*ferries* erected the poor supported, without the assessment and collection of taxes."[28] Nowhere did people require more in the way of facilities and services. In 1824 the Grand Jury of Pensacola complained that the city jail was so insecure that "the facility with which [prisoners] may escape is calculated rather to increase than to suppress the violation of the laws." Three years later Pensacola still had no facilities in which to confine prisoners and released them "in preference to allowing them to starve, no provision having been made for their support." While requests for federal support to build courthouses and jails flowed in a steady stream to Washington, the several counties took up the question of tax levies. Opposition was intense. A public meeting in Pensacola, called to protest the tax levied by the court of Escambia County, passed a strong resolution: "Taxes . . . are excessive, oppressive and unnecessary, and ought not to be tolerated." The editor later commented that the county had been organized and taxes levied for three years, but not one cent had been collected, and, not surprisingly, the county treasury was empty.[29] With growth and economic development came gradual acceptance of taxation. The levies were those customarily found on the frontier: polls, black and white; entertainment, such as taverns, billiard tables, "showmen of all descriptions"; luxury vehicles like carriages; license fees for peddlers, doctors, and lawyers. Prosperity expanded the list. By 1845 tax lists in some counties included "wharfs," money at interest, cattle, and cotton. The changes testify to the maturing agricultural economy of the territory about to become a state.[30]

The different sections of Florida created varied societies. St. Augustine had been the center of social, economic, and political life in the days of the Spanish empire. Much of this influence waned with the departure of a portion of the Spanish community to Cuba and the influx of Americans into Middle Florida. It survived in some forms, however, and especially in the theater. Several performances took place each year.[31] Pen-

28. St. Augustine *East Florida Herald*, Sept. 20, 1823.

29. Pensacola *Gazette*, March 13, 1824; Dec. 1, 1826; June 12, 1824; Feb. 18, 1826. St. Augustine *Florida Herald*, May 5, June 30, 1830, reflects opposition in the eastern part of the territory.

30. J. Randall Stanley, *History of Jackson County* (n.p., 1950), 30–31; David Yancey Thomas, "A History of Banking in Florida," table 2, PKY.

31. William G. Dodd, "Theatrical Entertainment in Early Florida," *FHQ*, 25 (1946): 121–74, has pieced the story together in great detail from the newspapers and other accounts.

sacola had musical entertainment, and an ensemble performed a Mozart symphony there in 1822. Both St. Augustine and Pensacola made much of their locations as ports of call. The arrivals of ships offered the opportunity for social activities, especially balls. Key West, a kind of resort in winter, also had balls and formal dinner parties with horseback rides on the beach. But the elite society of the territory gravitated to the new capital at Tallahassee. The new Americans dominated the government, and the attendant planter society that emerged in the 1820's was basically an extension of the cotton frontier of the Deep South. Great balls highlighted the social season. Horse racing was the favored sport of gentlemen (bets in specie only, please). The Magnolia *Advertiser*'s description of a ball in 1829 to honor the territorial delegate, Joseph M. White, expressed the pride of people in their rapid progress. The whole affair "presented in forcible contrast, the change which the short period of two years has wrought, where the track of civilization has scarcely been seen, and the howling of the wilderness and the roaring of the wild beasts, has given place to the refinements of civilized life—the sounds of music of the enlivening dance."[32]

Religion and churches reached into every section of Florida. Blacks made up a substantial proportion of some of the Protestant congregations. In 1839 the Methodist preacher Peter Haskew reported from St. Joseph that his mission congregation contained sixty-five black members and only fourteen white. The blacks faithfully attended his services, he wrote, while the white parishioners went to lectures on phrenology. Haskew prayed hard for his black members, and he concluded that "the coloured class is a tolerable passable class, taking so many together." Organized schooling was rarely found. With the revelation in 1824 that only 80 of 350 children in St. Augustine of school age received any kind of formal instruction, energetic church people organized Sunday classes to provide basic schooling. "Sunday instruction," as it was called, fitted the child to read the Bible and other religious and temperance tracts that circulated in the churches. Minimal as it was, such teaching was significant for children in towns.[33] Private academies in the towns provided al-

---

32. Magnolia *Advertiser*, April 24, 1829. Kenneth Scott, "The City of Wreckers: Two Key West Letters of 1838," *FHQ*, 25 (1946): 196–97, describes social life in Key West; Lizzie Brown, "Lizzie Brown's Tallahassee," ed. Bertram H. Groene, *FHQ*, 48 (1969): 155–75, does the same for Tallahassee.

33. Peter Haskew, "A St. Joseph Diary of 1839," *FHQ*, 17 (1938): 132, 140; St. Augustine *East Florida Herald*, July 31, 1824.

most the only opportunities for real education. Public schools languished on the editorial pages of newspapers. In 1832 a public school opened in St. Augustine for the male and female children of taxpayers, but it foundered on the opposition of property holders to the taxes necessary to support the institution. The school closed in five months, terminating the educational opportunities of 120 youngsters. In the countryside, education on an organized basis made no headway.[34]

Florida's development from 1835 to 1850 opened on a period of prosperity. By 1835 the basic problems that had plagued territorial Florida seemed on the way to solution: the land system was in operation; the federal government had financed a number of badly needed public works in transportation and communication; the Indian population was in process of "removal" to the West. In these days of heady prosperity, a few of Florida's leaders seized the most powerful economic institutions of the day and employed them for their own ends. Their activity was a striking feature of Florida's enduring frontier. One such institution was the bank. Banks, like almost everything else in Florida, were sectional. Prior to American occupation the British trading firm of Panton, Leslie & Company had provided whatever banking facilities existed. With its disappearance, Floridians looked for replacements. That the territory was so large, the settlement so sparse, transportation so rudimentary, and economic development so nominal proved no deterrent. The Legislative Council acted favorably on the demand for banks, and only Governor Duval's continued vetoes postponed the appearance of a banking institution until 1828, when the Legislative Council passed a bill over his veto. This was only the first of many banks. Between 1828 and 1839 the Legislative Council chartered eighteen banks, of which three became significant. The Union Bank of Florida, centered in Tallahassee, was the largest. Essentially a planter's bank, its charter provided that a board of appraisers appointed by the governor might lend money on land and slaves. Residents of Middle Florida owned almost all the stock of the

34. T. Frederick Davis, "Pioneer Florida, A Free Public School in St. Augustine, 1832," *FHQ*, 22 (1944): 200–07. At about the same time, a Mr. Ashman established in St. Augustine a school for some twenty to thirty blacks, most of them the children of slaves (p. 207). James O. Knauss, "Education in Florida, 1821–1829," *FHQ*, 3, no. 4 (1925): 22–35, is complete.

bank. The bank opened for business in January 1835, just in time to participate in the prosperous middle years of the decade.[35] The Bank of Pensacola was also a locally owned institution chartered to meet the needs of its section, especially the funding of transportation facilities to a remote agricultural hinterland. A Pensacola editor wrote,

> Pensacola is the natural mart for about ten or twelve thousand bales of Cotton raised in Alabama, but owing to our entire want of bank facilities, until within the last two or three years, this Cotton has found its way to the Alabama on the west and the Chattahoochie on the east. Now, however, we possess those facilities, in the operations of one of the soundest institutions in the Southern country.[36]

Having secured a bank, Pensacola's entrepreneurs sought to construct a railroad into Georgia and Alabama. In East Florida, northern capitalists dominated the Southern Life Insurance and Trust Company of St. Augustine. This bank had wide authority; a member of Congress once remarked that it had "every power except that of killing Indians."[37] The bank established branches at commercial centers like Apalachicola, St. Joseph, and emerging Jacksonville, thus giving it claim to serve all sections. In actual point of fact, it served its stockholders, most of who lived in New York City.

Florida's banks flourished in the flush times of the mid-1830's. Their loans spurred new purchases of land and slaves; their discounts assisted commercial transactions that flowed freely on a crest of high agricultural prices. This prosperity ended abruptly. The war against the Indians struck at the economy of East Florida and indirectly at the Southern Life Insurance and Trust Company. The other banks continued in operation, to be struck down in the panic of 1837 and its subsequent depression. The panic and depression were two events in which all Florida's sections shared equally. The Florida banking experience provided much evidence to support the indictments of hard money Jacksonians: favoritism, irresponsible management, and reckless loans without proper security. Florida entered the Union in 1845 without a single banking institution.[38]

35. Kathryn T. Abbey, "The Union Bank of Tallahassee," *FHQ*, 15 (1937): 207–31.
36. Pensacola *Gazette*, Oct. 8, 1836.
37. Quoted in St. Augustine *Florida Herald*, Dec. 11, 1840, quoted in Sidney Walter Martin, *Florida during the Territorial Days* (Athens, Ga., 1944), 153.
38. Thomas, "Banking in Florida," is a detailed discussion of Florida's territorial banks. Also see Martin, *Florida during the Territorial Days*, 144–64.

Another special feature of Florida's frontier experience was railroad construction. Why such a poor, sparsely settled territory, which constantly appealed to the federal government for assistance, should actively promote the most advanced transportation technology of the day invites our attention. That railroads appeared in Florida with banks was no accident. Railroads demanded capital in sums unavailable on the frontier unless through outside investment or a bank in the most prosperous of times. Geography also played a part. The land was level, if sometimes wet and marshy. Harsh winters imposed no demands. Furthermore, the nature of Florida's developing agricultural economy placed a premium on a transporatation facility that could ship bulk cargo—synonymous for cotton—a relatively short distance overland to a deep water port. Florida had a number of such ports on the Gulf by the 1830's, but most of them lay underused because there were no navigable rivers of significance to the hinterland. A railroad—even a short one—would perform economic miracles. So a few ambitious, far-sighted entrepreneurs seized upon railroads as a solution to the territory's problems of transportation. The flush times of the early and mid-1830's provided an attractive economic setting and ready capital for those disposed to dream such dreams.

In 1831 the Florida Legislative Council asked that the engineers surveying a proposed trans-Florida canal also explore the possibility of a railroad. Thereafter an increasing number of applications for railroad charters came before the legislature. Between 1830 and 1860 Florida's government gave charters to at least twenty companies for railroad construction. This is not surprising. What is astonishing is that by 1840 enterprising companies had constructed and put into operation four railroads in territorial Florida. Not all four were still in existence in 1840, nor did they ever operate simultaneously, but each had operated, if only for a short period. One was a line from Tallahassee to St. Marks near the Gulf; the short-lived but spectacular development of the town of St. Joseph promoted two railroads, to run from that port to the Apalachicola River (via Lake Wimico) and to Iola; and, the fourth, a short line from Arcadia to Pensacola Bay.[39]

The first and longest lived of these railroad lines served the cotton in-

---

39. T. Frederick Davis, "Pioneer Florida, The First Railroads," *FHQ*, 23 (1944): 177–83. Congress passed an omnibus railroad bill for the territory of Florida in 1837, offering an eighty-foot right of way through public lands, with the privilege of using the building materials thereon for construction. 5 Stat. 144–46 (Jan. 31, 1837).

terests in Middle Florida and was intended to provide rapid transportation to a port on the Gulf of Mexico. After the usual number of reorganizations and name changes, the Tallahassee Railroad Company emerged in 1834 with a land grant of five hundred thousand acres and a right of way to the Gulf. In its early organization and financing, the railroad owed much to its association with the Union Bank of Tallahassee. Construction began in January 1835. The twenty-three-mile stretch from Tallahassee to St. Marks went into operation in 1836, and the company extended the line to Port Leon in 1839. Physically, the railroad reflected an infant state of technology. A large work force of laborers and slaves laid pine rails on wooden crossties, and strips of iron were nailed on top of the rails. The cars were small, box-shaped affairs in which the passengers—where there were provisions for such—rode on back-to-back benches facing the sides of the car. Other Florida railroads—and railroads everywhere, for that matter—looked much the same. This project had the support of several of the most prominent men in Middle Florida, especially Richard Keith Call, entrepreneur, planter, militia general, and twice territorial governor. The railroad was a notable economic success. No longer did the planters of Middle Florida haul their baled cotton to the Gulf in wagons over frontier trails. The Tallahassee–St. Marks line carried thirty to forty thousand bales of cotton annually to the Gulf, first by mule and, after 1837, by steam locomotive. Slaves owned by the company performed much of the labor in construction and later operation. Port Leon was an early railroad town, built by the railroad company where the tracks ended at deep water on the St. Marks River. Within sixty years similar towns could be found throughout the Far West.[40]

Promoters associated with the town of St. Joseph constructed two railroads. Their town building had its roots in the St. Joseph–Apalachicola rivalry. In 1835 the United States Supreme Court gave clear title to the town of Apalachicola to a land company. Some residents refused to pay the company's price and left to start their own town, which they named St. Joseph. The new town flourished on a tide of prosperity and one of the most aggressive promotional campaigns in the urban dimension of the American frontier experience. But the "Saints"—as they came to be called—had built their town on the Bay of St. Joseph,

40. Herbert J. Doherty, Jr., *Richard Keith Call, Southern Unionist* (Gainesville, 1961), 87–92; Whitman, "Transportation in Territorial Florida," 43–44.

a site that was scenic but not commercially sound, for it lacked a trade connection with the interior. Planners intended that the first St. Joseph railroad of eight miles would run from the town to Lake Wimico, where ships could move by water to the Apalachicola River. Hundreds of carpenters and laborers rushed the project to completion, and in September 1836, in a triumphant gesture, a locomotive pulled twelve cars and three hundred passengers from St. Joseph to the lake in twenty-five minutes. But the lake proved too shallow for large vessels, and, despite the railroad connection, the town did not benefit economically. In the end the new trade route, including the rail line, had to be abandoned. A far more ambitious railroad project replaced it, a line from St. Joseph north to Iola on the Apalachicola. Once more the Saints pressed the plan to a conclusion, this time in the face of growing economic depression. The thirty-mile line opened in 1839, the same year that the town hosted the Territorial Constitutional Convention. Both were the high points in St. Joseph's history. The railroad did not divert the cotton trade from the port of Apalachicola, cotton prices fell, the economy slumped, and depression followed. A yellow fever epidemic in the summer of 1841 closed the town. It never reopened. Scavengers tore down the buildings and ripped up the iron rails from the tracks for use elsewhere.[41]

Florida's railroads were the work of some of the boldest and most gifted promoters on the trans-Appalachian frontier. In 1840 both the Iola–St. Joseph and the Tallahassee–St. Marks lines were in operation. Horses and mules drew the first trains, making them more closely related to urban trolley cars than to the steam trains of the future. The few accounts of trips on Florida's railroads tend to stress hazards and uncertainties: the cars derailed, the tracks disappeared into the marsh, the iron bands curled up and had to be held down by a trainman running ahead.[42] Gauges varied, as did charges. Where in competition with water routes, rail charges were low and competitive, but where there was no competition, companies levied whatever the market would bear. In the midst of confusion, humor, and venality, the conclusion was unmistakable: railroads were a revolution. The results were evident by

41. St. Joseph *Times*, April 27, Oct. 8, 1839; Feb. 19, 1840; James O. Knauss, "St. Joseph: An Episode of the Economic and Political History of Florida," *FHQ*, 5 (1927): 182–83; 6 (1927): 3–20.

42. Comte de Castelnau, "Essay on Middle Florida, 1837, 1838," *FHQ*, 26 (1948): 215–16.

1840. Railroads had made St. Joseph a great port city, or so thought envious Pensacolans as they planned their own railroad, a line from Pensacola north to Georgia that would transform the sleepy town with the big harbor into a great world port. Commented the *Gazette*, "*A new country is to be created* by this system of internal improvement, and resources of wealth are to be developed which had otherwise been destined to be dormant forever."[43] This was a vision of the future that would soon embrace large portions of the frontier areas of the trans-Appalachian West and, in another generation, the Pacific Coast.

Balanced against the prosperity of banks and railroads were years of chaos and economic depression. The war against the Seminoles was responsible for the chaos. Up to the arrival of the Americans, life for these five thousand Indian people was good. The Indians had space in which to move about, plentiful supplies of game and fish (both freshwater and saltwater), lands for agriculture, and a policy of benevolent indifference on the part of the Spanish. The Americans who came after 1819 did not propose to permit this life style to continue. Their impulse for acquisition of land made conflict inevitable. Floridians now seized upon a new phrase just making its appearance as a national policy and began planning for the removal of the Seminoles west of the Mississippi River. Negotiations for removal went on over a dozen years, while the American population enlarged and expanded. The pressure for removal increased with the flush times of the 1830's. In 1833 the federal and territorial authorities extracted a removal treaty from a delegation of Seminole chiefs, and, as the American agents began to press that the Seminole tribe fulfill the terms of the treaty, hostilities increased. Organized attacks by the Indians in late 1835 marked the opening of the war.

Frontier people had lived in fear of an Indian war since Daniel Boone cut the Wilderness Road. The violence of Kentucky's "dark and bloody ground" had lost nothing in the retelling over the intervening years. At the same time, the white man's impulse to dispossess the Indian of his land had grown overpowering, and his vague contempt for the Indian's "irresponsible" life style mixed in strange proportions with fear. When it came, the reality of the Indian war in Florida was fully as bad as the folklore and intensified by a total lack of preparedness. "It is inconceivable what Florida is destined to suffer from its defenseless state," com-

43. Pensacola *Gazette*, Oct. 28, 1837.

mented the *Gazette*. The Indians attacked the isolated agricultural settlements and, after death and fire, retired to the fastness of the swamps. In
the first winter of the war, such attacks destroyed sixteen plantations
south and west of St. Augustine, each employing more than one
hundred slaves.[44] Friction between the regular army and the territorial
militia did nothing to promote the war effort, and the struggle for military preferment became a prominent feature of the conflict. Sporadically
intense, the war dragged on and on. "Indians were a strong force in the
city's life," the St. Augustine *Herald* commented in 1840; later the same
year, "Though we cannot say the Indians are *masters* of the country, they
are masters of all the lives of passing travellers."[45] For the better part of
six years the Seminole War had an enormous impact on government,
economy, courts and the administration of justice, and the availability of
services throughout the territory. As late as the autumn of 1843, the
report on the election returns for Dade County noted that "in consequence of the destruction of the County seat, and the Total Abandon-
ment of the County (until within a few months past) the Clerk has not
deemed it safe to reside in that County."[46] The war introduced its own
variations of sectionalism. A few people and places benefited enormously
from the long and determined if not entirely successful campaign waged
by the United States Army. Merchants and wagoners profited and cities
prospered, especially the town of Jacksonville, which became a supply
center. The profits of the towns embittered the displaced agriculturists,
who found their lives completely disrupted. As part of its military operations, the army constructed several roads in Middle and East Florida, all
heading south—into Seminole country. After the destruction of millions
of dollars in property, hundreds of lives on both sides, and several military reputations, the war drew to a close. The United States Army lured
Chief Osceola to a parlay under a flag of truce and captured him; other
Indians fell victim to the same ruse, and some surrendered voluntarily.
The military high command declared the war over in 1842. The Seminole War found the territory in prosperity and left it in economic stagnation and depression. Not even military roads could make up the difference. In 1842 the western country and the nation as a whole was

44. Pensacola *Gazette*, June 4, 1836; Ruth Danenhower Wilson, "The Bulow Plantation,
    1821–1835," *FHQ*, 23 (1945): 227.
45. St. Augustine *Florida Herald*, Feb. 27, Dec. 31, 1840.
46. Dade County, Election Report 1843, in WPA Dade County History (HRS), PKY.

gripped in a prolonged depression that was especially severe for southern agricultural staples. But the slow growth of Florida, compared with Michigan, reflected her struggle against one adversity after another (see table 5).

Table 5. Growth of Florida, 1820–50

	1820	*1830*	*1840*	*1850*
Florida	ca. 11,000	34,730	54,477	87,445
Michigan	8,896	31,639	212,267	397,654

Sources: James Grant Forbes, *Sketches, Historical and Topographical, of the Floridas; More Particularly of East Florida* (1821; rpt. ed., Gainesville, 1964), 142; *Historical Statistics of the United States, Colonial Times to 1957* (Washington, 1960), 13.

Congress voted a Military Land Act that gave land bounties to veterans and helped to renew immigration. By the spring of 1843 the *Herald* commented of war-ravaged East Florida, "A tide of emigration is flowing in, and the wilds of Florida are giving place to the busy hum of civilization."[47] Some of these new settlements lay initially outside the institutions of organized government. The Indian River settlement began in 1842 with the usual frontier activities, centered around building and clearing. In 1844 a group of pioneers met to establish a government and provide for the common defense. Those present chose three of their members to serve as a committee of arbitration to settle disputes within the community. They also organized a militia and elected officers. Within months the governor and legislature laid off St. Lucie County, and the settlers elected the first board of commissioners. The new settlement was agricultural, with a specialty in citrus. The most prosperous planter imported a house from Savannah, bringing it down the coast by schooner. In the end, the colony did not succeed. Citrus trees take several years to yield productively, and the settlers lacked the resources or an alternative means of livelihood for the interim. Indian unrest complicated the situation, and the settlement broke up in 1849.[48]

Sectionalism continued to dominate frontier Florida from 1830 to 1850, for the events that shaped the development of the territory (statehood came in 1845) affected with varying force each of these three regions—four if one includes Key West—and led to strains and tensions

47. St. Augustine *Florida Herald*, May 15, 1843.
48. Joseph D. Cushman, Jr., "The Indian River Settlement: 1842–1849," *FHQ*, 43 (1964): 21–35. Among other things, the settlers enacted regulations to forbid the importing of diseased orange trees (p. 24).

among them. The prosperity of the middle 1830's was unequal: Middle Florida expanded and flowered; East Florida prospered until the devastation of the citrus industry by a hard freeze in 1835; West Florida stood still. The impact of the Seminole War was uneven: East Florida suffered severe physical destruction, loss of life, economic and institutional upheaval; Middle Florida also felt the war's impact, but to a lesser degree; West Florida was largely untouched. Each section continued to regard its own special interests above those of the territory as a whole.[49]

The experience of Florida was different from that of much of the trans-Appalachian West. The varied sectional nature of the territory produced confusion and conflict that grew rather than dissipated. War and depression resulted in widespread retreat from the frontier. Deserted settlements, abandoned houses, and the remains of human habitations dotted the territory. Florida demonstrates the degree to which the institutional framework established all over the trans-Appalachian frontier depended upon growth. Legislatures and the executive laid off and organized counties, designed to be in operation by the time the settlers arrived. This system anticipated the needs of the early settlers for roads, ferries, and recording facilities; it provided jobs for officeholders. At the same time, its effectiveness depended on continued settlement. In most areas of the trans-Appalachian West in the period from 1830 to 1850 the system worked. In Florida it did not work at all. The war ended immigration and cut short economic development. The organization of counties continued, but the counties did not grow. On its establishment in 1836, Dade County had ten families, about enough for a jury. An offshoot of Monroe County, it lay in the remote southeastern part of the territory, a region of scrub palmetto and sandy soil. Its most prominent feature was the Everglades. The population of the county did not increase, and the few had to assume the burdens of goverment: jury duty on a regular basis and the construction of a courthouse and jail. New counties benefited the entrepreneur and politician. There were numerous openings in the hierarchy of bureaucracy. For the active town promoter, every new county was a new county seat, with attendant opportunities for all town

49. As late as 1837, a group of Floridians petitioned for separate statehood for East Florida. Memorial to Congress by Citizens of East Florida, Feb. 5, 1838, in *TP*, 25: 469–75.

dwellers: professional people, mechanics, merchants. For ordinary citizens, this was no consolation for "the multiplication of expenses, duties, inconveniences, &c." they endured.[50]

American institutions in Florida replaced the remnants of Spain's domination, but, for all their influence, they had a fumbling quality about them. The court system was constantly in flux and dislocated; the laws were ever changing and confused. Taxes were not levied, and where levied could not be collected. As a result, the most necessary public buildings, such as jails and courthouses, remained unbuilt. Hampered by the confusion of the Seminole War, Floridians were not markedly successful in adopting American institutions to their tropical setting. A new departure in Florida's growth (however modest) was the noteworthy work of a few entrepreneurs. This territory/state with small, scattered population undertook economic development through the establishment of the newest and most powerful enterprises of the age: banks and railroads. A few individuals served as the driving force. They formed a sharp contrast to the other areas of the frontier Southwest and Northwest in this period, where the major thrust of development was the sheer mass of immigration. On most of the trans-Appalachian frontier individual men of enterprise were active in town planning, in establishing mills, plantations, and factories, and, of course, on the land, but so dramatic and so rapid was the pace of settlement that masses of people submerged their influence. In Florida the contributions of a few—while not always successful in sheer economic terms—were remarkable for their boldness, innovation, and widespread influence.

50. Key West *Enquirer*, Feb. 27, 1836; William A. Whitehead to Delegate White, Feb. 26, 1836, in *TP*, 25: 238–40, enclosing a "petition and remonstrance" against the division of Monroe County (pp. 240–43).

II

Arkansas:
A Frontier More West Than South

On his voyage down the Ohio and Mississippi rivers in 1814, Thomas Bolling Robertson of Louisiana "fell in with a canoe navigated by a man and two women." Robertson engaged the man in conversation. Yes, he was originally from North Carolina, then Tennessee, and most recently from Kentucky. Where were they headed? Arkansas was the reply. Why? The man was firm in his reasons: "That they might *live*, they had heretofore only breathed, that the lands there were fresh & good and there was spring water, that they would set down on Congress Land & purchase when it should be offered for sale." The canoe cast off and headed up the White River to a world that Robertson called "situated on the extreme verge of civilized inhabitation."[1]

Arkansas was a reincarnation of the American frontier traditionally associated with places like Kentucky after 1775 and Michigan after 1815. In Arkansas the early frontier experience reappeared and lived on until well into the nineteenth century, immune from the innovations of technology and forces of movement that overtook other frontiers after 1815. While people north and south of the Ohio moved aggressively to seize the land, to place it under cultivation, and to pursue commercial agriculture, Arkansans hunted, trapped, grazed livestock, and generally pursued a lonely, solitary existence, consistent with their location in the

---

1. Thomas Bolling Robertson, "Journal of a Tour down the Ohio and Mississippi," Thomas Bolling Robertson Letters, Walter Prichard Collection, folder 12, LSU.

most remote frontier of the West. Amidst their isolation, the people of Arkansas shared a number of common characteristics: a single-minded materialism; a tendency to unite in groups, linked by kinship, for self-protection and their own self-interest; and an inclination to violence widespread among all elements of society that endured. Their limited world was like that of medieval lords, with personal estates over which they ruled, armed forces, economic self-sufficiency, and ill-disguised contempt for higher authority and any interference with their lives. Sometimes they had fields under cultivation, but often they simply hunted and trapped, without "even so much as a garden." In disposition, they varied from kind and good-hearted to vicious. Reflecting the latter, the Flanigan family attempted "by every means in their power to discourage immigration and to injure newcomers. . . . The men respected no law, human or divine, but were slaves to their own selfish lusts and brutish habits." More often, the first Arkansans were primitive but agreeable. Russell W. Benedict described the Wyley clan in these terms:

> Their habits and manner of living was the same as the Indians. They had no knowledge of Letters or Books, and were wonderfully ignorant and as full of superstitions as their feeble minds were capable of, believing in Witches, Ghosts, Hobgoblins, Evil eyes, and all such traditions, but with all their weaknesses, whims, and follies this family were kind, friendly, inoffensive, harmless and perfectly honest. They did not farm, had no fences around their shanty habitations, and appeared to have lived a roving, rambling life ever since the battle of Bunker Hill when they fled to this wilderness.[2]

In the years after 1815 the arrival of ambitious men who sought to reenact in Arkansas the experience of the Great Migration in Mississippi and Alabama diluted this primitive society. The new arrivals—officeholders, merchants, and aspiring planters—succeeded in their objectives, but only very gradually, and only after a long struggle against nature and human resistance to change. Even as a frontier, Arkansas was unknown. The Arkansas Territory had about it the same air of mystery that the Americas held for navigators of the early sixteenth century. In 1820 Cephas Washburn, a missionary headed to Arkansas, inquired about his destination at Walnut Hills (later Vicksburg), Mississippi. People shook their heads in disbelief that any such place existed. Washburn wrote,

2. Quoted in Ted R. Worley, "Story of the Early Settlement in Central Arkansas," *ArHQ*, 10 (1951): 128–29.

"At that time Arkansas was a perfect *terra incognita*. The way to get there was unknown; and what it was, or was like, if you get there, was still more an unrevealed mystery."[3] Even those already in the territory were sometimes not sure where they were. Land movement was almost impossible, and, on water, the canoe for people and flatboat for cargo were the rule. Joab Hardin's ferry on the White River in 1818, "consisting of two small canoes lashed together with a few split clapboards laid across," was one example of local transportation facilities.[4]

This was the region and these were the fourteen thousand people to whom Congress gave a territorial government in 1819. The act of organization was based on the Ordinance of 1787 and provided for the usual offices and their prerogatives. One special feature was the adoption of the laws of the Missouri Territory, a step presumably consistent with the area's experience as a part of Missouri. The course of government for the Arkansas Territory was uncertain and hesitant. Between 1819 and 1830 lack of continuity, factionalism, and violence characterized both the executive and judicial branches. Three men held the office of governor during this period, and each was absent from the territory for a good portion of his tenure. Two of the original three justices appeared only briefly in the territory and served no useful function, so the judiciary lay in disarray. A dissident faction gathered around the secretary, Robert Crittenden, almost from the day of his appearance in the territory in July 1819, and the divisive and violent nature of Arkansas politics grew with each passing year. A duel in 1819 left dead a man who was a brigadier general, the commander of the territorial militia, and a recently elected delegate to the territorial assembly. Nor was the judicial branch of the government exempt from the practice of dueling. In 1824 one superior court judge killed another over a point of principle that arose in a card game. Three years later the territorial secretary killed a territorial delegate in an affair of honor. To a greater degree than in other territories, violence in Arkansas involved some of the leading public officeholders.[5]

Government in Arkansas, as in the other enduring frontiers, was very important at all levels: local, territorial, and national. Officials were, accordingly, the focus of public attention. Unlike Michigan, and to a cer-

3. Quoted in Walter Moffatt, "Transportation in Arkansas, 1819–1840," *ArHQ*, 15 (1956): 187.
4. Worley, "Story of the Early Settlement in Central Arkansas," 123.
5. Lonnie J. White, "Arkansas Territorial Politics, 1824–1827," *ArHQ*, 20 (1961): 17–38.

tain extent Florida, Arkansas was unlucky in the appointments that came its way. The governors were not distinguished by talents in compromise or leadership, or even by success in begging from the federal government. James Miller, the first governor, delayed his departure for Arkansas in 1819 until he could fit up an elaborate barge, with his name and official motto emblazoned in gold letters. His voyage up the Arkansas River ever farther into the wilderness had about it something of the air of the Spanish conquistadores carrying the Old World to the New. Miller was a professional soldier, and the only thing of lasting value that he brought with him was weapons: four hundred stand of arms, forty thousand rounds of "fixed ammunition," and "fifty horsemen pistols."[6] He spent as little time as possible in the territory. In his absence the secretary Robert Crittenden filled the office and promoted his own interests. The favorite project of the second territorial governor, George Izard, was the militia. The scattered nature of the population made effective organization impossible, but he devoted lavish attention to consideration of the appropriate uniform. The commissioned officers of the Izard County Battalion, for example, wore "a round hat, and a plume 15 inches in length; a deep blue cotton hunting frock, fringed with red, with a waist belt four inches in width, to buckle or button before; pantaloons of the same, the seams welted in red; white vest; and shall wear around the neck a black silk handkerchief or black stock."[7] There is no record of what the enlisted men wore—if there were any enlisted men. The collective contributions of the governors to the territory lay in the few place-names they left scattered on the land. There was little or nothing else.

The General Assembly was neither more statesmanlike in approaching the problems of the territory nor more effective in solving them. For the better part of a decade it engaged in time-consuming debates over the infinite variety of questions that seemed to concern frontiers everywhere, ranging from adultery to wolf bounties. The Arkansas assembly devoted most of its time to three issues: creating new counties, changing the

6. Journal of the Legislative Council and the House of Representatives, 1819–40, ESR, Arkansas, p. 13.
7. Little Rock *Arkansas Gazette*, May 21, 1828. The *Gazette* of Oct. 20, 1830, carried a long caricature of a militia muster. The county militia muster was a standard target for humorous pieces, e.g., A. B. Longstreet's *Georgia Scenes* (1835). Most of the accounts appeared in literary magazines or newspapers farther to the east; it is unusual to see a lampooning article so close to home.

court system, and petitioning the federal government for assistance. In 1829 one honest member introduced a resolution to the effect that since the General Assembly had debated for so long and no end was in sight, its members should be paid for only the first thirty days of the session. It would, he concluded, "be unjust to draw from the Treasury of the Territory Arkansas compensation for services rendered since the expiration of the said thirty days." His colleagues rose up to defeat the resolution decisively: Yeas, one; Nays, twenty-two. Salaries for officials and legislators dominated the budget of the territory. In the year 1825–26, for example, the budget included compensation to the members of the legislature: $4,073.75; salaries of civil officers: $7,603.00; cost of criminal prosecutions, jail fees, and grand jurors: $1,582.15½. Salaries and court fees added up to $13,258.90½ out of a total budget for the territory of $14,740.68.[8]

Like the legislators of Michigan and Florida, Arkansans loved to tinker with their legal code and courts. The legislature organized, abolished, and reorganized the county courts on a regular basis. The index of the laws of the territory shows the staggering amount of debate and legislation on the court system: 31 entries for chancery proceedings, 14 for circuit courts, 21 for county courts, and a total of 128 under the heading "Judicial Proceedings." The law on the duties of the justice of the peace covered twenty-eight pages; that on the territorial militia, thirty-one pages.[9] There were certainly many courts. The scheduled time of the sessions of the superior, circuit, and county courts for 1834 filled a full column of the newspaper. Simply put, the superior court held two terms in Little Rock, in January and July; there were four circuit courts, and one met twice annually in each county; the county courts convened quarterly. In spite of this interest and elaborate structure, justice was sometimes delayed. When the Crawford County Circuit Court met in February 1835, after a lapse of two years, the docket numbered more than two hundred cases.[10]

8. Journal of the Legislative Council, pp. 202, 51, 112. The same proportions of distribution may be found in the territorial budget for 1827–29, printed in the Little Rock *Arkansas Gazette*, Nov. 10, 1829. The appointments of the legislature were hardly luxurious. As late as 1827, the assets of the assembly consisted of five plain tables, four pitchers, twelve tin tumblers, six inkstands, four sandboxes, and four benches. *Ibid.*
9. Laws of the Arkansas Territory, 1835, ESR, Arkansas, pp. 355–82.
10. Little Rock *Arkansas Gazette*, Jan. 21, 1834; Little Rock *Arkansas Advocate*, Feb. 27, 1835. The court should have met twice a year.

The American Indian was another concern of legislators and the object of much legislation. At the time of territorial organization there were about fourteen thousand white settlers and about the same number of Indians. Because of its western location, Arkansas became the homeland of thousands of Indians expelled from the cotton lands east of the Mississippi by the forces of the Great Migration and the operation of Indian removal. Many of the territory's immigrants, especially after 1829, were Indians on their way west. In the early days the economy of the territory rested largely on the maintenance of Indians. Supplies and rations for Ft. Gibson and Ft. Smith provided both a market for agricultural produce and a reason for steamboat traffic on the Arkansas. The presence of a large number of Indians removed from areas to the east also gave rise to much uneasiness. The assembly passed several laws to reduce contact between the red and white peoples, prohibiting the sale of liquor and even of horses to Indians. Anyone with one-quarter or more Indian blood could not give court testimony on criminal cases. In few other territories were the laws separating the two civilizations so strong or so numerous and the restrictions on Indians so rigorous. Embodying the opinions of its constituencies, the assembly called the Cherokees a "restless, dissatisfied, insolent, and ambitious tribe, engaged in constant intrigues with neighboring tribes, to foment difficulties." The federal government must move with energy and vigor to control the Indian peoples by surrounding them by white settlements. This would have the effect, concluded the assembly's memorial of 1827, "of promoting their own civilization and knowledge of agriculture."[11]

Arkansans constantly asserted that they represented the onward march of a superior civilization. Looking over the state of white settlement in town and countryside, some Native Americans were not convinced. Nu-Tah-R-Tuh of the Cherokee delegation saw comments on the superiority of white civilization in the *Arkansas Gazette* and replied "To the man who makes the paper talk every week at Little Rock":

> Brother, you seem very desirous of the civilization of our people. I thank you in my own name, and in their name, for these benevolent wishes. But what is civilization? Is it a practical knowledge of agriculture? Then I am willing to compare the farms and gardens of this nation with those of the mass of white population in the Territory. The

11. Journal of the Legislative Council, p. 117.

advantages will be on our side. Does Civilization consist in good and comfortable buildings? Here, if the comparison be made, we shall have the advantage over the mass of your people. Does it consist in possessing stocks? We are willing to compare. Does it consist in the style of diet and clothing? Here, also for economy and comfort we are willing to compare. Does it consist in morality and religion? Our people have built, wholly at their own expense, the only Meeting-house in the Territory; and though the number of truly religious people is small, and though many immoral practices prevail, yet I believe we might compare with your very best settlements in these respects. Does it consist in schools and education of youth? I believe a larger portion of our youth can read and write than of those in your own settlements. Two permanent Schools, wholly supported by ourselves, will go into operation in a few days. Does it consist in hospitality? We are proud of our hospitable character. —If civilization consists in any of the above, then, Brother, do not tell about hemming us in, by your settlements, to civilize us. But if civilization consists in pitched battles, to murder one another, or in shooting our neighbors and brothers, in streets and places of public resort, then we are in a woeful state of barbarism. Brother, I have done.[12]

The influence of government spread through the Arkansas Territory by way of the county. At every session the legislature added to the few counties inherited from Missouri. Indeed, one of the characteristics of government in Arkansas was the energy with which the legislature created new counties and the governor named officers for counties that had no roads, no towns, and scarcely any people. In 1820 Crawford County had a population of fewer than five hundred people; in 1827 Lafayette, St. Francis, and Lovely counties had only a handful; in 1829 Jackson County had fifty taxpayers. The census of 1835 listed the population of Jackson County at 333; Pike, 449; Hot Spring, 458; Miller, 350; Monroe, 461; and estimated the number of inhabitants in Scott County at fewer than one hundred. Another four counties had fewer than one thousand people within their borders. The reason for the impulse to organize large areas with few people is not clear. County organization gave the illusion of growth, and government helped to attract immigrants. Perhaps the legislature hoped to meet the needs of a few scattered settlers for a court system. Yet the impression persists that the number of counties expanded for the sake of officeholders. In comparison to the

12. Little Rock Arkansas Gazette, April 23, 1828, quoted in Ina Gabler, "Lovely's Purchase and Lovely County," ArHQ, 19 (1960): 36–37.

small population of Arkansas, the number of officeholders was large. Every county had what the law allowed.[13] The budgets of the larger and more centrally located counties, published annually in the *Arkansas Gazette*, showed the income and expenditure for the year. The major items of income were tax collections (based on land) and license fees for merchants, peddlers, tavern keepers, and others, and, in addition, the occasional fines assessed and collected by the county courts. The principal expenditures were for the support of the bureaucracy: courts and court-related costs such as expenses for the grand jury, elections and election returns, and the maintenance of the road viewers. As late as 1826 only one county—Hempstead—supported paupers.[14]

At the same time that public administration on both territorial and county levels absorbed virtually their entire respective incomes, the counties and territory constantly petitioned the federal government for aid in maintaining roads and schools. At both the executive and legislative levels, Arkansas was a beggar. The territory sent forth petitions for every known form of support, from roads to rivers to courthouses to jails; the assembly even requested funds for printing a digest of the territory's growing body of laws. Congress, generous in a time of prosperity, provided much assistance. The Little Rock–Memphis Road, opened in 1828, cost the federal government $267,482. It was a large commitment to so remote a territory.[15]

Arkansas began its economic life with the fur trade and passed only gradually through this stage. The continued presence of large numbers of Indians tended to augment the trading nature of the economy. Jacob Barkman began to engage in trade at about the time of the War of 1812. With a boat made from a big pine tree, Barkman set out from Arkadel-

13. A list of offices appointed in 1826–27 alone is printed in Little Rock *Arkansas Gazette*, July 10, 1827; a roster of justices of the peace in 1830 is in *ibid.*, March 23, 1830; the census of 1835 is in *ibid.*, Aug. 25, 1835.

14. County budgets that are especially useful in assessing county priorities for expenditures and the way in which these changed or did not change over time are Phillips and Miller (Little Rock *Arkansas Gazette*, Dec. 3, 24, 1822); Clark and Pulaski (Little Rock *Arkansas Gazette*, Feb. 12, March 11, 1823); and Hempstead, Pulaski, and Clark (Little Rock *Arkansas Gazette*, March 28, 1826; March 27, 1827; April 11, 1826; Jan. 9, 1827). Annual expenditures published elsewhere often lacked a detailed breakdown of precisely what the expense was for, simply noting a disbursement, the person, and date.

15. Waddy William Moore, "Territorial Arkansas, 1819–1836" (Ph.D., North Carolina, 1962), ch. 6.

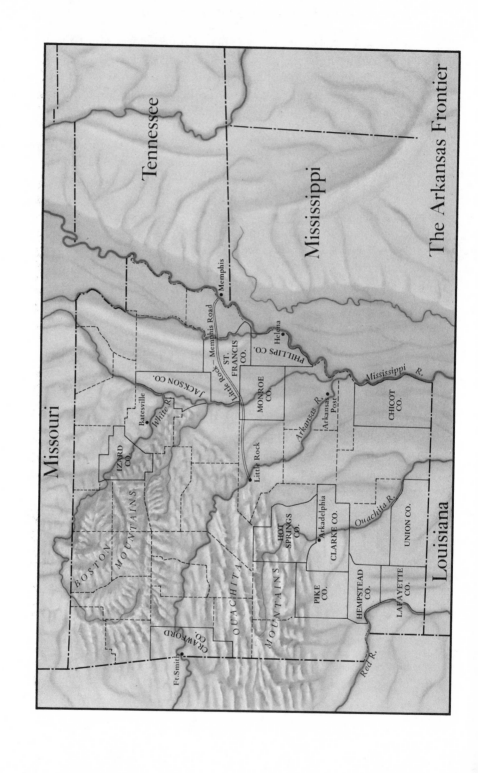

The Arkansas Frontier

phia for New Orleans with a cargo of bear's oil, skins, pelts, and tallow. Soon he was making the trip on a regular basis, returning with goods needed by the early settlers: crosscut saws, handsaws, cotton cards, powder, lead, and shot.[16] The Great Migration of 1815 turned much of the frontier South to cotton cultivation, but not Arkansas. The *Gazette* commented in 1819 that Arkansas had plenty of lawyers but needed more farmers. The lands were good—"as rich as human avarice can desire"—yet immigrants were few, and even where agriculture was established, production lagged. Much of the food consumed was imported into the territory at a high cost. Some merchants bought flour on speculation, holding barrels until the river closed and the price climbed accordingly.[17] Arkansas exhibited to a high degree the lack of specialization that characterized the early frontier economy. Most people had more than one source of income. Agriculturists also hunted and trapped, surveyed, and served as minor officials wherever possible. Even those who lived in Little Rock displayed a wide range of occupations.[18]

Cotton cultivation gradually began south of the Arkansas River. Reports of cotton crops and prices appeared regularly in the newspapers. The term "planter," with its economic and social implications, entered the Arkansas vocabulary and spread. Arkansas Post, bypassed as the territorial capital, re-emerged as a center of the cotton trade. "Our little town is all in a bustle," was the report in 1826. "Cotton, the great staple of our country, is crowding in from every quarter. Boats arrive every day at our landing, with the rich production of the climate." Loaded wagons arrived from the interior with the staple and carried home seed for the coming year. The leading Arkansas Post merchant, Frederick Notribe, had his own gin and general store. He bought cotton at New Orleans prices and offered a "large assortment of DRY GOODS, HARDWARE, and GROCERIES" for cash or produce, probably on credit. By 1830 cotton

16. "Early Reminiscences by an Early Settler of Clark County," Myra McAlmont Vaughan Collection, AHC.

17. Arkansas Post *Arkansas Gazette*, Nov. 20, 1819; Little Rock *Arkansas Gazette*, Feb. 3, 1824; Feb. 24, 1821; Aug. 14, 1824; Jan. 1, 1825. (The *Arkansas Gazette* was published at Arkansas Post from 1819 to 1821.) John C. Luttig to Jean Antoine, April 16, 1815, printed in *ArHQ*, 1 (1942): 151–55, suggests the primitive state of the economy, with dependence upon trade amidst barter conditions.

18. John Lewis Ferguson, "William E. Woodruff and the Territory of Arkansas, 1819–1836" (Ph.D., Tulane, 1960), 51–55, discusses this dimension of the Arkansas economy. Woodruff was the editor of the *Arkansas Gazette*.

dominated the agricultural news of the region to the virtual exclusion of other crops, even corn.[19]

The central fact about life in Arkansas Territory during its first decade remained the slow pace of settlement and economic development. Arkansas's lands were often suitable for cotton cultivation, the bounty warrants brought many settlers in search of their free tracts, and the *Arkansas Gazette* advertised the virtues of the territory in a manner equal to anything its most ardent supporters could require. Yet the territory did not grow. Too many negative forces were at work everywhere. It was remote. The extended swamps in eastern Arkansas forced the new settler to confront some of the most inhospitable land in the territory. The Indians were numerous, disinclined to move, and a barrier to stability and expansion—or so it was thought. Navigation of many of the watercourses was hazardous, at a time when the people of the territory moved—when and where they moved at all—by water. Finally old Spanish claims clouded the title of some of the most attractive lands in the eastern part of the territory. Arkansas was presumably no place for the energetic aggressive agriculturalist, especially one with capital. Lands in Alabama, Mississippi, and Louisiana had much more of everything to offer.[20]

A principal reason for the slow settlement and economic development of Arkansas was the lack of transportation facilities. The territory had a large river system leading to its interior and, most important, the Arkansas River itself, bisecting the territory from east to west and leading directly to the Mississippi and New Orleans. It also had, along the watercourses, much wet and overflowed land that made land transportation and even communication difficult and subjected the hardy traveller who braved these conditions to clouds of insects and wet feet. Between Little Rock and Arkansas Post, for example, the green-headed horsefly was so bad that people travelled long stretches at a gallop to avoid the pest, sometimes stopping to light fires to smoke the flies off the horses. Occasionally horses died from the ordeal. The *Gazette* carried news of men who left the road, became lost, and wandered for days in the wilderness.

19. Quoted in Jackson (Missouri) *Independent Patriot*, March 15, 1826; see also Little Rock *Arkansas Gazette*, Oct. 8, 1822; Dec. 12, 1825; Sept. 18, 1827.
20. The reasons for slow immigration and economic development are discussed in detail in Lura Mae Fitzrandolph, "The History of Arkansas to 1836" (M.A., Wisconsin, 1935), chs. 7 and 9; and in John Bradley Mason, "Early Immigration to Arkansas" (M.A., Louisiana State, 1942), ch. 4.

Mail service was irregular. Little Rock, the political and economic center of the territory, was once cut off from the East for more than two months. In 1828 contractors completed the long-awaited Little Rock–Memphis Road, but parts of it were under water for three months of each year.[21]

Arkansas depended almost exclusively on water transportation in the 1820's. The territorial period opened on the keelboat and the flatboat and eagerly welcomed the steamboat. The arrival of the steamboat *Comet* at Arkansas Post in 1821 and of the *Eagle* at Little Rock in 1822 were among the most dramatic events of the decade. The *Gazette* declared that the *Eagle*'s docking "opens a new and interesting era in the navigation and commerce of the Arkansas." To the extent that Arkansas participated in the life of the nation in the 1820's—and it did so only marginally—it did so because of steamboat communication. The impact of steam transportation was felt throughout the territory. The supplies and men for the garrisons at Ft. Smith, Ft. Gibson, and the Dwight Mission made steamboat traffic profitable, and Little Rock became the principal stop on the voyage upriver. Steamboat service reduced prices of groceries and merchandise, especially after 1825. The price of groceries at Batesville, for example, fell by half within a year of the arrival of the first steamboat. Gradually the vessels found cargoes for the return trip to New Orleans, at first furs and hides, and, by the middle of the decade, cotton. The arriving immigrants came by steamboat; for those intending to bring substantial quantities of household goods, overland transportation was almost impossible. After 1829 Indians moving to their new lands in the West provided much of the upriver business. By 1833 Little Rock had so many arrivals and departures that the local newspapers began to print a register.[22]

The proliferation of county government and the arrival of steamboats did little to change the nature of Arkansas society. Difficult as it is to characterize a society scattered over a large area and on the basis of limited evidence, the impression of a primitive, violent, self-sufficient, isolated world remains. The continued importance of hunting, trapping, and subsistence emphasizes the slow development of the economy. The

21. Walter Moffatt, "Transportation in Arkansas, 1819–1840," *ArHQ*, 15 (1956): 187–91; Little Rock *Arkansas Gazette*, Jan. 27, 1824; Sept. 9, 1829.
22. Moffatt, "Transportation in Arkansas," 194–98; Little Rock *Arkansas Gazette*, March 19, 1822; Little Rock *Arkansas Advocate*, Oct. 20, 1830.

open land to the west and contact with Indian peoples prolonged the early stage of economic development, as trading continued to be profitable business despite the laws passed by territorial legislatures forbidding contact between American and Indian societies. Perhaps the traditional frontier antipathy toward the Indians that often provoked violence infused the society as a whole. Whatever the reasons, Arkansas had more than its share of bloodshed. Almost everyone went armed. The columns of the *Arkansas Gazette* carried numerous accounts of the violence and mayhem that human beings committed against one another, much of it in the name of personal honor. And this condition was hardly confined to the people in the woods; it extended to the streets of the capital and included the leading public figures of the territory. So to the usual attacks on Indians, horse stealing, counterfeiting, gambling, and random assaults on black people, must be added the continuing violence of elected public officials. Indeed, some of the leading presidential appointees participated in it. And to these affairs of honor have to be appended the self-appointed mobs that dispensed unofficial punishment in the name of law and order.[23]

C. F. M. Noland, a literate Arkansan who was also a good shot, made a tour of the territory in 1830. One of the results was a series of articles for the Little Rock *Arkansas Advocate*, a new paper in the capital city. "Arkansas is at this time, the only new Western Country to be settled," wrote Noland in the autumn of 1830. It was a nice, tidy statement. Arkansas was still the West. It was certainly new, although not nearly as "new" as a decade before. Noland's accounts suggested, among other things, the great variation in topography, attendant economic development, and the direction of society in the several counties. But everywhere there were great strides in physical amenities. As evidence, he noted that "fifteen years ago and beyond the immediate neighborhood of the Post of Arkansas, there was but one family which enjoyed the luxury of a glass window. . . . Now, most of our farmers occupy comfortable

23. Walter Moffatt, "Out West in Arkansas, 1819–1840," *ArHQ*, 17 (1958): 33–44. Ted R. Worley, "The Story of Alfred W. Arrington," *ArHQ*, 14 (1955): 318–23, documents a particularly brutal example of vigilante justice. An account of the tendency to settle personal slights by beatings or whippings is in "Extracts from Reminiscences of John R. Homer Scott," Vaughan Collection.

houses, and a glass window no longer excites astonishment." The *Advocate*'s witty editor, Albert Pike, joined in celebrating the conquest or at least taming of "a matted and mighty forest" by "the towering wave of emigration." Pike took sharp exception to the continued criticism of the territory's location and the condition of its society. "There seems to be an idea among our brethren of the quill, that we in Arkansas are entirely out of the world," he wrote. "One editor says that Little Rock is a place somewhat west of sunset." Pike went on to assure his colleagues that the sun did indeed rise and set in Little Rock: "It is true that we are pretty well to the leeward, but we are not *quite* on the edge of the world." His was the confidence of a man writing in a period of prosperity and expansion.[24] The population statistics for the territory (state after 1836) reflect the accelerated growth of the territory after 1830 (see table 6).

Table 6. Growth of the Enduring Frontiers, 1820–50

	1820	*1830*	*1840*	*1850*
Arkansas	14,273	30,388	97,574	209,897
Michigan	8,896	31,639	212,267	397,654
Florida	ca. 11,000	34,730	54,477	87,445

Sources: *Historical Statistics of the United States, Colonial Times to 1957* (Washington, 1960), 13; James Grant Forbes, *Sketches, Historical and Topographical of the Floridas; More Particularly of East Florida* (1821; rpt. ed., Gainesville, 1964), 142.

Whether Noland and Pike celebrated the triumphs of the past or prophesied the future, in 1830 Arkansas stood on the threshold of unprecedented physical expansion and agricultural prosperity. The reasons for these were better transportation routes, especially roads; the establishment of a number of stage lines, which often ran late, but ran nonetheless; and the arrival of men of capital, with gangs of slaves, who purchased large tracts of land and settled down to the business of raising cotton. Sure signs of prosperity crowded the territory's newspapers: more advertisements for runaway slaves; more lawyers' cards; more steamboat arrivals. Little Rock, which welcomed its first steamboat in 1822, docked one hundred steamboats in the month of June 1837. It was a figure that symbolized a decade of physical expansion and, by the yardsticks of the day, progress.[25]

In the period from 1830 to 1850 distinctive societies appeared in

24. Little Rock *Arkansas Advocate*, Nov. 3, June 9, 1830; March 7, 1834; July 24, 1835.
25. Fitzrandolph, "The History of Arkansas to 1836," ch. 10; Little Rock *Arkansas Gazette*, July 4, 1837.

various sections of Arkansas. A planter class slowly emerged in the south
and east, with large-scale cotton cultivation and slavery its foundations.
Not until the 1830's, however, did the cotton exports downriver justify
its characterization as a southern civilization, with planters, lawyer class,
and wealth based on land and land speculation. This trend received impetus in the early years of the decade with the rise of cotton prices and
the opening of the Red River Valley. Supported by the federal government, Captain Henry Shreve sought to break through the heretofore impassable "Red River raft," an entangled obstacle of logs, trees, flotsam,
and mud that projected upstream for more than one hundred miles. The
success of his efforts opened the Red River Valley to immigration. "The
Red River Country is growing rapidly into notice," the *Gazette* reported
in 1834. "From the vast number of movers many of them with large
droves of negroes, who have been almost daily passing through our town
for the south for two or three months past, we imagine that country is
settling as fast as any other section of the Territory, and perhaps faster."
And a correspondent in Hempstead County commented of the immigrants, "I think that we can safely calculate on an emigration to the
Red river country, surpassing, in wealth, enterprize, and industry, the
emigration of former years."[26]

At the same time, a different society emerged in north and west Arkansas. This was a region of small independent farmers, cultivating corn
and grains, grazing large herds of livestock, isolated by geography and
economy from the cotton interests to the east. The differences were evident by 1836, when the Little Rock *Times*, describing the territory for
prospective immigrants, treated the two sections separately. The southern and eastern counties "were considered the great cotton region."
Lands to "the north and north-western counties" were "somewhat
broken, but interspersed with innumerable vallies and small water cour-
ses" where agriculturalists "raised corn, vegetables, and fruits."[27] Batesville was a center of northern economic and political influence. According to the argument of the *News*, "substantial comforts" were available
for the whole population in northern Arkansas, "as well in the mansions
of the rich as in the cottages of the poor." The independent yeoman in
this healthy climate contrasted with the "inhabitant of the tropics," the

26. Little Rock *Arkansas Gazette*, Dec. 2, 1834; Moore, "Territorial Arkansas," 167–70. On
the emergence of cotton culture along the Mississippi, see Ted R. Worley, "Helena on
the Mississippi," *ArHQ*, 13 (1945): 1–15.
27. Little Rock *Times*, April 25, 1836.

"products of his burning clime," and the "negro who ministers to his wants."[28]

The areas north and west of the Arkansas River concentrated on traditional frontier staples—corn and beef. C. F. M. Noland found the large herds a part of the livelihood of pioneers everywhere. He wrote, "In a few years a farmer here, will from a small number of cows, acquire a stock, the increase of which will not only gratify him, but create a sigh of regret, that he had not, at an earlier period of his life, come to the country so congenial to the increase of his means." The rising Indian immigration provided a ready market at Ft. Towson and Ft. Smith. The *Gazette* remarked that "the subsistence of such a vast number of Indians will give profitable employment to our farmers, by furnishing an excellent market for all the beef, pork, corn, etc. that they can raise." On numerous occasions the quantities purchased by the Indian agents reached several hundred thousand pounds.[29]

Northern Arkansas continued to depend on the keelboat and flatboat to move its commodities to market. In 1841 Batesville served as the departure point for a large "number of flat boats that have been sent down the river this season, loaded with stock, and produce of various kinds. One firm, of this place, alone has sent off twelve, loaded principally with stock; we are informed that in all, about thirty have been sent down this season and a number more are fitting out." The next season traffic was even heavier, with emphasis on the export of the corn crop to the rest of the state. Trade by water involved risks, for it depended on sufficient water levels. A fall in the river in the winter of 1842–43, the result of no rain for two months, left the town of Batesville "almost destitute of the necessaries of life."[30]

For all its cotton, steamboats, and plantation dreams, Arkansas in

28. Batesville *News*, June 24, 1841.
29. Little Rock *Arkansas Advocate*, Nov. 3, 1830; Aug. 22, 1832; Little Rock *Arkansas Gazette*, Feb. 23, 1831. The significance of livestock grazing as a stage in the development of the frontier South is explored in Frank L. Owsley, "The Pattern of Migration and Settlement on the Southern Frontier," *JSH*, 11 (1945): 147–76. The territory of Arkansas provides strong support for Owsley's theories.
30. Batesville *News*, Jan. 21, 1841; Dec. 1, 1842; see also Feb. 25, 1841; and Nov. 3, 1842. In the midst of the transition to commercial agriculture, which continued to depend on water transportation and river improvements, it is surprising to find the newspaper of a Mississippi River town saying, early as 1837, "In a few years, rail ways will be constructed in every direction, and the produce of an immense extent of back country will find its way to our markets." Helena *Constitutional Journal*, April 6, 1837. Arkansas had no railroads until the 1850's.

1840 was still western and not southern. In this, it differed dramatically from the cotton frontiers across the Mississippi River. Its needs were those shared by the western country: order in society, transportation and communication, and government assistance. Territory and state importuned the federal government to support clearing her rivers, building her roads, and so forth. On the eve of statehood in 1836, the Little Rock *Times* spoke of an identification with

> the growing interests of the West. What may we not expect in a few years more, when immense tracts of land in Illinois, Missouri, and Arkansas are taken up and improved? One continual stream of emigration continues pouring within our borders—an emigration of worthy and respectable citizens, adding to an already bold and enterprising population, would ere long raise the character of the West second to no section of the Union. The struggles now making by the eastern and northern States to secure the Western commerce already shows its importance; and there is no longer a doubt remaining that the West will, in a few years, be considered by far the most important part of the United States.[31]

Arkansas in the 1840's was still in the process of development. Much of the territory was primitive. Frederick Gerstaecker saw this world as he wandered from cabin to cabin, through a trackless and untouched wilderness. Men lived for the hunt, the freedom and exhilaration of the chase. Those who took to agriculture did so solely for survival, while herds of livestock in the woods gave them an economic hedge against the vanishing game. These people were generally content with their lot. The land returned subsistence for little work. Gerstaecker commented, "The western settlers, and particularly those in the south-western states, are not very fond of hard work; in those wild regions they prefer rearing cattle and shooting, to agriculture, and are loth to undertake the hard work of felling trees and clearing land."[32] Others also noted this reluctance to hard labor, at the same time that a commercial agriculture made its appearance. "Corn, wheat, potatoes, and nearly all other grains and vegetables flourish in all parts of the state, where the indolence of men can be aroused to their cultivation," wrote A. Fowler on the prospects of the Little Rock region in 1841. "Our industrious and enterprizing

---

31. Little Rock *Times*, April 18, 1835.
32. Frederick Gerstaecker, *Wild Sports in the Far West* (Boston, 1864), 164–65.

farmers are yet but few. The hunter race is gradually disappearing before the more useful energies of the planter."[33]

For those areas longer settled that considered themselves part of the greater South, the decade of the 1840's represented a new high point in progress. The spirit of the cotton South centered in Little Rock, one of the oldest settlements and the focus of economic, political, and social life of the territory. But some observers found Little Rock and its surroundings—along with the territory as a whole—still maturing. Fowler wrote of it in 1841, "As to the Society, it is generally far behind that of Tennessee—owing principally to the thinness of the settlements. It is however improving; and in this city, and some other places, is decidedly good."[34] Certainly the earlier frontier society had undergone a transformation and passed on to something else. Yet the maturing of this society only served to highlight the sharp contrast with the solitude and isolation of the hill country visited by Gerstaecker and the gradual evolution of the staple crop society in Columbia and Union counties.

Two major concerns were shared by the various societies that emerged in Arkansas after 1830: moral behavior and slavery. To promote what they referred to as "the morality of the people," editors attacked gambling and disorder. Antigambling societies appeared in eastern Arkansas and, following the examples in Mississippi in 1834, took vigorous actions against individuals suspected of gambling activities. Many observers viewed the outlawing of gambling as the key to domestic tranquility and argued that its suppression would cleanse society. After a violent outburst against gaming in Little Rock, "everything is quiet and peaceable—no swaggering drunkards infest our streets—no midnight broils, noisy debauches, and coffee houses filled with depraved drunken gamblers, now disturb our rest." Whether gambling was the linchpin to a moral society—with the twin evils of drunkenness and dissipation—was never proven conclusively, but citizen groups thought so and attacked these sins with the law and, if necessary, without it, and sometimes even in violation of it.[35]

33. A. Fowler to John S. Russwurm, Feb. 13, 1841, John S. Russwurm Papers, box 1, TSLA.
34. Fowler to Russwurm, Feb. 13, 1841, Russwurm Papers, box 1.
35. Little Rock *Arkansas Gazette*, Aug. 11, 1835; Little Rock *Arkansas Advocate*, Sept. 22, 1830; Little Rock *Times*, Aug. 8, 1835. The constitution of the Hempstead Anti-Gaming Society is printed in *ibid.*, Aug. 15, 1835.

Some of the activitity that took place against gambling was violent, but this was hardly the only example of physical violence in the name of morality. Vigilantism had a strong vogue in Arkansas in the 1830's, and its rise marks, in part, the transition from individual violence to violence as an institutional form. Organized groups took action (sometimes violent) against those suspected of crimes—gamblers, robbers, murderers—and other undesirables. Their activities had the support of the community—or at least the articulate elements of the community. Those working for the growth of the territory and its refurbished image had little patience with "due process" or the legal niceties that enabled suspected criminals to escape what they regarded as just punishment. "To resort to our laws for protection, seems to be worse than useless" was a prevailing opinion among the pacesetters of public opinion. Juries were too lenient; jails were easy to break out of. These criminal elements "ought to be hunted down as wild beasts, and their carcasses left as food for the buzzards." The solution was "not to trouble our courts or juries with them." The press applauded vigilante activities, including execution without trial.[36] The solution involved the same element of lawless violence that presumably the territory was most anxious to rid itself of. Of course, most of those dealt with so summarily were without friends, influence, or property in the community where they were apprehended, and the violence against them was a crime for which no one individual was responsible. It was much easier to hang a vagrant for a suspected murder than charge a member of the legislature with manslaughter for killing another in a duel.[37]

Recreational activities in Arkansas were likewise physical and occasionally brutal. In spite of the outcry against it, the urge to gamble was powerful. Men wagered on anything and everything. Horse racing was extremely popular, made the more so by the social activities of those it brought to Little Rock from all parts of the state. In the north and west, hunting was not only a business, it was a passion. Other entertainment tended sometimes to cross the line from rough-and-ready to barbaric. The Fourth of July celebration at Batesville in 1842, for example, featured a bear-baiting contest, in which a two-year-old bear "and *poor at*

36. Little Rock *Arkansas Gazette*, April 7, Sept. 29, 1835; Little Rock *Times*, Oct. 19, 1835.
37. Moffatt, "Out West in Arkansas," documents the violent side of life in early Arkansas. Moffatt's is the only account I found to address the question of sex crimes on the frontier.

that, was *pitted* against all the dogs in town, and we have a good many." The bear died of wounds, and the celebrants went home contented with the events of the day.[38]

All Arkansas societies agreed on the need to control the growing black population that became more numerous with the development of commercial agriculture and the rise of cotton culture. The territorial legislature passed the usual restrictive legislation, and municipalities supplemented these with their own local ordinances. By 1850 a legal network circumscribed the lives of slaves in the most minute detail. Free blacks were scarcely better off. In Little Rock, for example, free blacks and mulattoes over sixteen years of age (male and female) had to post bonds annually to guarantee good behavior.[39] Amidst the customary institutional structures of a slave society, one extraordinary event took place. During elections at the town of Columbia (Chicot County) in 1836, a black man appeared at the polls and, in the words of an eyewitness account, "claimed the right to vote." The judges refused. An altercation followed in which the black man, Bunch, allegedly "resorted to violent measures." One townsman was stabbed; irate citizens hung Bunch.[40]

By the year 1850 Arkansas had come a long way from the *terra incognita* noted by Thomas Bolling Robertson. Yet despite its cotton, slaves, and two hundred thousand people, the state bore the imprint of the West rather than the South. Perhaps this was due to the long experience with Indians and the proximity of Texas and Indian Territory, perhaps to the geography that sharply divided societies. Urban development in the state offered a gamut of sectional allegiances, running from Helena's world of cotton and docks on the Mississippi to Ft. Smith, a staging area for the distant Far West, to Batesville, representing the values of a grazing and agricultural rather than a cotton society. So the distinction was not so much between Arkansas and other frontiers as within Arkansas itself. In this sense, sectionalism defied political boundaries. The political allegiance that united a territory in its dependence upon the federal government for services had faded with statehood. The experience of Arkansas reinforces the significance of people on the enduring frontiers.

38. Batesville *News*, July 7, 1842.
39. Little Rock *Arkansas Gazette*, Feb. 25, 1834; Jan. 12, 1836. On restrictive legislation in other towns, see Helena *Constitutional Journal*, March 25, 1836; Batesville *News*, April 8, 1841.
40. Helena *Constitutional Journal*, Aug. 11, 1836.

Large-scale institutions for economic growth, such as banks and
railroads, were not important here. Local interests dominated the attention of public men and the press at the expense of national issues. Despite violence, vigilantism, and its timeless submersion in the forces of
nature, Arkansas matured in a long-sweeping motion of consistent
growth. If people answered the demands for education and religion more
slowly than the demands for racetracks and a strong legal code, this was
nothing unusal on the trans-Appalachian frontier. But it was typically
Arkansan that these ameliorations in the frontier condition came later in
Arkansas than elsewhere.

V

The Second Great Migration
1830–50

The years from 1830 to 1850 were the climax of an impulse to expansion
as old as the American nation. The pioneer men and women who followed Boone's Wilderness Road in 1775 were the first generation of the
trans-Appalachian frontier. Their children drifted down the Ohio and
Mississippi rivers in 1815, to the Boon's Lick country, the Sangamon
River Valley, or to Madison County at the Great Bend of the Tennessee.
Now their grandchildren together with large numbers of foreign immigrants took part in a third generation of movement, to distant Arkansas, Michigan, or perhaps to Wisconsin and Iowa. Like the First Great
Migration, this Second Great Migration involved many people over a
vast area. It changed the economic and political form of the nation,
settled much of the remaining trans-Appalachian West, filled in the
country to the Indian lands, and brought the pioneer almost to the edge
of the Great Plains. The Second Great Migration built on the experiences of the First. The institutional framework that dated from before
1815 continued in use, suggesting the continuity rather than the differences of this frontier experience. But there were differences. A common institutional base in the form of the legacies of the ordinances of
1785 and 1787, county government, and the common law could not hide
the rise of tensions and mistrust among different areas of the country and
within smaller sectional societies, between those areas long settled now
moved into a stable and prosperous society and those at the far end of
the scale in an early frontier condition. The frontier of the South was in-

creasingly black, specifically in those areas of Mississippi along the great river. The growing implications of national expansion brought the nation once again face to face with Negro slavery, that peculiar institution that had troubled American democracy since the signing of the Declaration of Independence. By 1850 this issue could no longer be evaded.

The immigrants to these new frontiers found themselves at once linked to a national economy. The days of self-sufficiency and a long, drawn-out transition to a market economy had passed. The new pioneers moved as rapidly as possible to commercial agriculture and, accordingly to dependence on a larger marketplace. The period from 1830 to 1850 witnessed widespread fluctuations in the economic condition of the nation that made their influences felt in the western country. It began with prosperity, speculation in real estate, high prices for staple agricultural products, optimism, confidence, and the spread of banking institutions to even the most remote frontiers. The financial crisis of 1837 changed this scene dramatically, and the subsequent depression was long and deep. Cotton prices sank to their lowest figure from the invention of the cotton gin to the opening of the Civil War, and prices for corn, wheat, and livestock plunged in similar fashion. Hard times came to the entire nation, and not least to the frontiers. The decade of the 1840's was one of gradual recovery. Some of the newer frontiers, especially those in western Illinois, Iowa, and Wisconsin, emerged as the most rapidly growing parts of the western country.

By and large, this was still an agricultural world. A dominant feature in this last generation of movement was the emphasis on great staple crops. Cotton remained of continuing importance on the frontiers of the South, whether in Arkansas or the New Counties of Alabama and Mississippi. Cotton culture was the measure of the progress of a society, and the planter continued to represent the highest level of economic and social achievement, even in the newest settlements. Thus the South was determined to retain its right of access with slave property to the next frontier, the territories of Kansas and Nebraska. In the last frontiers of the Old Northwest, corn was the first crop, but the settlers soon shifted to wheat for shipment across the Great Lakes or down the Mississippi. Or they grew corn and livestock for commercial purposes. The fat lands of Illinois, Wisconsin, and Iowa fed the growing urban centers of the West and East and began to assist in feeding Europe. The economy became diversified. Lumbering offered spectacular economic opportunities on the frontiers in Wisconsin and Michigan and became the economic basis of several Iowa river towns. Mining, too, was a significant feature of settlement, economic development, and institutional structure in some areas of the Northwest. All reflected expanded economic opportunities associated with this generation of movement on the trans-Appalachian frontier.

Even before 1850 expansion to the limits of the trans-Appalachian frontier no longer sufficed for the citizens of a continental nation. Texas attracted heavy immigration in the 1840's. The West Coast of the continent was a new magnet, distant but widely publicized by explorers, traders, diplomats, and a war against Mexico. Its attractions drew people from the trans-Appalachian frontier, even those portions settled in the last generation. Movement to Oregon and California had become a routine—albeit sufficiently exciting to make it an adventure—complete with guidebooks of great detail and towns where the pioneer might procure supplies and advice in equal portions. The climax of this new movement to a distant West came with the discovery of gold in California in 1848. Seamen from Massachusetts, lumberjacks from Wisconsin, farmers from Iowa, all joined in the rush across the continent, overwhelming the Spanish and Indian civilizations of the Far West. Gold drew thousands across the continent in 1849 to a frontier experience markedly different from that west of the Appalachians. The rush to California symbolized the end of the frontier in the trans-Appalachian West.

12

The New Counties
of Alabama and Mississippi:
A Frontier More South Than West

From the beginning of American settlement west of the Appalachians, the presence of large and powerful Indian tribes had shaped the frontier of the South. The War of 1812 and the First Great Migration changed this condition only in part. Substantial portions of the states of Georgia, Alabama, and Mississippi remained in the possession of Indians after 1815. The mass of immigrants that went south and west left pockets of Indian settlements on lands that soon became immensely attractive for cotton cultivation. Pressure for complete Indian removal now began to build throughout the South. By the late 1820's Indian removal had become a central issue in the domestic politics of all three states, its supporters stressing that the Georgia cession of her lands to the public domain in 1802 committed the federal government to remove the Indians; that the several tribes and individual Indians represented a threat to the safety of the white settlements; that the entire growth and prosperity of states—synonymous with increase in population—hung on the occupation of the Indian lands, so solemnly guaranteed by the federal government to their aboriginal inhabitants.[1] Whatever the public pronouncements, the real reason was the profitability of cotton. In spite of the lower prices of the 1820's, nothing could diminish the significance of

---

1. Michael David Green, "Federal-State Conflict over the Administration of Indian Policy: Georgia, Alabama, and the Creeks, 1824–1834" (Ph.D., Iowa, 1973), analyzes the conflict between state and federal governments over the removal of one tribe.

cotton for the South. Cotton cultivation was the economic, social, and political force of the age, for frontier and long-settled sections alike.

In response to these pressures, the federal government forced a series of removal treaties upon the Indians of the South: on the Choctaws in 1830, on the Chickasaws and the Creeks in 1832, and, in 1835, on the Cherokees. All provided for removal west of the Mississippi.[2] Beginning in 1830, then, and at regular intervals for the next half-dozen years, great new tracts of land in the heart of the cotton kingdom became available for settlement and cultivation. The result was the appearance of a new frontier, or series of frontiers. People referred to the new lands variously as the "Indian Nation," the "Choctaw Cession," or the "Chickasaw Purchase"; for most, it was the "New Counties." This was a world in which things were both substantially similar and remarkably different. In many ways frontier experience here was a continuation of established patterns. The great forces at large on the frontier were the traditional ones of cotton, steamboat, slave labor, rich land, and, toward the end of the period, the railroad. Initially conspicuous by their absence, institutions quickly appeared on the scene. "In the older settlements we find stable government, fixed institutions, stereotyped habits and notions, with highways giving facility of communication, with interlacing family and neighborhood relations, with social and religious ties," wrote J. L. M. Curry, from the perspective of fifty-odd years. He continued, "In the new, unoccupied territory, the settler is confronted by enfelled forests, absence of private ownership of land, county and municipal institutions unorganized, schools and churches just beginning to exist, and by newcomers, entire strangers to one another."[3] The people and the land were indeed new. The institutions were not. They were the structures of county and state government, a well-organized court system, and agriculture with cotton as a staple crop. All of these were old and familiar ways of doing things. And people did them rapidly after (and sometimes even before) the settlement of the New Counties.

There was also something new in this frontier. What took place was occupation, cultivation, and development of frontiers within the frame-

2. Mary E. Young, *Redskins, Ruffle-shirts, and Rednecks: Indian Allotments in Alabama and Mississippi, 1830–1860* (Norman, 1961), tells the story of the treaties and the struggle for the individual tracts of land given the Indians. The fight for the spoils eventually corrupted almost everyone involved.

3. J. L. M. Curry, "Reminiscences of Talladega," *AHQ*, 8 (1946): 351–52.

work of well-organized and established state governments. The state legislature simply imposed many institutions on the New Counties as part of its routine business: county organization, taxes, and the state's court structure. No longer was the state government and its tool—the judiciary—the remote creation that it had been for so many on the early trans-Appalachian frontiers. The circuit court was a prominent part of the institutional structure of the New Counties. The New Counties blended the frontier experience with the growth of a state, the presence of an unsettled and newly occupied region lying adjacent to a settled country where institutions had been established and functioning for a decade. This was the rapid settlement and institutional development of a frontier where the proximity and institutional strength of long-settled areas and the continuing cycle of the agricultural experience minimized the sharp features of frontier life. It was what we might call an "instant" society, in which longer-settled regions molded neighboring frontier areas.

The upper Creek lands, lying east of the Coosa River across Alabama and into Georgia, were one of the most attractive Indian cessions. No sooner was the treaty signed than the inevitable flow of speculators, surveyors, and bureaucrats from the Indian Office began to engulf the new country. These new arrivals found many others already on the land: squatters, who lived in defiance of the Indians and federal government alike; squaw men, who lived with the Indian tribes and hoped to profit from the treaty by land, money, or both; traders, who circulated among tribes and sold them whiskey or other goods; their more permanent brethren, who had made their log huts into doggeries, where Indians might come to purchase liquor, trade for tools, sell furs, or simply pass the time of day. Most of these groups shared a common characteristic: they exploited the Indians for a livelihood. Among the new arrivals, farmers and those connected with agriculture predominated. Some were men of means from Alabama, Georgia, and the Upper South, who weighed the opportunities of the New Counties against those available in the older agricultural settlements.

Thomas Law was one of the many landlookers who crossed the cession line from Columbus (Georgia) to Montgomery (Alabama) in the fall of 1834. He intended to move from Darlington District (South Carolina) to the New Counties of Alabama, provided prospects were sufficiently attractive. Law kept a journal of his trip, and he also wrote a detailed letter to his brother William. It was a chronicle of the land, its early occupants, and his fellow travellers. He passed nights "with some of the Indian traders, as they are scattered all over the nation to purchase up the Indian Reservations, with little shops or stores consisting of a few coarse goods & groceries." His bed consisted of "some fodder spread down on a dirt floor & a blanket spread over it with our cloaks for covering." Food was plain, with "plenty of the substantials—meat & bread & a little *coffee sweetened with molasses.*" Most of his comments concerned the land. It was mixed in quality, he wrote. "Speculators in Indian lands," as he termed them, were already in possession of some choice tracts, excellent lands that "would produce 1,000 to 1,200 weight per acre of cotton & twenty-five or thirty if not more: corn." These two crops were the yardsticks of land value, and the productiveness he conjectured fitted the description of choice lands everywhere on the trans-Appalachian frontier since men came over the Wilderness Road in 1775: fertile, level, well watered. The good lands might be purchased for $2.50 to $4.00 per acre, with credit. Thomas thought that he might buy in the Creek Cession. His brother James surely would, he reported, unless he found better lands in "the older parts of the State" to the west. Thomas Law intended to cross the Black Belt to the Choctaw Cession and inspect the lands there. "There is no scarcity of company—we are continually on the road, and I scarcely pass a day without falling in with some traveller," he concluded. Like any frontier in process of settlement, society was narrowly concerned with economic advancement. "There are nothing but a parcel of Indians and speculators for society," Law wrote, "& what is life, with the mines of Perue, without the sweets of special friendship— and in such a place as that, men would be your friends no longer than you would be gain to them, in a pecuniary point of view."[4]

As had been the case since the first trans-Appalachian frontier in Kentucky and Tennessee, the land was the attraction, this time stretching in

4. Thomas C. Law to Capt. William Law, Sept. 20, 1834; Law, "Journal of Travel to the Western Counties—from September 2ᵈ 1834," ADAH. Law's account suggested, among other things, the extensive development of the Black Belt over the previous ten years. He crossed Greene, Lowndes, Perry, and Dallas counties. He commented that "the houses generally very fine & taste displayed in everything—& health, wealth & contentment" and concluded, "The crops in these lands surpass anything I ever beheld" (entry for Sept. 24).

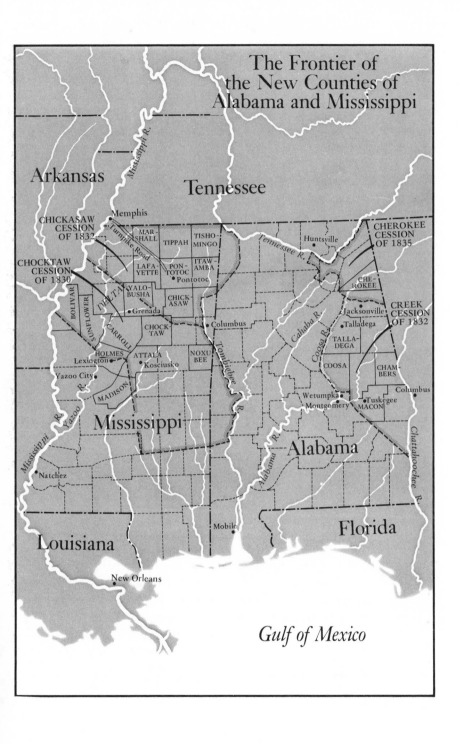

The Frontier of
the New Counties of
Alabama and Mississippi

Arkansas

Tennessee

CHICKASAW
CESSION
OF 1832

CHOCKTAW
CESSION
OF 1830

Memphis

Turnpike Road

MAR-
SHALL

TIPPAH

TISHO-
MINGO

Huntsville

CHEROKEE
CESSION
OF 1835

LAFA-
YETTE

PON-
TOTOC

ITAW-
AMBA

Pontotoc

CHE-
ROKEE

DELTA

YALO-
BUSHA

CHICK-
ASAW

Jacksonville

CREEK
CESSION
OF 1832

BOLIVAR

Grenada

Columbus

Cahaba R.

Talladega

SUNFLOWER

CHOCK-
TAW

TALLA-
DEGA

Coosa R.

CARROLL

HOLMES

ATTALA

NOXU-
BEE

COOSA

Lexington

Kosciusko

CHAM-
BERS

Yazoo City

Tombigbee R.

Columbus

MADISON

Yazoo R.

Wetumpka

Tuskegee

Montgomery

MACON

Mississippi

Alabama

Alabama R.

Mississippi R.

Natchez

Mobile

Florida

Chattahoochee R.

Louisiana

New Orleans

Gulf of Mexico

blocks across northern Georgia, Alabama, and Mississippi. The Creek Cession of Alabama was representative of all the new lands in its variety. Pine uplands, fertile river valleys wet with overflow, and level prairies were present in abundant quantities. The Creeks had farmed some of the land, perhaps in the hopes of avoiding removal by adopting the white man's ways. Their clearings lay scattered throughout the purchase. The land viewers remarked on them, noting the poor agricultural techniques of the Indian but citing the "Indian old fields" as evidence of fertility of the land. "Upon the whole I think it is a very good poor man's country," wrote Joel Spigeuer in 1833. Presumably he intended to convey the sense that the land lacked the uniform fertility of the level Black Belt, which would have led to its immediate engrossment by large planters with slave labor. That it was a "poor man's country" did not mean, however, that the land was suitable only for a noncommercial, isolated, self-sufficient economy. Spigeuer continued, "The greatest objection I have to settling there now is, you are compelled to play squat, that is to set down upon government land. It is not yet known when they will be offered for sale." He wished to buy land, expected to pay a reasonable price, and wanted the assurance of clear title. In truth, the "poor man's country" was an opportunity for aggressive, ambitious men, with some capital, to become wealthy.[5] Landlookers like Law and Spigeuer were hard-headed, practical men. They wasted no time describing the beauty of the land in its natural state, but focused their attention on the cotton fields of the future.

Just as the land varied in quality, so did the patterns of settlement on it. Cotton prices rose steadily in the mid-1830's, and southern agriculturists responded energetically. Immigrants came in a steady stream to Coosa County, by horse, in wagons, on foot, a few by the newly established stage lines that already linked centers of population. One participant described this restless energy and its impact on Tuskegee, the new county seat of Macon County: "Immigrants were pouring in with a ceaseless tide. Stage coaches filled with travellers, and among them, the 'Land Sharks' ready to swallow up the home of the redmen, or the white, as opportunity might offer. . . . Houses were going up as if by magic, fields were being cleared, and crops planted." The new immigrants crowded into the so-called hotels in the new county seats and

5. Joel Spigeuer to William K. Oliver, June 3, 1833, quoted in George E. Brewer, "History of Coosa County," *AHQ*, 4 (1942): 36.

market towns. In the country those with shelter provided accommodation for the newcomers and charged for their services. Smooth-curved frontier lines on modern maps disguise the scattered nature of these settlements. Such was the variation in the land that some portions of the cession were still unoccupied at the opening of the Civil War.[6]

John Evans's father moved from Wayne County (Mississippi) to the Choctaw Cession in February 1832. By the autumn of that year, Evans related, "the new purchase, as it was called, filled up rapidly from different portions of the country." The young boys in the family did a full day's work, "clearing up the forest and opening lands for agricultural purposes." There were no postal routes until the establishment of a stage line. It ran once a month. Social intercourse was equally rare. Religion was important as a social institution. In the absence of church buildings, families held services in farmhouses. Evans remembered, with a touch of asperity, "There is no question that the preacher's family fared better than any other in the county. In a word they were supplied with everything in the way of living and clothing." In the first years of settlement, families like the Evanses worked hard for what they ate and wore.[7]

Institutions appeared almost simultaneously with settlement. In the New Counties courts began to function. The commissioners court managed the traditional frontier administrative and economic concerns of roads, bridges, and ferries; supervised elections, taxes, and licensing; made provisions for the poor; located the county seat; and constructed the necessary public buildings. Local elections were an early proving ground for ambitious politicians. There were several elective offices. The commissioners of Coosa County, organized in 1834, called an election in February "for a sheriff, clerk of circuit court, clerk of county court, an assessor and tax collector, and four commissioners of roads and revenues for the county. On the same day, Asbury Coker was appointed by an

6. Brewer, "History of Coosa County," 80; H. M. King, "Historical Sketches of Macon County," *AHQ*, 18 (1956): 213–14. Contrasts in the rate of settlement and economic growth appear in two unpublished master's theses at the University of Alabama. Marylee Reynolds, "A Social and Economic History of Sumter County, Alabama, in the Antebellum Period" (1953), is the story of a county laid off from the Choctaw Cession that "almost overnight, became the most populous county of Alabama" (p. 42); and Dewey Maurice Johnson, "History of Coffee County, Alabama, 1840–1871" (1947), is the account of a county that grew very slowly and lay almost unoccupied at the beginning of the Civil War.

7. John H. Evans, "Reminiscences of Olden Times, 1809–1850," ADAH; William T. Lewis, "The Centennial History of Winston County," *ibid.*

Act to take a census of the county." As early as 1836, the commissioners levied a tax for the support of the poor, and "Wm. Robertson was allowed ten dollars per month for keeping one pauper."[8]

The organization of county government and legal machinery flowed from state statutes. A new aspect of institutional development was the almost immediate extension of the circuit court system into the New Counties, taking justice out of the hands of local friends and placing it in the hands of remote strangers. Settlers came out to view these all-powerful figures on court day. "On our arrival at the court ground we found all the county officers present; also a very large portion of the white settlers in the county had come out to see and make the acquaintance of their new Judge and solicitor, who were entire strangers to settlers in the county," wrote Evan Goodwin Richards of early Chambers County. The grand Jury met under one tree; the judge presided under another. The deliberations, though often improvised, conveyed a sense of dignity that was designed to reassure the population, and perhaps also to intimidate them. Later courthouses would be built—when the struggle over the location of the county seat was sufficiently protracted, several courthouses might be built—along with jails, and other physical reminders of the omnipresent legal system and its courts. On this court day in Chambers County there were no cases, but the people went home sensing that they had seen law and justice. The affair was reassuring, impressive, and perhaps a little awesome in terms of the part that law and the courts would play in their lives. The court in the woods under the great oak was heir to an enormous body of law and could affect the lives of settlers in the most remote confines of the newly established counties.[9]

In an earlier day people complained of the slowness of the arrival of the court system. Now courts appeared almost with the first field of cotton. The new court system did not lack for business. Litigation moved right along with the settlers and increased with the accumulation of property. Property in the frontiers of the New Counties was readily identifiable— land, slaves, and cotton—and litigation over these articles lasted until mid-century and later. In a long American tradition, the principal beneficiaries were lawyers. They came with the first settlers, spied out the

8. Brewer, "History of Coosa County," 37, 40–41. Governor John Gayle's conflict with the federal government had delayed the organization of the county.
9. E. G. Richards, "Reminiscences of the Early Days in Chambers County," *AHQ*, 4 (1942): 420.

most likely embryonic town—preferably the county seat—hung out a shingle and commenced practice. Their services were everywhere in demand. The first lawyer came to Talladega in 1833, at the time of the first sitting of the circuit court. There is little evidence that people did not find all the court services they wanted. Counties took pride in the skills of their lawyers, the most prominent of their professional men. Lawyers of "wit, grace, and intellect" suggested the high tone and prosperity of this group. They shared with the ministers and doctors the duty of setting the standards of refinement and morality for the community. Distinctions of wealth and influence appeared rapidly in the New Counties, and these professionals exercised widespread influence.[10]

The law was (at least technically) a universal and impersonal instrument. It touched all peoples on the frontier, however remote and invisible they may have been. In a maturing society, blacks increasingly appeared as objects of litigation and also as witnesses. Slaves were one of the principal forms of property throughout the South by 1830, and their value grew thereafter. So the white population brought them before the courts, the objects of a legal struggle, sometimes in a sale, or an inheritance and estate, or a marriage portion—a common form of dowry was land and slaves sufficient to establish an economic unit of production. Slaves could be mortgaged or made security for other kinds of loans, and, as such, they were recoverable in a suit at law. Or they might be attached for nonpayment of obligations such as taxes, for they were generally the most valuable part of any estate, and certainly the most negotiable. Blacks also formed a significant proportion of the population; in several counties they outnumbered whites. This circumstance produced related fears—an economic one, over the loss of the slave as property, and a physical one, over the loss of control of the slave. With their universal presence, slaves sometimes appeared in court as witnesses, where they testified under threat of flogging for false testimony, "or such other punishment as the court shall think proper, not extending to life and limb." Preservation of the value of slave property was always important. Any slave charged with serious crime would be defended in court by the best legal talent the master could summon. Conviction meant a hasty sale and removal from the region. When the Talladega court charged a slave named Milly with murder, her master quickly sent her off to the West.

10. Wellington Vandiver, "Pioneer Talladega, Its Minutes and Memories," *AHQ*, 16 (1954): 16, 105, 112; Curry, "Reminiscences of Talladega," 350, 361.

He was not about to risk a propety valued at one thousand dollars in a court, even in pursuit of law and order.[11]

Many legal proceedings in the New Counties involved Indians. The contest was even more unequal than in the case of blacks. The Indian had no master interested in protecting him as a piece of property. Not only was the Indian in an adversary position by his very presence in the court—given the nature of white-Indian tensions—but he frequently had land that the white man wanted. The path to the courtroom was well marked. It began with trade at one of the endless groceries or grog shops set up illegally for the express purpose of soliciting the Indian's business. The commodities stocked and traded were like those in trading posts one hundred years before: liquor, tools, bright cloth, and beads. At first the Indians had something to trade: furs, meat, the products of the forest that he knew better than anyone how to harvest. Then came the great land cessions. The Indian had money or land now, not that he clearly understood the value of money or its place in the transactions of white society. But certainly the storekeeper was solicitous enough of him. After the money ran out, credit was the next step, not that the Indian understood credit either. When payment was not forthcoming, the storekeeper took the Indian to court. The court became a useful instrument to get at the Indian's property and land—in a world where white men conversant with the law coveted the land. The Indian was unable to defend it. All the character and physical traits of a great warrior counted for little against the whiteman's powerful intruments of legal warfare. With his little property gone and his land on the block at a sheriff's sale, the Indian left the country. Thus the local and state courts were the latest, and perhaps the final, instruments of enforced removal in this generation.[12]

In spite of the protection provided by law and courts, some elements in society expressed unhappiness with the confused state of criminal law and the lack of vigor in its enforcement. "All communities, for protection of themselves and property, wish to have laws, and honest men who never violate them, are never heard to complain of either their strictness or

11. *Aiken's Digest*, quoted in Vandiver, "Pioneer Talladega, Its Minutes and Memories," 26, 29. The speed with which state law, state legal institutions, and state courts came to the New Counties is in striking contrast with, say, James Duane Doty in Michigan's far western frontier about the same time, i.e., the early and mid-1830's.
12. Vandiver, "Pioneer Talladega, Its Minutes and Memories," 29, 61–63.

their enforcement when infringed," commented the Jacksonville (Alabama) *Republican* in 1838. "A little more law, a little better enforced, that we have a little better order."[13] Added to this concern was the fear that the law had become so sophisticated that it contained loopholes through which alleged criminals might escape a deserved punishment. The response was an outbreak of vigorous vigilante activity in the mid-1830's in both Mississippi and Alabama, in long-settled and cultured areas, such as Natchez and Madison County, as well as in the New Counties, like Chambers and Cherokee. In a timeless tradition, vigilante groups of local citizens came together and dispensed extra-legal justice. Their presence coincided with the high tide of immigration in 1835 and 1836, the climax of motion, turbulence, and restlessness.[14]

At first the targets of "slick law" were thieves and gamblers whose activities seemed beyond the reach of institutional law. Spontaneous vigilante groups gradually took on qualities of permanence and began to dictate morality in the areas where they ruled. Newcomers who declined to join the organization found themselves numbered among its enemies or even victims. Vigilante activities included attacks on those who were different; members used "slick law" to settle personal feuds. J. D. Anthony of Cherokee County called it "this pioneer monster of corruption." Some remembered later that members of the "slick company" included rascals who had joined simply to protect their own illegal activities. Eventually a few of those victimized by "slick law" instituted lawsuits for damages against vigilante companies and helped to force their dissolution.[15]

Economic development was largely agricultural. Corn was the basic frontier subsistence crop; cotton was the cash crop. The route to market was overland to water. The journey was sometimes difficult, with six or more mules to move half a dozen bales over "execrable" winter roads. It was little wonder that road construction and repair occupied so much of the county commissioners' time. Once on water, all routes led south to

13. Jacksonville *Republican*, May 24, 1838.
14. Huntsville *Southern Advocate*, Dec. 1, 1835.
15. Richards, "Reminiscences of the Early Days in Chambers County," 434–37; Rev. J. D. Anthony, "Cherokee County, Alabama: Reminiscences of Its Early Settlement," *AHQ*, 8 (1946): 333–34. James W. Bragg, "Captain Slick, Arbiter of Early Alabama Morals," *AR*, 11 (1958): 125–34, is a general account. Mary Effie Cameron, "The Summer of 1835 in Mississippi History" (M.A., Mississippi, 1931), describes similar vigilante activities in Mississippi and raises the question of why the greatest violence took place not only on the frontiers of the New Counties but also in the longer-settled parts of the state like Vicksburg and Natchez.

the great rivers, the Coosa, Alabama, and, finally, the port of Mobile. This pattern led to the rise of a series of river towns with a great many merchants and commission agents. In the flush times of the 1830's villages and hinterland alike prospered as flatboats and canoes with marketable crops crowded the rivers. At least one substantial urban center sprang up. Wetumpka lay at the head of navigation on the Coosa. As geography and the limits of technology funnelled cotton and supplies through it, this town became the commercial center of the New Counties. All roads in eastern Alabama seemed to lead there, and even counties in western Georgia fell within its economic orbit. In all seasons of the year wagons lined Wetumpka's muddy streets. By 1840 the town had three thousand people and a striving business. Had the projected railroad been completed—it was doomed by the financial crisis of 1837—Wetumpka might have become the first city of the state.[16]

A commercial economy also flourished outside the principal towns. Its center was the small crossroads store. Simmons Grocery in Macon County was one of many. An observer described it in 1833 in these terms: "It's contents, about ten bars of soap, one keg of powder, one jug of whiskey, six strings of glass beads, one piece of blue calico, and one of red, one small keg of pigtail tobacco, a few bars of lead, and a three string fiddle." The population at the time was a mixture of red and white, and the stores were stocked accordingly, with a good deal of powder, lead, and liquor. As the Indians scattered or became impoverished, the clientele changed to white settlers. The contents of the stores also changed. Ezekiel Abner Powell, in his reminiscence of the New Counties in western Alabama, described the system of country merchandising that catered to the new immigrants: "At almost every crossroad in the county you would find a store, and these country stores were filled almost exclusively with dry goods: all of which had been bought on a credit."[17]

16. Brewer, "History of Coosa County," 56–63; Curry, "Reminiscences of Talladega," 357.
17. King, "Historical Sketches of Macon County," 203; Ezekiel Abner Powell, "Fifty-five Years in West Alabama," AHQ, 4 (1942): 508. The crossroads store in the South met the needs for local services before widespread transportation facilities made possible frequent visits to town. In this, it was one with the nation. What has been distinctly southern is the concentration, in the twentieth century, on trade with blacks, the poorest social group and the last to acquire the automobile. Much of the trade with blacks was done on a credit basis, against year-end settlement with the landowner. Thus, through a full century, the clientele of the small crossroads store has changed from red to white to black.

A society supported by cotton culture, backed by the statute book, and shaped by the dominant tone of the settled parts of the states quickly emerged and passed through the frontier stage. Cotton was the only crop for which a market (however low the price) existed. It brought in the funds that could be used to purchase necessities and luxury items from local merchants; it marked progress upward in the economic and social scale to a new coach, custom-cut broadcloth, or the acquisition of more land and slaves. The end product was a world like that settled for a generation. It had much in common with the older parts of the Southwest, both in terms of heritage (many settlers in the New Counties came from there) and ambitions for the future (the settler in the New Counties wanted to be like them). Not surprisingly, the new society was much like the old in its institutions and values. W. J. Cash's frontier planter tried to emulate the Charleston aristocracy as soon as possible. A high point of his achievements was the marriage of his daughter to a "Charleston gentleman."[18]

Year later frontier planters discoursed much on the morality and civilized nature of the population of their areas. Of the influences here, churches were dominant. They appeared on the scene soon after settlement, a tribute to the dedication of the ministers and the religious enthusiasm of the time. Blacks formed a substantial proportion of many of the early congregations. With the mere presence of churches and ministers no longer a rarity, doctrinal differences (between denominations, and sometimes within denominations) became increasingly important.[19] Schooling was of lesser importance, but it did exist. Despite state legislation, the common or public school was rare. Where found, it lasted for perhaps a three-month term. Generally "incompetent men" taught in the early Cherokee County schools, and for some years "the schools. . . on the south side of the Coosa, in Cherokee, were schools only in name." John Evans remembered that his early school in the Choctaw Cession had both white and Indian students. The first teacher was a man named Hennessey, of whom Evans wrote, "He was a splendid scholar and a perfect thrashing machine."[20]

18. W. J. Cash, *The Mind of the South* (New York, 1941), 14–17.
19. Richards, "Reminiscences of the Early Days in Chambers County," 427.
20. Anthony, "Cherokee County, Alabama: Reminiscences of Its Early Settlement," 328; Evans, "Reminiscences of Olden Times"; see also Brewer, "History of Coosa County," 158. On a school in Dallas County in 1838, see Philip Gosse, *Letters from Alabama*, cited in Lucille B. Griffith, *History of Alabama, 1540–1900* (Northport, Ala., 1962), 114–15, which suggests that even in the prosperous Black Belt counties the process of

For the new immigrants, maturity endowed the pioneer beginnings with great significance. One great holiday served as a reminder of the pioneer past. On the Fourth of July all elements of society convened to give thanks. In day-long celebrations, town and country paid tribute to the ideals and achievements of the past and proclaimed their hopes for the future. It was a day of speeches, parades, a public dinner, solemn toasts. Upon this occasion local leaders spoke to their constituents about their common world. It was a time to celebrate country, state, county, and themselves. The importance of the celebration was not diluted by a variety of competing attractions, for the day was the social occasion of the year. The Fourth of July ceremonies also enhanced the public reputations of the local elites, for the various public roles in the celebration were carefully parcelled out. Ambitious politicians paraded to the speaker's rostrum. Military organizations performed one of their few remaining significant functions. Fourth of July celebrations had one other virtue: description, toasts, even long speeches, found their way into print, and so serve as sources for the historian. In this way, these occasions present an annual account that is one of our most complete records of growth on the frontier.[21]

The northern part of the state of Mississippi opened for settlement at the same time and under the same circumstances. The Choctaw Cession of 1830 and Chickasaw Cession of 1832 removed Indians from almost half of the state. Between 1833 and 1836 the number of counties in Mississippi doubled, and the legislature eventually added another fourteen from the Indian cessions. The result was a large sectional division in the state, with the New Counties constantly struggling for representation and recognition of their interests.[22] The differences in land were just as great as in Alabama: piney hills and uplands in the northeast, levelling off to rolling fields and dropping abruptly to a floodplain of incredible

---

education was a makeshift one, with windswept log cabins for schoolhouses, itinerant masters, and indifferent pupils whose interests lay far from their lessons.

21. Only John William Ward's *Andrew Jackson: Symbol for an Age* (New York, 1955), begins to explore the possibilities of this annual outpouring of local sentiment. A study of Fourth of July orations would be especially revealing for the frontier, for they represent one of the few common declarations.

22. Jack Davison Ramsey, "New County Representation in Mississippi from 1830 to 1840" (M.A., Mississippi, 1931), esp. ch. 2.

fertility. This was the Delta of the Mississippi, renown for its richness, annual flooding, and disease. The Delta was the most striking of the new lands opened by Indian treaty in the 1830's. The settlement and growth of Sunflower-Leflore counties—the legislature laid off Leflore County in 1871—provide examples. By 1840 a rush of immigrants claimed half the land of what would become Leflore County, principally the rich tracts along the Yazoo River. The remainder was settled slowly, and a considerable amount of land remained unsold at the time of the Civil War. The new settlers found their lands wet and level, subject to annual flooding, and almost tropical in their luxuriant growth. The counties of Sunflower-Leflore lay isolated from the East and depended on the Mississippi and its tributaries for contact with the outside world.

The first arrivals spent much time on the question of communication, but roads developed slowly and imperfectly. In 1838 the board of police of Bolivar County ordered a road cut through what would later (1844) become Sunflower County. It was a track three feet wide and clearly marked, to run from the Mississippi to a point on the Yazoo River. This and subsequent roads had to be hacked out from the thick covering of cane and vines, and vegetation grew so rapidly in the moist warm climate that the task was never completed. Almost all so-called roads were impassable in the winter rainy season, especially for wagons. During the wet winter months those settlers inland of the river lapsed into self-contained isolation reminiscent of the earliest days of settlement on the trans-Appalachian frontier. The Delta region prospered within the context of the depression of the early 1840's. Aside from the small market center of Greenwood, towns did not develop. The county of Leflore had no railroad connection in 1860, and conditions of travel and trade were only marginally better than twenty years before. Conditions in this Delta country created a new kind of frontier society, in which the dominant feature was slave labor. An overwhelmingly agricultural, simple society developed around the cultivation of cotton, access to market for a staple product, and control of the numerically dominant black population. In 1860 the black population in Sunflower County was seventy-eight percent of the total; in what would become Leflore, sixty-three percent. According to the returns of the census taker for that year, the county had neither church nor school. A more complex society never evolved because it seemed unnecessary. The one that existed could grow cotton for export in abundant quantities. Aside from institutions for cotton cultivation and control of the black population, the rest of the society was formless.[23]

Bolivar County, organized in 1836, was another Delta county dominated by its number of blacks and the production of cotton by slave labor. These demographic characteristics of the population and the astonishing rise in productivity can be seen in table 7. The population remained rural and determinedly agricultural. As the production of cotton increased, so did the predominance of the slave population. Towns did not develop in Bolivar County. Professional people were largely unknown. In 1850 the county had one merchant, five doctors, and not a single lawyer. Cultural development was nonexistent. Those sufficiently affluent to do so spent much of their time elsewhere, far from the dangerous diseases of this tropical low country.[24]

Table 7. Growth of Bolivar County, Mississippi, 1840–60

	1840	*1850*	*1860*
white population	384	395	1,393
slaves	971	2,180	9,078
cotton production (bales of 400 lbs.)	288	4,723	33,452
slaves owned by each slaveholder	21	32	35

Sources: Anna Alice Kamper, "A Social and Economic History of Ante-Bellum Bolivar County, Mississippi" (M.A., Alabama, 1942), ch. 2; Joseph Kennedy, comp., *Population of the United States in 1860, Compiled from the Original Returns of the Eighth Census under the Direction of the Secretary of the Interior* (Washington, 1864), 1: 265, 267; 2: 85.

High water was another challenge of the Delta frontier. The universal response was the levee. At first each planter built his own, using slave labor. These barriers against floodwaters were "small, crooked, crude levees, in which stumps and logs were covered up with limbs, brush, and other debris—totally without bed preparation or muck ditch—a temporary and hastily constructed levee across the bayous and flats and along ridges." Given the nature of a flood and the size of the river, indi-

23. Willie D. Halsell, "Migration into, and Settlement of, Leflore County, 1833–1876," *JMH*, 9 (1947): 219–37. Halsell concludes that Leflore County in 1876 was "little more than a frontier" (p. 237).

24. Anna Alice Kamper, "A Social and Economic History of Ante-Bellum Bolivar County, Mississippi" (M.A., Alabama, 1942), ch. 2.

vidual levees of such primitive construction were inadequate. As men occupied the lands bordering the rivers, they began to join together in
order to plan a collective protection from the threat of high water. The
need for levees eventually made their construction an official matter. The
board of police of Bolivar County divided the county into levee districts
in 1838 and assigned inspectors to each. Between August and December
1838 the board of police supervised the construction of its first levee,
sixty feet at base and twenty feet at top, with "no timber in the body or
on the sides, and made three feet above the highest water mark." By
1850 the county had built eighty-five miles of levee, for which a firm tax
base had been established. The board gave the work to a contractor,
preferring professional to the conscripted labor used on roads. Under the
impetus of levee construction and high cotton prices, this part of the
Delta settled rapidly in the 1850's.[25]

The first stages of settlement of the new Indian Cessions attracted
many small farmers. Not all graduated to great white houses with pillars, overlooking vast fields tended by slave labor. One of those who
remained a small farmer, Lawrence Ferdinand Steel, left a record of his
day-to-day activities for twelve years. Steel moved into the Choctaw
Cession in 1836. He was then twenty-four years old, with little formal
schooling, some experience in storekeeping and on a flatboat, and responsibility for a family of four. He never owned slaves to help in cultivating his 170 acres in northern Carroll County. His account conveys a
picture of continuous hard labor, from 5 A.M. until sunset, five and one-
half days a week. Saturday afternoon he went to market in the town of
Grenada, five miles away. Sunday he devoted to religious affairs. Over
the ten years from 1836 to 1846 little changed on the Steel farm. Times
were hard. Cotton and corn were the basic crops. Cotton was the cash
crop, but it produced little cash. In 1839, for example, Steel harvested
enough for five bales (in addition to 350 bushels of corn). The cotton
brought in $171.41, and watermelons another $30. His cash outlay for
the year was $73.78, plus $57 for two cows and a calf. He performed
several kinds of labor during the year: in the fields on his crops; on roads
as a part of his tax obligation; in the construction of farm buildings, such
as a cotton pen, springhouse, stable, and wagon shelter. Church affairs
and exchanges of work and equipment brought Steel into contact with

25. Walter Sillers, Sr., "Flood Control in Bolivar County, 1838–1924," *JHM*, 9 (1947):
3–6.

other farmers. According to his account, he took little or no interest in politics except to attend Harrison rallies during the campaign of 1840. The newspapers in the northern counties of Mississippi already expressed concern over the growing abolition movement. Steel did not share their concern, at least to the extent of committing his thoughts to paper. He felt the economic depression, which sent cotton prices to record lows, but his stakes were small. He did not seem threatened by the many sheriff's sales announced in the columns of newspapers around the state from 1837 to 1841. If cotton prices had been twice as high and his income twice as great, Steel's life style would have changed little. He might have added some livestock to his herd and bought dresses for his mother and sister, but he could scarcely have afforded a slave.[26]

That region later known as the Delta was not the only area opened to settlement in northern Mississippi in the 1830's. The Chickasaw Cession at Pontotoc—the last of the great cessions in Mississippi—was another. The legislature laid off Pontotoc County from this cession in 1836. The commissioners selected a county seat, also named Pontotoc, and shortly a newspaper, the Pontotoc *Chickasaw Union*, began publication. Pontotoc had a bank, a branch of the Agricultural Bank of Natchez, almost as soon as it had a hotel. It was "a log building run up for the reception of the *strong boxes*, and the accomodation of the cashier," but it performed necessary banking functions in a time of prosperity and optimism. Immigrants surged into the New Counties to create the proverbial "land-office business" in real estate. The *Union* noted by advertisement and editorial "the progress of the LAND SALES—THE LOCATION OF RESERVATIONS—THE LOCATIONS OF SEATS OF JUSTICE OF THE TEN NEW COUNTIES INTO WHICH THE CHICKASAW CESSION HAS BEEN DIVIDED; and the progress of improvements in them, individually as well as collectively." As the agriculturalists and enterpreneurs poured in, plans for the Pontotoc-Aberdeen Railroad (to connect the interior to the Tombigbee River) moved forward.[27]

26. Edward M. Steel, Jr., "A Pioneer Farmer in the Choctaw Purchase," *JHM*, 16 (1954): 229–41. Steel also read Blackstone and composed poetry in his leisure moments, but the traditional frontier interests—e.g., weather, crop prices, location, and soil—dominate his account.

27. Pontotoc *Chickasaw Union*, July 1, 1836. Two detailed descriptions of the New Counties in northern Mississippi are "North Mississippi—The Chickasaw Counties," Pontotoc *Chickasaw Union*, Dec. 7, 1837; "A Ride through the Choctaw Nation," Columbus *Democrat*, Aug. 5, 1837.

A brief history of the early development of Pontotoc County identifies most of the issues that concerned early settlers, as well as the institutional framework established earlier for county organization and carried largely intact into Mississippi's north in the 1830's. The county benefited much from the assistance of the federal government. In order to accommodate purchases at the new Pontotoc land office and to remove the Indians, the government cut a road from Pontotoc to Memphis. The Turnpike Road—as it was known—had a quality of construction superior to that of the usual county road. In 1839 commissioners appointed to examine the turnpike described it thus: "The road is opened 50 feet wide and good framed bridges built across the creeks and the branches bridged with good puncheon bridges, and the road causewayed where it runs through post-oak flats; the causeway 12 feet wide, and each side of the road ditched 18 feet apart." After the removal of the Indians, the government turned the road over to the proprietors of the adjoining lands, who were given permission to charge a toll in order to defray the cost of maintenance. Although the road deteriorated in quality, it remained an important route of access to a town of growing commercial importance.[28]

The Probate Court of Pontotoc County also went into operation in 1836. Its duties included recording stock marks and the bonds posted by elected officials. Ministers of the gospel appeared before the court, presented their credentials, and received authorization to "solemnize the Rite of Matrimony within this State according to Law." The Reverend James B. Stafford of the Presbyterian Church was first, followed by the Reverend Robert Bell of the Cumberland Presbyterians. By 1839 both the Methodists and Baptists had ministers so authorized. The main business of the probate court, however, was wills and estates. The court appointed administrators of estates, a position of great trust and responsibility. The guardians and administrators named were frequently women, almost always in their capacity as the widows of the deceased. Even the earliest pioneers had estates, goods and chattels that they had brought to the new Mississippi counties, in addition to what they had accumulated there. The inventory of an estate in 1838 disclosed large quantities of household necessaries—tables, chairs, dishes, pots, pans, plus books and the products of the farm. These included livestock—two sows and pigs,

---

28. Pontotoc County History, in WPA Historical Project (HRS), Source Materials for Mississippi History, vol. 58, pt. 3, p. 105. This description is taken from "old records found in the basement of the Pontotoc courthouse. . . ."

two cows and calves, one "old cow," two yearlings, fifty bushels of corn (valued at $37.50), and 450 pounds of bacon ($56.25). But the striking feature of the estate is that the major portion of its value of $1,744 was in four slaves: two women (Duffy, $500; Nancy, $450), and two children ($350 each). Their total value was $1,650. As in the older sections of the South, land and slaves were the most valuable property, and on the frontier slaves were proportionately the greater, for land was relatively inexpensive. It would, of course, go up in value, with clearing, improvements, and cultivation, transportation improvements, and more settlements. Slaves were already of premium value. A slave commanded roughly the same price in Pontotoc County as in the city of Natchez.[29]

County justices of the peace also began their duties in 1836. Their business was handling misdemeanors. The transfer of more serious affairs to the state courts gave an increasingly local air to county court proceedings. The justice of the peace courts considered a number of cases involving blacks and Indians. The Indians almost never appeared, and the court convicted and fined them *in absentia*. The erosion of the jurisdiction of the local court did nothing to reduce the role of the lawyers. Land and land titles formed a core of business. One commentator on law and lawyers in early Pontotoc County wrote, "The cases of difficulty in perfecting titles under the pre-emption laws, the irregularity of the public sales, and the conflicts with the Indian locations of land, were innumerable." Lawyers "attended" at the county courts, Pontotoc of course, but also Tishomingo, Tippah, Marshall, Lafayette, Yalobusha, Chickasaw, and Monroe, as well as the "High Court of Errors and Appeals, Superior Court of Chancery, and U.S. District for Mississippi." Legal notices filled the columns of newspapers as the profits of legal confusion extended to editors.[30]

The society that emerged included small farmers like Steel, a few large agriculturalists who would have styled themselves planters, and the mixed occupations carried on in the few towns. The unifying theme of

29. Minutes of Probate Court, Pontotoc County, 1836–49, in Pontotoc County History, vol. 58, pt. 3, pp. 375–83; Inventory of Estates, in *ibid.*, 384–86. As for the value of land, the January 1836 public sale of Chickasaw lands at the Pontotoc land office resulted in the disposal of 266,442 acres at an average of slightly less than $1.70 an acre. The figures on the land sale are from the Pontotoc *Chickasaw Union*, July 1, 1836. The price of land at the subsequent private sale was the minimum $1.25 per acre.

30. The Bar, in Pontotoc County History, vol. 58, pt. 3, pp. 204, 390–91. On legal notices, see, for example, Pontotoc *Chickasaw Union*, Feb. 8, 1838.

the society was agriculture, and the activities of the people in the small towns supported the agricultural population. The distribution of the population of Attala County is a case in point. Formed in 1833 from the Choctaw Cession, the county's population in 1840 was 3,029 whites, 1,083 blacks, 194 taxed Indians: total, 4,306. According to the census marshall, the "pursuits of our citizens" broke down into the following categories for the white population: 1,343 in agriculture; 33 in "manufactures and trades"; 9 in "learned professions"; and 2 "in commerce." Those in nonagricultural categories were presumably linked to agriculture, with the "manufactures" in cotton gins; the "learned professions" sorted out land titles, drew up wills, and probated estates; and those in "commerce" concerned themselves with the shipment of cotton to market. The vast majority of the blacks were also in the agricultural sphere.[31]

New County agriculture was repetitive in its techniques and crops. There was little agricultural experimentation, crop rotation, or elaborate fertilizers. These were the prerogatives of the educated and well-to-do, leisured agriculturists in the older sections. In the New Counties the basic instruments were slave labor and draft animals, and with them the plow and the hoe. The crops remained cotton for cash and corn for the sustenance of men and animals. The rich land of the New Counties gave forth abundantly. In 1839 Noxubee County, organized six years earlier, produced twenty to twenty-five thousand bales of cotton. This crop was worth perhaps one million dollars, even at depressed prices. Wheat was an important secondary crop in Holmes, Carroll, and Choctaw counties. "We are fast marching to the plains of commercial independence, when a country not yet seven years old is able to raise the staff of life in abundance besides making enough cotton bales to wall a fortress," wrote the editor of the Yazoo City paper.[32] The style of life for the early settlers was as plain as the agriculture. A man travelling through Holmes

31. Kosciusko *Central Register*, Aug. 8, 1840. Edward Lee McMillan, "A Social and Economic History of Kosciusko, Mississippi" (M.A., Mississippi, 1951), records the growth of the county seat of Attala County and reflects the few social and cultural amenities available in such towns until the Civil War and after. Kosciusko, for example, had no public or free schools before 1870. In 1857 William Dodd, a wealthy citizen of the town, rented books at five cents a day to those who sought reading materials (p. 26).

32. Early History of Agriculture, in Pontotoc County History, vol. 58, pt. 3, pp. 2–9; Macon *Intelligencer*, Dec. 14, 1838; Yazoo City *Whig and Political Register*, Aug. 9, 1839.

County in 1839 spent the night in "the *Mansion House* of the plantation, a cabin with two rooms and passage between, the one room was occupied by barrels of pork, flour, the plough and its appendages, a few old saddles, some peas spread on the floor, etc. The other served as a parlour, dining room, chamber, etc."[33] This primitive condition was the experience of both the small farmers and the large-scale planters with their gangs of slaves and extensive landholdings. The great architectural displays that became associated with the antebellum aristocracy were the products of the 1850's, a more leisured, more self-assured society, far enough from its frontier antecedents to treasure and revere them without wishing to experience them again.

Crime and punishment in Mississippi's New Counties were much the same as elsewhere. The more structured court system lent an air of judiciary authority, but the punishment was brutal. The circuit court in Holmes County, organized in 1833, found George Treece guilty of horse stealing in 1839 and handed down the most humane sentence the law allowed: "To be branded in the right hand with the letter T, receive thirty-nine lashes on the bare back, fined in the sum of five dollars, be incarcerated for three months, and stand in the pillory for one half hour for three successive days." In the face of such appalling brutality, the frontier editor in Holmes County pleaded for mercy, a quality not associated with frontier justice. His conclusion: better not stand before the court "poor" and "friendless." He went on to lay such brutal conditions to institutional progress: "In olden times, when there were no physicians, there was no sickness; when there were no lawyers, dissensions and litigation did not exist—when there were no BANKS there were no debts. In our country, when there was no pillory, there was no subject for that disgraceful mode of punishment." Six years after its organization the county had medicine, law, and justice. The editor thought that the result did not signify progress.[34]

The struggle to create a more complex society in the New Counties is focused in the experiences of Josiah Hinds in Itawamba County. The legislature laid off Itawamba in 1836. Hinds moved there with his family in 1839. "We are among strangers, in a strange land, and in a wilde[r]ness, where but a short time since was heard the yell of the savage,

33. Lexington *Union*, July 20, 1839.
34. Lexington *Union*, May 4, 1839.

and where the hoot of the owl and the prowl of the wolf is still heard," he wrote of his situation in 1840. "We are almost in the woods—one cabbin only to shelter us and our little ones, and a rail pen for a smoke house and kitchen, a few neighbours who are kind but ignorant, no churches erected for the worship of God." Religion was the dominant force in Hinds's life, and he entered wholeheartedly into revivals, church building, and temperance. He fought the Devil and the Baptists— between whom he saw only shades of difference—with the same vehemence. He was savage in his judgments of others, particularly on religious grounds. His principles of life were hard work and strict discipline. He expected the same of his family. Hinds displayed his sense of purpose most strongly in religious matters. "This day was appointed for class meeting," he wrote. "No one attended but two black men. I was wonderfully blessed in reading the word of God to those two black men." Yet Hinds wanted something more than religious purity. He wanted a world of varied social opportunities for himself and his children. This he did not find. In 1846, after seven years in Itawamba County, he offered this comment:

> My children is growing up like the wild ass'es colt, and I cannot help myself. Education is but little prized by my neighbours, although honest and industrious, yet there is little or no disposition manifested in the acquirement of knowledge, and if the corn and cotton grows to perfection (which it seldom does), it is enough, provided it brings a fare price, and hog meat is at hand to boil with the greens.[35]

The frontier experience of the New Counties, taken as a whole, varied little from the Great Migration of the previous generation, at least from the Great Migration in the South. An earlier generation had laid down patterns for establishing a society in all its forms. People going onto the land knew what to cultivate and how to market it. They would find a familiar court system and legal code. The presence of so many settlers from other parts of Alabama and Mississippi strengthened continuity. There were Indians on the land, but they were an inconvenience—and, in the case of land warrants, an opportunity—rather than a danger. The

35. Josiah Hinds, "The Journal of Josiah Hinds, April 24, 1839–July 10, 1863," ed. Newton Haskin James (M.A., Mississippi, 1939); quotations are from the entries for Oct. 27, 1840; July 24, 1842; and Aug. 24, 1846.

Native Americans left their presence on the records of the county courts and in the observations of travellers, but aside from place-names, by the end of the decade little else had survived. This Second Great Migration into the New Counties was a smooth continuation (for the most part) of the dominant features of southern society whose outlines had been laid down in an earlier generation. Steamboats, cotton, slavery, and the land were still at the center of this most agricultural of the southern frontiers.

But the frontier of the New Counties also differed from the First Great Migration. In spite of the hectic nature of movement in the 1830's, there was a more leisured, almost calculated air about it. People like the Laws of South Carolina approached their immigration as businessmen. They spied out the land with the cool detachment of military officers planning a campaign. There was little of the rush and intense competition that drove prices of land to unheard-of levels in 1818 and 1819. There was ample land to go around in the New Counties and in the older Black Belt settlements, of varying quality and at varying prices. What all this added up to was a world much more southern than western. The basic issues were the price of cotton, the institution of slavery, and a market for the staples. The people in the New Counties shared these values with those everywhere who felt themselves part of a southern civilization. They created a society that changed little in its institutional framework and development up to 1861. The New Counties settled and grew, becoming ever more set in their collective ways. The population was increasingly black; the market crop remained cotton. The frontier condition gradually faded into a world that was always rural and always engaged in commercial agriculture. With the frontier of the New Counties, the sharp sense of a dividing line that separates the frontier period from what follows fades. In this sense, the frontier goes on forever, or passes unremarked into a rural world that is much like the frontier. In many ways, this was an agricultural immigration from one rural society to another rather than a frontier experience.

13

The Last Frontier
of the Old Northwest:
Illinois, Wisconsin, and Iowa

Massive numbers and great varieties of peoples characterized the last frontier of the Old Northwest. They came from the earlier trans-Appalachian frontiers in the Ohio Valley, from New York and New England, from the Atlantic Coast and Pennsylvania, and, finally, from Europe. A generation of pioneers travelled west by steamer on the Great Lakes, through newly constructed canals, and even by way of an expanding railroad system. Their numbers reflected the growth of the Republic and the rising immigration from Europe.[1] Consider, for example, the population figures for the new territories of Wisconsin and Iowa, organized in 1836 and 1838 respectively, as given in table 8.

Information about the newest frontier was widely available and included instructions on how to make the trip west, how to purchase land, and even how to farm. Albert M. Lea's *Notes on Wisconsin Territory, with a Map* (1836) served as a reference work and guide to the new Wisconsin

---

1. The South Bend *Northwestern Pioneer* and the Maumee *Express* remind us that western Michigan, northern Indiana, and northwestern Ohio were also frontiers in the 1830's. The *Pioneer* editor's "longing for a steamboat to blow its long black nose" (April 25, 1831) places him in the tradition of all those frontiers that eagerly awaited steam transportation. On the occupation of northwestern Ohio, see Martin R. Kaatz, "The Settlement of the Black Swamp of Northwestern Ohio: Early Days," *Northwest Ohio Quarterly*, 25 (1952–53): 122–36, 143–56, 201–17; on northern Indiana, three articles by Leon M. Gordon, II: "The Influence of River Transportation on St. Joseph and Elkhart Counties, 1830–60," *IMH*, 46 (1950): 283–96; "Effects of the Michigan Road on Northern Indiana, 1830–60," *IMH*, 46 (1950): 377–402; and "Settlements in Northwestern Indiana, 1830–60," *IMH*, 47 (1961): 37–52.

Table 8. Growth of Wisconsin and
Iowa, 1836–50

	Wisconsin	Iowa
1836	11,683	10,531
1838	18,139	22,859
1840	30,945	43,112
1842	44,478	. . . . .
1844	. . . . .	75,152
1846	155,277	102,388
1847	210,546	116,454
1850	305,390	192,214

Sources: Alice E. Smith, *The History of Wisconsin: From Explo-
ration to Statehood* (Madison, 1973, 466; John A. T. Hull,
Census of Iowa for 1880 with Other Historical and Statistical Data
(Des Moines, 1883), 168.

Territory; John Plumbe, Jr.'s *Sketches of Iowa and Wisconsin Taken during a
Residence of Three Years in Those Territories* (1839) did the same for Iowa.
More maps were in circulation than ever before. The numbers of published travel accounts by visitors—foreign and American—increased in
proportion to the ease of travel and high interest in the western country.
Letters from friends and relatives to those in the old home added to the
pool of information. These written works publicized the new West and,
at the same time, alleviated the fear of an unknown and hostile land.
Hundreds of thousands from varied places and of varied stations responded to the invitation.

Andrew Fitz of Marblehead (Massachusetts), who went west in 1837,
travelled by sloop and steamboat to New York, railroad and canal to
Pittsburgh, thence down the Ohio and up the Mississippi to the Illinois
River and Fulton County (Illinois). Fitz paid $150 for a claim, describing
it in these terms: "A house containing one large room one door one window but no glass a small building stable a good well of pure water stoned
up 15 acres under fense and had been cultivated three years and seventeen hundred rails split on it." The next spring he planted corn and potatoes. The crops exceeded all his expectations. Buoyed by confidence in
the new country, Fitz purchased another eighty acres ("It is all timber
but first rate Land"), three cows ("one which I intend to kill"), a yoke of
oxen, one horse, and sixteen hogs. He found several New England
friends, and all rejoiced in their good health and prosperity. A well-

organized county government had already laid out several roads. Fitz lived near a town (two and a half miles away), a Methodist Society, and a camp meeting in the summer. He had a fortunate location, for the county road "runs by my door and is travelled very much wich is great company for my wife and we have two nabours one at both sides of us."[2]

This new agricultural frontier also attracted men without means, seeking financial rewards in exchange for their youth and energy. They moved west impelled by the same forces that in the near future would send young people by the thousands to California in search for gold. One such adventurer was Aristarchus Cone, who came from New England by way of Pennsylvania. Cone and a companion crossed the Mississippi into Iowa in 1837 and, shouldering their packs, started walking through the tall prairie grass toward the setting sun. They found a beautiful and empty land, with "no shelter nothing to eat musquitoes thick you could stir them with a stick." The two men made a claim and paid fifty cents to have it recorded by the local recorder of claims. They boarded two and a half miles from their land with a man named Johnson who kept a large supply of whiskey to sell to the Indians. Cone and his friend had to start from the beginning: "Here I was on the Prairie without any thing for a House I built a fire and lay on the ground with a Bufalow Skin for a bed plenty of Shelter for myself and things." In the fine autumn weather the two men explored the country and built a shelter large enough to satisfy the regulations of the local claims association. Cone spent the winter in Ohio but returned to Iowa and his claim the next spring. When his partner arrived with four yoke of oxen, the two men began to break prairie. Of the experience, Cone later wrote: "We had to wade through grass as high as our heads in the morning we would get as wet as if we had been in the River." They lived in a tent through the summer. When the weather turned cold, they built "a Rail Pen and filled the cracks with Hay and Hay and dirt on the top for a roof." The shelter burned down, and, the following day, six inches of snow fell. Cone remembered, with a degree of sarcasm, "We began to realize the pleasures settling in a new country we were on the extream Frontier not a solitary settler West of us to the Paciffic Ocean and but

2. Andrew Fitz to Daniel Weed, Nov. 13, 1837, Daniel Weed Collection, ISHL. Fitz's wife Nancy, from a New England seaport town, apparently did not know how to ride a horse and remained bound to the house.

few settlers here." They built a log cabin—"I presume we felt prouder of our Home than many would be with one that cost Thousands"—brought provisions in from Illinois, and saw the winter through. Cone had most of the experiences that the early frontier settler recalled. The staple of the diet was the corn dodger: "I shall call the years 1838 and 1839 the Corn Dodger Period." He suffered from the ague: "I did not much care whether I lived or died I had lost all ambition." In March 1839 Cone headed across the prairie on his first visit to the mill, a round trip that would take five days: "It was like starting out on a voiage to sea a man had to take his provisions along for fear he might not make a Port when it came night Harbors are few and far between at this time." Cone persevered. From these lean beginnings he built a prosperous farm in Muscatine County that was still his sixty-five years later.[3]

Foreigners represented another distinct group of immigrants to this newest agricultural frontier. In the generation after 1830 increasingly large numbers of European agriculturists came to this country and often went directly to the frontiers of Illinois, Wisconsin, Michigan, and Iowa. The census of 1850 recorded that in Wisconsin one-third of the 305,390 residents were not born in America. In general foreign immigrants were surprised—almost staggered—by the opportunity for landownership. The German-born Johann Frederick Diederichs described in detail how he could achieve financial independence on his eighty acres. Within a year, he thought, he would have some surplus to sell. For all his enthusiasm, Diederichs emphasized that foreign immigrants would need money to get started. Another German national, Johann Diefenthaeler, agreed on the need for capital as well as on the prospects of the new land. To those who would follow, he offered a list of things to bring: crockery, wood saws, strong steerhides, songbooks, parts to make thresing flails. The ladies especially wanted door locks, a blue skein of yarn, and silk for a dress. Diefenthaeler concluded, "Bring anything you want, for your baggage will not be inspected." Scandinavians, Swiss, and Dutch joined the Germans. Large numbers of English and Irish formed a significant if less conspicuous part of the immigration. Oswald Ragatz, a Swiss who settled in Sauk County (Wisconsin) in 1842, offered a benediction on the experience of the immigrant with the land. "Each night found us utterly

---

3. Aristarchus Cone, "The Memories of Aristarchus Cone," ed. Mildred Throne, *IJH*, 49 (1951): 51–72. Cone includes in his memoirs a recipe for corn dodgers (p. 67).

fatigued," he wrote. "But we were exultant—it was all ours, and we were converting sheer wilderness into a smiling habitable land. There is a deep thrill of such effort—it causes a leaping of the heart incomprehensible to one who has not had the experience." And, in conclusion, "Thus, Sauk prairie did, indeed, become our promised land."[4]

Fitz, Cone, Diederichs, Diefenthaeler, and Ragatz suggest the variety and scope of immigration to the West, as well as the services available in this period, hitherto unknown. From the docks of New York City and the villages along the Erie Canal to the prairies of western Illinois and eastern Iowa, catering to the needs of the frontier immigrant had become a large business, involving food, shelter, transporatation, and, closer to the final destination, seed, tools, and stock. The immigrant had several options in transportation. He might walk or ride on horseback with his family, leading a wagon filled with their goods. Or he might take his family and household west by one or more of the several kinds of public transportation available, including coastal ships, canals, steamboats, stages, and even railroads. It cost Andrew Fitz nearly three hundred dollars to transport his family and two thousand pounds of baggage from Marblehead to Fulton County, but no one walked a step of the way. Aristarchus Cone, by contrast, took a steamboat up the Illinois River to Peoria, then walked west into Iowa, carrying his belongings in a small bundle.[5] On the distant frontiers, men made a business of hauling immigrants to farm sites, building cabins, digging wells, or building fences. Some made a living by providing these services; others supplemented

4. Alice E. Smith, *The History of Wisconsin: From Exploration to Statehood* (Madison, 1973), 488–93; Joh. Fr. Diederichs, "Letters and Diary of Joh. Fr. Diederichs," *WMH,* 7 (1923–24): 360, 368; Johann Diefenthaeler letter, Jan. 16, 1844, SHSW; Oswald Ragatz, "Memoirs of a Sauk Swiss," *WMH,* 19 (1935–36): 213–19. Ragatz noted that Swiss ministers would not come to serve the growing Swiss community unless the immigrants guaranteed their salaries. In the course of their experiences on the frontier, these immigrants eventually had to come to terms with the traditional American institutions of county government, county court, common school, and even politics. See, for example, Theodore C. Blegen, *Norwegian Migration to America: The American Transition* (Northfield, Minn., 1940).

5. Fitz to Weed, Nov. 13, 1837, Weed Collection; Cone, "Memories," 56–57. Andrew Fitz noted that his trip west was delayed three hours when the train on which he was riding in Pennsylvania hit a horse, derailing several cars. Another account of a family trip west is in the Peoria *Register,* Oct. 28, 1837. The first railroad in Illinois was the portion of the Northern Cross line from Meredosia to Springfield, opened in 1839. H. J. Stratton, "The Northern Cross Railroad," *JISHS,* 28 (1938): 15–25.

their farm resources by catering to the needs of immigrants who could afford to pay for them.[6]

Breaking new prairie became an important occupation. This was the first pioneer generation for whom the prairie experience was almost universal. There had been prairies before, but it was possible to avoid them. Now they lay all around. The prairie land was flat in some places, gently rolling in others. Wild flowers bloomed in profusion in the spring. The Chicago *American* called them "these glorious gardens of nature" and saluted "their gaudy and fantastic dress." The prairies were also treeless and hard to drain, so the prospective agriculturist found himself working in mud through the growing season. The sod was tough, demanding several teams and a strong plow. So difficult was the task of breaking prairie for the individual farmer that many hired it done and so created a new business of plowing up the prairie at so much an acre. The new settler could also hire fencing. From the scarcity of timber for fencing, sod fences appeared. According to one account, they were more expensive than wooden fencing, "but it is better, being permanent, if well made, and of course requiring no repairs."[7]

The costs of transportation to the new land and breaking the prairie were only the beginnings of the expenses involved in farming. Sooner or later the prospective farmer had to acquire title to the land. Here, too, he found a wide range of options. A "claim" might be bought in a price range from twenty to one thousand dollars, depending on whether the purchaser was buying uncertain rights to a tract of raw unimproved land or a secure title to a farm with large portions cleared, under cultivation, and perhaps fenced. Some sort of suitable house and other farm buildings had to be constructed. The pioneer might do this himself or hire it done, sometimes in exchange for labor or other services. A cash outlay, however, was almost always necessary to acquire livestock. What did it

6. Mary Blanche Tibbitts, "The Development of a Pioneer Wisconsin Farm during the Thirties and Forties" (M.A., Wisconsin, 1925), *passim;* a briefer account that touches many of the same points is Ezra Henry Pieper, "The Settlement of De Kalb, Du Page, Kane, and Kendall Counties to 1850" (M.A., Illinois, 1926), ch. 4.

7. Chicago *American,* Oct. 31, 1835; Peoria *Register,* July 1, 1837. An extended description of these prairie lands is found in Allan G. Bogue, *From Prairie to Corn Belt: Farming on the Illinois and Iowa Prairies in the Nineteenth Century* (Chicago, 1963), 1–7. An especially insightful treatment of the Iowa prairie is David George Kinnett, "Locating in the Garden of the World: The Prairie Factor, 1830–1860," 1973, unpublished paper in the possession of the author.

cost to make a farm on the last frontier of the Old Northwest? Obviously the figure varied, depending on a man's capital and how he wanted to spend it, for many of the costs could still be met by labor instead of cash. George Holland came to Iowa with a team of horses and $2.50 in his pocket. He made a farm by hard work. Aristarchus Cone, if anything, had less. Others, such as Andrew Fitz, expended capital instead of labor. The German immigrant Johann Frederick Diederichs sent a detailed analysis of costs to friends in his homeland to assist those following. He estimated that in Wisconsin in 1848 the pioneer needed five hundred dollars to settle on "wild land," and two thousand dollars would buy a fine farm. The lands of the west were not free, but in this early period, most of the basic features of pioneering—housing, fencing, breaking land—could still be paid for by labor. It was possible to make something out of nothing. Many did it—by hard work. But there was no denying that prairie agriculture was more and more a business, and subject to the forces that affected other businesses.[8]

In spite of the costs (capital and labor) in farm making, the feeling persisted that this agricultural frontier was a good place for people of limited means. Many who went west voiced this sentiment. Wrote Stephen Eames, "The chance here for poor people who are willing to live in a log cabin ware raged clothes and shake a little with the Ague is first rate for if they work they can raise corn wheat and sauce of all kinds in abundance, cattle and hogs are kept much easyer than at the east." Cyrus Aldrich wrote in the same vein: "This is the Country for a poor man, no mistake, corn 20 cts. per Bush. wages $1¼ per day—for a rich man too, money is worth 12 per cent." Emma Sprague summed up the opportunities in describing her new home in Grant County (Wisconsin): "I do think that a man with small means can do better in this country than at the east if they can get here with a span of horses and waggon and 100 dollars to buy 80 acres of land or 50 dollars to enter 40 and good health and plenty of ambition they are sure to make a good place in a little time."[9]

8. George and Sarah Holland to Thomas and Elizabeth Cary, Aug. 2, 1843, Thomas Cary Collection, SHSI; Diederichs, "Letters and Diary," 368. The issue of farm-making costs is examined in Bogue, *From Prairie to Corn Belt*, 169–70, with emphasis on the increased costs of a later generation of pioneer farmers as machinery became more necessary to farm operations.

9. Stephen Eames to Wm. and Olive Plumb, Aug. 23, 1840, in Stephen Eames, Bascom Letters, IHS-U; Cyrus Aldrich to Nath'l Spaulding, April 22, 1838, Cyrus Aldrich

Along with diversity in immigration and options in economic expenditures went increasing standardization in institutional life. The pattern continued to be the guidelines laid down by the Ordinance of 1787, along with the basic instruments of county government, the common law, and the court system. These were already well known to almost everyone except the European immigrants. One important variation emerged. The press for lands across the broad expanses of the new prairies and the sense of competition raised by the large numbers in motion gave rise to a new concept in land rights. Known as the "claim," it was not based on government title but on the traditional concept that land belonged to those who were there, now given institutional form. When the pioneer had fulfilled certain minimum conditions testifying to his commitment to the land, he registered his claim with a local recorder. A claim conveyed the right (protected by local custom) to purchase a tract of land with improvements at the minimum price at the time of public sale. Morris Sleight described this arrangement as early as 1834. "I can by going one mile from this place where I am now take as much land as I choose, say a mile square, run a Plough Furrow around it, and the place is then mine," he wrote. "No man will presume to intrude. . . . This is an arrangement among the settlers, that they will not bid against each other; anything to the contrary they have declared Club Law, and are determined to put it in force."[10] Most of the time making a claim involved more than simply a plowed furrow. An early settler in Mercer County (Illinois) plowed up fifteen acres of prairie and planted a corn crop to make his claim. He also laid down four logs for a cabin foundation. He then returned the following April to plant another crop. He made a second trip east over the summer, and his claim was still valid when he came back in September. In this fashion land might be held for several years—depending on how rapidly the government could place it in market—and great improvements made. The value of the farm rose with the settlement of the area. Thus, by the time the early settler (or the person to whom he sold his claim) bought the tract at the minimum price, the land might already be worth ten dollars an acre. The concept of the claim lasted throughout the period. As late as 1849 P. C. Haynes wrote from Appanoose County (Iowa) that such claims were "al-

Collection, CHS; Emma Sprague letter, Dec. 4, 1842, SHSW. A similar declaration is in Morris Sleight to his wife, July 9, 1834, Morris Sleight Papers, CHS.
10. Sleight to James Russell, July 7, 1834, Sleight Papers.

most as good as deeds" and protected by the threat of tar and feathers.[11]

The rules of the Prophetstown Club on the Rock River in Illinois, organized at a public meeting in August 1837, suggest the institutional form of claims associations—or clubs, as they were sometimes called. The preamble to a formal "constitution" (for so it was entitled) recited the reasons for its existence: "Whereas conflicting claims have arisen between some of the citizens residing on government lands, and whereas many individuals have much larger claims than necessary for common farming purposes, therefore, we, the subscribers to preserve order, peace and harmony deem it expedient to form an association." In addition to naming officers, the articles laid down a number of specific regulations for holding land claims. No settler could hold more than half a section of land, and this to include not more than eighty acres of timber. Settlers must register their claims, giving specific boundaries, with the recorder, and pay a fee of twenty-five cents. A committee of three investigated and adjudicated disputes between and among claimants, with an appeal to the whole committee of fifteen. Settlers had to make improvements—"by plowing, fencing or building"—within three months of recording their claims. The improvements necessary to retain rights to the claim were a matter of local practice, varying from place to place. That the organizing committee directed the publication of the proceedings in three newspapers suggests confidence in the universal acceptance of such an institution.[12] Claims associations were, strictly speaking, conspiracies. The association provided for collusion and threats of violence at public sales in order to ensure that the claims of their members might be purchased at the minimum price. But settlers vigorously defended the use of the institution, citing the rights of original claimants, the defenseless condition of their families, and the rapacious character of evil speculators who would outbid them at public auctions and take not only the land but the hard-earned improvements at a price just beyond what the legitimate settler could afford to pay.[13]

11. Peoria *Register*, July 1, Oct. 28, 1837; P. C. Haynes to his father and mother, May 6, 1849, Peril Columbus Haynes Family Letters, SHSI.
12. Peoria *Register*, Oct. 7, 1837. Bogue has concluded that land speculation was a basic force behind the organization and operation of these institutions. He also notes the significance of timber lands in claims club activities. *From Prairie to Corn Belt*, 31–39.
13. The constitution of the early claims club of Des Moines County (Iowa), along with a virgorous defense of this institution, is in "Early Land Claims in Des Moines County," *IJHP*, 10 (1912): 255–60.

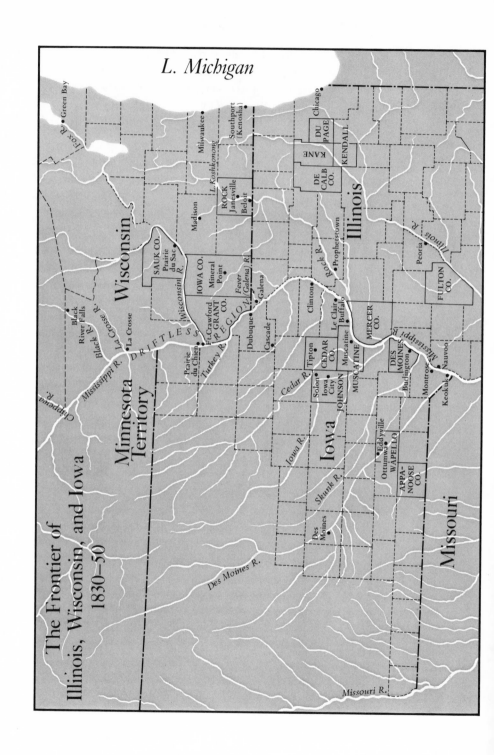

The Frontier of Illinois, Wisconsin, and Iowa 1830–50

Between 1830 and 1850 technological changes, institutional stability, and large numbers of people foreshortened the frontier experience of the Old Northwest. The transition to commercial agriculture was particularly rapid. Staple agricultural products—especially wheat, corn, and livestock—found a ready market. Central to this development was the evolution of a transportation system to give access to markets and the rise of a series of important urban centers. Two groups of cities appeared on principal water routes. One group lay along the western edge of Lake Michigan, serving the frontiers of northern Illinois and Wisconsin; the second, on the west bank of the Mississippi River with extensions up the Wisconsin, Rock, and Illinois rivers, met the needs of Iowa Territory. Chicago was the largest and most important of the rising commercial centers that date from the period 1830 to 1850. Located at the foot of Lake Michigan and by turns a fur-trading post and fort, in 1830 it was still a tiny village of traders, Indians, and soldiers. In the following decade, however, factors influencing expansion everywhere—the opening of the Erie Canal, steam navigation on the lakes, rapid settlement and development of Michigan, northern Indiana, and northern Illinois—gave this village an enormous impulse to growth. Soon it was the fastest-growing urban center in the western world. Chicago was more than new blocks of wooden shanties, town site speculation, and a busy waterfront; it was a symbol of America's energetic materialistic growth. Visitors from America and abroad came to see and comment. Amidst the rutted streets, droves of hogs, and grog shops, new immigrants and wagons piled high with goods headed inland. The rise of Chicago reflected the settlement and agricultural production of the hinterland with which it was in partnership. "This country, from Lake Michigan to the Illinois and Mississippi is not now uninhabited, uncultivated region, but the immigrant has broken upon the stillness which reigned there,—molested the forest grove, and turned up the rich soil to the sun," commented the Chicago *American* in the summer of 1835. It concluded, "Those fields which yesterday were but broad wastes, are now waving with corn, and enriching the cultivator with plentious harvests."[14]

Every autumn wagons rumbled into Chicago from as far distant as the

14. Chicago *American*, June 27, 1835. On Chicago as a market for agricultural produce, see Edwin John Peckous, "The History of Downers Grove, Illinois, from 1832–1873" (M.A., Illinois, 1956), 25–26; and Pieper, "The Settlement of De Kalb, Du Page, Kane, and Kendall Counties," 90–91.

Rock River Valley and southern Wisconsin. Of his trip to Chicago in 1840, the Wisconsin pioneer Frederick Starin wrote, "It was truly surprising to see the number of teams and loads of produce that are daily entering the city & oncoming out to find such detestably execrable roads, over which we empty as we were . . . could scarcely pass without miring."[15] Chicago, Milwaukee, Dubuque, Burlington, and Keokuk depended on wagon roads to the interior—for settlers headed west, for commodities on their way to market. Under the circumstances, impetus for road construction assumed a new urgency.[16]

As in Michigan and Florida, the federal government built several roads on the grounds of national defense. In the spring of 1832 the Sauk war leader Black Hawk recrossed the Mississippi into Illinois to occupy lands from which the tribe had been expelled the year before. Black Hawk protested the treaty of cession (1804) as fraudulent, but his declared purpose in returning was to raise a crop of corn to support the tribe. Fed by failure of communication, the traditional distrust between the two civilizations, a terrified countryside, and the ambitions of Illinois politicians, the so-called Black Hawk War ended in the virtual annihilation of Black Hawk's band, which included many women and children. Although the military aspects of the uprising were soon over, the war provided a good excuse for the large-scale intervention of the federal government in road construction, and federal troops built several important roads in the territories of Wisconsin and Iowa. The war had another important feature: under the terms of peace, a Sauk and Fox land cession opened much of eastern Iowa to white occupation.

The varieties of the frontier experience in this last frontier of the Old Northwest emerge in the story of George W. Ogden. Born in New York State in 1810, Ogden came to Wisconsin Territory in the autumn of 1836. On arriving, he and one of his brothers—eventually three joined him—went into the wagon building and repair business in Milwaukee, where, according to his own account, they prospered. Ogden felt the at-

---

15. Frederick J. Starin, "Diary of a Journey to Wisconsin in 1840," *WMH*, 6 (1922–23): 91.
16. W. Turrentine Jackson, "The Army Engineers as Road Builders in Territorial Iowa," *IJH*, 47 (1949): 15–33; Jacob Van Der Zee, "Roads and Highways of Territorial Iowa," *IJHP*, 3 (1905): 175–225, esp. map on p. 183. Edwin D. Karn, "Roadmaking in Wisconsin Territory" (M. A., Wisconsin, 1959), is an excellent study.

traction of the land, however, and soon left the city for the prairie in Rock County, where he established a claim and settled down to the pioneer life in a "shanty" of his own construction. In his first few years Ogden witnessed the transformation of the region. When he arrived, a large band of Indians camped across the river from him. He watched their canoes move up and down the river, even into Lake Koshkonong, in search of fish and wild fowl. In the evening the Indians would sometimes come to trade game and fish for tobacco. But gradually the Indians vanished from the scene. In their place came the landlookers, ambitious hard-riding men—driven by a certain sense of competition—who rode over the prairie, stopping by Ogden's cabin for something to eat and an exchange of information. In general, he welcomed their arrival.

The new agricultural enterprise was an endless source of work. Ogden settled on the land in August, and during the fall he cut twelve tons of hay from the prairie. He broke the prairie right up to the time the ground froze. The Ogden brothers traded work with other early arrivals; George split rails in return for breaking prairie, and everyone worked during house raisings and prairie fires. The Ogdens bought and borrowed from other settlers such items as a dressed buckskin, a rifle for hunting, or a horse for travel. Seasonal duties commanded their attention, too. In the fall prairie fires were a constant threat, especially to hay. In the winter snow and cold winds drove Ogden and his brothers indoors for long spells, where they cobbled, mended, whittled tools and axe handles, did the laundry, and took baths. In the spring came new construction duties: fences, a corn crib, ox shed, and a horse stable. The main business was planting and harvesting. The principal crops were vegetables, oats, wheat, and corn. Although nearby Janesville had been named the county seat, Ogden make his large purchases in Chicago. On one trip he spent more than $150 for, among others, "one yoke of oxen, plough, barrel of pork, one of flour, part of barrel of salt, and other fixings." He built a new house and found a market for his beans at the local gristmill in Beloit. The economic cycle of the next few years was much the same. Ogden hired a Mr. Davis to do much of his harvesting and paid him in shares. Ogden also sold a part of his claim. In September 1841, four years after his arrival on the land, he carried a load of wheat to Chicago. His agricultural enterprise was now well under way, his land and the country itself had been transformed from wilderness to farm, and around him other claims were experiencing a similar evolution. By 1841 there were rumors of a steamboat on the river, and Ogden had already built a skiff and chopped logs for a wharf.

Ogden also participated in a wide range of other activities. The news that Janesville was to be the county seat stimulated his interest in government. Soon thereafter he attended the election of county officials. He himself convened a meeting of his neighbors in order to name the prairie—they named it Prairie du Lac—and to draw up a petition for a post office. In autumn 1838 Ogden signed a petition "for a Territorial road from Geneva Lake to Madison, to pass by here." He and his neighbors agreed "to appoint some person to go to Madison with our road petition, and lobby there a spell." The legislature approved the petition for a road but declined to act on the request for a ferry as beyond its jurisdiction, so the petitioners appealed to the county commissioners. In the summer of 1838 the federal government established a post office at Prairie du Lac. Ogden and several others built a cabin to serve as the post office and named it Grainfield. Road surveyors came through in the winter of 1838, plotting the road to Beloit. At about the same time Ogden paid his first taxes. "Esqr. Brown came along today collecting taxes our tax was $1.75," he wrote.

Ogden and his brothers also helped to create a society. Contact with his neighbors was constant from the beginning of settlement. He and his neighbor Churchill hunted, bartered and traded work, and when Ogden was ill, having cut his leg with an axe—"two inches deep to the bone, about three inches above the ancle"—Mrs. Churchill made regular visits, for which he expressed much appreciation. In March 1838 Ogden began to attend "a Methodist meeting," and in late May recorded a visit by a preacher. As the land viewers came and went, succeeded by settler families, Ogden's world changed. Some of his friends, like the Churchills, left, but other families moved in. In 1839 Ogden was a member of a committee to make plans for a Fourth of July celebration. On the appointed day, "All hands went independence. We had a first rate independence. an oration delivered by D. F. Kimball. it went off right. I carried Amanda to the ball. We were honored by the presence of Gov. Dodge." The next year Ogden helped to organize a school district. Financed by a tax levy, he and others arranged for the construction of a schoolhouse eighteen feet square. The extended transformation of his world had reached a bench mark by the end of 1841. The first wilderness experience was behind. The new society had many signs of permanence.[17]

Wapello County (Iowa) in 1850 was a larger frontier, larger not only in area but in range of experience, and a different frontier, farther west and at a later date. Because of a delayed resolution of the Indian title, Wapello County could not be legally settled until 1843. The great land rush of that year—anticipating later scenes in the Oklahoma Territory—brought a substantial population to the new county. Wapello County posed for a census portrait after seven years of settlement. In 1850 Wapello was agricultural. The census classified seventy-eight percent of the men as farmers, and many others worked in what might be called supporting industries. Of the 2,067 men declaring occupations, only eight identified themselves as ministers, seven as schoolteachers. The average value of the land was $5.74 an acre, a fourfold increase over the minimum government price. This rapid rise in land values flowed from the factors influencing growth: crowded settlements, improvements, roads and ferries, access to schools, and churches. The productive farms raised and sold corn and hogs and grazed large numbers of milk cows. The Des Moines River, cutting through the county, was an easy avenue of access. Within eighteen months of the first legal settlement, voters elected a board of commissioners; the board assessed taxes by July 4, 1844. The district court convened in Ottumwa on September 14, 1844. Farmers were the dominant economic group in the county, but the civic leaders tended to be people involved in trades and professions: merchants, millers, lawyers, and physicians. Urban development was already evident in the villages of Ottumwa and Eddyville, which provided services for the countryside by 1850 and where these people lived and worked.[18]

The new frontier of the Old Northwest offered alternative ways of making a living. Mining was an important economic activity in southwestern Wisconsin and northeastern Iowa from the late 1820's to the mid-1840's. In this hard and rocky land of bluffs and valleys, permanent settlements began in the so-called Driftless Region as early as 1822. The settlers left

17. This account is based on George W. Ogden, Diary, 1837–41, SHSW.
18. Mildred Throne, "A Population Study of an Iowa County in 1850," *IJH*, 57 (1959): 305–30. Throne comments of Turner's image of a single-file procession to the frontier: "In Iowa, this procession was hardly single file—the movers trod on each other's heels, or walked side by side" (p. 330).

tracts of fertile and unsettled prairies behind as they went out to the lead diggings and squatted on government land. By 1830 a large concentration of people engaged in mining, smelting, and exporting lead ore. These tenants at will dug up every mining site within a hundred miles. A few started farms and did a thriving business with the miners. At first the miners prospered, but the price of lead dropped abruptly in 1829, initiating a temporary period of stagnation and hard times. Renewed high prices in the 1830's brought an immigration of miners from Cornwall and Yorkshire. Economic prosperity lasted until the 1840's, when the mines played out. After this agriculture became progressively more important in the local economy.[19]

Mining brought variations in the traditional patterns associated with an agricultural fronter, specifically with respect to urban growth, transportation, and government. The rapid influx of a large number of immigrants accelerated the rise of towns. In 1828, for example, prospectors struck lead outcroppings; a year later a thousand people celebrated the Fourth of July in the new town of Mineral Point. Built almost overnight, Mineral Point became the focal point of the lead industry in what would become in time southwestern Wisconsin. In 1830 it was the county seat for Iowa County (Michigan) and in 1834 became the site of a district land office. Galena (Illinois) grew almost as rapidly. The Galena *Advertiser* had columns with legal notices, cards of lawyers side by side with those for blacksmiths, and advertisements for dry goods stores, indicating the nature and direction of the town's business. Miners and middlemen exported lead downriver to St. Louis. The attendant commercial transactions meant good business for the region's lawyers. The *Miner's Journal* commented on the rising number of professionals of this class: "The business of the court here has very rapidly increased within the last year. The immense number of business transactions have swollen the civil docket to a large size, and invited the talents of the country to attend the courts here."[20]

19. The literature on the lead region of Illinois, Wisconsin, and Iowa is voluminous, especially for Wisconsin. The most complete account is Joseph Schafer, *The Wisconsin Lead Region* (Madison, 1932). One of the best specialized studies is Mary Josephine Read, "A Population Study of the Driftless Hill Land during the Pioneer Period, 1832–1860" (Ph.D., Wisconsin, 1941).

20. David Dirk Van Tassel, "Democracy, Frontier, and Mineral Point: A Study of the Influence of the Frontier on a Wisconsin Mining Town" (M.S., Wisconsin, 1951); Galena *Advertiser*, Dec. 14, 1829; Galena *Miner's Journal*, May 9, 1829; *Galenian*, May 16, 1832.

The town of Dubuque appeared across the river on the Iowa side somewhat later, but under the same circumstances. The first flood of legal immigrants settled on the site of this village in 1833, then still a part of Michigan Territory. On the town's third birthday, the Dubuque *Visitor* offered to the outside world an account of the 35 blocks and 280 town lots, "all of which are occupied by homes and gardens. The village contains about one thousand inhabitants, and two hundred and fifty buildings of different descriptions; among which are fifteen dry good stores, and one Methodist meeting house. A large Catholic church is now building, and preparation is being made for a Presbyterian church."[21] Dubuque was the last of the three major lead district towns. The accidents of time and settlement patterns divided the lead region among three political units: one was the distant corner of a state; two others were new territories, one of them west of the Mississippi River. But the political distinctions were not significant. The lead-mining towns were very similar in nature; they appeared as quickly as the mining population moved in, prospered and stagnated with the lead trade, whose wants they catered to, and gradually underwent a transformation to an agricultural economy, along with the countryside around them.

Lead made special demands on transportation facilities. The lead region had to trade to survive; its products could not be consumed. Unlike strictly agricultural frontiers, there could be no long period of self-sufficiency while new immigrants drove up land values and provided a market for surplus crops. There was no lead market nearer than St. Louis, and the bulk of the cargo placed a premium on water transportation. Galena on the Fever (later Galena) River and Dubuque on the Mississippi had excellent locations. Galena fancied itself a "port" in the late 1820's, and the "Marine List" in the local paper testifies to the importance of this commercial contact with urban centers downstream. Galena's record for 1830 showed vessels arriving at two- or three-day intervals in the spring when traffic first resumed. Incoming cargoes included foodstuffs—pork, flour, dried fruit—iron bars, one box of books, and two thousand fruit trees. Commercial life at Dubuque followed the same pattern.[22]

Mining attracted a transient, sometimes turbulent population. The special demands of mining and the early settlement fostered confusion.

21. Dubuque *Visitor*, May 11, 1836.
22. Galena *Advertiser*, April 5, 1830; Dubuque *Visitor*, May 11, 1836.

No orderly rectangular survey system had laid off the land and showed the boundaries of tracts to pioneers. Miners were intensely interested in small claims of a few hundred feet. Even a few acres might represent a fortune in lead ore. So the questions of ownership and procedure that after mid-century appeared all over the mountain West and California were anticipated in the lead region of the upper Mississippi Valley: how were claims to be laid out? how was the land to be claimed? how much land could an individual miner claim? when was a claim vacated? how should disputes between and among miners be resolved? A governing body drew up special rules and posted them around the camps. These local customs—for so they may be considered—had the force of law in the mining district. Even after county government appeared in the late 1820's, these customs continued to meet the special needs of a mining community. The miners east of the river carried the regulations across the Mississippi to the new "diggings" on the Iowa side in 1830. Those published at the Dubuque Mines on June 17, 1830, offer a fair example:

> We, a committee, having been chosen to draft certain rules and regulations, by which we, as miners, will be governed; and, having duly considered the subject, do unanimously agree that we will be governed by the regulations on the east side of the Mississippi River, with the following exceptions, to wit:
>
> ARTICLE I. That each, and every man shall hold two hundred yards square of ground by working said ground one day in six.
>
> ARTICLE II. —We further agree, that there shall be chosen by the majority of the miners present, a person who shall hold this article, and who shall grant letters of arbitration, on application being made, and that said letter [of] arbitration shall be obligatory on the parties concerned so applying.
>
> To the above, we the undersigned subscribe.
>
> J. L. Langworthy
&c[23]

Lumbering was a second significant new economic enterprise, its appearance and prosperity demonstrating a perfect blending of supply and demand. The crush of settlers from 1830 to 1850 created an enormous demand for building materials. This need was evident as early as the first lead-mining settlements. Rough pine planking brought thirty-five to forty dollars per thousand board feet in Galena in 1828 and was in short

23. Quoted in John C. Parrish, "Langworthys of Early Dubuque and Their Contributions to Local History," *IJHP*, 8 (1910): 317.

supply. The thriving town of Dubuque suffered from a shortage of lumber that "has hitherto retarded its progress. A large number of buildings, which would otherwise have been erected, have necessarily been delayed on that account; and many emigrants have been obliged to return down the river for want of horses." As agriculturists moved out onto the Illinois and Iowa prairies, the demand for building materials intensified, for the land provided little in the way of natural timber. George Ogden of rural Rock County (Wisconsin) traded a pair of oxen for eight thousand feet of lumber, flooring, and siding.[24] At the same time this demand arose, the land north of the Wisconsin River to the Arctic Circle stood an unbroken forest. It now remained to tap this great resource, move it south, and place it in the hands of its potential users. The American frontier rarely lacked men of enterprise, especially where the exploitation of natural resources was concerned. The Wisconsin pine lands were no exception. Much timberland passed into private hands as part of the speculative flurry of the mid-1830's. At the same time, entrepreneurs organized some ten to fifteen lumber companies on a small scale, probably with no more than fifteen to twenty-five men each. Parties in search of attractive sites began to move upriver from Prairie du Chien (Wisconsin River) and La Crosse (junction of the Mississippi, Black, and La Crosse rivers). The race for logs, mill sites, and profits had begun. Much of this frenzied economic activity took place on land that still belonged to the federal government and, in many cases, had not even been surveyed.[25]

Sawmills began to go up along the banks of the major Wisconsin rivers. The first mills were primitive water-powered affairs, small in size and capacity, with up-and-down saws, waterwheels, and dams made of brush and stone. The work was seasonal, concentrated in the winter months, with supplies brought in by sled from Dubuque or Galena; as the loggers moved to year-round operation, keelboats brought in men and supplies. The lumber frontier expanded enormously in the decade of the 1840's. In 1842 a group of Mormons brought large log rafts down the Black River to the Mississippi and down the Mississippi to Nauvoo, thus

24. Galena *Miner's Journal*, Aug. 30, 1828; Dubuque *Visitor*, June 1, 1836; Ogden, Diary, entry for Oct. 10, 1840.

25. Robert F. Fries, *Empire in Pine: The Story of Lumbering in Wisconsin, 1830–1900* (Madison, 1951), ch. 2. Lumbering required skilled labor, and, as it grew, so did the search for skilled woodsmen in the East.

demonstrating a new technique for moving lumber. Others copied their methods, and, as early as 1843, more than three million board feet came down the Black. Next year the number of mills had increased to eight. In 1847 thirteen mills were in operation, and the output exceeded 6.25 million board feet. Rafting expanded rapidly to include steam towboats. By 1850 great lumber rafts moved on all the major Wisconsin rivers— down the Mississippi to sawmills in Iowa and markets from St. Louis to New Orleans, down the shore of Lake Michigan to Chicago. The center of the Wisconsin lumber industry gradually focused on the Chippewa River Valley, where lay one-sixth of the pine forest west of the Appalachians. The lumber frontier was far removed from agriculture. It employed single men for the most part, subjecting them to extended hardships and dangers. The camp was the center of activity. As in other exploitive industries, men on the lumber frontier tended to be transient, and permanent communities evolved only slowly. The center of social and cultural life on the Black River was Black River Falls, with its tavern, one-term school, and church. The mix of population in 1849 indicates the nature of its economic activity: 375–400 men, 35 couples, 25 single women.[26]

The demand for wood created by settlement on the prairie carried the lumbering undustry into Iowa. There the resources wre neither as extensive nor as rich as in Wisconsin, but the industry appeared to meet the demand. As early as 1831, the first sawmill appeared on the Turkey River, opposite Ft. Crawford. The number of mills increased with settlement. In the autumn of 1836 Dubuque had "five saw mills and two grists in our neighborhood, but the demand is greater than can be supplied." Lumber came from the northeastern corner of the Hawkeye country and increasingly from the Wisconsin pineries. By the middle of the 1840's this new source of timber was so productive that it was no longer profitable to import lumber from the East. The lumber industry was a significant factor in the economic development of Iowa river towns, especially Dubuque and Muscatine.[27]

Manufacturing also appeared on the last large-scale frontier of the Old Northwest, adding another new dimension to the rapid and varied eco-

26. Horace Samuel Merrill, "An Early History of the Black River Falls Region" (M.A., Wisconsin, 1933), ch. 3; Selma Sather Casberg, "The Lumbering Industry of La Crosse, Wisconsin, 1841–1905" (M.A., Wisconsin, 1953), ch. 1.
27. Dubuque *Visitor*, Nov. 9, 1836; Lyda Belthuis, "The Lumber Industry in Eastern Iowa," *IJHP*, 46 (1948): 121–35.

nomic development of the region. The existence of industry on the frontier was not new; it had been present in various forms since the first trans-Appalachian frontier. But the terms "manufacturing" and "industry" can be misleading. Early industrial workers functioned in such a limited sphere and with such small output that they were more a local convenience than a basic unit of the economy. The first processing industry to serve the frontier was the mill, which became an important economic institution, a significant force in the neighborhood (and a substantial living for its owner, setting on foot a race for the best mill sites), and an early center of social activities. In the period from 1830 to 1850 the importance of mills—especially sawmills and gristmills—increased in accordance with the greater demands of a large population. This early dependence on mills was typical of early frontiers.

The changing nature of the frontier experience—the foreshortening of the process, especially in economic development and the rise of societies—was also evident in the acceleration of manufacturing. Large numbers of people and their demands for goods, growing urban centers, expanding transportation facilities, large-scale agricultural production that led to a surplus of commodities, all combined to spur the rise of industry. As the products of the newest frontier appeared in greater variety, so did the manufacturing processes. Wisconsin is a case in point. It began with a lead industry in the late 1820's, became an important wheat producer by 1840, branched into lumber in the 1840's, and in the 1850's went into the extraction and manufacture of other minerals on a large scale. The area was distinguished not only for its natural abundance, but also for the variety of these natural gifts. In 1840 the population of the four-year-old territory was 30,945; its industrial development was centered in the processing industries. The next decade brought dramatic changes. The population of the state—for so it became in 1848—increased to 305,390 in 1850. Some forty percent of the value of manufactured products concentrated in flour milling and lumber, processing the basic products of the frontier economy. Other significant enterprises included, in decreasing order, construction materials, iron, wagons, boots and shoes, furniture, and agricultural implements.[28]

28. Margaret Walsh, *The Manufacturing Frontier: Pioneer Industry in Antebellum Wisconsin, 1830–1860* (Madison, 1972), ch. 1, esp. pp. 1–25, maps 1–4, tables 4 and 5. A useful visual description of the variety of industry in early southwestern Wisconsin is a map in Herman R. Friis, "The David Dale Owen Map of Southwestern Wisconsin," *Prologue*, 1 (1969): 28.

With steamboats, wagons, and immigrant trains pouring into the western country came the drive to preserve older values and the need to ensure an orderly and what people at the time liked to call a "civilized" society. Institutionalized religion was a focal point of this effort. Religion no longer carried solace for the lonely and hope for the dispossessed. The religion on the cutting edge of the newest frontier was strongly institutionalized. Denominational identity was important. Those chosen for missionary activity here worked along traditional lines with specific landmarks of progress: the establishment of a church, always with a Sunday school; the establishment of auxiliaries, such as prayer meetings, ladies' groups, and regular revivals; and, finally, the construction of a church building. The issues of Sabbath observance and temperance went hand in hand with theology. Already the prohibition of strong drink had become a cornerstone for church membership in several denominations. The minister came to the frontier as a transforming agent, carrying not only theology but also civilization. In the first trans-Appalachian frontier the minister was often one of the people; now he was often apart from them. In spite of the alleged moral darkness and physical hardships of the western country, volunteers were numerous. The speed and volume of missionary activity was remarkable. As early as 1840 missionaries worked hard in the new Wisconsin Territory. Here these messengers from the East encountered the various societies associated with mining, lumbering, and agriculture, and increasingly, they found urban centers. Each presented its own array of challenges. In general, all societies tended to be transient and unsettled, intensely directed to the pursuit of wealth. Furthermore, they were often free of traditional restraints, especially those all-male societies of mining and lumbering camps.[29]

The part played by the Congregationalists may be taken to represent the increasingly institutional and formal nature of frontier religion. This

29. Charles J. Kennedy, "The Congregationalists and the Presbyterians on the Wisconsin Frontier" (Ph.D., Wisconsin, 1940), chs. 1 and 3; Lois Marie Craig, "The Role of the Missionary on the Wisconsin Frontier (1825–1840)" (M.A., Wisconsin, 1949), chs. 4 and 5. An insight into the financial hardships of frontier ministers may be obtained from the letters and diary of Elihu Springer, ISHL. Springer was a Methodist circuit rider in Illinois. His first year, 1833, he travelled four thousand miles, and his income—"quarterage" plus missionary funds—came to $61.16. He wrote of coffee, tea, and sugar as luxuries, at a time when even the most humble cabin would have enjoyed such articles. His is a poignant account of dedication and self-sacrifice that involved his family equally.

denomination was especially influential on the Iowa frontier. Its most important leader, Asa Turner, reached the New England settlement near Burlington just as the territory was organized. His call in 1843 for assistance from the East found a response in a group of men from Andover-Newton Theological Seminary who became known as the "Iowa Band." The best known of the Iowa Congregationalists after Turner was William Salter, renowned both for his longevity (he died at Burlington in 1910) and for his prolific writings. One of those who labored faithfully for Turner and Salter was a young New Englander, Ebenezer Alden. Alden first organized a Congregational Church in the town of Solon (Johnson County)—it consisted of five members—but he left soon for Tipton (Cedar County), a more promising community. In 1844 Alden estimated Tipton's population at seventy-five individuals, including twenty-five men, "almost all professed infidels & Universalists. A hard place isn't it." He urged forward plans to build a church, "but we moved slowly in this Western world. 215 dollars have been subscribed to put up this building—$8.00 in cash I believe the remainder in work—produce—timber etc." Alden added, "You see how much money is in circulation." He looked askance at the new society in the West. "The amount of coffee & tobacco used here would be incredible to you. The spitting here at singing school especially would be a caution to those who have to clean up in the morning," he commented. Towns such as Tipton and Cascade (he had compared notes with the Congregational minister there) "are generally pretty wicked at first. But as the country grows older a new class of people moves in, 2 years may put an entirely new face upon things here. I hope God will change the place before that time." He cooperated with the Methodists, but reluctantly. Of the denominational competition he wrote, "The best way to preserve peace is to be complaisant, courteous, yielding, & unite sometimes, but still you must be as independent of them & all other sects as you can." Alden wrote to his father, "It should be remembered that there is no lack of 'preachers' here. The great difficulty I have met with has been to arrange my appointments for preaching, as to not conflict with some of them." The high point of the year 1844 was the appearance of the revered Turner himself to preach to the new congregation. The results were not entirely successful, Alden reported:

> We had a large congregation yesterday but there was a good deal of confusion on account of the number of small children present & in the

344 *The Second Great Migration 1830–50*

evening someone set the prairie on fire close by so that we were disturbed by it. The prairie is on fire now right out a half a mile before my window. Br. Turner did not enjoy the day much & was a good deal disconcerted in preaching so that we did not see so great results as we had hoped for & as he saw up at Br. Salter's place a week before.[30]

The Catholic Church was also vigorous in parts of the Old Northwest. From Prairie du Sac (Wisconsin) a priest wrote that Protestant strength overshadowed his church, "for the Protestants are more numerous and prosperous, their churches are simple, and their meager rites cost almost nothing. Their mission bureaus are numerous and strong; consequently they flood the country with their missionaries and emissaries. The opposite is the case among the Catholics."[31] In truth, the Protestants were everywhere, but where Catholics chose to organize, they also made their mark. Nowhere was this more evident than in northeastern Iowa. Bishop Mathias Loras established a diocese at Dubuque in 1838, and its influence radiated into the countryside and the small towns. Bishop Loras bought lands, encouraged immigration, consecrated churches, and appealed for missionaries and money from his superiors in the East and in Europe. He became the most important single force for organized immigration into the northeastern part of Iowa.[32]

By the time the advance into the last frontier of the Old Northwest began in the 1830's, the concept of the common school, which provided equal opportunity for education of all children at public expense, was widespread. It was a period of great national interest in education and examination of the ways in which the people of the Republic should be trained to meet their duties as responsible citizens. Although not without its critics, the doctrine of a universal education had a substantial degree of acceptance in the Old Northwest.[33] The experiences of both Iowa and

---

30. Ebenezer Alden to his father, Feb. 3, March 1844; Alden to his parents, Feb. 22, 1844; Alden to his mother, Nov. 4, 1844, Ebenezer Alden Letters, SHSI. On the high educational standards for Congregational ministers—even in the West—note that George N. Smith was refused a license to preach in Kalamazoo (Michigan) in 1834 because he lacked knowledge of Latin and Greek. J. Fraser Cocks, III, "George N. Smith: Reformer on the Frontier," *MH*, 52 (1968): 39.

31. Adelbert Inama, "Letters of the Reverend Adelbert Inama, O.P.," *WMH*, 12 (1928–29): 59.

32. For a discussion of Bishop Mathias Loras and his contributions to the Iowa frontier, see Loren Nelson Horton, "Roman Catholic Institutions and Their Influence in Early Dubuque," 1970, unpublished paper in possession of the author.

33. James M. Sears, "Teachers of the Old Northwest Territory 1830–1860, as Seen in Their Diaries and Papers (M.A., Wisconsin, 1964), ch. 1.

Wisconsin in this twenty-year period, however, show that despite laws for the support of common schools, these institutions developed slowly and were poorly supported. Urban centers led the way. Milwaukee had a school in 1836, but it was not a public school. Southport (Wisconsin, later incorporated as Kenosha) passed a free school law and opened a public school in 1849, but only after a long struggle against those who opposed it because of the cost. The presence of a public school was a cause for rejoicing among many parents. The itinerant Methodist circuit rider Elihu Springer reported from Milwaukee in 1847, "We have an excellent school here, where I send five children, free of charge. This I conceive to be an privilege for which I feel truly grateful, and one which I have never before, been permitted to enjoy, and which I hope to improve to advantage."[34] Generally speaking, public schooling beyond the "rate law," under which parents of pupils paid costs beyond state contributions, was not widespread until the decade of the 1850's. As the final step in the creation of educational institutions came the establishment of state universities. The first Wisconsin territorial legislature (1836) made provision for a university; the first Iowa Legislative Assembly (1847) did the same. Both institutions had extended periods of slow growth ahead, but the acts of founding exhibit the high aspirations of the pioneer peoples.[35]

Through the flood tide of immigration, the many new societies, and the emergence of a vast agricultural civilization ran the disturbing signs of an America approaching mid-century—and civil war. The vigorous nationalism that arose after 1815 reached a crescendo in the annexation of Texas and the Mexican War, but both, at the same time, divided the nation. Cultural egocentrism emerged in anti-Catholic sentiments, Mormon persecutions, and contempt for the inefficient Mexicans. The influx of immigrant peoples attracted suspicious glances, especially in their association with rising urban areas. North of the Ohio, the growing abolition movement, even as it divided and splintered within itself, began to divide the nation. The nation was in the process of change. The lands west of the Appalachians, and, more recently, the newest frontier of the Old Northwest, reflected these changes. Frontier peoples adopted, or brought with them, the ideology of the East as well as its technology,

34. Springer to his father, Nov. 9, 1847, Springer Letters.
35. For the case of Iowa, see Irving H. Hart, "The Governors of Iowa as Educational Leaders, 1838–1949," *IJH*, 54 (1956): 233–36; Vernon Carstensen, "The University as Head of the Iowa School System," *IJH*, 33 (1955): 213–24.

and they came to be aware of different peoples and societies in their midst. One-third of Wisconsin's population was foreign-born by 1850, and these immigrants had their own languages and customs. P. C. Haynes, on the other hand, who moved from Tennessee to Davis County (Iowa), hated "Yankees." So did the Langworthys of Dubuque. A hundred miles to the southwest, Johnson County had a thriving antislavery society.[36] The frontier had long exhibited more than its share of intolerance. The rising national tensions of this period did nothing to assuage this instinct, and, if anything, only intensified it.

36. Haynes to his brother, Dec. 3, 1851, Haynes Family Letters; Lucius H. Langworthy, "Sketches of the Early Settlement of the West by Lucius H. Langworthy," *IJHP*, 8 (1910): 362. The Johnson County (Iowa) Anti-Slavery Society reported more than one hundred members at its meeting in 1844. Iowa City *Iowa Standard*, Sept. 12, 1844.

VI

The First American Frontier

By 1850 the lands west of the Appalachians, which had contained only a handful of settlers in Kentucky in 1775, had a population of more than six million. The new land settlements stretched west to Des Moines, north to the Wisconsin River, south to the Gulf of Mexico. The trans-Appalachian frontier had expanded to meet the frontier of the Texas Republic and now prepared—with the help of the railroad—to unite with the new western states on the shores of the Pacific Ocean. The admission of California in 1850 marked the close of one era and the opening of another. The Great West—from the Appalachians to the Missouri River—had made an enormous impact upon the nation, especially in the last generation. Its politicians were among the nation's leaders; its agricultural production was larger than that of many European nations. The people who lived west of the Appalachians in 1850 would have enjoyed such observations, for they were always intent upon growth and material wealth. The seventy-five years of expansion after 1775 gave them much of both. If the West still lagged in literature and the arts and in providing for schools for its young people, it may be thought of as much like the new American nation after 1775, when the Americans found that cultural achievement and a distinctively American civilization were not as easy to achieve as political independence. The western country after 1775 also discovered that economic gratification was more easily achieved than were cultural amenities. First it sought security and stability, then wealth, and, finally, an improvement in quality of life. Throughout, the frontier offered an abundance of the most fertile agricultural lands in the world to compensate for its lack of cultural amenities.

Among the many changes over seventy-five years, two themes continued. From the very beginning, the frontier had towns. Some of these became great cities; others faded from sight. But all had an impact on the people who lived in and around them. Attention singles out a Cincinnati, Chicago, St. Louis, or New Orleans, but the real urban center of the frontier was the small town. This was the heart of the service enterprise that made the town indispensable in the age of agriculture. It was the center of professional life—such as it was—and professional people came to set the tone for town and countryside alike. Thousands of such towns appeared. Each was a microcosm of the urban experience. Although towns surely played a central role in the development of the trans-Appalachian West, our view of them has been conditioned by the survival of records they themselves made possible. Travellers stayed in towns and described them at length, if not always favorably. People who lived in towns were more likely to leave accounts of their activities, and their records were also more easily preserved than the records of those who struggled quietly in the countryside. Municipal governments also left records of what they did and why. Following these sources, historians have tended to focus on the urban experience at the expense of the rural. In the end, however, even those who lived in the countryside and wrote of their experiences testified to the impact of the town on their political, economic, social, and cultural lives.

From the beginning of permanent American settlements west of the mountains, men struggled for political leadership. The desire to lead is as old as human nature, but on the frontier it was closely associated with the drive for economic advantage. Men went to the frontier to improve themselves economically, but such was the nature of the land that the pioneers were forced to call on government to do many things for them. Those in control of the apparatus of government obviously had an enormous influence. Like economic development, politics took place at several levels: federal, state, territory, county, and township. In the drive for office, frontier people did not lose sight of the importance of local government to their world. From the time of the establishment of Kentucky County in 1776, politics at the county level was a beehive of activity. Like the influence of small towns, local politics was unobtrusive but pervasive. But, at the same time, local politics often reflected political divisions on the larger level. Whatever the circumstances—and they often changed—politics was as much a part of the trans-Appalachian frontier experience as corn and cotton.

So, too, was the closing of the frontier. Men and women no sooner began to settle the lands west of the mountains than differences in rate of development appeared. The quality of land, good management, and luck all played a part, but whatever the determining forces, distinctions appeared and grew over time. Some areas matured and passed beyond the frontier stage rapidly; others lagged behind. Whatever the rate, as the frontier was constantly opening in the form of new land settlements, so it was constantly closing, to be succeeded by a world that was rural rather than frontier. By the beginning of the Civil War most of the trans-Appalachian areas considered in this study had passed beyond the frontier stage. The ways in which they did this and the forces involved are an important part of the panorama of experiences in the trans-Appalachian West over seventy-five years.

14

The Urban Dimension

In 1796 Francis Baily toured the new country west of the Appalachians. The Treaty of Greenville had opened to settlement a portion of the land north of the Ohio River, and the frontier was in motion. Baily felt this impulse as he talked to settlers, examined the country for its agricultural prospects, and hunted the abundant wildlife. One fine autumn day he accompanied a friend and several companions into the woods to establish a new settlement. The young man had chosen a site on the Little Miami, where he and his companions intended to lay out a town. The morning after their arrival, Baily wrote, "Nothing was to be heard but the noise of the axe resounding through the woods." Before nightfall the men had raised a cabin from the wilderness. The town was named Waynesville in honor of General Anthony Wayne. Its energetic proprietor had laid off a square in the middle of the proposed village that, Baily recounted, "he told me, with a degree of exulting pride, he intended to a courthouse, or for some public building for the meeting of the legislature; for he has already fallen into that flattering idea which every founder of a new settlement entertains, that his town will at some future time be the seat of government." Such were the hopes that fashioned innumerable towns along the Ohio and its tributaries. Even Baily had to admit that within "a short time I saw quite a little town rise from the desert; and in several places gardens were actually laid out, and the walks formed." He was impressed. "When once a town is settled in this way, its rapidity towards greater improvement and perfection is very great," he wrote, "and

351

I have no doubt but that this town, at the foundation of which I have just been witness, will at some future period make a great figure in the history of its country."[1]

Waynesville was only one of many. From the time of the first settlements on the trans-Appalachian frontier, people came together in an urban setting. The first permanent settlement, Harrodsburg, was, in a sense, the first town; other stations were also urban in form and purpose. Just as the Americans had behind them in 1775 more than one hundred and sixty-five years of experience in new land settling, cultivating, and wilderness survival, so they also had extensive experience in town building. Between 1775 and 1850 they built on these urban experiences. Although the urban dimension changed over these three generations, a few basic ingredients endured. Towns remained service centers for the agricultural hinterland—or mining, or lumber, as the case might be. They came into being, grew, prospered, or withered as they met the needs of their rural constituency. The forces that kept them alive came from outside the city limits. It might be the federal government in the form of a land office, Indian agency, or a post office. Or it might be the local government, if the town were selected as a county seat. These official functions meant people, and the town prospered in like proportion. Or it might be the impulse to commerce. Towns catered to the needs of large numbers of people and were usually the centers of trade. There were specific reasons for what happened to a frontier town, and these related directly to what went on around it. Town and hinterland were wedded to each other. Pioneers transported this relationship across the mountains with towns themselves, much as other institutions and institutional relationships that made the trip through the Cumberland Gap and along the Wilderness Road, down the Ohio, or up the Mississippi. It was one of the paradoxes of the trans-Appalachian frontier experience that while three generations of farmers sought land and embraced the agrarian life as the avenue to wealth and independence, they needed towns. They

1. Francis Baily, *Journal of a Tour in Unsettled Parts of North America in 1796 & 1797* (London, 1856), 206–19. Waynesville survives as a small village between Dayton and Cincinnati.

recognized that towns performed certain necessary functions, and they used and supported them in spite of their resentment of townspeople, whom they came to feel exploited the countryside.

Certain physical features and occupational types were standard in towns of the hinterland from Pittsburgh to Iowa City, from Detroit to Blakeley (Alabama): the dry goods store and the saloon (or "grocery"), the miller, blacksmith, wainwright, and eventually the schoolteacher and minister of the gospel. Where the town was lucky enough to be a center of government, there were public buildings and public officials. Routes of transportation were never far distant from the well-ordered town. Roads, canals, and especially rivers and navigable streams of any and every kind became funnels through which people, supplies, and commodities moved. The central role played by transportation routes in urban development can be seen geographically and chronologically from Pittsburgh at the confluence of the Monongahela and Allegheny, to Chicago at the foot of Lake Michigan; to Dubuque, Davenport, and Burlington on the west bank of the Mississippi River. Urban development on the cotton frontier differed in degree, for the plantation performed many of the services provided by towns north of the Ohio, but in the South the town was still an important center of government functions, economic enterprise, and professional services. Plantations, especially, required assistance in the several economic transactions necessary to market their crops of cotton, rice, and sugar. Urban development on the southern frontier up to 1815 was marked by single, even exotic, urban centers, like New Orleans, Natchez, and St. Augustine. In the north, by contrast, there were many towns, all very much alike.[2]

Over the three generations from 1775 to 1850 town planning (if such it could be called) on the frontier was remarkably similar in form. Planners—in most cases synonymous for founders and entrepreneurs—laid out their towns in a grid or checkerboard pattern. Throughout the frontier of the trans-Appalachian West the geometric pattern of towns was the same: rectangular blocks, streets in straight lines, and intersections at right angles. The reasons seem clear. Frontier planners did not seek beauty or innovation so much as the familiar. Gridiron plans

---

2. The basic starting point for a consideration of the urban frontier are the studies of Fulmer Mood and James C. Malin. See especially Malin, *The Grassland of North America: Prolegomena to Its History with Addenda and Postscript* (Gloucester, 1967), 318–22.

were simple to understand, easy to survey, and readily enlarged as the town grew.[3]

Towns were functional. They existed to meet the needs of the time. The first priority of the new settlers on the trans-Appalachian frontier was physical security, so many of the first urban centers were military outposts. This was true of the French fur-trading villages; it was true of the Kentucky stations. In Kentucky and Tennessee, and later north of the Ohio, people came together for mutual protection and perhaps also for mutual reassurance in their struggle against the wilderness. The Ohio Company of Associates founded a town, Marietta, to serve as a center of company authority, and as a focus for school and church. The French also had their own towns; Vincennes, Kaskaskia, Cahokia, and Detroit offered protection against the dangers of the wilderness and were centers of society and the church.

Within these frontier towns municipal services appeared slowly. By 1850 most towns had taken some steps toward a water system, but few had street lights, and almost none had even a modest system for the disposal of sewage. That the volunteer fire department was found everywhere gave recognition to a grave danger to town life if not strong protection from it. At an early stage most towns had paid constables, and, in the frontier tradition of government influence in economic life, among the most important municipal offices was that of supervisor of weights and measures, as towns sought to ensure a degree of integrity in the economic transactions within their limits.[4]

In spite of their many contributions to the frontier, towns did not spring spontaneously into life. They were the creations of ambitious promoters and speculators. These entrepreneurs planted and nurtured their urban centers like a farmer tending a crop of corn or cotton. If the hinterland called the frontier town into existence, then the town promoter served as interested midwife. He knew the factors that made for successful towns, and he did not wait for them to coalesce. Instead he took

3. John W. Reps, *Town Planning in Frontier America* (Princeton, 1969), ch. 12. On Baily's growing distaste for the grid system, see his comment in *Journal of a Tour*, 226–27.
4. On the services available in selected Ohio and Mississippi river valley towns, see Richard C. Wade, *The Urban Frontier: The Rise of Western Cities, 1790–1830* (Cambridge, 1959). Town improvements varied according to the circumstances and ambitions of the town fathers. The town of Madison (Indiana), for example, had a waterworks system that went into operation in 1814 and functioned for three years. Emory O. Muncie, "A History of Jefferson County, Indiana" (M.A., Indiana, 1932), 59.

whatever steps were necessary to bring them about, naturally if possible, artificially if necessary. He knew full well the value of transportation routes. He recognized the value of a government office or newspapers. Anyone with a semblance to title (or prospects of one) who would give free lots to the first few hardy settlers, cut their construction thirst with a barrel of whiskey, and trust to providence thereafter could go into the town-building business. Many did. Most of these entrepreneurs went about it in a more organized way than Francis Baily's friend. Advertising was the usual first step. Jacob Myers laid off a town on Slate Creek in Kentucky in 1788, for example, and his advertisement in the *Kentucky Gazette* emphasized the large streets and the "public ground, sufficient for Courthouse, Meeting house and Schoolhouse." Everyone settled in the town on July 1, 1789, would be entitled to free in and out lots. Additional land might be purchased for cash or mill stones, "and the ballance in castings and bar iron." Myers continued:

> The advantages of a Town with a public road through it to the Eastern states, and Navigable waters from it to the ohio, must be obvious to every person. Those who wish to become settlers will please to meet me at Strodes station on monday the eighteenth inst. where I will attend with surveyor chain carriers &c. in order to proceed to the laying off said Town. As soon as a crop of corn is raised on said land, I will erect a Grist mill, and further intend, as soon as possible, to erect iron works and slitting mill on the waters of slate creek.[5]

Proprietors displayed varying degrees of endurance. Some sold their lots and hastily departed; others stayed to grow up with their creations. Special kinds of towns eventually appeared, towns in the lead-mining regions, towns in the northern lumber camps, towns established by communities of like-minded immigrant groups, some native and some foreign. In the first generation of the urban development on the trans-Appalachian frontier, however, most towns came into existence to meet the needs of a slowly expanding agricultural people. They reflected the capacity, intelligence, good judgment, and luck of the founder.

One of the most determined of the early town builders north of the Ohio was Bezaleel Wells, who laid out the town of Steubenville in 1797. His advertisement in the Pittsburgh *Gazette* emphasized that the town

5. Lexington *Kentucky Gazette*, Aug. 9, 1788. In the same issue David Leitch advertised a proposed town on the upper Blue Licks, suggesting that competition was already a part of town building.

would be the seat of government for Jefferson County. He pointed out the availability of a sawmill close to the site and noted the abundance of materials for building construction. Wells also established two ferries across the Ohio to assist the growth of his village. Aside from his great manor house (the rival of Harmon Blennerhassett's and Thomas Worthington's as the great estates in the early Northwest Territory), the development of the town followed closely the usual form of the period: a tannery (1798, a second tannery in 1802), distillery (1798), gristmill and sawmill (1802), and, at the end of five years, a population of three hundred persons with several stores, a hotel, and a land office. The land office helped to make the town a center of immigration and commercial activity for northeastern Ohio. In order to continue this growth, Wells gave land for a courthouse, jail, and other county buildings at a nominal fee; he also contributed a lot for the city hall. This was a process repeated throughout the Northwest Territory in areas of immigration and growth, but not always with such success.[6]

In the period from 1775 to 1815 urbanization was a fragile thing. In truth, the numbers of people and stream of settlement were too thin to support many urban centers. The population was not sufficient to create a continuing demand for the services of many towns. Some cities, like Cincinnati, Louisville, and St. Louis, gained size and strength as they solidified their positions as the entrepôts of a growing agricultural hinterland. New Orleans became a great port, or close to it, profiting from its location as the terminus of a trade that began on the upper waters of the Ohio, Kentucky, Cumberland, and Tennessee. An occasional urban phenomenon like Natchez remained an exception to almost every rule, both in its growth and in the quality of its life and people.

6. Edward Thornton Heald, "Bezaleel Wells, Founder of Canton and Steubenville, Ohio" (M.A., Case–Western Reserve, 1942), ch. 3. Heald's excellent study compares this urbanization experience to that of Chillicothe and Cleveland. Heald also analyzes Wells's other ventures into town building: Canton, which suffered from its lack of a good navigational outlet to the Ohio, a much more modest success in the short run and far more significant in the long run; and Madison, which failed in its struggle to become the seat of Wayne County (Wooster won) and declined. Heald notes that it was the failure of Madison that prompted Wells to move from town promotion to banking and manufacturing (p. 169). This study is important because it became the basis of Heald's five-volume history of Stark County, which in turn formed the centerpiece of Elkins's and McKitrick's essay on the Turner thesis in the Old Northwest. On the growth of Steubenville, see Steubenville *Western Herald*, 1806–08, and Edward J. Smith letter, Nov. 8, 1804, OHS.

Far more characteristic in size and services were villages like Brookville (Indiana) and Shawneetown (Illinois). John Test, an energetic and
ambitious lawyer, brought his wife to the Brookville settlement in 1808.
He remembered that "it was with much difficulty that we made our way
through a newly cut road, whose scarcely removed stumps formed considerable barrier to our approach to our new residence. On each side of
this road was an impenetrable wilderness, so dense, so dark, that the
small specks of sunshine that pierced their way looked like stars glim-
mering in a dark lake." After a long journey the party at last reached a
log cabin settlement. Refreshed by the pause, Test's wife suggested that
they all go into the village for dinner at the hotel, apparently expecting
accommodations like those that she had known in the East. Test explained, "She little dreamed we were in the very heart of the village, and
that four or five cabins made up the number of its houses." When informed of the true state of affairs, she burst into tears, for she was "accustomed to all the refinements and delicacies of life." Her condition was
not soothed by the arrival of sympathetic neighbors, "dressed in striped
cotton of their own manufacturing coarse in the extreme and all barefooted."[7]

Shawneetown came into existence to serve the early frontier—trade in
furs and the manufacture of salt—and stayed to minister to and equip
thousands of agricultural pioneers. Located on the north bank of the
Ohio just downstream from the mouth of the Wabash, it was convenient
to the considerable saline industry centered in springs a score of miles to
the north. Shawneetown prospered with the price of salt (which remained high until 1815) and began to pick up some of the increasing
trade in agricultural commodities that moved down the Ohio and Mississippi to New Orleans. A road laid out to the west connected Shawneetown with Kaskaskia and then St. Louis. In a period before the spread of
steam power on the western waters, those who wished to transport
goods or even baggage to St. Louis had to land at Shawneetown and
proceed overland. As a port of entry the town provided useful employment for those in the transportation business, renting, selling, servicing
vehicles and animals for the trip west. In 1812 Congress established a
federal land office at Shawneetown, assuring a clientele for trade and future employment for large numbers of lawyers. A town government

7. John Test, "Reminiscences," IHS.

emerged and levied taxes, designated a graveyard, put up a jail, and made plans for a stray pen. It became an important influence in the lives of the residents, especially with its authority for promoting improvements. When the legislature organized Gallatin County in 1812, Shawneetown was named the county seat and three years later acknowledged its new status with a courthouse.[8]

Shawneetown alternately prospered and suffered from the presence of the river. It was regularly inundated by the Ohio in the spring and endured severe fevers in the autumn. Even though located on the main route of travel west, the town did not grow much, and, like other frontier villages up and down the Ohio, it was not a thing of beauty. Travellers had nothing kind to say about its physical appearance, hospitality, or the quality of its accommodations. Indeed the miscellany of people and buildings looked as if they had been left by recently receding floodwaters. The gentleman planter-politician from Louisiana, Thomas Bolling Robertson, landed at Shawneetown on a

> lovely night, the moon shown bright but it could impart no beauty to the scene. Figure to yourself 40 log huts which you might take for large hen houses or small stables, strung along the banks for half a mile and you will form a correct idea of Shawneetown. It is overflowed every year the inhabitants driven back to the hills about a mile and the buildings such as are worth it made fast to trees & stumps.[9]

Yet with all the slighting comments about it, Shawneetown was the most important urban center on the Ohio between Louisville and St. Louis. If anything, its growth picked up after 1815 with the economic impact of the Great Migration. The influx of travellers brought a demand for accommodations. Taverns, inns, and even hotels appeared in response. Skilled tradesmen also set up shops: the presence of saddle and harness makers, hatters, tailors, watchmakers, cabinetmakers, and specialists in eyeglasses attested to the town's importance. As the inflated prices of salt fell with the end of the war, the land business increased and the town became a banking center. Chartered in 1816 at an early period of banking mania, the Shawneetown Bank became a symbol of the town's prosperity and permanence. And so it continued, as long as speculation in land and banking currency continued. With the panic of 1819 and the

8. Mary Katherine Kershaw, "Early History of Shawneetown, Illinois, from 1812 to 1832" (M.A., Illinois, 1941), ch. 1.
9. Thomas Bolling Robertson to M. B. Robertson, June 1814, Thomas Bolling Robertson Letters, Walter Prichard Collection, folder 12, LSU.

slowing of the Great Migration, the town stagnated and watched immigration and urban growth pass to other towns farther to the interior.[10]

Seemingly beyond the influence of local entrepreneurial talents, leadership in government and civic affairs, and the vagaries of nature, one urban center dominated the trans-Appalachian frontier, at least after 1803. New Orleans was the mouth of the funnel through which drained the growing trade of the trans-Appalachian frontier as well as some of the longer-settled areas. Governor William C. C. Claiborne called it "a great, and growing city." He went on, "The commerce of the Western Country concentrates at this place, and there appears to me a moral certainty, that in ten years, it will rival Philadelphia or New York." He was right. In spite of swamps and floods the city's location was strategic and made it the most important urban center on the trans-Appalachian frontier. For prosperity, New Orleans needed a strong trade from the interior. The opening of the Mississippi to American trade in 1795 and, to an even greater degree, the sale of the Louisiana Territory to the United States in 1803 assured its future importance. Although it had been continuously occupied since its establishment in 1718, New Orleans had assumed a variety of shapes and sizes in the intervening three generations. Fires had levelled the city as recently as 1788 and 1794. Viewing the newly rebuilt city in 1804, one observer called it "a cluster of clumsy irregular looking wooden Houses . . . without a solitary decent looking building to relieve the prospect; the levee covered with all the filthy ordure of the City." Thomas Nicholls, the author of that description, might have excepted the New Cabildo from his general indictment of the city's architecture, but he was right about the odor. The city was filled with the smells of the river, the vapors of the surrounding swamps, and the remainders of the most recent floodwaters, and it lacked sanitary facilities adequate to clean up the mess.[11]

---

10. Kershaw, "Early History of Shawneetown, Illinois," chs. 3 and 4. A description of the town's society—such as it was—is in chapter 6.
11. Governor William C. C. Claiborne to Thomas Jefferson, Jan. 16, 1804, in *TP*, 9: 161; Thomas C. Nicholls, "Reminiscences," LSU. Reps, *Town Planning in Frontier America*, 98–105, devotes much attention to New Orleans. Of special interest are transcripts of the cabildo records (in English translation) for the period 1769–1803, New Orleans Public Library. These suggest the Spanish institutional structure and the way that the city fathers attempted to deal with the special opportunities and problems presented by the location of their town. Among the latter should be numbered overflowed lands, a large black population, and the presence of many transients, in later years especially Americans.

Along with the stench of decay came the unmistakable smell of profits. The waterfront was a hive of activity. Already the wharves were piled high with the agricultural products of the interior: hogsheads of tobacco from Kentucky, flour from the Miami River Valley by way of Cincinnati, furs and lead from Missouri and the Illinois country, bales of cotton from the Natchez region, sugar and indigo from the adjacent plantations, lumber, long a staple export of Louisiana, all awaiting shipment to the distant corners of the world, not to mention the foodstuffs and provisions that had to be imported to feed the city and nearby plantations. Hogs, corn, and wheat from the Ohio Valley were there in large quantities. Stacked side by side with these were the imported luxury goods from Europe, destined for the plantations upriver, especially those in the Natchez region. At intervals there stood or squatted bands of black slaves, their movements accompanied by the harsh grating sounds of chain metal, sold or awaiting sale, their final destinations the fields and forests upriver. European war, American peace, and the settlement of the backcountry would multiply these exports and imports, which in turn would nurture numerous fortunes for the large planters, merchants, shipowners, bankers, and Yankee financiers.[12]

The surge of movement to the trans-Appalachian frontier after the Treaty of Ghent had its own urban development. Among the most thriving crops planted in the western country after 1815 were town sites. Small urban centers sprang up like Indian corn, almost as widespread and rapidly growing. Newspapers were filled with announcements of their births, although few public notices could be found of their deaths. Like the towns on the earlier trans-Appalachian frontier, they were the creation of no spontaneous demand, but, in most cases, the carefully contrived creatures of promoters, and they often grew very rapidly. One frontier editor wrote of a new town that it would "spring up like others of our western cities, *out of the woods,* and will in all probability like many of them, be visited by the steamboat, before the stumps of the forest have disappeared from its streets."[13] If they were rich with promise, the new towns were also raw. Timothy Flint, a traveller who saw much of

12. John G. Clark, *New Orleans, 1718–1812: An Economic History* (Baton Rouge, 1970), chs. 14–16, correctly notes the relationship of New Orleans to its hinterland.
13. St. Augustine *East Florida Herald,* Jan. 10, 1824, on Tallahassee.

the western country after 1815, described an Indiana town in these terms: "The deep and rich bottom, the trees of which had but just been cut down, was so muddy, that my feet sank at every step in the mud. Huge beech and sycamore trunks of trees so impeded these avenues and streets, that were to be, that I doubt if a chaise could have made its way, by day light and the most careful driving, amidst the logs."[14] A town founded after 1815 fell generally into one of three categories: it might be specifically laid out as a center of government, state, territory, or county; it might be established as a service center for immigrants on the way west; or it might be a small community of like-minded peoples, held together by family ties.

The most successful of the government towns in the Old Northwest was Indianapolis. Judge Finch remembered people settling on the site of the future capital in 1820. The next year the commissioners laid out the town on an expanse of trees and underbrush. Andrew TenBrook found a single two-story house there in 1822. The population in 1823, according to one account, consisted of about ninety families. With the usual optimism of the day, one editor declared the village to be "in a rapid state of improvements: and as much can be said in favor of the morality and industry of its inhabitants, as of any other town in the state." More to the point were the agricultural attractions of surrounding Marion County and the large number of mills: "Four saw mills in operation in the county, three of which are within less than a mile and a half of town— There are also two grist mills within the same distance, and several more grist and saw mills are now building, together with carding machines, etc." The establishment of an Indianapolis newspaper in late 1823 provided a medium for endless reports of progress and growth. The editor praised "the rapid expansion of inhabited territory, and the great increase of population, will of course produce more business every year." When the *Journal* wrote these words the town had been established for three and a half years. On March 7, 1826, the population of the town was reported as 760; a year later, about one thousand. A description of Indianapolis in 1827 noted: "There are now 25 brick, 60 frame, and

14. Timothy Flint, *Recollections of the Last Ten Years in the Valley of the Mississippi* (Boston, 1826), 59. Another detailed description of town founding and promotion is Morris Birkbeck, *Notes on a Journey in America from the Coasts of Virginia to the Territory of Illinois* (Philadelphia, 1817), 103–05. An amusing contemporary account of town promotion is the "City of Skunksburg," Detroit *Gazette*, Nov. 19, 1819.

about 80 hewn log homes and cabins in town. The public buildings are, a Court House, 60 feet by 45, a Jail, and Meeting Houses belonging to the Presbyterian, Baptist, and Methodist societies."[15] Improvements continued with immigration, especially in the fall season, when most people moved. In 1828 the town was officially seven years old. Stumps still dotted the streets, but like much of agricultural Indiana and the New Purchase, Indianapolis was no longer a raw frontier settlement. Isaiah Osborn described it to his brother: "The place begins to look like a town. There are about a thousand acres cut smooth, ten stores, six taverns, a court house which cost $15,000, many fine houses, and six weeks back had in it 1,066 inhabitants, lots worth $100 and the place somewhat sickly but improving."[16]

Indianapolis was a creation of the state legislature, a happy accident of geography—for a capital must be centrally located—for those who profited. Other towns had a less assured future, although they were no less the product of geographic considerations: natural—an attractive site on a navigable river; or man made—the center of a new county and a likely site for the location of the county seat. In the interim the new town could become a base for immigrants who always needed advice and supplies. Crawfordsville (Indiana), laid out in 1822, served as a focal point for people headed to the Wabash country. Here were the goods and services for an immigrant people. After the first land sale, settlers came in great numbers. "Fresh arrivals of movers were the constant topics of conversation," an early schoolmaster remembered. "New log cabins widened the limits of the town, and spread over the circumjacent country." Crawfordsville and its supporters waxed fat and happy on the flood tide of immigration. Within a year the town had a federal land office, a tavern "in a two story log house," "a little grocery," two retail stores, two physicians, one lawyer, two cabinet shops, a tannery, and a blacksmith. The town was named the county seat of Montgomery County. The excitement of early growth was long remembered, although time may have dulled the sore muscles and physical exhaustion that accompanied taming the new country. The schoolmaster recalled

15. John G. Finch, "Reminiscences," IHS; Evansville *Gazette*, April 30, 1823; Indianapolis *Indiana Journal*, Feb. 1, March 8, 1825; March 7, 1826; Feb. 20, 1827.
16. O. William Sickels to Daniel Gold, July 15, 1828, ISL; Isaiah Osborn to brother John, Jan. 13, 1828, "Old Indianapolis Letter," *IMH*, 4 (1908): 28.

the new country with delight: "We cleared land, rolled logs, and burned brush, blazed out paths from one neighbor's cabin to another, and from one settlement to another—made and used handmills and hominy mortars—hunted deer, turkies, otter, and raccoons—caught fish, dug ginseng, hunted bees, and the like, and—lived on the fat of the land."[17]

The mass immigration of people after 1815 moved farther inland in a series of reflexive spasms, like expanding waves of an incoming tide. Success and growth begat competition. Soon Crawfordsville—and the immigrant towns of the north and west like it—had their competitors: newer towns, rawer, stumps higher in the streets, log cabins without false fronts, immense forests on both sides. But they were closer to the expanding frontier. As the new towns grew, urban centers that had earlier experienced explosive growth or others that had long served as entrepôts on a former frontier now stagnated and even lost population. With the opening of the New Purchase and its rapid occupation, the old urban centers like Brookville, Princeton, Corydon, and even Vincennes seemed to stand still. In the midst of prosperity and movement, the impulse to growth and "progress" had passed farther to the interior. In time these new interior towns suffered a similar fate. In January 1826, the Indiana legislature laid off Tippecanoe County and commissioners located the county seat at a new village called Lafayette. If the inhabitants of the new county "were like angels' visits, 'few and far between,' " it did not long remain so. Lafayette now began a period of substantial growth, gradually outstripping its rivals to the south in pace of improvements. Within three years, hard on the heels of Lafayette, came Logansport, founded in 1828 and made the seat of Cass County in 1829. The proprietors of Logansport saw the torch of progress passed to them. In 1828 the little village "situated as it then was, in the heart of the Indian country, almost, we may say, 40 miles from the settlement" saw great physical growth; the next year more than forty buildings were constructed, including four of brick, one of them, designed as a Masonic Hall, twenty-five by fifty feet. The *Times* of Logansport summarized the impulse of progress to which it was now the local heir: the New Purchase, opened in 1818, had one hundred thousand inhabitants, twenty-two

17. Sandford C. Cox, *Recollections of the Early Settlement of the Wabash Valley* (Lafayette, Ind., 1860), 19.

counties, and forty towns with a population of 800–1200. It concluded, "The backwoods may well be said to be receding."[18]

A third kind of urban growth was associated with innumerable small towns that were almost family communities. An example was the village of New Salem, located twenty miles north and west of Springfield (Illinois). New Salem was the village of the Rutledge and Camron families, who came to the Sangamon country in 1825 or 1826. They entered lands on the Sangamon River in 1828 and there established the first mill. Settlers came from miles around to get their corn ground into rough flour, and the village grew up around the mill. And, of course, where people appeared in numbers, there also came others who wished to cater to their needs. A store opened in 1829; soon thereafter, a grocery, to meet the thirst of country men who had come to trade. The same year a post office opened, giving the town a kind of official status. It grew slowly, with the addition of new family groups and the traditional trades.[19] Little distinguished it from a score of other frontier villages that met the needs of the surrounding countryside; similar small towns provided the urban experience of large numbers of people in the trans-Appalachian west.

To bring order to the little villages that grew up as a result of the Great Migration, town governments were organized and a series of ordinances passed that tended to be similar throughout the trans-Appalachian West, at least in terms of the problems they dealt with. First order of priority was to prevent the discharge of firearms and stop racing of horses within the town limits; there was to be no fighting or rioting; shortly thereafter people were directed to keep pigs off the streets and establish market days, remove piles of dirt, lumber, manure, and "dead or putrid" animal carcasses. Whether the villages organized sooner or later after their settlement, and whether the surrounding countryside was crowded or deserted, the ordinances were virtually interchangeable. Some were concerned with preservation of order; others were directed toward health and sanitation (a new area of interest on the trans-Appalachian frontier and indeed in the nation as a whole); a third group might be loosely defined as directed to civic improvements. The

18. Logansport *Potawattomie & Miami Times*, Oct. 10, 1829. A description of Lafayette is in the Indianapolis *Indiana Journal*, March 5, 1829.
19. Marjorie Ruth Paullin, "New Salem: A Typical Frontier Settlement" (M.A., Illinois, 1942), chs. 1 and 2.

regulation of the economy in terms of the market, its location, functioning and hours, as well as control of weights and measures, was often extensive. Those associated with urban centers on the trans-Appalachian frontier after 1815, whether as residents or farmers who patronized towns, felt the impact of town government.[20]

The cotton frontier also had a kind of urban development. Its center was the plantation, a complex economic and social entity featuring, as it did, large-scale landholding, commercial economy with an export cash crop, and often several slaves. The plantation had different economic needs from northern towns and produced a relatively self-sufficient society. On the plantation social intercourse involved visits, dances, and dinners with the owners of nearby plantations rather than participation in those institutions associated with the rise of towns and concentration of population—churches, schools, public lectures, theatricals, and public libraries. Yet even the largest and most prosperous plantations were associated with urban areas because only in such centers could their economic needs and desires for stability be met. The economic needs of plantations were those of large cotton exporters and closely tied them to major ports rather than country towns, for only a New Orleans or Mobile could ship bulk cotton to Europe or the northeast in this period, provide long-term credit on the basis of cotton receipts, serve as a center for importing luxury goods—more than just the "fresh goods" advertised in country newspapers—and negotiate for a transoceanic trading economy. Quantities of corn, pork, whiskey, cotton goods, machinery, and other manufactured items might come down the Mississippi River from the Ohio Valley, sometimes directly to the plantation, sometimes through the small market towns (often county seats), and, in the case of Louisiana at least, by way of New Orleans.

The triumph of the cotton kingdom brought changes in the kinds, the regularity, and, above all, the volume of transportation. This was the first golden age of water transportation—with its successes and failures. The widespread service of the steamboat created a new world: the rush for a steamboat docking, then regular service; yards to build and repair

20. As examples, see Columbus *Gazette*, June 11, July 9, 23, 1818; Edwardsville *Spectator*, June 26, 1819. See also Lexington *Kentucky Gazette*, April 4, 1791, for regulations on wooden chimneys and slaughterhouses.

boats; and the aura of adventure inspired by the stalwart captains and crews who braved the treacherous waters of the Red, Tombigbee, and Alabama rivers to carry the loads of baled cotton to the sea. These were the heroic figures of the new age, and they were so celebrated by the town fathers upriver. In the world of the cotton frontier, water transportation was everything. Baled cotton might be moved a score of miles over rutted roads in jolting wagons, at risk to animals, equipment, and men commensurate with the profit to be gained, but to transport cotton long distances overland was out of the question. So the business of new towns on the cotton frontier catered to the needs of the surrounding planters, and initially this meant supplying transportation, financing (in larger towns, perhaps a branch bank), legal advice, storage, and goods and foodstuffs brought in for the plantation. The circumstance made fortunes for shippers-merchants-factors, men who acted as agents for the planters upriver, on whom the planters were dependent for sales, receipts, and (sometimes) credit. These middlemen in the great ports of the South became wealthy and powerful. So the cotton frontier was oriented to the large deep water ports or towns with direct access to a deep water port. The Great Migration of postwar America and the attendant rise of cotton culture changed New Orleans from a bustling, growing city into one of the great ports of the world. Similarly the expansion of settlement in its river hinterland transformed Mobile from a sleepy Spanish town to a thriving port. Like its Louisiana counterpart, it owed growth to the new Indian cessions in Alabama.

These cities were old and well established. Not so well known was the effort of others to break their monopoly. Among the towns that tried was Blakeley (incorporated 1814), a small but ambitious port on the northeastern corner of Mobile Bay. In the period immediately after 1815, with the great migration to Alabama under way, many thought that Blakeley might replace Mobile as the principal Alabama port. Blakeley was a new town constructed to meet a commercial need, or, more properly, to capitalize on the prosperity of the cotton frontier. Its rise coincided with the territory's, "the tide of emigration into the Alabama, irresistible, as the full and majestic waters of her own great streams." To these new arrivals the town offered its "advantages." These included

> our immediate connexion with the seaboard, and the ease with which the abundant production of our rich and fertile soil can be sent to the great marts of trade in any quantities of the world, the great staple ar-

ticles of commerce which our Territory produces, more especially the article of Cotton . . . ; and our advantage for vast improvement in the extension and facilities of trade, point out the ALABAMA TERRITORY as the abode of future wealth, happiness and grandeur.

The heart of the town was commerce: the importation of goods for upriver consumption; export of cotton to the northeast and Europe. Central to this interest was the ship traffic, the arteries of Blakeley's life-blood. The "full and correct report of all arrival and departure of vessels" was a necessary duty of the local paper, and the "Marine List" ran for column after column. Construction of small boats for the coastal and river trade promised not only enlarged trade but also industry. The launching of the *Tensa* in the spring of 1819, "intended to ply on the Tombigbee, Alabama and Coosa rivers," provided the Blakeley editor with a chance to discourse on the disadvantages of barge traffic ("mighty uncertainty") and the need for small steamboats to get far upriver. The commercial activity of late 1818 and early 1819—coinciding with the most prosperous cotton prices—seemed to justify the town's expectations. Ships from Boston, New York, and New Orleans (most of them by way of Mobile) were docked at the wharves. Commodities unloaded from these were much like those for any frontier village, except for the large quantities and varieties of spirits (rum, gin, brandy, cordials, ale). From Boston came cranberries, kegs of mackerel and salmon, Irish potatoes, and casks of cheese; from New York, "Spanish Segars," medicines and soaps, buckshot and musket balls, anvils, vices, and nails. And almost everywhere merchants had posted the notice "Cash paid for COT-TON." Blakeley's busy wharves and large warehouses suffered severely from the drop in prices that began in 1819 and the subsequent depression of agriculture. The town never realized its ambition to overtake Mobile, and this thriving urban center went into decline and eventually vanished from the map altogether.[21]

Alexandria (Louisiana) was a well-established interior town, located on the Red River, the commercial center for a growing agricultural hinterland. Founded between 1805 and 1810 and chartered in 1818, Alexandria was the head of navigation on the Red River from July to January every year. Thus, for six months, it was the outfitting and staging town

21. Blakeley *Sun*, Dec. 12, 15, 18, 1818; Feb. 9, April 20, 1819. James C. Parker, "Blakeley: A Frontier Seaport," *AR*, 27 (1974): 39–51, is a complete account of Blakeley's rise and fall.

for risky but profitable steamboat trips upriver to ambitious and more remote villages such as Natchitoches. For the other half year, low water forced all commercial traffic to stop at its wharves. Alexandria's extensive hinterland had flatlands for cotton cultivation and hill country for grazing.[22] There was no doubt, however, where the economic interests of the town lay, at least in the period of the Great Migration. Under the heading "COTTON," the *Louisiana Herald* described it:

> There is, probably, no word in the English language that excites more interest in this part of the world, than the word COTTON; for if we except the weather and the enquiry for the news, it forms the primary subject of conversation in all companies; it occupies the thoughts by night and by day, and no doubt many pleasing dreams of wealth employ the midnight hour, arising from anticipating the sale of this staple commodity.

News of cotton prices and steamboats dominated public interest. Several steamboats from New Orleans made regular calls, generally with cargoes of foodstuffs, "flour, bacon, lard, pork, butter, cheese, &c." Hard times on the cotton frontier came to Alexandria in the 1820's. Ambitious planters had purchased land and slaves on credit. New Orleans moneylenders had lent large sums in the parish, at ten to thirty percent. In the early 1820's the sheriff sold several properties to satisfy debts, and strong feelings against New Orleans "Shylocks" surfaced. The cases of debtors filled the docket of the district court.[23]

Much of the care and attention of the town centered on its self-improvement in easily definable and practical ways. Citizens of the village elected a board of trustees in 1820, and thereafter the board closely managed town affairs. It placed a tax on freehold estates, suppressed gaming, taxed billiard tables, and regulated the marketing of produce by requiring that all goods be sold in a public market. Eventually the trustees extended this same broad control over draymen—whose fees they set—and appointed an overseer of the town streets (like overseers in rural road districts) and night watchmen. By 1824 elected town officials included a tax collector, three assessors, and five fire wardens. Every effort was made to preserve order. The court hung two men on the basis

22. G. P. Whittington, "Rapides Parish, Louisiana," *LHQ*, 16 (1933): 427–40.
23. Alexandria *Louisiana Herald*, Nov. 3, 1821; March 23, 1820; March 3, 1824.

of "presumptive evidence; which was doubtless strong and well connected." The victims asserted their innocence to the end. Leading citizens urged that the town clean out the riffraff and idlers, both men and women, "who are able to work, that have neither trade, profession or property and live idly and frequent grog shops, gambling houses &c &c." Rapides Parish demanded the attention of its "civil officers . . . in ferreting out the idle and abandoned—it is peculiarly exposed to the machinations of negro stealers, horse thieves and other of the *corps des chevaliers d'industri.*"[24]

The expansionist years of the cotton frontier also witnessed the founding and rapid growth of a series of new towns. These sprouted in the newly opened Indian cessions of the postwar period. Several appeared in central Alabama, in that area later known as the Black Belt. Selma (settled in 1816), Montgomery (1817), and Marion (1817) had similar experiences. To begin with, each was a county seat—Montgomery did not become the state capital until 1846—and so assured of serving as the political, administrative, economic, and eventually social center of an agricultural area. Each town began as a town site speculation, located on a waterway. Each underwent the traditional physical changes as a clearing emerged in the forests—promoters laid off and sold lots, log cabins were built, and rival towns had to be met and overcome. All three towns were closely associated with the cotton culture. Growth was steady by the early 1820's. Buildings were constructed, and population—black and white—increased. The towns became the center of a society that engaged in large-scale cotton cultivation with slave labor. The men engaged in this process needed an orderly society, and their towns had the institutions to establish and keep order. The period of experimentation in institutions had taken place somewhere else at an earlier stage. By this time men knew what they wanted. There was much emphasis on preserving the peace. Stringent local regulations, curfews, and nightly patrols completely controlled the slave population. The excesses of the towns came rather from the gentry: gambling, horse races, confrontations over honor. That men were quick to take personal affront and resort to physical violence did not seem to them to contradict their quest for order. The cultural development was also that associated with

24. Alexandria *Louisiana Herald*, Oct. 7, March 24, Aug. 12, 1820; April 23, 1823; April 7, 1824; July 1, 1820; July 27, 1825.

economic wealth: private schools, theatricals, and literary clubs. As the rich agricultural hinterland provided support for large numbers of professional people, these towns attracted many doctors and lawyers.[25]

In sharp contrast to the similarities among the urban centers of the cotton frontier were the varieties of Florida, where the sectional nature of the territory, the diversity of geography, and vast distances gave rise to a wide variety of urban experiences. First there were three urban centers: St. Augustine, with its Spanish heritage, trying to adjust to the arrival of the Americans, becoming increasingly dependent on trade to the north; Pensacola, with its great harbor and slow growth, the patient wait for an elusive stimulus, always just beyond the horizon, now to be brought on by railroads, now by the federal government, now perhaps the lumber industry or tourism; and, finally, the new town, Tallahassee, the artificial creation to serve government and, as it turned out, the market and social center of prosperous staple plantation agriculture. To the distant south, Key West was a tropical port whose greatest formative influences were disease and the salvage business. Both boomed in this period, and Key West went its own way to its own kind of success.

Added to these were a wonderful variety of other towns. Apalachicola, a vigorous port on the Gulf, was typical of so many villages that rose in response to the demands of cotton cultivation. At the outlet of a large river system, Apalachicola experienced a steady growth and a seasonal cycle of business typical of such port cities. Others were more exotic. St. Marks was one of the first railroad towns in the country. The creation of the railroad, the village prospered with the railroad and disappeared with it, or rather was taken apart piece by piece and carried elsewhere to be reassembled. And, of course, there was St. Joseph, the entrepreneurial marvel of the age. The child of a feud over land titles, St. Joseph became the fastest growing urban center of the Southeast. It created railroads, hosted the Constitutional Convention of 1839, and succumbed to natural and economic storms with the same intensity with

---

25. Clanton W. Williams, "Early Ante-Bellum Montgomery: A Black Belt Constituency," *JSH*, 7 (1941): 495–525; Williams, "Conservatism in Old Montgomery, 1817–1861," *AR*, 10 (1957): 96–110; Williams, ed., "Extracts from the Records of the City of Montgomery," *AR*, 1 (1948): 128–42; Weymouth T. Jordan, "Early Ante-Bellum Marion, Alabama: A Black Belt Town," *AHQ*, 5 (1943): 12–31. On the federal government's experiences in town site development in Alabama, see Robert Nesbit, "The Federal Government as Townsite Speculator," *Explorations in Economic History*, 7 (1970): 293–312.

which it lived. This was a variety of urban centers unmatched anywhere on the continent at the time.

The great surge of energy that ushered in the last generation of large-scale movement on the trans-Appalachian frontier produced much urban development. A national mania for speculation in real estate character-ized the mid-1830's, and Michigan was the greatest center of the specula-tive art in the western country. Newspapers displayed the endless op-portunities of the day. As everywhere on the trans-Appalachian frontier, city lots, it seemed, were more common than corn and wheat. Every inlet on either of the two lakes, every promontory on the two roads run-ning east and west, the falls of every river leading inland, every prospec-tive county seat, or indeed any vacant field, all were prospective town sites. The proprietor needed a smooth tongue, a suitable location, and the help of a number of urban fixtures—a mill and a hotel, a few stores, plus artisans and mechanics to serve the farmers from the countryside—to begin the village's career. W. Forbes talked of building mills on his property in Allegan County (Michigan)—not to assist farmers in the sur-rounding countryside but as a real estate speculation. He wrote:

> After these mills are a going and a blacksmith and a carpenter shop es-
> tablished this will form the nucleus or a beginning of a village and then
> my property would rise from the value of 3 Dollars p. acre to that of
> $100 or more as in many similar instances in this country, such a thing
> requires only a beginning and some natural advantages, and a proper
> range of country around it. I know ground bought 4 years ago for 1–¼
> $ now will sell for 100.

Thousands of others shared Forbes's vision. Agriculture was the road to independence, but it meant a lifetime of backbreaking physical labor. The way to a life of wealth and leisure lay through the manipulation of paper: banks, town building, and railroads. All had great impetus in the mid-1830's; all were found on the frontier; all were associated with urban development.[26]

26. W. Forbes to James Forbes, April 10, 1835, W. Forbes Collection, MHC. Malcolm J. Rohrbough, *The Land Office Business: The Settlement and Administration of American Public Lands, 1789–1837* (New York, 1968), 242–44, 248–49, describes the large-scale specula-tion in town sites associated with the 1830's. A clever spoof on town founding that emphasizes speculation rather than response to need is "Origin of a Town," Little Rock *Arkansas Advocate*, Oct. 30, 1830.

Of the urban centers associated with the period 1830 to 1850, one stands as dominant, both in the speed of its growth and in its impact on a large portion of the trans-Appalachian frontier. Chicago was, as late as 1830, a fur-trading post where hogs ran at large in the streets. With the close of the Black Hawk War it felt the impulse of growth, responding to the settlement of western Illinois and southern Wisconsin. By 1835 and 1836 it had become the fastest-growing city in the country, and real estate changed hands with a single-minded frenzy as fortunes were made and lost within hours. Chicago came to symbolize the ultimate in urban development. It combined access to water transportation on the lakes and, by easy portage, to the rivers to the interior with a location that would make it the center of railroad networks. Its location and leadership were such that it made the transition from the steamboat to the railroad with uninterrupted growth. Its success is visible on all hands today. Of greater importance for the expanding agricultural frontier than the question of speculation was the impact of Chicago on the surrounding countryside. It quickly became the commercial center. For the first few years commercial transactions were predominantly in one direction: toward the new western settlements. In 1836, for example, Chicago's imports were valued at $325,203; her exports at a mere $1,000. It took time for the hinterland so recently settled to produce crops for trade. Wheat was first exported in 1839, and grain rapidly became the principal export commodity. By 1841 the wheat surplus was so large that not enough vessels could be found for its shipment. Wheat-laden wagons struggling into the city over poor roads made worse by heavy traffic became a daily sight. Sometimes the lines were eighty wagons long. The growth of this trade in the middle of a depression was truly astonishing and touched hoteliers, farmers, and merchants, who found a ready market for their goods and services. The rise of Chicago's trade was one of the most dramatic features of the transformation of the new West in this period.[27] Trade statistics demonstrate its growth (see table 9).

There was only one Chicago, but the word "town" encompassed a wide variety of activity on the frontieer. The so-called towns that appeared in the 1830's ranged from the large and respectable to developments that were more urban in name than in reality. Fourteen "towns"

27. James Fiske Lee, "Transportation—A Factor in the Development of Northern Illinois previous to 1860," *JISHS*, 10 (1917–18): 17–28.

Table 9. Rise of the Port of Chicago,
1836–45

	Imports	Exports
1836	$ 325,203	$ 1,000
1837	373,677	10,000
1838	379,174	16,044
1839	630,980	38,843
1840	562,106	228,635
1841	564,347	348,862
1842	664,347	659,305
1843	971,849	682,210
1844	1,686,416	785,504
1845	2,043,445	1,543,510

Source: James Fiske Lee, "Transportation—A Factor in the Development of Northern Illinois previous to 1860," *JISHS,* 10 (1917–18): 27, n. 16.

were identified in Peoria County (Illinois) in 1837, for example. Peoria itself had about three hundred houses and a population of 1,900; all in all, it was a substantial village on the Illinois River. But other urban centers and their improvements included Alliton, "1 house and ferry"; Kickapoo, "1 house"; Hudson, "ferry house"; Kingston, "1 house"; Harkness, "4 or 5 houses"; and others at a similar stage of development.[28] Granted that decentralized conditions and difficulties of transportation—three to five miles was obviously a far distance for someone on foot or horseback or by wagon—encouraged the establishment of a great many towns, but these little places were hardly more than sites on the prairie, established presumably with the expectation that the accidents of future patterns of settlement would make them into something permanent.

The settlement of the last frontier of the Old Northwest provided a new dimension in the form of a wider range of economic activity. New economic enterprises appeared, and, for each, a new form of urban development. Galena (Illinois), Mineral Point (Wisconsin), and Dubuque (Iowa) all began with lead mining. Galena, like the others, reached a high degree of urbanization because of the nature of the economic enterprise that it served: a large concentration of population producing a commodity that offered opportunities for affluence but at the same time demanded good transportation facilities to move a bulk cargo. Galena

28. Peoria *Register,* April 8, 1837.

emphasized its connection with river transportation, and the local newspapers regularly published a "Marine List." By 1830 the spring traffic was heavy enough for several steamboat arrivals and departures each week. Arriving steamboats brought foodstuffs (dried fruit, flour, green apples, bacon, pork, and sardines) and departed carrying lead to St. Louis.[29] These were not the only urban centers associated with lead mining, merely the largest. Smaller towns grew up in the "diggings" to meet more local needs. Later, in the decade of the 1840's, similarly specialized towns appeared around lumbering operations. Located at the falls of streams that provided the waterpower to run the sawmills, they had their own special characteristics to match the specialized nature of the economic enterprise that they served.[30]

Movement of large numbers of people to the western side of the Mississippi River, especially after the conclusion of the Black Hawk War in 1832 and the subsequent land cession in Iowa, led to the establishment of a number of towns on the Iowa side of the river: Dubuque, which served the lead-mining business; others of lasting importance like Davenport and Burlington; and some of a more passing fancy, still the wonders of that age and of great promise for the future, places such as Lyons, Buffalo, and Montrose. Their rise may be described in general terms. The Mississippi River was a unifying force in the establishment of all of them. Keokuk and Montrose depended on the rapids; another set of navigation obstacles served Davenport and Le Claire. The proprietors built their towns on a narrow flood plain, with the bluffs of the river valley hemming them in and thus exposing them to floods. Ferries were an early form of economic activity, for the river not only served as an avenue of trade but also an obstacle to movement. To the west lay the great prairies of Iowa. Dubuque's avenue to the interior was steep and precipitous; Davenport's characterized by the gradual ascent. In every case the motive of town founding was profit, but in the source of that profit these towns varied enormously. Dubuque lay adjacent to the lead outcroppings. Davenport appeared on the site of a former Indian trading post; Antoine Le Claire, the interpreter after whom the town was named, had clear title to two sections of land given him for services in treaty negotiations. Towns differed greatly in their development, too. Some stagnated

29. Galena *Advertiser*, April 5, 1830.
30. Selma Sather Casberg, "The Lumbering Industry of La Crosse, Wisconsin, 1841–1905" (M.A., Wisconsin, 1953), is a study of one such town.

and failed, at least in the long run. Others prospered from unexpected sources: Davenport became a resort center for those coming north to escape the heat and disease of the southern summers; Dubuque and Burlington benefited from the establishment of federal land offices; and several towns profited from the arrival of railroads in the 1850's, which crossed the river at Davenport (first railroad bridge), Dubuque, Burlington, and later Clinton. A town on the river in 1860 without the prospect of a railroad was virtually doomed. The services provided by these towns generally responded to the growth of the countryside and agriculture. Most towns rapidly passed through the early stage of a few houses, with mills, hotels, and ferries, and moved on to a newer stage as suppliers and marketers for those in the interior, selling building materials, machinery, and foodstuffs, and marketing grains and meat downriver, and, with the arrival of railroads, in Chicago.[31]

Town building in the 1840's changed, partly the result of the slowed growth of the economy generally and partly the result of changing geography, for the settlements that moved toward the center of Iowa edged farther and farther out onto the prairies. Most of the new towns were still located on sizable streams. They were also determinedly agricultural, as the settlement of Iowa was pre-eminently an agricultural experience. The towns in Wapello County provide a good example. Ottumwa (and nearby Eddyville) grew in response to the needs for economic and institutional development. It was located on the Des Moines River, but this was never an important artery to the interior, and not until the arrival of the railroad in 1859 did the town grow rapidly. Ottumwa provided the services that the expanding agricultural population demanded and also served as the center of the professional classes—doctors, lawyers, merchants, and millers—that would provide the leadership for the county. Ottumwa was only one of many county seats that appeared and prospered with the expansion of settlement into Iowa.[32]

Inland from the Mississippi and beyond the dominant force of water

31. Loren N. Horton, Historical Specialist, State Historical Society of Iowa, Iowa City, is my source for information on Iowa's river towns. His study of the founding, growth, planning, and ultimate form of these urban centers promises to be the standard work on the subject.

32. Mildred Throne, "A Population Study of an Iowa County in 1850," *IJH*, 57 (1959): 324–30. Throne comments, "And certainly in Wapello County, and in many other parts of Iowa, another type of pioneer came along with the farmer—the town builder" (p. 330).

transportation, a series of prairie towns sprang up in the wake of westward settlement. These were also economic in focus. Tipton (Iowa), the
county seat of Cedar County, is a good example. Ebenezer Alden, Congregational minister, was a witness to—indeed a participant in—the
urban growth of a part of eastern Iowa. Alden originally settled in Solon
(Johnson County) in 1844. Of this town, he wrote: "Solon was 'staked
out' for a town but it never certainly was named after its proprietors. By
a town we mean here a little plat of ground, divided up into lots, laid out
by authority of the legislature. The lots in Solon were bid off but never
paid for and the town stakes will this winter be pulled up." Alden also
pulled up his stakes. He moved to Tipton, then the center of an agricultural community located on an attractive prairie. The town was three
years old and contained "12 to 15 frame houses *painted white*, 3 lawyers,
1 physician etc." Tipton was "a right smart place" in the summertime,
according to Alden. The progress of urban growth was from east to
west, largely along the lines of length of settlement, or so Alden described it. Burlington, he wrote, "is in advance of what it is here. More
frame houses & barns. In the n. part of Johnson County I know of but 4
frame houses." People in Tipton had a sufficiency, if not the luxury associated with Iowa City. Already a sense of difference between town and
country had appeared. "As to hardships those who live in Bloomington,
Iowa City, are like city folks everywhere, a 'little stuck up' above the
country people." In late 1844 Alden described the character of Tipton
and its people in these terms:

> In the towns there is a great deal of extravagance in dress, just as there
> is in their suppers when they have a party. You can see all kinds of
> dress in Cedar County even. The Scotch plaid thrown over the shoul-
> ders, Eastern ladies dressed well enough not to attract attention in any
> congregation and hoosier bonnets of all description. There are all kinds
> of people with a great many different kinds of ways. There is a great
> deal more familiarity here than in the East. People don't always take off
> their hats so much when they go into a house and do not always put a
> Mr. before a man's name.

Alden founded a church and stayed in the town, recording his impres-
sions in long letters to his parents. The town grew steadily. In three
years, Alden estimated that the population of the village increased from
75 to 140 "or upwards." Among the new improvements: "an apothecaries

shop—opened the past year—a new store soon to be opened—7 buildings—6 houses & a school house put in the last year."[33]

By the middle of the nineteenth century, towns on the trans-Appalachian frontier were important and influential. In a sense, they had always been so, whether their initial purpose was military or economic. From the Bluegrass of Kentucky and the first Ohio River towns to the prairies of Illinois and Iowa and the lead-mining camps of the Driftless Region, towns had always been a part of the frontier experience. Those that had initially provided security lived on to provide the countryside around them with an array of goods and services. By 1850 towns were already centers of education and religion; in the next generation they would become the arbiters of taste, manners, and morals. In the last half of the nineteenth century towns across the trans-Appalachian West would have a decisive influence on those who grew up in or adjacent to them. People would identify with them, dislike, or perhaps even hate their constricting pressures. But all would be shaped by them.[34] Towns were one of the lasting legacies of the frontier experience from 1775 to 1850.

33. Ebenezer Alden to his parents, Feb. 3, 22, Dec. 24, 1844; Feb. 12, 1847, Ebenezer Alden Letters, SHSI.

34. On the significance of towns in the lives of people in the last half of the nineteenth century, see Lewis Atherton, *Main Street on the Middle Border* (Bloomington, 1954). A personal account is the first meeting of the country boy, Hamlin Garland, and his colleagues with the city boys. It ended in a fight. The occasion was a visit to town for the Fourth of July celebration. *Boy Life on the Prairie* (1899), ch. 11.

15

The Changing
Political Experience

The political life of the trans-Appalachian frontier began with its first permanent settlements. From the beginning, the challenges of the wilderness demanded that people organize and pool their resources to perform tasks that individuals could not carry out alone. In the course of this organization, some men led and others followed; such was the nature of things. The Anglo-Americans were political creatures. They inherited their interest in politics and political affairs from their English ancestors and carried it across the ocean to the New World, where political life underwent changes as time and circumstances dictated. Some form of politics gradually came to permeate the English colonies, from New England to Georgia, as the ministers of the Crown after 1763 knew well. This interest in political affairs did not necessarily indicate widespread participation, for all colonial societies were deferential ones (the frontier perhaps less so but not entirely excepted), and men acknowledged traditional leaders and forms of leadership. By the time that the conflict with England came into focus, the Anglo-Americans had much experience in politics, and at a high level of sophistication, as their private and public arguments in the quarrel with Great Britain before 1775 show and their public documents thereafter—the Declaration of Independence, the Articles of Confederation, and the Constitution of 1787—testify.

Between 1775 and 1850 the political life of the trans-Appalachian frontier embraced three distinct experiences. Although each had its separate characteristics, no one was mutually exclusive; although the transition from one to another may be measured in chronological terms, the three coexisted in the later years, especially as the settlements of the trans-Appalachian West grew in size and over time to encompass several stages of development. In the first twenty years, from 1775 to 1795, political life was characterized by an informal spontaneity closely associated with the frontier's immediate needs for survival and security. The large numbers of people that went west after 1795 (especially after 1784 in Kentucky), the Northwest Ordinance, and a temporary accommodation with the several Indian tribes after 1795 wrought great changes in the informal nature of politics. Groups and institutions began to play a larger part. And, especially with the imposition of political boundaries, a second stage of political life came to coexist with the first: the organization of Kentucky County in 1776 and later, in enlarged form, the promulgation of the Ordinance of 1787, led to the presence, for the first time on the frontier, of a corps of appointed officials. Politics and the struggle for political preferment now took place at several levels: township, county, and territory. Finally, a third stage came into focus: in both the 1790's and later again in the mid-1820's the practical politics directed at specific frontier needs underwent a transformation, and a strong ideological strain emerged. Political principles became a dominant feature of political life on the trans-Appalachian frontier and took the form of factions, or what people called political parties.

The earliest settlers carried politics across the mountains, with their rifles, shot pouches, and axes. For the first several years a special concept of leadership gave focus to political life and the search for positions of leadership. A few leaders, chosen in an informal way, met the immediate requirements of the frontier settlements that they served. They provided physical protection from the Indians in the form of stations or forts, negotiations, and, if necessary, punitive expeditions to enforce the will of the Americans. Leaders in stations and on military expeditions directed the economic and military affairs for those settlers who lived or fought within their jurisdiction or authority. They often did so arbitrarily, as befits a people at war. Those who did not like the arrangements could go elsewhere.

Throughout these early years, politics was personal and individual. It was the work of individuals chosen for positions of leadership among fellow frontiersmen not so much different from themselves in education, social standing, and economic position. These people often knew one another personally. Militiamen elected officers and then observed them in battle. In short, the frontiersmen had ample opportunity to judge the performance of men in the position tendered them. This personal form of leadership owed much to the small and dispersed nature of the population, which brought people together in small groups of mutual dependence. It also owed much to their preoccupation with military matters. People moved and settled in military patterns, a direct result of their concern for constant physical security from the Indians. James Harrod was the first such leader on the trans-Appalachian frontier, for he directed the laying out of the settlement that bore his name and led the expedition that laid it out. Judge Richard Henderson was an early political leader whose views on political leadership were more long range. He intended to establish a government with himself at the head, in a form reminiscent of forms of government in the older colonies. Other frontier leaders were entrepreneurs like Benjamin Logan who founded stations and gave their names to them. In virtually every case, the practical needs of their constituents were paramount. By whatever name that they gave to it, the first settlers pursued an informal voluntary association in search of common ends. Political life was practical, informal, even spontaneous.

A major transition in the nature of politics took place following the end of the Revolution. This transition reflected, in part, larger numbers of people. Kentucky began to grow and grow rapidly—from twelve thousand to fifty thousand people in four years. The change also flowed, in part, from the establishment of political units that began with the organization of Kentucky County in 1776. In addition to the authority of military leadership and economic proprietorship, power was now also rooted in the continuing influence of Virginia. The officials of this Virginia county court were only the first of a huge corps of appointed officials who would fill public office on the trans-Appalachian frontier. Joining them were the surveyors of land claims and, after 1779, the all-powerful land commissioners. This group of leaders achieved prominence and power through its control of the machinery of what Virginia recognized as a legitimate form of government, and, in the final analysis, their impact on the frontier was much stronger than that of the early Indian fighters and pathfinders. John Floyd was one of this new group, although he had been in and around Kentucky longer than most of them.

A member of the Virginia gentry class, he used his influence in the Old Dominion to enhance his prospects in Kentucky County. His service as a surveyor was a sign of the transference of Virginia leadership west of the mountains. Men like Floyd and Isaac Shelby, who became the first governor of the commonwealth in 1792, were an increasingly prominent feature of the Kentucky scene after peace with Great Britain.[1]

Throughout the decade before statehood (1792) politics became increasingly multidimensional, for at the same time that the political arena enlarged, vigorous political struggles continued at the county level. The influence of the county was wide and lasting. The county court passed judgment on a far range of economic, political, and social matters that directly affected the lives of frontier people, ranging from questions of morality to taxes. Members of the county courts tended to appoint their own successors. As a self-contained political unit with enormous influence, the county became the focal point of politics. This influence and the importance of political struggles at the county level continued up to the Civil War and even into the twentieth century.[2]

Most of all, this transition in the nature of politics was accompanied by a change in the nature of the political process, in the struggle for leadership, and in the issues at stake in a New World that was no longer quite so new. The survival of the trans-Appalachian frontiers was no longer in question; it seemed assured. Matters of stability and property began to replace matters of military and economic survival. The issue was the institutional form of the new settlements. In short, people began to debate the kind of world in which they wanted to live, and the focus of the debate was understandably directed toward political power and preferment. The debate included questions of land claims (especially those granted by Virginia to favorite sons), taxes, slavery, law and lawyers, all items that determined the nature of society, the distribution of wealth, and the locus of power. This political debate—if it may be so described—was about the future of the commonwealth. It engaged the important minds of the day and drew the interest of Kentucky's citizens everywhere. As the jurist Harry Innes wrote in 1791, "The people of

1. Patricia Watlington, *The Partisan Spirit: Kentucky Politics, 1779–1792* (New York, 1972), 35–37; Paul W. Beasley, "The Life and Times of Isaac Shelby, 1750–1826" (Ph.D., Kentucky, 1968), ch. 5.
2. On the continuing influence of the county court in Kentucky, see Robert M. Ireland, *The County Courts in Ante-bellum Kentucky* (Lexington, 1972).

Kentucky are all turned Politicians from the highest in Office to the Peasant."[3]

In the struggle to shape the future of the commonwealth of Kentucky, men used the traditional political techniques,· only on a larger scale: public meetings and resolutions, remonstrances, petitions, and letters to the editor. The *Kentucky Gazette* became an open forum for a broad spectrum of political views. A series of large-scale meetings covering the entire district of Kentucky convened, beginning at Danville in 1784 and extending up through the Constitutional Convention of 1792. In its use of large-scale political techniques, the convention may be said to exemplify the transition from the first frontier political experience to the second.

The commonwealth of Kentucky entered the Union of States in 1792. Statehood, and the diplomatic triumphs and greater security from the Indians achieved by 1795 changed the nature of the political process and, in a sense wrote an end to the early political style on the trans-Appalachian frontier. Size, new political units, and the growing complexity of a world (or parts of it) no longer frontier had terminated the personal and pragmatic nature of the first frontier political experience. The primacy of military leadership and the search for security were gradually succeeded by struggle for control over the levers of economic power, at the local, county, and state levels. At the same time, the thrust for security had passed on to other, newer frontiers—across the river in portions of the Northwest Territory and in the settlements found on both sides of the Mississippi. The personal nature of politics would be repeated on every subsequent frontier experience to the Pacific Ocean. It was a necessary first step in establishing conditions under which the occupation of the country might be carried out.

The year 1787 introduced another kind of political leader and political authority on the trans-Appalachian frontier, or at least did so on a new scale. Under the provisions of the Northwest Ordinance—which eventually spread over most of the trans-Appalachian frontier—the territorial governor emerged as an appointed leader with an enormous range of political power, both on matters of governance and appointment. Given the nature of the position as defined in the ordinance, and adding the dis-

3. Harry Innes to Thomas Jefferson, Aug. 27, 1791, quoted in Watlington, *The Partisan Spirit*, 215.

tances involved, officers in the territories (especially the governor) wielded great influence. With his authority to lay off counties and appoint local officials, the governor had enormous patronage to dispense. Not surprisingly, the political life of a territory (and its intrigue as well) revolved around the governor, and most chief executives developed factions (and later parties) with their office as the base of strength. From this point the territory's political experience rapidly divided into those who supported the governor and hoped to benefit from his political largesse and those who opposed him and hoped to bring about his downfall. The situation was somewhat parallel to that produced by the appearance of the first county officials from Virginia and North Carolina west of the mountains after 1776, but the influence and authority of the territorial governor dwarfed the significance of any county official, for the governor could lay off counties and appoint their officeholders. Just as the passage to statehood removed this arbitrary power of the territorial governors, so, too, in time, the county bureaucracy became elective rather than appointive, but in some places this shift did not occur until well into the nineteenth century.[4]

The contrasting styles of politics and governance in the use of the new power and authority under the Northwest Ordinance can be seen in the experiences of the Territory Northwest of the Ohio and the first fruits of the ordinance within the Louisiana Purchase, Orleans Territory. Arthur St. Clair, first governor of the Northwest Territory, brought his own political style to his new appointment. St. Clair was basically unsympathetic to the aspirations of frontier people for more participation in the political processes. In this view, he shared the skepticism of some national leaders about the capacity of the many to govern themselves. His arbitrary direction of the affairs of the territory in a period dominated by a concern for survival aroused little hostility. For the most part, he gave effective leadership in these years to a decentralized and sparsely settled territory. Until at least 1795 the Northwest Territory and its people were still engaged in a struggle for survival against internal and external threats, especially the Indian menace and the accompanying machinations of the British. Here St. Clair failed his constituents, for he suffered one of the most devastating military defeats in the history of the nation.

4. Jack Ericson Eblen, *The First and Second United States Empires* (Pittsburgh, 1968), ch. 4. Arthur St. Clair, governor of the Northwest Territory, appointed some seven hundred officeholders, about half of these in the militia (p. 123).

The authority of his office was not weakened, however, for St. Clair was still governor, with all the governor's rights and privileges. His experience is an interesting contrast to that of the first political figures in Kentucky and Tennessee, whose military reputations counted for everything, and who were successful or quickly replaced.

Gradually the Indian threat subsided. The settlements along the Ohio River grew and prospered, and a concern for stability replaced the overwhelming concern for security. Population increased, resulting both in a division of the territory and in the advance of Ohio to the second stage of government. Effective opposition to Arthur St. Clair stemmed from these changing circumstances. St. Clair's leadership, arbitrary and dictatorial as befitted a territory in a state of siege, was not appropriate for the larger numbers of people in a territory at peace. The organization of the legislature meant political campaigns throughout the territory, and the legislature itself became a forum for opposition to the governor. St. Clair, who as an appointed governor in a territory concerned most of all about security had been flexible, was now almost reactionary. The times had changed; and as Ohio entered the second stage of political experience on the frontier, the nature of politics changed, too.

Across the Mississippi River in the Louisiana Purchase, another political story unfolded. In Orleans Territory (organized in 1804 from Lower Louisiana) the political drama was complicated by a host of factors that played little or not part in the Old Northwest. Inherent in the conflict between French and Americans were divisions between old inhabitants and new arrivals and between Catholics and Protestants. Differences between the two cultures were pervasive, extending from fights between Creoles and Americans over which dance tunes should be played at balls to conflict over basic institutional questions, such as civil versus common law. In addition, language differences reduced communication and intensified the estrangement between the two groups. The site of these several conflicts was a growing city (by the standards of the day), and, for almost the first time, political divisions were based on ethnic concerns. New Orleans had several living areas—new suburbs appeared with the arrival of the Americans after 1803—and the city supported several newspapers of various political persuasions. Each editor entered vigorously into a controversy centered around the administration of Governor William C. C. Claiborne, who, as the American governor of essentially French territory, came to symbolize government of a majority by a minority. Although only twenty-eight years of age when he became acting governor (Jefferson made him governor in 1804), Claiborne had already served as a clerk in Congress, judge in Tennessee, congressman from Tennessee, and governor of the Mississippi Territory. He had his own political style and his approach to politics and political conflict. Guided by the policy of his superiors in Washington who wished to do nothing to upset the newest Americans in Louisiana, Claiborne adopted the posture of neutrality amidst the swirling conflicts. In so doing, of course, he neglected the opportunity to use the power and authority of his office to build his own political support and served, instead, as the target for all disaffected groups. In a typically unpartisan act, for example, Claiborne awarded the public printing contract to James Bradford and the *Orleans Gazette*, although Bradford constantly abused him and his administration in print. Claiborne endured Bradford's attacks for three years before giving his patronage to the more friendly and understanding *Louisiana Courier*. In addition to the press, weapons in the struggle included petitions, remonstrances, and pamphlets. Whether Claiborne's neutrality was his own personal style, his interpretation of the wishes of his superiors, or simply the aloofness of a federal official is not entirely clear. The opposition press could not bring down the governor, but it could and did make his life uncomfortable and his posture defensive.

At the center of the controversy was the loyalty of Louisiana and her citizens to the United States. The issue was the more pressing as the territory lay on the exposed southern flank of a nation enlarged by the recent purchase of Louisiana and increasingly embroiled in the affairs of western Europe. This was an involvement that might lead to an armed confrontation with the British navy. Also in question was the readiness of Orleans for statehood and the acceptance of republican principles implied in admission to the Union. Most of the *anciens habitants* wanted statehood, for they wished to manage their own affairs with a minimum of interference from the alien Americans. President Jefferson and Secretary of State Madison felt that the territory of Orleans was not ready for statehood. Claiborne concurred with the views of his superiors. The president named a majority of Americans to the Legislative Council. Some of the older French nominees were reluctant to serve when asked, and the French expressed understandable irritation at their underrepresentation. The American governor now directed the affairs of

French Louisiana with a minority representation for the French. The Americans were democrats, however, and they could not escape their own principles. Three months after government with the council began, Congress—perhaps seeking a compromise on the statehood issue— promoted Orleans Territory to the second grade of territorial government and provided for the election of a lower house. When the election took place in October 1805, the French elected all their candidates. The legislature—at least the lower house—was now at odds with the American governor. The focal point of the conflict was the legislature's passage of a bill to make civil law the law of the territory. Claiborne vetoed this bill that represented the will of a majority of the territory's people. Thus, political conflict in Orleans Territory extended well beyond the question of personalities and the search for power and preferment under a generally accepted framework of institutions to basic questions of institutional and cultural identification.[5]

Throughout the political experience from 1775 to 1815, and with echoes to almost 1850, ran the theme of the successful military experience as the mark of personal leadership and the foundation of a call upon the electorate for office. This old frontier tradition dated back to George Washington and continued through the early settlement experience in Kentucky, Tennessee, and the Northwest Territory.[6] In the course of these three generations, innumerable political aspirants sought success on the battlefield. Great success and extraordinary political careers came to a few such as William Henry Harrison, Andrew Jackson, and others lesser known like John Tipton of Indiana. Riding to the fore on renewed conflict with the Indians and British for which he was at least partially himself responsible, William Henry Harrison proved an enormously effective practitioner of the old political rule that a military triumph against the universal public enemy gives the ultimate leverage in political life. Harrison even provided a variation on the theme by claiming a victory at Tippecanoe that far exceeded the actual military results of the battle. Still, the burning of the village by Harrison's troops broke Te-

5. George Dargo, *Jefferson's Louisiana: Politics and the Clash of Legal Traditions* (Cambridge, 1975), ch. 2, esp. pp. 38–41.
6. This theme of military service as a prerequisite for public office endured long in Kentucky and on the frontier generally. As late as 1794, James Lemon published a letter defending his early return from an Indian campaign. Lexington *Kentucky Gazette*, Jan. 25, 1794. Or note the case of Thomas Lewis, a candidate for public office, in *ibid.*, March 12, 1791.

cumseh's aura of invincibility and forever laid to rest the vision of a great Indian alliance. The West rushed toward the War of 1812 on a flood tide of spirited optimism. This conflict brought much trouble and little satisfaction to the trans-Appalachian frontier, but it did produce one military leader who symbolized the strength and virtues of the frontier in the public mind. Andrew Jackson emerged from Tennessee to win impressive military victories over the British and the Indian enemies. The frustrations of the war and the brilliance of Jackson's leadership merged at New Orleans, where the great American victory mitigated the disappointments of the war and sealed Jackson's reputation as military leader, and, in the course of time, civil leader.

The Great Migration in the postwar years enlarged the opportunities for aspiring politicians, new offices, and new wealth on the trans-Appalachian frontier. Most of all, it brought numbers. The mass of people who moved to the western country necessitated an increasing number of large-scale political units. Territories passed in regular succession to statehood, and both were political arenas. The West was a place of opportunity in law and in politics as well as in land. The many elective state offices from governor down provided ample scope for the talents of young and ambitious politicians. Larger-scale contests for a larger constituency brought greater rewards. It also brought more competition. Federal patronage in the form of the land business, Indian affairs, and the postal service offered opportunities for reward. When Noah Noble received the appointment as receiver of the land office at Indianapolis over fifty other applicants, one editor summed up a political truth of the day. "Ah, those 'loaves and fishes' of Uncle Sam's," he wrote, "they're enticing."[7]

Amidst the larger numbers of people, the growing impersonality of politics, and the rising competition for preferment through federal patronage, much of the old personal nature of politics survived. To succeed in political life, one best have militia command, service in the War of 1812 and against the Indians, an avenue to federal patronage, and the right family ties and connections. The widely scattered nature of the population on the trans-Appalachian frontier worked to the continued advantage of those who could bring even modest leverage to bear in search of preferment. John Messinger, for example, exercised influence in

7. Richmond (Indiana) *Public Ledger*, Dec. 3, 1825.

the Illinois Territory through his father-in-law, Congressman Matthew Lyon of Kentucky, who provided him with suitable employment and patronage opportunities.[8] In spite of the growth of the trans-Appalachian frontier and the new political units being organized across its breadth, some aspects of the political experience were one with what had gone before.

The personal nature of politics of the first period of frontier experience and the opportunity to benefit from federal patronage that emerged in the second and the enduring significance of military reputation characteristic of both can be seen in the political career of John Tipton. Born in a log cabin on the East Tennessee frontier in 1786, Tipton began his political career with his appointment as a justice of the peace for Harrison County (Indiana) in 1811 and concluded it in the United States Senate in 1839. Over this generation, he exhibited the full range of the frontier political experience and its changes. When the Tipton family moved from Tennessee to Indiana in 1807, settlements were few. The Greenville Treaty line marked the edge of settlement from the east; the Wabash River was the center of population in the west. In between lay a few scattered villages, most along the Ohio River. The great forests of southern Indiana grew undisturbed. The major economic enterprise of the region was the fur trade. Jeffersonville, site of the new federal land office, and Vincennes, the territorial capital, were the only centers of urban life. The first settlers were small farmers, merchants, and government officials. This was the frontier world that John Tipton entered to seek his fortune.

Tipton first operated a ferry on the Ohio in Harrison County, opposite the mouth of the Salt River. Carrying immigrants and their belongings was a lucrative business, and it was also a good way to meet people. Tipton's physical strength, directness of manner, and outspokenness were qualities admitted by frontier people. In 1811 the governor of Indiana Territory apppointed John Tipton a justice of the peace, his first public office. His participation in Harrison's punitive expedition against the Tippecanoe campground in the autumn of that year was most significant for his political career. Tipton fought brilliantly and established himself as a brave, confident, and aggressive military commander. He was rewarded with a commission and was later elected cap-

8. See the John Messinger Papers, ISHL, for correspondence between Messinger and Matthew Lyon over patronage.

tain of a rifle company. For a full decade, talk of Tecumseh had brought apprehensive glances from Indiana settlers. Now that threat had ended, and John Tipton had played a significant role. His subsequent military rise was rapid, from lieutenant colonel (1813) to colonel (1814) in the War of 1812 and to a commission as brigadier general in 1817. Thereafter he was always General Tipton.

Tipton was also active on other fronts. In 1814 he purchased a sixty-two-acre farm on the Ohio. In his capacity as deputy sheriff, militia officer, and justice of the peace he often visited the county seat of Corydon, named territorial capital in 1813. In 1816 he moved to Corydon and opened a tavern in his home. All these activities widened his circle of acquaintances. County voters elected him sheriff in 1816, and, in addition to holding other public offices, he was a member of the committee to select the site of the new state capital. He also served two terms in the Indiana House of Representatives. In 1823, after failing in his quest for various federal offices, John Tipton accepted a position as federal agent to the Indians on the upper Wabash. Ft. Wayne was remote and primitive, but the office was one of power and influence. Among other duties, Tipton controlled the licensing of Indian traders and the enforcement of trade regulations, and he disbursed annuities and gifts to the several Indian tribes. In response to treaties of cession, he also directed the evacuation of the Indians, an exercise that involved provisioning and transportation. In 1828 Tipton forced the removal of the agency from Ft. Wayne to Logansport, where he and his friends controlled the land on which the town had been laid out. His influence as a dispenser of patronage also increased. By 1830 he controlled the appointment of two subagents, one or more interpreters, two millers, a gunsmith, two blacksmiths, three assistants and ten laborers, plus contracts to purchase food, lumber, and agricultural implements.

On the death of James Noble in 1831, John Tipton became a candidate for the United States Senate. The election took place in the Indiana legislature. His opponents were men like him, but all had more education and more political experience. Tipton had the finest military background, however, a reputation for honesty and integrity in an office generally characterized by malfeasance, and powerful support around the state built up over many years through his access to federal patronage. He won on the seventh ballot. Next year the legislature elected him to a full six-year term. His decision not to seek re-election in 1838 was based in part on poor health. It also grew out of the changes that had taken place in politics and political style in the trans-Appalachian West. By 1838 the sources of Tipton's power and the personal nature of his influence had become obsolete in the face of the strength of the new party politics and a new emphasis on ideology.[9]

The slowed pace of expansion and growth that followed the panic of 1819—a sorting-out process—coincided with a transition in the style and format of political life on the trans-Appalachian frontier. At issue was the change of politics from personal to ideological. This change encompassed two distinct time periods: the 1790's and mid-1820's. People who found unity in matters of political principle first combined in institutionalized form in the 1790's, and these groups were called political parties. Political parties on the frontier were not indigenous; they came across the mountains like iron, firearms, tools, and other eastern goods. Principles and expectations of officeholding united the so-called parties east and west of the mountains, who had taken the names Federalists and Democratic-Republicans. In a practical sense the Democratic-Republican triumph in the election of 1800 carried most of the frontier into the camp of Thomas Jefferson and his followers. There it remained for almost a generation, with little conflict over principle and much over personal ambition of leaders in search of office.

By the middle of the 1820's a new political experience built around political parties was in process of developing. The election of 1824 saw the last of the old-style politics, and the election of 1828 the first of the new. At the time of the election of 1824 the direction of national political life was not clear, and the contest for president was still fought largely on the basis of personality and sectional identification. The election of 1824 was important because it was the first vigorously contested election in twenty-four years. It offered the national electorate an assortment of candidates from a much wider range of backgrounds than had heretofore been the case. For the first time the trans-Appalachian West had its representatives, not one but two. Andrew Jackson had a strong following. General Jackson's views on the issues of the day were not entirely clear,

9. Paul Wallace Gates, introd. to John Tipton, *The John Tipton Papers*, ed. Nellie A. Robertson and Dorothy Riker (3 vols., Indianapolis, 1942), forms the basis of this discussion.

but he had fought the Indians and the British with great success. He was the most universally acknowledged American military hero since George Washington. His identification with the Tennessee frontier also gave him claims on the West. Henry Clay, of Kentucky, deliberately attempted to portray himself as a spokesman of western interests, and his so-called American System, with its emphasis on internal improvements, had widespread appeal in frontier settlements. William H. Crawford of Georgia had strong support in the South, and elsewhere, John Quincy Adams, the New Englander, commanded respect. Adams was a vigorous nationalist who favored using the authority of the federal government to solve many of the problems associated with frontier life. He had successfully acquired Florida—and covered up the diplomatic indiscretions of Andrew Jackson while doing so—and his program of federal internal improvements had obvious attractions for the western country. Despite the qualities of the candidates, however, interest in the election was mild. Newspapers and politicians responded slowly and in measured tones to the noises of political strife drifting across the mountains. Elections at the local level were still very important, and, in many places, the largest share of interest went to local candidates. Here frontier people felt themselves directly affected by the outcome.[10]

At the heart of the new politics were emerging political parties based on something people at the time called principles. The most important party and principles were associated with Andrew Jackson. That Jackson would become synonymous with ideology seems contradictory, for he himself had a political apprenticeship grounded in the old-style personal politics of the frontier. He emerged as the protégé of John Sevier of Tennessee and made his own reputation by defeating the Creeks at Horseshoe Bend and the British at New Orleans. After 1824, however, other forces worked to give impetus to Jackson and his followers and to build a party ideology around him. The first was a deep sense of grievance at what they felt was the subversion of the political process in the election of 1824. "Bargain and corruption," the phrase used to describe the alleged arrangement under which Henry Clay threw his support to John Quincy Adams and Adams in payment made Clay his heir apparent as secretary of state, was devoutly believed by many, including Old Hick-

10. The Evansville *Gazette*, for example, showed an interest in elections at all levels. See March 24, July 1, 1824. Both this paper and the Corydon *Indiana Gazette* supported Adams.

ory himself. So Andrew Jackson cast himself in the role as spokesman for honesty and integrity in government. A second factor in the emergence of ideology was the changing nature of America. The postwar boom and the attendant impulses of the Great Migration created large-scale economic enterprise in the form of banks (of which the Second Bank of the United States was the largest) and the emerging factory system. At the same time, frontier people became accustomed to a considerable degree of economic gratification, and the Second Bank of the United States, an eastern-controlled corporate colossus that restricted the expansionist plans of western entrepreneurs, seemed to stand in their way. It became the enemy. Jackson's veto of the bill to recharter the bank in 1832 would be consistent with his views and with western opinion.

If the sound of political battle had diminished by the time it crossed the mountains, the revolution of the Jacksonians was no less profound on the frontier. The issues were not new, but what happened in terms of political style was not only real but far reaching. From the opening of their campaigns in 1824 the Jacksonians had organized. Politics was no longer a casual game to be played every two or four years. It was a full-time business, and the stakes were, accordingly, high. Professional politicians—for so, in a sense, they were—kept the issues of the day constantly before the electorate. In this fashion the Jacksonians moved to destroy any semblance of neutrality or nonpartisanship in political life. A favorite weapon in the new politics was the press. The Jacksonians used the press wherever possible, and they set a new standard in rewarding editors for faithful service. With so many appointments in Indian agencies, the land business, and post offices, the new spoils system directly affected the frontier. The electorate in the West generally favored Jackson for his exploits against the Indians and his removal policy. In Alabama and Mississippi sentiment in his favor was overwhelming for these reasons.[11] At the same time, Old Hickory's policies of the bank veto and hard money, simplicity and honesty in government, and his constant reference to the virtues of the agrarian life made him popular throughout the frontier of the trans-Appalachian West.

The re-emergence of political parties brought to the fore once more a concern that dated back to the days of the founding fathers. Politics was an unsettling element in a society or societies already concerned about

11. Edwin A. Miles, *Jacksonian Democracy in Mississippi* (Chapel Hill, 1960).

questions of order. From the beginning of settlement, some people had voiced uneasiness about the unstructured nature of the frontier. This voice had become louder and more influential as the frontier passed beyond the condition in which survival was the primary concern to the stage dominated by the desire for greater stability. The search for more order on the frontier was constant. Into this uncertain world came politics, with its divisions, factions, bitterness, occasional violence, and the activities of election day itself. The whole election process loosed elements of rowdyism and boisterousness, not infrequently lubricated with corn whiskey. The *Indiana Gazette* commented that an election in Corydon in 1820 "exhibited such a degraded state of society, as outrages all the usual principles of civilization, or rules of social order and morality." The emergence of political parties intensified the competition at election time. Achille Murat, a French relative of the fabled Bonaparte, described an election about 1830 in Jefferson County (Florida) in these terms:

> The whiskey, however, (not exactly the "nectar of the gods"), all this time going its rounds; towards evening all have, more or less, disposed of their sober qualities, and it is rare that the sovereign people abdicate power without a general set-to, where nobody can he heard, . . . and from which all who claim the enviable distinction of possessing a vehicle take very good care to keep aloof.

In 1834 the Grand Jury of Jefferson and Madison counties (Florida) publicly deplored "the violence of *party spirit*," noting especially that those guilty of violent acts expected to be shielded from punishment by their political friends and allies.[12]

The one national political event that drew the attention of people on frontiers everywhere was the election of 1840. Many who wrote at that time remarked on its parades, rallies, and speeches. Lovira Hart of Michigan walked to Lapeer to cast his vote for the Whig party. Ferdinand Steel of Mississippi recorded his reactions to the campaign. George Ogden of the Wisconsin Territory responded to the intensified political pulse of the territory by attending political rallies and actively support-

12. Corydon *Indiana Gazette*, Aug. 10, 1820; Tallahassee *Floridian*, Dec. 6, 1834; the *Floridian*'s solution was to hold elections less frequently. Murat is quoted in James Owen Knauss, "The Growth of Florida's Election Laws," *FHQ*, 5, no. 1 (1926): 7–8. See also Sandford C. Cox's description of an 1828 election gathering in Indiana in *Recollections of the Early Settlement of the Wabash Valley* (Lafayette, Ind., 1860), 17. "The Pioneers of Jefferson County—Reminiscences of James B. Lewis, Esq.," ISL, emphasizes the more physical aspects of the electoral process.

ing a candidate. Why? Part of the interest was the strain imposed on American society—including the frontier—by the panic of 1837 and the subsequent depression. The first real opportunity for the Whigs to capture the presidency led to an all-out campaign by Whig editors and vigorous counterattacks by their Democratic colleagues. The "log cabin and hard cider" cry of the supporters of Harrison may have captured the interest and imagination of the Western voters. Mass rallies, torchlight parades, and songs probably increased participation by offering another attractive form of socializing. William Henry Harrison had a large following on the frontier, and if younger voters could not remember the Battle of Tippecanoe, older men and editors could always be found who would remind them afresh of the debts the Republic owed to the general and the reasons for supporting him at the polls. The strong turnout at the election in the autumn of 1840 suggests a response to an intense political campaign that was felt even on the most remote and distant frontiers.

Throughout the trans-Appalachian frontier there runs another basic question: did the average frontiersman really care about politics? Mastering the land was a time-consuming business. Local government might play a significant part at a certain stage, in road construction and other public works, especially, in the South, in levee building. But national affairs were remote. An editor of the Maumee (Ohio) *Express*, at the far northwestern corner of the state, put the case in these terms:

> Occupying, as we do, a frontier position in the great American republic—at a great distance from the political metropolis of the country—with limited means of obtaining the earliest information concerning the political movements of the different parties—having no important offices in our immediate vicinity—living in a section of the country where the lines of party distinctions have not been drawn with any degree of certainty, and possessing moderate talents, and a small degree of information upon political subjects, we were not long in forseeing the entire futility of an attempt to make our paper a leading political journal.[13]

Party men might change the editor's mind with suitable financial inducements in the form of printing patronage. But could the party and the edi-

13. Maumee *Express*, April 5, 1837.

tor induce any enthusiasm in the mass of people engaged in making a living? Of those few accounts of frontier people that have survived, few mention politics. Fewer still display more than passing notice of national political affairs. The impression persists that a dramatic event like the election of 1840, the issue of Indian removal, or a grave economic crisis was necessary to make the American pioneer into a political partisan.

16

The Closing of the Frontier

Poets, novelists, editors, and Fourth of July orators have celebrated the opening of the frontier. Few have noted its close. The frontier did pass, however, and almost invariably to other regions farther west. "At different periods in our history, the 'Far West' has been differently located," wrote one Indiana editor. "At one time Indiana was the far west; at another . . . the Mississippi but now, it has been determined, that no point short of half a mile this side of sundown deserves the appellation."[1] The time was 1837. The editor's hyperbole aside, the opening of new land settlements had carefully marked signposts. Where before there had been open space or wilderness were now clearings, log cabins, and the first tentative cultivation of the soil. Where once there was nothing, there was now something, at least in terms of American occupation. Institutional manifestations gradually appeared: government, militia, courts, and the law. Latin phrases echoed off bare courthouse walls, and the frontier people embraced the doctrines of Sir William Blackstone, if they did not entirely understand them. The minister came and organized a church. Public-minded citizens raised their voices in support of a school. All these marks could be found sooner or later on most frontiers.

---

1. Logansport *Canal Telegraph*, June 24, 1837, quoted in Virginia Lowell Mauck, "Population Movements in Northern Indiana before 1850" (M.A., Indiana, 1948), 1.

No such clear signposts marked the closing of the frontier. The struggle to clear, plant, harvest, and trade merged in varying degrees and at varying speeds into a rural world much like that elsewhere, whether east of the Appalachians or in the longer-settled parts of the West. No dramatic discoveries marked its passing; no folklore, legends or celebrations marked its quiet disappearance. The agricultural world of the late eighteenth and nineteenth centuries was not necessarily an orderly or precise one. It is not surprising that little difference could be found in outward appearance between some farms that had been under cultivation for half a century and others only a few years old. The change was in the hearts and minds of the people who experienced the entire cycle. Generally speaking, the frontier of the trans-Appalachian West from 1775 to 1850 was an experience of high expectations. The great prize was the land. This was a continuing theme running throughout the three generations of immigrants. Pioneers expected to find rich land and make it their own. It was this expectation that carried them through the hard struggle of the first few years, when the forest wilderness, the canebrakes, or the prairie land had to be subdued yard by yard. In addition to land, a vision also drove people forward. It was the sense that the structure of the New World was not in final form and that something important might come out of it for them. As a more permanent world of institutions took shape around them, they came to realize that the New World was no longer so new. It had aged, counting not in years, but in the occupation and clearing of the land, the establishment of a county court, the acceptance of the common law, the taxes that accompanied these changes, the gradual appearance and spread of roads, and in economic relationships that had changed from spontaneous to permanent. A new society had been shaped. This portion of the frontier had become an agricultural society much like agricultural societies elsewhere.

What were the reactions of people to this transition? Some surely rejoiced, the more so if the struggle for survival had been long and hard. Lovira Hart in Tuscola County (Michigan) must have welcomed a sense of progress in the struggle for economic survival, an assurance that the land would provide and that the margin of existence was no longer so thin. For some, the change was less welcome. The expectation of a bright future—landownership and perhaps something more, vague and undefinable but nonetheless more—had been the driving force behind the years of hard work. Now, with a competence achieved, the limits of the hitherto unlimited future revealed themselves with unsettling clarity. What lay ahead were years of labor on the farm to preserve what had been won or to improve on it. People no longer had the illusion of progress, of "getting ahead," as frontier editors liked to call it. The future was now filled with the monotony of repetitious hard work. Edward Eggleston's *Hoosier Schoolmaster* (1871) and Hamlin Garland's *A Son of the Middle Border* (1917) captured the way younger people reacted to a future on the land. They had not experienced the early years of struggle and the glow of accomplishment that went into making a farm, and saw nothing but work and more work. The difference in outlook between the first pioneers and their children led Lovira Hart to plant potatoes, his daughter to cultivate flowers. It was a sense of frustration that sent large numbers to fight a war with Mexico and later to the gold fields of California. It was no accident that these dramatic responses to the opportunity to try something new came at a time when so much of the frontier struggle of the trans-Appalachian West was drawing to a close. Nor was it surprising that the most numerous participants were young people.

The varieties of frontiers gave rise to the varieties of societies and, accordingly, several different ways in which these would pass through the frontier stage. Among the several variables that would come into play here, a major distinction should be made immediately between urban and rural areas. The urban frontiers had different bench marks of development. The arrival of the institutions of government, law, and the courts, and the emergence of a society were readily recognizable. Peoples in urban centers felt, in a direct way, the structure of institutions. For most, it was a welcome condition, for the economic opportunities associated with urban life thrived on stability and order. The concentration of people that produced economic advantage also created problems. Rowdiness, drunkenness, gambling, and the possibility of violence threatened the orderly rise of urban centers, and city ordinances, the sheriff and jail, and, in some places, vigilante movements, emerged to control them. It is noteworthy that much of the mob violence on the trans-Appalachian frontier associated with the period of the mid-1830's took place in towns. Perhaps this urban society felt most threatened, had the most to lose, and so was most determined to act; at the same time, it was in urban centers that large numbers of people could be brought together, organized, and activated in pursuit of a common goal. In towns it was order and stability that most clearly marked the transition out of the frontier stage into something beyond, for this was the critical condition for the pursuit of commerce and orderly growth. Growth and institutional maturity brought changes. Some did not like these new forms of society, especially the more complicated bureaucratic nature of the new urban world. It was a world of the constable, the tax collector, the alderman, countless regulations and strictures, and often economic planning, with market restrictions and price fixing. Liked or not, they came to all urban centers sooner or later.[2]

For the rural societies that were more typical of these seventy-five years in the trans-Appalachian West, the bench mark noting the end of the frontier condition was the sale of surplus crops and the coming of commercial agriculture. With commercial agriculture—in the South this meant cotton—the economic world of these people west of the mountains changed from one of subsistence and independence to one based on a cash economy and interdependence. This interdependence was seen as early as the embargo of 1807 and was felt severely during the economic crises of 1819 and 1837, which affected the farmer and all those dependent on him—the mechanic, tradesman, minister, lawyer, and even the teacher.

Before 1815 physical growth in the form of tangible improvements was also a key bench mark in the maturity of a frontier. The first trans-Appalachian frontier experience was closely associated with deep woods and canebrakes and demanded much physical labor to prepare the land for cultivation or even to let in the sun. The pioneer struggled to achieve the basic necessities of life. He lived in a world whose dominant features were still vast spaces, few people, marginal communication, and subsistence agriculture. This struggle began in 1775 in Kentucky in the vicinity of Harrodsburg, whence it continued over a widening area through the Revolutionary War and the great expansion of the 1780's to statehood and the opening of the Mississippi to American commerce. By 1795 the prosperity of the Bluegrass region, the Nashville Basin, and the Natchez District, all now settled for almost a generation, was especially striking.[3]

---

2. For one objection to the new order in society, see "The Pioneer's Lament," Jackson *Mississippian*, Jan. 10, 1834.
3. To cite only a few historians on the closing of the first trans-Appalachian frontier, Pratt Byrd, "The Kentucky Frontier in 1792," *FCHQ*, 25 (1951): 183–84, says that by 1792 Kentucky "had advanced beyond the stage of the rough, crude frontier." Patricia Watlington, *The Partisan Spirit: Kentucky Politics, 1779–1792* (New York, 1972), declares,

As early as 1793 the *Kentucky Gazette*—published at Lexington in the heart of the Bluegrass—carried advertisements for "Country Seats" with substantial improvements. One included twenty-six acres of land cleared and fenced, eighteen acres in pasture, a garden, two orchards (apple, peach, and cherry trees), a "two story BRICK HOUSE and Kitchen, with a Pump of good water at the door; also a large and convenient framed Barn with stabling for twenty horses."[4] Or, physical progress might be measured in a general way by the number of farms, with the many fields under cultivation, that a traveller could see as he passed along. The Reverend David Barron, who journeyed through northern Kentucky in 1795, noted the superior crops and agricultural production of the region. "The improvements that have been in these counties since their settmt: must surprise a Traveller, and at the same time indicate the future greatness thereof," he wrote. Or, improvement might be represented by numbers of people and their dwellings, such as François André Michaux found along the northern banks of the Ohio in 1802. "Till the years 1796 and 1797 the banks of the Ohio were so little populated that they scarcely consisted of thirty families in the space of four hundred miles," he wrote. As a result of recent heavy immigration from Pennsylvania and Virginia, he continued, "the plantations are now so increased, that they are not farther than two or three miles distant from each other, and when on the river we always had a view of some of them."[5]

The development of institutions also changed the shape of the frontier experience for the individual settlers. The pioneer's institutional needs

---

"Between May and December 1784 it had become obvious that Kentucky was no longer a frontier" (p. 69). She quotes Humphrey Marshall, Kentucky's early historian, to support her argument. Tennessee passed through the frontier stage after the War of 1812, according to Thomas P. Abernethy, *From Frontier to Plantation in Tennessee: A Study in Frontier Democracy* (Chapel Hill, 1932), 226. North of the Ohio, Robert Leslie Jones notes Ohio's rapid progress in agricultural development but goes on to comment that the state as a whole did not pass through the frontier period until the 1820's, "except for the late settling swampy northwest section." "Ohio Agriculture in History," *OHQ*, 65 (1956): 232, 233. William Baskerville Hamilton states that the Natchez District was already passing the "frontier stage" when the United States first established organized government in 1798. "American Beginnings in the Old Southwest: The Mississippi Phase" (Ph.D., Duke, 1937), 264.

4. Lexington *Kentucky Gazette*, Feb. 16, 1793.
5. "Journal of David Barron," Lyman C. Draper Collections, 12 CC 179, SHSW; François André Michaux, "Travels to the West of the Allegheny Mountains, in the States of Ohio, Kentucky, and Tennessee," in Reuben Gold Thwaites, ed., *Early Western Travels, 1748–1846* (32 vols., Cleveland, 1904–07), 3: 189.

were a direct response to the primitive world in which he found himself. He wanted protection from the Indians, good land titles, communications, and a market for his surplus crops. To the extent that these could be supplied, he had achieved maturity. In this first period, directed to survival and stability, he got government, the militia, the law, and the courts. Added to these was the Ordinance of 1787, reinforcing the influence of the federal government through its control of so much institutional machinery. Yet the expansion of people into a variety of isolated places across the length and breadth of the trans-Appalachian West spread population thinly and led to much subsistence economic activity and a delay in institutional development. It also placed great strains on communication. The bureaucracy at all levels, county (roads and bridges), territorial (county courts), and federal (Indian relations and mail delivery) moved hesitatingly to meet the needs of a diffuse people in a vast wilderness. Minimal achievements gave a sense of accomplishment and a new departure. One Alabama editor rejoiced in 1821 at just such changes. "Our state is now beginning to assume the regularities of society—government is organized—roads cleared out—mails established—the spirit of navigation improving—communication with other states facilitated," he wrote; "All tend to give us a decided ascendency over our former condition."[6]

The years after 1815 brought a new frontier experience, at least in terms of the character of the agricultural frontier and the pace at which people passed through the frontier stage. To begin with, this extended period brought a number of dramatic changes in technology. The frontier of the trans-Appalachian West always reflected the world around it, even if this world lay across the mountains. The strength of this reflection varied, of course. It was strong in matters of technology. When steamboats appeared on the rivers and canals in the East, they penetrated to the western waters as soon as the opportunities for profit would admit. Canals were also significant, especially the Erie Canal, in bringing about the rise of large-scale commercial agriculture on the Great Lakes. This development, in turn, led to the rapid settlement and economic growth of the last frontier of the Old Northwest, oriented around the rise of Chicago and other less well known lake ports. Commercial agriculture now came earlier to the pioneer, and it also came easier. The

6. Cahaba *Press and Alabama State Intelligencer*, Jan. 6, 1821.

pace of this economic transformation quickened with the large-scale development of cotton culture on the southern frontier, even in its remote and newest areas. Thomas Law rode through the Black Belt only ten years after the first settlements. On the north side of the Alabama River, he wrote, he had "passed some fine plantations & staid this night at an old dutchman's." His host "lived in a very good house & at one of the most beautiful places I ever beheld." The next day, as he moved north and west into the heart of the Black Belt, Law noted that "the crops in these lands surpass any thing I ever beheld."[7] Improvements in communication and transportation also had the effect of elevating the interests of people from the local to the state and regional. This condition was especially evident in the New Counties of Alabama and Mississippi, which immediately achieved a community of interests (land, slaves, and cotton) with longer-settled parts of their states and with the South generally.

The rise of the cotton frontier introduced a type of settler clearly beyond the frontier period. This was the eastern aristocrat, who left the worn-out lands of the Tidewater and came out to new and fresher lands. One of the most elegant and genteel was Thomas Smith Gregory Dabney, descendant of a Huguenot family settled in Virginia since the middle of the seventeenth century. In 1835 Dabney, age thirty-seven, left his plantation "Elmington" and his native state for a new life in the cotton lands of the Southwest. His departure was the occasion for a great testimonial dinner in his honor, reported in detail in the Richmond newspapers. The new seat of the Dabney estate—and home for his family and large slave population—was Hinds County, Mississippi. Over a number of years, as the opportunity presented itself, he bought a total of four thousand acres "from half a dozen small farmers." In a leaky log cabin, he settled down to a pioneer life as an aristocrat. Dabney was the product of three or four generations of the Virginia aristocracy. Hinds County was formed in 1821 out of the Indian cession at the Treaty of Doak's Stand (1820). Although settled for fifteen years, the site of the state's capital, and already a large-scale producer of cotton, it was not the world from which Dabney emigrated.

With his well-developed sense of *noblesse oblige*, Dabney assisted his economically less fortunate neighbors and succeeded only in arousing

7. Thomas C. Law, "Journal of Travel to the Western Counties—from September 2ᵈ 1834," ADAH; the entries are for Sept. 23 and 24.

their hostility. To the invitation to a house-raising, or to help a neighbor whose fields were overgrown with weeds, he would respond with twenty slaves. Mounted on his horse and impeccably gloved, he would direct the work of his labor force. He put up houses in record time and cleared choked fields, but he never called on his neighbors for their aid. As a result, he found himself disliked, and for reasons that he could not understand. He received no more invitations for assistance. His daughter later tried to explain the meeting of two new societies: "The plainer classes in Virginia, like those in England, from whom they were descended, recognized the difference between themselves and the higher classes, and did not aspire to social equality. But in Mississippi the tone was different. They resented anything like superiority in breeding. Thomas Dabney was considered cold and haughty." Hinds County was a well-settled county in central Mississippi, but it was not yet Tidewater Virginia.

Dabney's purchase of the holdings of small farmers represented a new stage in the economic development of the area. Large-scale agriculture grounded on slave labor had taken over from a less efficient, less profitable system. Large-scale capital investment moved into an area where institutions were formed—at least with respect to government and law. Cotton was already the money crop, as it was farther to the north in the New Counties. This was an early state of settlement in a physical sense, but it was no frontier. There was much going on that was still of a developing nature: road building, clearing the land, drinage, placing large tracts under cultivation for the first time. Dabney tried to apportion the work at "Burleigh" in such a way as to clear one hundred acres of new land each year for cotton cultivation. So to consolidation of land and capital must be added some of the same functions—or a combination of the functions—that we associate with the frontier period. Perhaps the arrival of people like Dabney took some of the influence away from towns, transferring the center of society, economy, and influence over the life of the county to several large-scale, institutionally self-sufficient agricultural units known as plantations. This postfrontier experience—if we may call it that—was especially characteristic of the cotton South and, more specifically, of the new cessions in Mississippi and Alabama. Here large-scale capital investment and commercial agriculture followed hard on the heels of the first pioneers.[8]

8. Susan Dabney Smedes, *A Southern Planter* (New York, 1890), 17–68; quotations are from pp. 47 and 67. Others, including Jefferson Davis, repeated Dabney's experience.

In the early stages of development, the thrust for economic gratification dominated life in the western country. It was the vision that sent new immigrants across the mountains. It emerges from the glowing letters that those who had triumphed over early obstacles sent home to their parents and friends. In 1836 John Humphries of Parke County (Indiana) tried to explain to a Virginia relative what he had done in the past several years and what kind of life he had made for himself and his family. The bench marks were largely physical and material. He had carved out a farm of 170 acres, with six horses, nine cows, "a good stock of Hogs," and an orchard of one hundred fruit trees, he wrote. He was constructing a stable and had timbers laid for a barn. In defense of his large family, Humphries wrote that "this is a verry prolific country." He recited the improvements of the countryside like a Fourth of July orator: "20 years ago there was not a white man in it it now contained from 6 to 8000 inhabitants." Aside from the urban center of Rockville with its many buildings, "we are about to obtain Charters for putting up a County Seminary and a Steam Mill." As for the economy, "hog is our staple and is suppos^d that there was near $100,000 worth sold in Parke County this season." "I tell you my Friends," he concluded, "it is literally true every Man sets under his own Vine and Fig tree and none to make them afraid."[9]

The achievement of economic abundance with a commercial economy, institutional security, and the closing of the frontier did not mean a dramatic change in values or in the quality of life for many people in the western country. The passing of the frontier and the substitution of a rural world was part of the same broad river. Nor did it give any assurance of the quality of the society. Mary Carter Hovey, a minister's wife in Montgomery County (Indiana), wrote about these circumstances in 1832. What surprised her was the contrast between the affluent conditions of many people—she called them "wealthy" and said they "lived quite genteelly"—and their ignorance and illiteracy. "This is a large and rich settlement where we are," she continued. "I know of three [women] who live within half a mile of us that do not know [how to read] a word,

9. John Humphries to Samuel Blackwood, Jan. 7, 1836, ISL. Cf. the editorial comment in the Jackson *Mississippian* (Jan. 10, 1834) that people in that part of the country focused their interest on dollars and cents, and the comment in the Maumee *Express* (June 24, 1837) that the "accumulation of property is the governing principle" of life in northwest Ohio.

who are mothers of large families and disposed to let their children grow up in the same way."[10] Sometimes the same indifference could be found with respect to simple physical improvements, sanitation, and cleanliness. Ellen Bigelow wrote of a settlement on the Illinois prairie in which log houses lay surrounded by "a bed of mud, which is todden in and around the house without the slightest regard for comfort or cleanliness." These families who lived in their "wretched hovels" had estates "worth $30,000 or $40,000 owning vast herds of cattle and immense farms which produced almost spontaneously every comfort and luxury of life."[11]

A theme that constantly emerges from the whole range of the frontier experience in the trans-Appalachian West is that life was not simple. Travellers noted the inhabitants of lonely cabins in the woods, whose life style and expectations had changed little, if at all, since the outbreak of the American Revolution, and whose institutional needs and interaction with society were minimal. Such descriptions tend to deceive. From the beginning of the first palisaded station in Kentucky, frontier peoples were dependent upon one another and upon the institutions that they created or that others imposed upon them. This was a two-way development: on the one hand were the needs of the pioneers, on the other was the force of the institutions, whether in response to needs or not, whether welcome or not. The county court involved almost everyone; the law was close behind. The need for some kinds of economic transactions, even the most modest barter, was a part of the trans-Appalachian frontier from the very beginning and grew with each passing decade. Commercial men and bureaucrats became important in this world. Merchants took produce and sent it downriver, and so the frontiersman had to deal with them. Lovira Hart had to come to terms with the bureaucrats of Tuscola County over taxes and roads. He knew full well the price that he had to pay: three days to Lapeer and back. But he had to pay it all the

10. Mary Carter Hovey to her mother and sisters, May 12, 1832, Edmund O. Hovey Correspondence, ISL. This description is reminiscent of Edward Eggleston's *Hoosier Schoolmaster* (1871), in which characters lived in ignorance and intellectual poverty on rich bottomland said to be worth one hundred dollars an acre.

11. Ellen Bigelow, "Letters Written by a Peoria Woman in 1835," *JISHS*, 22 (1929–30): 349–50. A similar account in Wisconsin is Frederick J. Starin, "Diary of a Journey to Wisconsin in 1840," *WMH*, 6 (1922–23): 87.

same. Thus, from the beginnings of settlement to the west of the mountains, life took on an interlocking quality about it that belied the simple picture of the individual against the wilderness. Men depended on their friends, relatives, and neighbors. They also depended on institutions to help them, whether to defend them from Indians, build roads, recover property in a suit of law, or, finally, probate a will disposing of their property. They paid a price for this dependence.

The presence of an institutional framework on the frontier was not necessarily related to economic conditions or even to physical appearance. After 1815 the institutions of court, law, and county government awaited the settler almost everywhere. They provided a sense of order and also some necessary services. This did not mean that such benefits accrued to everyone on the frontier; not did it mean that all those there chose to take advantage of them. A full set of institutions existed along with extreme conditions of poverty—as in the mid-twentieth century. The kinds of facilities and institutions available to people must be measured against the kind of society that people hoped to create. There was little point in lamenting the absence of schools or churches if settlers did not really want them or, alternatively, wanted them but were not prepared to establish and support them. The institutions related to quality of life, cultural matters, and education changed less over seventy-five years than any others, except perhaps for the basic structure of government under the county and the Ordinance of 1787. Even as late as 1850 the concept of a public school supported by the state and local taxation was only in its first stages. On the eve of the Civil War the quality of life in rural agricultural America was much like that on the agricultural frontier. Both focused on economic advantage. Beyond that, the variations had become a matter of degree.

At whatever level of development, the strong impression persists that the frontier was one of enormous abundance for almost all those who experienced it. Life was full and rich if not luxurious. Accounts from Kentucky to Wisconsin tell of hardship, some privation, and difficult winters with inadequate shelter, but not of starvation or famine. In spite of early trials, this was a frontier of abundance, and this condition presumably disposed it to adopt institutions and forms that had worked in the past. There was no need to change. Along with abundance came optimism. Both were grounded in the seemingly inexhaustible rich lands of the trans-Appalachian West. On the frontiers of the trans-Mississippi

West—whether the agricultural frontier of the Great Plains, with its scant rainfall and heartbreak, or the mining frontier of the Rockies and the Far West—failures equalled successes. The story of the people, societies, and institutions across the Mississippi would be very different. But the frontier experience of the trans-Appalachian West is a story of repeated successes. Indeed, one searches in vain for other frontiers that produced so much for so many in so short a time. The great outpouring of county histories in the 1880's and 1890's celebrated this experience. It was an appropriate occasion, for most of those who participated thought, in retrospect, that they had done well. In light of the standards and values of the age, and of later frontier experiences, they had.

Bibliography

Like much of the early frontier experience west of the Appalachians, history is a collective enterprise. Historians borrow from and build on each other. It may not be quite the same as raising a barn or shucking corn, but the sense of collective indebtedness remains. This book owes much to what others have written. This is not to say that it agrees with what other historians have said; in many instances, it does not. Still, I am much in their debt.

At the same time, the literature of the trans-Appalachian West is simply too vast to acknowledge everything written in the field or even all that I have read. Where I have drawn directly on articles or monographs, I have cited them. Beyond this direct acknowledgment lies a vast body of material that is impossible to list in its entirety. Most of the fourteen states considered here have multivolume, multiauthored state histories. Some date from the 1920's; others are so recent that they are still incomplete. Every state has a single-volume history; most have several, written at regular intervals over the last half century. Each state also has an historical quarterly, and several have more than one. The students of the trans-Appalachian frontier should supplement the articles and documents found therein with other state publications and other series of printed historical materials.

Special note should be taken of the several collections of materials prepared by the Historical Records Survey (HRS), a division of the Works Progress Administration. These range from bibliographies of source materials in local archives and depositories to verbatim transcripts of county and local records (sometimes in translation). Projects in the state of Mississippi, for example, included a county history for each of Mississippi's counties, some running to as many as five volumes. Here and elsewhere, the quality of the work varies, but the Historical Records Survey has made accessible large quantities of historical materials.

Special note should also be taken of the Early State Records on Microfilm

(ERS). Beginning in 1941, the Library of Congress and the University of North Carolina jointly located and microfilmed early state legislative proceedings. After 1945 the project was expanded to include statutory laws; constitutional, administrative, and executive documents; court records; and local records. Eventually the project included more than 2,500,000 pages of records on 160,000 feet of microfilm. See Lillian A. Hamrick, ed., *A Guide to the Microfilm Collections of the Early State Records* (Washington, 1950). The Early State Records used in this study are listed below.

ALABAMA

Journal of the Legislative Council, 1818; Journal of the Senate, 1819–32; Journal of the House of Representatives, 1819–28.

ARKANSAS

Journal of the Legislative Council and the House of Representatives, 1819–40; Laws of the Arkansas Territory, 1835.

FLORIDA

Journal of the Legislative Council, 1822–38; Journal of the Legislative Council and the Senate, 1839–48; Journal of the House of Representatives, 1839–46.

ILLINOIS

Journal of the House of Representatives, 1812; Journal of the Territorial Legislature, 1814–15, 1817–18; Journal of the Legislative Council, 1814–18; Journal of the Senate, 1818–19; Journal of the House of Representatives, 1819.

INDIANA

Journals of the General Assembly of Indiana Territory, 1805–15; Legislative Council Proceedings, 1808, 1811, 1812–13.

MICHIGAN

Governor and Judges, Journal of Proceedings in Their Legislative Capacity, 1805, 1808–10; "Rough Minutes," 1810–12; Journal of the Legislative Council, 1824–35; Some of the Acts of the Territory of Michigan, 1816.

MISSISSIPPI

Journal of the Upper House, 1800–17; Statutes of the Mississippi Territory, 1807; Journal of the Legislative Council, 1815–16, 1817; Journal of the Senate, 1817–18; Unbound notes on 1809–10 session; Journal of the House of Representatives, 1811–12, 1813; Statutes of the Mississippi Territory, 1816.

MISSOURI

Journal of the Proceedings of the Legislature of the Territory of Louisiana, 1806–11; Laws of the Territory of Louisiana, 1808; A Digest of the Laws of Missouri Territory, 1818; Journal of the Proceedings of the Legislature of the Territory of Missouri, 1812–17; Journal of the House of Representatives, 1818–19.

OHIO

Journal of the Governors and Judges, 1795; Journal of the House, 1795–1801; Journal of the Legislative Council, 1800–01; Laws of the United States North-West of the Ohio, 1796.

WISCONSIN

Journal of the Council, 1836–42; Journal of the House of Representatives, 1836–44; Statutes of the Territory of Wisconsin, 1839.

MANUSCRIPTS

The manuscript collections covering the trans-Appalachian frontier are extensive and found in several depositories. I have listed here those that I found most useful. Some are cited in the footnotes of this study; others are not.

ALABAMA

Alabama Department of Archives and History (ADAH), Montgomery
Matthew Blue Papers; William H. Cather Collection, especially "A Brief Historical Sketch of St. Clair County"; John H. Evans, "Reminiscences of Olden Times, 1809–1850"; Eliza Chotard Gould, "Autobiography"; Thomas C. Law, "Journal of Travel to the Western Counties—from September 2ᵈ 1834," and Letter to Capt. William Law, Sept. 20, 1834; William T. Lewis, "The Centennial History of Winston County"; T. N. Martin, "Historical Sketch of Chickasaw County"; Alexander B. Meek Collection; Israel Pickens Papers; A. C. Ramsey, "A Sketch of the Life and Times of Rev. A. C. Ramsey . . ."; Charles Tait and Family Papers; John Williams Walker Papers.

ADAH has a large collection of court records for Alabama counties. Note especially the following: Benton County: Court Records, 1833–53. Bibb County: Minutes, 1818–37; Record of the Superior Court, 1819–; Orphans Court, Minutes, 1818; Administrator's Account, 1821–31. Chambers County: Miscellaneous Probate Court Records, 1836–76. Madison County: Orphans Court, Minutes, 1810–19; Superior Court of Law and Equity, 1810–12; Superior Court, Appearance Docket, 1811–16; Superior Court of Law and Equity, 1811–19. Montgomery County: Commissioners Court, Transcript Minutes, 1817–45; Orphans Court, Minutes, 1817–23; Probate Court, 1820–52. Perry County: Commissioners Court, Minutes, 1820–32. Sumter County: Commissioners Court, Minutes, 1833–36. Talladega County: Execution Dockets, 1833–; Fee Books, 1837–43; Circuit Court, Records, Appearance Docket, 1833–39; Subpoena Dockets, 1833–38; Trial Dockets, 1833–38; Commissioners Court, 1833–48; Estray Book, 1833. Tallapoosa County: Commissioners Court, Minutes, 1836–46. Washington County: Superior Court, 1802–11.

ARKANSAS

Arkansas History Commission (AHC), Little Rock
Arkansas County, Abstract of Records of the Probate Court; Myra McAlmont Vaughan Collection, especially a copy of the Notary Public Records kept by

André Fagot at Arkansas Post, 1809–12, "Early Reminiscences by an Early Settler of Clark County," and "Extracts from Reminiscences by John R. Homer Scott"; "Diary of Maria Watkins: Journey of Shelbyville to Little Rock, 1820–27."

DISTRICT OF COLUMBIA
Manuscript Division, Library of Congress, Washington, D.C.
Northwest Territory, Miscellaneous Documents; Thomas Rodney Papers; J.N.T., "Settlements on the Mississippi, April 1776"; West Florida Papers, 1799–1827.

FLORIDA
P. K. Yonge Library of Florida History (PKY), University of Florida, Gainesville
George Colee Correspondence; T. Frederick Davis Papers; James David Glunt Papers, especially John Faulk Correspondence and Horatio S. Dexter Correspondence; Hillsborough County, Record Book, 1837–39; David Yancey Thomas, "A History of Banking in Florida."
    Several WPA transcripts (HRS) are useful: City of St. Augustine Ordinances Also Minutes, Vol. I, July 13, 1821–March 7, 1831; Dade County, Election Report 1843; Fernandina; History of Madison County; Jefferson County, 1827–1910; Madison County, County Commissioners Proceedings and Mortgage Book "A"; Monroe County, Short History of Monroe County; Narrative of a Voyage to the Spanish Main in the Ship 'Two Friends'; Santa Rosa County.

ILLINOIS
Chicago Historical Society (CHS), Chicago
Cyrus Aldrich Collection; Benjamin F. Barker Collection; Samuel Burton Collection; Edward Coles Papers; Ninian Edwards Papers; John Estabrooks Collection; O. L. Ingraham Collection; Elias Kent Kane Collection; Griswold C. Morgan Collection; Cecil C. Moss, "Reminiscences"; Morris Sleight Papers.

Illinois Historical Survey (IHS-U), University of Illinois Library, Urbana
Bloxham Letters; Edward Coles Letters; Stephen Eames, Bascom Letters; Ninian Edwards Papers; Williams-Woodbury Collection.

Illinois State Historical Library (ISHL), Springfield
Sarah Aiken Letter; Sidney Breese Papers; Daniel Brush, "Autobiographical Memoir, 1813–1861"; Carlyle Circuit, Day Book 1836, Journals 1836–37, 1840–42; Greene County, Poor Book, 1824–26; William Hempstead Letters; Elijah Iles, Account Books; "Illinois Women"; Jefferson County, Commissioners Court, 1819; P. N. Lewis and John Limkins, "Sketch of the Early Days of Naples"; Laura A. McKee, Diary, 1837–48; Richard Lee Mason, "Journey from Philadelphia to Illinois and Missouri, 1819"; "Memoranda on the Road," by a Gentleman of Maryland; John Messinger Papers; North Stonington Colony; John Phelps, "Reminiscences"; Harry Riggin Family Papers; John Russell Family Papers; Sangamon County, Commissioners Court, Record Book A, 1821–26; Shale Creek Baptist Church, Bond County, Minutes, 1818–45; Elihu Springer,

Letters 1834–59, Diary 1840–43; James W. Stephenson Papers; Daniel Weed Collection; William Wilson Papers; James B. Woollard Papers.

INDIANA

Indiana Historical Society (IHS), Indianapolis
Charles Alling, "Early Settlers on Upper Big Creek"; John Arnold, "Early History of Rush County Courts"; William H. English Collection; John G. Finch, "Reminiscences"; Nathan D. Gallion Papers; John Kennedy Graham, Diary, 1825–26; John Ingle Papers; Charles K. Laird, Diary, 1820; Nicholas McCarty, Day Book, 1826–27; Ira Meater, "Early Reminiscences of Parke Co."; Erastus Nevins, "Reminiscences"; Hosea Smith Letters, 1810–14; John Test, "Reminiscences"; Samuel Vance Papers; Samuel Williams Letters.

Indiana State Library (ISL), Indianapolis
T. V. Denny Letters; Barton Griffiths Correspondence; Joseph Hayes, "Life"; Edmund O. Hovey Correspondence; John Humphries Letter to Samuel Blackwood, 1836; "The Pioneers of Jefferson County—Reminiscences of James B. Lewis, Esq."; Little Pigeon Creek Baptist Church, Minute Book, 1816–40; William McCutcheon Letters; "A History of Thomas Morrison"; Peter Pressey Letters; Archibald Shaw, "Autobiography"; O. William Sickels Letter to Daniel Gold, 1828; John Vawter, "Early History of Madison."

IOWA

State Historical Society of Iowa (SHSI), Iowa City
Ebenezer Alden Letters; Thomas Cary Collection; William Duncan Letters, 1837; Samuel Goodnow Letter, 1837; Peril Columbus Haynes Family Letters; David Olmstead Letters.

KENTUCKY

Margaret I. King Library (MIK), University of Kentucky, Lexington
Bourbon County: Wills, vols. A-B, 1786–1805; Order Book, 1786–93. Jefferson County: Court Orders, Minute Book A, 1780–83; Minute Book #1, 1784–85. Mercer County: Circuit Court, Judgements (Suits), 1780–1801; County Court, Marriage Bonds, 1786–94; Deed Books; Will Books; County Court, Order Books.

LOUISIANA

Department of Archives, Louisiana State University Library (LSU), Baton Rouge
Bensen Family Papers; Richard Butler Collection; John P. Combs Ledger; Concordia Parish Collections, 1794–1896; J. Fair Hardin Collection; David Mills Letter, 1818; Natchitoches Parish Collection; Thomas C. Nicholls, "Reminiscences"; Opelousas District Papers; William T. Palfrey Papers; Thomas Bolling Robertson Letters, Walter Prichard Collection; St. Helena Parish Records; Alonzo Snyder Papers; James Sterrett Letters, 1802–10; Nathaniel Evans and Family Papers, Merritt M. Shilg Memorial Collection; Zachariah Taliaferro, "Catahoula Parish."

The following police jury minutes are also useful: Avoyelles Parish, 1821–88;

East Feliciana Parish, 1818–22; Lafayette Parish, 1823–57 (typewritten); Point Coupeé Parish, 1829–40 (in French); St. Charles Parish, 1811–17 (typewritten in French); St. Helena Parish, 1813 (typewritten); St. Landry Parish, 1811–19 (hand transcribed); Terrebonne Parish, 1822–47.

New Orleans Public Library, New Orleans
Ordinances and Resolutions of the City Council of New Orleans, 1805–15; Transcripts of the Cabildo Records, 1769–1803.

MICHIGAN
Michigan Historical Collections (MHC), Bentley Historical Library, University of Michigan, Ann Arbor
John Allen Family Letters; Berrien County, Niles Township, Commissioner of Highways, 1839; Kingsley Scott Bingham Papers; Chauncy Bird Collection; William Boyd Family Papers; Ebenezer Laken Brown, "The Beginning of Schoolcraft"; John Bryan Letter; Richard A. Bury, Diary, 1853; Carter Collection; Elizabeth Margaret Chandler Papers; Clinton Baptist Church, Records, 1832–42; Clinton Presbyterian Church, Records, 1834–; David Mack Cooper, Scrapbook, 1812; John Cooper Papers; Philip Cumings, Diary; Lorenzo Davis Collection; Dennis Family Papers; Sophia Perrin Fellows, "Reminiscences"; W. Forbes Collection; Charles Foster, Diary, 1836–39; James Fraser Letters; Morell Goodrich, "Reminiscences"; Lovira Hart Collections; Clarissa Hayes Letters; Augustus S. Johnson, "Autobiography"; Munnis Kenny, Diary, 1828; Livingston County, Tuscola Township, Records of Township Meetings, 1838–; Marshall Congregational Church, Minutes, 1832–; Ezra Maynard Letters; Navarre Family Records; Oakland County, Journal of the Board of Supervisors, 1827–44; "Recollections and Reminiscences of Early Life on Lake Superior"; St. Joseph's Presbytery, Records, 1834–46; William Schlatter, Diary, 1851–52; Shaiwassee Baptist Missionary Board, Records, 1840; Cornelius G. Shaw, Diary, 1847–48; Thaddeus Smith, Record of Serving Summons and Subpoenas, 1834–36; William W. Spaulding, Diary, 1844; William Watts Letters; O. Wilder, Journal; Ypsilanti Township, Highway Commissioners 1827–31, Township Meetings 1828–33.

HRS: History of Genessee County; Macomb County, Board of Supervisors, Records, 1827–32; Ottawa County, Board of Supervisors, Records, Vol. A., 1839–; St. Clair County, Supervisors, Record, 1833–34

William L. Clements Library, University of Michigan, Ann Arbor
Lucius Lyon Papers, 1822–33; Southwest Territory Papers; Christopher Van Deventer Papers.

MISSISSIPPI
Mississippi Department of Archives and History, Jackson
WPA Historical Project (HRS), County histories of De Soto, Grenada, Jackson, Lowndes, and Pontotoc.

MISSOURI

State Historical Society of Missouri, University of Missouri Library, Columbia
Cape Girardeau, Court of Common Pleas, 1809; T. Frisel & Co., Jackson, Journal, 1818; Abiel Leonard Papers; St. Charles, Miscellaneous Papers, 1801–31; St. Charles District, Grand Jury Papers 1811, Tax Lists 1805; Ste. Genevieve Academy, Records, 1807–12; John Sappington Collection; Thomas A. Smith Papers.

OHIO

Ohio Historical Society (OHS), Columbus
Rosvelt Caulkins Letter, 1810; Jesup N. Couch, Diary, 1804–05; Walter Curtis, "Narrative"; John C. Deems, "Autobiography"; William Fitch Papers; Anna Strong Gillett, "A Memoir"; Charles Hammond Papers; John Harris, "Brief History of Stark County, 1806–"; Edward C. Lamson Collection; Jared Mansfield Papers; "Memorandum Book, 1805–10"; Charles E. Rice Collection; Edward J. Smith Letter, 1804; Tallmadge Stagecoach Records, 1816–36.

TENNESSEE

McClung Historical Collection (McHC), Lawson-McGhee Library, Knoxville
William Blount Papers; Hamilton District Court Papers; William B. Lenoir Papers; Charles McClung Papers.

Tennessee Historical Society, Nashville
H. Denison Letter, 1800, Miscellaneous Collections.

Tennessee State Library and Archives (TSLA), Nashville
Joseph Bartholomew Correspondence; Isaac Conger, Diary; Fergusson Family Papers; John Hutchins, "Memoirs"; Lawrence Family Papers; Levi Lee, Diary, 1813–31; Martha Philips Martin, "Memoirs," McIver Family Collection; Mill Creek Baptist Church, Minutes, 1797–; Miscellaneous Collections; John S. Russwurm Papers; Mary Smith, "Memoir"; Michael Woods Trimble, "Memoirs, 1788–1860."

University of Tennessee Library (UT), Knoxville
William B. Lenoir Papers, Special Collections; transcriptions of the following court records: Blount County: Court Records, Book 1, 1795–1804. Carroll County: County Court, Minute Books, 1826–33. Davidson County: Minute Book A, 1783–91. Jackson County: Ranger Book, 1817–60. Knox County: Superior Court, Minute Book 1, 1793–1808. Madison County: Circuit Court, Minute Book No. I, 1821–28. Tennessee Superior Court (Mero District): Pleas, 1803–05. Washington County: Superior Court Minutes, Vol. 1, 1791–1804. Weakley County: First Minute Book, 1827–35; Grant Book, 1794–1844. White County: Minutes of County Court, 1806–11.

WISCONSIN

State Historical Society of Wisconsin (SHSW), Madison
Harvey Brown, "Historical Record of the Brown Family from New York to Buffalo County, Wisconsin"; Johann Diefenthaeler Letter, 1844; Lyman C.

Draper Collections; Mrs. M. F. Fishburn, "Reminiscences of Pioneer Life in Eastern Iowa," 1845; Timothy Flint Letters to Abel Flint, 1815–22; David Giddings Papers; Josiah Harmar Letter to Henry Knox, 1787; Hugh Heward, "Journal of a Voyage, 1790"; Emmor Hickman Letter to William Sharpless, 1845; James C. Howard Papers; Morgan Jones, Diary, 1793; John Kerr, Journal, 1800; Mrs. Robert Murray, "From Boston to Wisconsin in 1838"; George W. Ogden, Diary, 1837–41; Martin Packman Letters; Sarah Pratt, Diary, 1844–47; Horace Rublee, "Reminiscences"; Emma Sprague Letter, 1842; "Benjamin Vancleve's Biographical Memoir from 1773."

NEWSPAPERS

This is a list of newspapers most useful for this study. It includes a few newspapers in more settled areas for purposes of contrast. Many of these runs are broken, and I have not listed newspapers with only two or three issues, such as those found in the miscellaneous collections (by state) in the Library of Congress. Where there are major changes in title or in place of publication, I have included separate listings.

ALABAMA

Blakeley *Sun*, 1818–19; Cahaba *Alabama Watchman*, 1820; Cahaba *Press and Alabama State Intelligencer*, 1821; Huntsville *Alabama Republican*, 1819–21; Huntsville *Southern Advocate*, 1834–37; Jacksonville *Republican*, 1837–39; St. Stephens *Halcyon and Tombeckbee Public Advertiser*, 1819–21; Selma *Courier*, 1827–29.

ARKANSAS

Arkansas Post *Arkansas Gazette*, 1819–21; Batesville *News*, 1840–43; Helena *Constitutional Journal*, 1836–37; Helena *Spy*, 1838; Little Rock *Arkansas Advocate*, 1830–37; Little Rock *Arkansas Gazette*, 1821–37; Little Rock *Times*, 1835–36.

FLORIDA

Jacksonville *Courier*, 1835–36; Key West *Enquirer*, 1834–36; Key West *Gazette*, 1831–32; Key West *Register and Commercial Advertiser*, 1829; Magnolia *Advertiser*, 1828–30; Pensacola *Floridian*, 1821–22, 1823; Pensacola *Gazette*, 1824–30, 1833, 1836–45; St. Augustine *East Florida Herald*, 1823–26; St. Augustine *Florida Gazette*, 1821; St. Augustine *Florida Herald*, 1829–30, 1832–45; St. Joseph *Times*, 1839–40; Tallahassee *Florida Advocate*, 1828–29; Tallahassee *Florida Intelligencer*, 1826; Tallahassee *Floridian and Advocate*, 1829–41.

ILLINOIS

Alton *Spectator*, 1832–34; Chicago *American*, 1835–37; Chicago *Democrat*, 1833–36; Edwardsville *Spectator*, 1819–20; Galena *Advertiser*, 1829–30; Galena *Miner's Journal*, 1828–29; *Galenian*, 1832–33; Kaskaskia *Illinois Herald*, 1814; Kaskaskia *Western Intelligencer*, 1816–19; Peoria *Register and North-western Gazetteer*, 1837–39; Springfield *Sangamo-Journal*, 1831–35; Vandalia *Illinois Intelligencer*, 1822–23.

INDIANA

Brookville *Enquirer*, 1819–25; Corydon *Indiana Gazette*, 1819–24; Evansville *Gazette*, 1822–25; Indianapolis *Indiana Journal*, 1825–30; Logansport *Potawattomie & Miami Times*, 1829–31; Richmond *Public Ledger*, 1824–25; Salem *Western Annotator*, 1829–31; South Bend *Northwestern Pioneer and St. Joseph's Intelligencer*, 1831–32; Vevay *Indiana Register*, 1824–25; Vincennes *Indiana Gazette*, 1804–05; Vincennes *Western Sun*, 1807–16.

IOWA

Bloomington *Herald*, 1840–42; Burlington *Hawkeye and Iowa Patriot*, 1841–43; Burlington *Herald*, 1840–43; Burlington (Wisconsin Territory) *Wisconsin Territorial Gazette*, 1837–39; Davenport *Iowa Sun and Davenport & Rock Island News*, 1838, Dubuque *Iowa News*, 1837–39; Dubuque *Visitor*, 1836; Fort Madison *Patriot*, 1838; Iowa City *Iowa Capitol Reporter*, 1841–45; Iowa City *Iowa Standard*, 1842–44.

KENTUCKY

Lexington *Kentucky Gazette*, 1787–98.

LOUISIANA

Alexandria *Louisiana Herald*, 1820–25; Baton Rouge *Gazette*, 1821–23; Baton Rouge *Republic*, 1822–23; New Orleans *Louisiana Gazette*, 1804–12; New Orleans *Moniteur de la Louisiane*, 1802–03; St. Francisville *Asylum*, 1821–25; St. Francisville *Louisiana Journal*, 1825–26; St. Francisville *Louisianian*, 1819–20.

MICHIGAN

Adrian *Michigan Whig*, 1838–40; Ann Arbor *Michigan Argus*, 1835–37; Ann Arbor *State Journal*, 1835–37; Ann Arbor *Western Emigrant*, 1830; Brighton *Livingston Courier*, 1843–46; Copper Harbor *Lake Superior and Miners Journal*, 1846–49; Detroit *Gazette*, 1817–26; Grand Rapids *Grand River Eagle*, 1847–48; Jonesville *Expositor*, 1840–43; Marshall *Western Statesman*, 1839–41; Monroe *Michigan Sentinel*, 1825–30, 1834–36; Monroe *Times*, 1836–37; Niles *Intelligencer*, 1838; White Pigeon *Michigan Statesman*, 1835.

MISSISSIPPI

Benton *Yazoo Banner*, 1838–40; Clinton *Gazette*, 1835–37; Columbus *Democrat*, 1837; Columbus *Southern Argus*, 1835; Grenada *Grenadian*, 1838; Grenada *Southern Reporter*, 1839; Hernando *Free Press*, 1839; Holly Springs *Marshall County Republican*, 1839; Holly Springs *Southern Banner*, 1839–41; Jackson *Mississippian*, 1834–37; Kosciusko *Central Register*, 1839–40; Lexington *Standard*, 1838; Lexington *Union*, 1838–40; Liberty *Piney Woods Planter*, 1838; Macon *Intelligencer*, 1838; Monticello *Gazette*, 1833; Monticello *Pearl River Advocate and Eastern Advertiser*, 1830; Natchez *Chronicle*, 1808–11; Natchez *Mississippi Herald*, 1803–04; Natchez *Mississippi Herald & Natchez Gazette*, 1804–07; Natchez *Mississippi Messenger*, 1807; Natchez *Mississippian*, 1808–10; Pontotoc *Chickasaw Union*, 1836–38; Port Gibson *Correspondent*, 1819–25; Raymond *Times*, 1837–40; Ripley *Transcript*, 1838; Yazoo City *Whig and Political Register*, 1839–40.

MISSOURI

Boonville *Western Emigrant*, 1839–40; Fayette *Missouri Intelligencer*, 1829; Fayette *Western Monitor*, 1829–30; Franklin *Missouri Intelligencer*, 1819–26; Jackson *Independent Patriot*, 1820–26; Jackson *Missouri Herald*, 1819–20; Kansas City *Enterprise*, 1855–57; St. Charles *Missourian*, 1820–22; St. Louis *Missouri Gazette*, 1808–21; St. Louis *Missouri Republican*, 1822–28.

OHIO

Chillicothe *Scioto Gazette*, 1800–11; Cincinnati *Centinel of the North-western Territory*, 1793–95; Cleveland *Gazette and Commercial Register*, 1818–20; Cleveland *Herald*, 1819–23; Columbus *Gazette*, 1817–18; Columbus *Western Intelligencer*, 1814–17; Hamilton *Miami Intelligencer*, 1814–16; Maumee *Express*, 1837–39; Steubenville *Western Herald*, 1806–08; Worthington *Western Intelligencer*, 1811–13; Zanesville *Express and Republican Standard*, 1813–16.

PENNSYLVANIA

Pittsburgh *Gazette*, 1786–97.

TENNESSEE

Knoxville *Gazette*, 1792–1803; Nashville *Tennessee Gazette*, 1800–07.

WISCONSIN

Green Bay *Intelligencer*, 1833–36; Milwaukee *Advertiser*, 1836–37.

UNPUBLISHED THESES, DISSERTATIONS, AND OTHER PAPERS

I owe an enormous intellectual debt to the authors of unpublished studies about the trans-Appalachian frontier. Each of these titles represents a major piece of work for the author, and most of them continue to reside unread and uncited on library shelves. Many I have cited in footnotes; some I have not. I hope that this list will, at least partially, discharge my obligations to these scholars and, at the same time, bring to light however briefly these useful studies of varying aspects of life in the trans-Appalachian West.

UNIVERSITY OF ALABAMA

Akens, David Strode. "Clarke County to 1860," M.A., 1956.

Bassett, Ariel Darvel. "A Social and Economic History of Kemper County, Mississippi in the AnteBellum Period," M.A., 1947.

Boozer, Jack Dwight. "Jacksonville, Alabama, 1833–1846," M.A., 1951.

Bragg, James William. "Frontier Entrepreneurs of Madison County, Alabama: The Bell Factory Enterprise, 1819–1842," M.A., 1958.

Cochran, John Perry. "James Asbury Tait and His Plantations," M.A., 1951.

Cooke, Leonard Calvert. "The Development of the Road System of Alabama," M.A., 1935.

Elliott, James E. "A History of Methodism in Western Alabama, 1819–1870," M.A., 1947.

Johnson, Dewey Maurice. "History of Coffee County, Alabama, 1840–1871," M.A., 1947.

Kamper, Anna Alice. "A Social and Economic History of Ante-Bellum Bolivar County, Mississippi," M.A., 1942.

Kelly, Samuel Bledsoe. "The Establishment of Local Government in Alabama," M.A., 1927.

Mason, Mary Glenn. "The Ante-Bellum History of Limestone County, Alabama," M.A., 1949.

Reynolds, Marylee. "A Social and Economic History of Sumter County, Alabama, in the Antebellum Period," M.A., 1953.

Roberts, Frances Cabaniss. "Background and Formative Period in the Great Bend and Madison County," Ph.D., 1956.

Watkins, Esther Belle. "Some Social and Economic Aspects of Ante-Bellum Neshoba County, Mississippi," M.A., 1942.

BALL STATE UNIVERSITY

Brady, Francis X. "W. G. and G. W. Ewing, Pioneer Mercantile Capitalists," Ed.D., 1965.

Hodges, Malcolm Maurice. "A Social History of Vincennes and Knox County, Indiana, from the Beginning to 1860," Ed.D., 1968.

BUTLER UNIVERSITY

Tobey, Jeanette. "Economic Life in Indiana, 1800–1816," M.A., 1948.

CASE–WESTERN RESERVE UNIVERSITY

Davidson, Kenneth E. "Forgotten Ohioian: Elijah Whittlesey, 1783–1863," Ph.D., 1953.

Heald, Edward Thornton. "Bezaleel Wells, Founder of Canton and Steubenville, Ohio," M.A., 1942.

UNIVERSITY OF CHICAGO

Attig, Chester Jacob. "The Institutional History of the Northwestern Territory, 1787–1802," Ph.D., 1921.

Galvin, Sister Eucharista. "The Influences and Conditions Affecting the Settlement of Minnesota, 1837–1860," Ph.D., 1929.

Harr, John Lauren. "The Ante-Bellum Southwest, 1815–1861," Ph.D., 1941.

DUKE UNIVERSITY

Hamilton, William Baskerville. "American Beginnings in the Old Southwest: The Mississippi Phase," Ph.D., 1937.

UNIVERSITY OF FLORIDA

Jones, Robert E. "The Methodist Circuit Rider in Territorial East Florida," M.A., 1952.

Lewis, Frank G. "A History of Education in St. Augustine, Florida, during the Territorial Period, 1821–1845," M.A., 1950.

Osbourn, Sandra Shaw. "Women in the Ohio Valley Frontier Culture," M.A., 1963.
Waite, Mariella Davidson. "Political Institutions in the Trans-Appalachian West, 1770–1800," Ph.D., 1961.

FLORIDA STATE UNIVERSITY
Bittle, George Cassel. "In the Defense of Florida: The Organized Florida Militia from 1821–1920," Ph.D., 1965.
Owens, Harry P. "Apalachicola before 1861," Ph.D., 1966.

GEORGE PEABODY COLLEGE
Holt, Albert C. "The Economic and Social Beginnings of Tennessee," Ph.D., 1923.

HARVARD UNIVERSITY
McNulty, John Wesley. "Chief Justice Sidney Breese and the Illinois Supreme Court—A Study of Law and Politics in the Old West," Ph.D., 1961.

UNIVERSITY OF ILLINOIS
Addis, Frank Raymond. "The Early History of Stark County, Illinois," M.A., 1949.
Allison, May. "Conditions in the Illinois Country, 1787–1800," M.A., 1907.
Chapman, Marion Lola. "The Establishment of Methodism in Central Illinois (1824–1840)," M.A., 1929.
Coard, Helen Clara. "The Illinois and Michigan Canal as an Influence on Westward Migration," M.A., 1941.
Harper, Josephine L. "John Reynolds, 'The Old Ranger' of Illinois, 1788–1865," Ph.D., 1949.
Kershaw, Mary Katherine. "Early History of Shawneetown, Illinois, from 1812 to 1832," M.A., 1941.
Mitchell, Ralph Vernon. "The Character of Lawlessness in Illinois to 1860," M.A., 1962.
Paullin, Marjorie Ruth. "New Salem: A Typical Frontier Settlement," M.A., 1942.
Peckous, Edwin John. "The History of Downers Grove, Illinois, from 1832–1873," M.A., 1956.
Pieper, Ezra Henry. "The Settlement of De Kalb, Du Page, Kane, and Kendall Counties to 1850," M.A., 1926.
Ramey, Nell Holland. "History of Early Roads in Illinois," M.A., 1948.
Sandmeyer, Elmer Clarence. "Methodism in Illinois before 1850," M.A., 1924.
Tevebaugh, John Leslie. "Frontier Mail: Illinois, 1800–1830," M.A., 1952.
———. "Merchant on the Western Frontier: William Morrison of Kaskaskia, 1790–1837," Ph.D., 1962.
Wrone, David Royer. "Prairie Press in Transition: The East Central Illinois Newspaper Scene, 1830–1870," Ph.D., 1964.

INDIANA UNIVERSITY

Anson, Bert. "The Fur Traders in Northern Indiana, 1796–1850," Ph.D., 1953.

Carmony, Donald F. "Indiana Public Finance, 1800–1826," Ph.D., 1940.

Coplen, Marion Wallace. "History of Kosciusko County, Indiana, to 1875," M.A., 1944.

Deen, Arthur. "Frontier Science in Kentucky and the Old Northwest, 1790–1860," Ph.D., 1938.

Dragert, Eva Ellen. "Indianapolis: The Culture of an Inland City," Ph.D., 1952.

Gordon, Leon Millard, II. "Transportation Facilities and the Growth of Northern Indiana, 1830–1860," M.A., 1949.

Hewes, Bernard A. "The Rise of the Pork Industry in Indiana," M.A., 1939.

Hisey, Stella J. "Harrison County, 1808–1825," M.A., 1937.

Humphreys, Bertha. "Guide to Early Indiana History," M.A., 1935.

Kuhn, Cecil LeRoy. "The Michigan Road," M.A., 1927.

Lang, Elfrieda W. H. "Immigration to Northern Indiana, 1800–1850," Ph.D., 1950.

Lawlis, Chelsea L. "Settlement and Economic Development of the Whitewater Valley, 1800–1900," Ph.D., 1956.

Mathis, Ray. "History of Brown County," M.A., 1936.

Mauck, Virginia Lowell. "Population Movements in Northern Indiana before 1850," M.A., 1948.

Muncie, Emery O. "A History of Jefferson County," M.A., 1932.

Owen, Mary Steele, "An Analysis of the Frontiersman Based on the Observations of Continental French Travellers," Ph.D., 1954.

Page, Katherine B. "Some Chapters in the Early History of Peoria, Illinois," M.A., 1936.

Prather, Geneal. "The Building of the Michigan Road," M.A., 1941.

Rediger, Lloyd Glenn. "Wilderness Road and the Ohio River, Routes of Emigration, 1783–1820," M.A., 1944.

Steck, Victor. "The Development of Huntington County," M.A., 1940.

Weicker, Jack Edward. "The Growth of Fort Wayne Industry, 1815 to 1860," M.A., 1950.

White, Harlan Scott. "Western Banking: Ideas and Practices before 1840," M.A., 1942.

UNIVERSITY OF IOWA

Boeck, George A. "An Early Iowa Community: Aspects of the Economic, Social and Political Development in Burlington, Iowa, 1833–1866," Ph.D., 1961.

Browning, Julia Anne. "The Frontier Settlements of the Early Thirties," M.A., 1933.

Erickson, Erling Arthur. "Banks and Politics before the Civil War: The Case of Iowa, 1836–1861," Ph.D., 1967.

Fleck, Byron Y. "The West as Viewed by Foreign Travellers, 1783–1840," Ph.D., 1950.

Green, Michael David. "Federal-State Conflict over the Administration of Indian Policy: Georgia, Alabama, and the Creeks, 1824–1834," Ph.D., 1973.

Haefner, John Henry. "The West as Seen through Frontier Biography," Ph.D., 1942.

Harris, Faye Erma. "A Frontier Community: The Economic, Social, and Political Development of Keokuk, Iowa from 1820 to 1866," Ph.D., 1965.

Horton, Loren Nelson. "Roman Catholic Institutions and Their Influence in Early Dubuque," 1970, unpublished paper in possession of the author.

Jones, Pamelia Pearl. "Social Life in Territorial Iowa," M.A., 1908.

Kinnett, David George. "Locating in the Garden of the World: The Prairie Factor, 1830–1860," 1973, unpublished paper in possession of the author.

O'Brien, Thomas B. "The Frontier of Settlement in 1850," M.A., 1935.

Pyle, Perry E. "Outlawry in Early Iowa," M.A., 1940.

Sener, William E. F. "The Frontier Life of 1840," M.A., 1938.

Shepherd, Helen Evans. "Social Origins of Cedar Rapids, Iowa, 1838–1861," M.A., 1947.

Swierenga, Robert Peter. "Pioneers and Profits: Land Speculation on the Iowa Frontier," Ph.D., 1965.

Throne, Mildred. "A History of Agriculture in Southern Iowa, 1830–1890," Ph.D., 1946.

Wunder, John Remley. "The Mississippi Territory's First Experience with American Legal Institutions: Sargent's Code, Its Adoption and Abolition, 1798–1803," M.A., 1970.

KENT STATE UNIVERSITY

Woehrmann, John Paul. "Ft. Wayne, Indiana Territory, 1794–1819: A Study of a Frontier Post," Ph.D., 1967.

UNIVERSITY OF KENTUCKY

Allen, Samuel Elwood, Jr. "Observations of Travellers in Kentucky, 1750–1850," M.A., 1950.

Beasley, Paul W. "The Life and Times of Isaac Shelby, 1750–1826," Ph.D., 1968.

Clay, William Wilson Hume. "Fleming County, Kentucky, 1773–1860," M.A., 1963.

Eagle, Delbert P. "Aspects of the Kentucky Frontier," M.A., 1938.

Howard, Hugh Asher. "Chapters in the Economic History of Knox County, Kentucky," M.A., 1937.

Royalty, Dale Maurice. "Banking, Politics, and the Commonwealth, Kentucky, 1800–1825," Ph.D., 1971.

Smith, Leland. "A History of the Tobacco Industry in Kentucky from 1783 to 1860," M.A., 1950.

Tachau, Mary K. Bonsteel. "The Federal Courts in Kentucky, 1789–1816," Ph.D., 1972.

Thacker, Joseph Allen, Jr. "The Kentucky Militia from 1792 to 1812," M.A., 1954.

LOUISIANA STATE UNIVERSITY
Brister, Elaine Holmes. "A History of Pineville, Louisiana," M.A., 1948.
Gillson, Gordon E. "The Development of a Military Frontier: The Story of Fort Adams and Its Hinterland," M.A., 1954.
Hair, Velma Lea. "History of Crowley, Louisiana," M.A., 1941.
Heidelberg, Nell Angela. "The Frontier in Mississippi," M.A., 1940.
Higginbotham, Sanford W. "Frontier Democracy in the Early Courts of Tennessee and Kentucky, 1772–1799," M.A., 1941.
Knipmeyer, William B. "Settlement Succession in Eastern French Louisiana," Ph.D., 1956.
Mason, John Bradley. "Early Immigration to Arkansas," M.A., 1942.
Miller, Marshall Stone, Jr. "The History of Fort Claiborne, Louisiana, 1804–1822," M.A., 1969.
Morazan, Ronald R. "A Translation of the Letters, Petitions, and Decrees of the Cabildo of New Orleans for the Year 1800," M.A., 1969.
Odom, Eunice Maxwell. "The Frontier in the Arkansas River Valley," M.A., 1938.
Phillips, Yvonne. "Settlement Succession in the Tensas Basin," Ph.D., 1952.
Suarez, Raleigh A., Jr. "Aspects of the Social History of Iberville Parish, 1850–1860," M.A., 1948.
Walker, David Allan. "A History of Commerce and Navigation on the Lower Mississippi," M.A., 1965.
White, Alice P. "Plantation Experiences of Joseph and Lavinia Erwin, 1807–1836," M.A., 1933.

UNIVERSITY OF MICHIGAN
Boertman, C. Steward. "The Sequence of Human Occupation in Wayne County, Kentucky; An Historical Study," Ph.D., 1934.
Davis, James Edward. "Demographic Characteristics of the American Frontier, 1800–1840," Ph.D., 1971.
George, Milton C. "The Settlement of the Connecticut Western Reserve of Ohio," Ph.D., 1950.
Kaatz, Martin R. "The Settlement of the Black Swamp of Northwestern Ohio," Ph.D., 1952.
Neithercut, Mark E. "The Development of the Portage Lake Mining District," B.A. (honors), 1974; copy in MHC.
Odle, Thomas D. "The American Grain Trade of the Great Lakes, 1825–1873," Ph.D., 1951.
Shirigian, John. "Lucius Lyon: His Place in Michigan History," Ph.D., 1960.

UNIVERSITY OF MISSISSIPPI
Bolton, Reuben Leon. "History of Prentiss County," M.A., 1935.
Boman, Martha. "A Social History of Jackson, Mississippi: 1821–1861, State Capital in the Old South," M.A., 1952.
Cameron, Mary Effie. "The Summer of 1835 in Mississippi History," M.A., 1931.

Fowler, Lula Mae. "History of Panola County, 1836–1860," M.A., 1960.

Hearn, Walter Carey. "Towns in Antebellum Mississippi," Ph.D., 1969.

Holder, Ray, ed. "The Autobiography of William Winans," M.A., 1936.

James, Newton Haskin, ed. "The Journal of Josiah Hinds, April 24, 1839–July 10, 1863," M.A., 1939.

McMillan, Edward Lee. "A Social and Economic History of Kosciusko, Mississippi," M.A., 1951.

Ramsey, Jack Davison. "New County Representation in Mississippi from 1830 to 1840," M.A., 1931.

Sabakka, Clement John. "A History of Lafayette County, Mississippi," M.A., 1973.

Stamphy, Herbert Glenn. "The Academy Movement in Mississippi during the Nineteenth Century," M.A., 1950.

Summers, Mary Floyd. "Tishomingo County, 1836–1860," M.A., 1957.

UNIVERSITY OF MISSOURI

Anderson, Hattie Mabel. "A Study of Frontier Democracy: The Social and Economic Bases of the Rise of the Jacksonian Group in Missouri, 1815–1828," Ph.D., 1935.

Dugger, Harold H. "Reading Interests and the Book Trade in Frontier Missouri," Ph.D., 1951.

English, William F. "The Pioneer Lawyer and Jurist in Missouri," Ph.D., 1943.

Foley, William E. "Territorial Politics in Frontier Missouri, 1804–1820," Ph.D., 1967.

Harris, James Griffith. "The Justice of the Peace in Missiouri, 1800–1845," M.A., 1948.

Hill, Leslie G. "The Pioneer Preacher in Missouri," M.A., 1948.

Kennedy, Mary Alice. "Business Career of Moses U. Payne, 1828–1870," M.A., 1944.

Lewis, Donald F. "Economic and Social Life in the French Villages in Missouri," M.A., 1936.

Ronnebaum, Sister Cheledonia. "Population and Settlement in Missouri, 1804–1820," M.A., 1936.

Scroggins, Albert Taylor, Jr. "Nathaniel Patton, Jr., and the *Missouri Intelligencer and Boon's Lick Advertiser*," Ph.D., 1961.

Swartzlow, Ruby Johnson. "The Early History of Lead Mining in Missouri," M.A., 1933.

Utz, Cornelius. "Life in Missouri, 1800–1840, as Pictured in Travellers' Accounts, Letters and Journals," M.A., 1933.

Westover, John Glendower. "The Evolution of the Missouri Militia, 1804–1919," Ph.D., 1948.

UNIVERSITY OF NEBRASKA

Beck, Paul Louis. "Daniel Drake and the Interior Valley," Ph.D., 1961.

UNIVERSITY OF NORTH CAROLINA
Moore, Waddy William. "Territorial Arkansas, 1819–1836," Ph.D., 1962.

OHIO STATE UNIVERSITY
Cramer, Clarence H. "The Career of Duncan McArthur," Ph.D., 1931.
Gordon, Francis Marion. "Early History of Hocking County," M.A., 1940.
Hansen, Ann H. "James Kilbourne, Ohio Pioneer," M.A., 1950.
Pitzer, Donald E. "Professional Revivalism in Nineteenth Century Ohio," Ph.D., 1966.
Still, John S. "The Life of Ethan Allen Brown," Ph.D., 1951.

PRINCETON UNIVERSITY
Gaver, James M. "The Boonesborough Experience: Revolution in the 'Dark and Bloody Ground,' " B.A., 1964.

UNIVERSITY OF TENNESSEE
Brandon, Helen Gould. "A History of Steward County, Tennessee," M.A., 1944.
Carmichael, Claudia J. "A History of Weakley County, Tennessee, through 1861," M.A., 1970.
Counce, Paul Atkins. "Social and Economic History of Kingsport before 1908," M.A., 1939.
Davidson, Elizabeth Huey. "The Life of William Blount," M.A., 1928.
Fink, Miriam. "Social and Economic History of Jonesboro, Tennessee, prior to the Civil War," M.A., 1934.
Gauding, Henry Hendricks. "Water Transportation in East Tennessee prior to the Civil War," M.A., 1933.
Ledford, Allen James. "Methodism in Tennessee, 1783–1866," M.A., 1941.
Merritt, Frank. "Selected Aspects of Early Carter County History, 1760–1861," M.A., 1950.
Rogers, William Flinn. "Life on the Kentucky-Tennessee Frontier near the End of the 18th Century," M.A., 1925.
Seeber, Raymond Clifford. "A History of Anderson County, Tennessee," M.A., 1928.
Slay, James Linwood. "A History of Bradley County, Tennessee, to 1801," M.A., 1967.

UNIVERSITY OF TEXAS
Walker, William A., Jr. "Tennessee, 1796–1821," Ph.D., 1959.

TULANE UNIVERSITY
Ferguson, John Lewis. "William E. Woodruff and the Territory of Arkansas, 1819–1836," Ph.D., 1960.

VANDERBILT UNIVERSITY

Applewhite, Joseph Davis. "Early Trade and Navigation on the Cumberland River," M.A., 1940.

Barbee, John D. "Navigation and River Improvement in Middle Tennessee," M.A., 1934.

Browning, Howard Miller. "Washington County Court: The Government of a Tennessee Frontier Community, 1778–1790," M.A., 1938.

Bryant, Gladys Eugenia. "Daniel Smith, Citizen of Tennessee Frontier," M.A., 1961.

Chappell, Gordon T. "The Life and Activities of John Coffee," Ph.D., 1941.

Cooke, John White. "Isaac Shelby, 1750–1796," M.A., 1959.

Des Champs, Margaret. "Pioneer Life in the Cumberland Country," M.A., 1946.

Kinard, Frances M. "Frontier Development of Williamson County, Tennessee," M.A., 1948.

McDonald, Kenneth. "Milling in Middle Tennessee, 1780–1860," M.A., 1938.

Moffat, Charles Hill. "The Life of Charles Tait," Ph.D., 1946.

Wagner, Mary Church. "The Settlement of Zion Community in Maury County, Tennessee, 1806–1860," M.A., 1945.

UNIVERSITY OF WISCONSIN

Casberg, Selma Sather. "The Lumbering Industry of La Crosse, Wisconsin, 1841–1905," M.A., 1953.

Cotton, Juliana Maria. "Social Life and Conditions in the Mississippi Valley, 1825–1840," M.A., 1926.

Craig, Lois Marie. "The Role of the Missionary on the Wisconsin Frontier (1825–1840)," M.A., 1949.

Fitzrandolph, Lura Mae. "The History of Arkansas to 1836," M.A., 1935.

Fix, Jacqueline A. "The Establishment of Wisconsin Territorial Newspapers, 1833–1848," M.A., 1961.

Karn, Edwin D. "Roadmaking in Wisconsin Territory," M.A., 1959.

Kennedy, Charles J. "The Congregationalists and the Presbyterians on the Wisconsin Frontier," Ph.D., 1940.

Liddle, Clifford S. "The Development of the Common School District in the Towns of La Grange, Linn, and Sugar Creek, Walworth County, Wisconsin," Ph.D., 1942.

McCluggage, Robert W. "The Fox-Wisconsin Waterway, 1836–1872: Land Speculation and Regional Rivalries, Politics and Private Enterprise," Ph.D., 1954.

Merrill, Horace Samuel. "An Early History of the Black River Falls Region," M.A., 1933.

Overy, David H., Jr. "Wisconsin Men, The Frontier Cycle, and the South," M.S., 1960.

Paullin, William T. "Money and Credit in Western Trade, 1816–1836," Ph.D., 1935.

Read, Mary Josephine. "A Population Study of the Driftless Hill Land during the Pioneer Period, 1832–1860," Ph.D., 1941.

Sears, James M. "Teachers of the Old Northwest Territory, 1830–1860, as Seen in Their Diaries and Papers," M.A., 1964.

Somerville, James K. "Wisconsin Territorial Politics as Reflected in the Contest to Elect a Delegate to Congress, 1835–1847," M.A., 1959.

Tibbitts, Mary Blanche. "The Development of a Pioneer Wisconsin Farm during the Thirties and Forties," M.A., 1925.

Van Tassel, David Dirk. "Democracy, Frontier, and Mineral Point: A Study of the Influence of the Frontier on a Wisconsin Mining Town," M.S., 1951.

Index

Wisconsin (*continued*)
  growth in, 373; politics in, 393-4. *See also*
  Lumbering; Mining; *counties, towns, and
  geographical designations by name*
Wisconsin River, 225, 331, 339, 347
Woods, Robert, 196, 217
Worley, Mr. (schoolteacher), 58
Worthington, Thomas, 104-5, 356

Worthington, William G. D., 248
Wyley family, 273

Yalobusha (Miss.), 316
Yazoo City (Miss.), 317
Yazoo River, 89, 158, 311
Ypsilanti (Mich.), 234

The Trans-Appalachian Frontier in 1775